I0866555

VITAGRAPH

VITAGRAPH

America's First Great Motion Picture Studio

Andrew A. Erish

UNIVERSITY PRESS OF KENTUCKY

Paperback edition 2022

Scholarly publisher for the Commonwealth,
serving Bellarmine University, Berea College, Centre
College of Kentucky, Eastern Kentucky University,
The Filson Historical Society, Georgetown College,
Kentucky Historical Society, Kentucky State University,
Morehead State University, Murray State University,
Northern Kentucky University, Spalding University,
Transylvania University, University of Kentucky,
University of Louisville, and Western Kentucky University.

Editorial and Sales Offices: The University Press of Kentucky
663 South Limestone Street, Lexington, Kentucky 40508-4008
www.kentuckypress.com

The Library of Congress has cataloged the hardcover edition as follows:

Names: Erish, Andrew A., 1958– author.
Title: Vitagraph : America's first great motion picture studio / Andrew A. Erish.
Description: Lexington : The University Press of Kentucky, [2021]. | Series: Screen classics | Includes bibliographical references and index.
Identifiers: LCCN 2021006502 | ISBN 9780813181196 (hardcover) | ISBN 9780813181226 (pdf) | ISBN 9780813181219 (epub)
Subjects: LCSH: Vitagraph Company of America.
Classification: LCC PN1999.V5 E75 2021 | DDC 384/.80973—dc23

ISBN 978-0-8131-9534-6 (pbk. : alk. paper)

This book is printed on acid-free paper meeting
the requirements of the American National Standard
for Permanence in Paper for Printed Library Materials.

Manufactured in the United States of America

ASSOCIATION of UNIVERSITY PRESSES

Member of the Association
of University Presses

Contents

Introduction

Mention "Vitagraph" to most film buffs and you are likely to receive one of three responses: "You must mean Vitaphone, the people that made the Bugs Bunny cartoons"; "You're saying it wrong, it's Biograph"; or an uncomprehending stare.

There was a time when *everyone* in the world who went to the movies knew that Vitagraph was the most popular maker of motion pictures.

If you've ever read any histories of the movies, watched documentaries that cover the beginning of motion pictures, or had to study the opening chapters of a textbook for a film history class, chances are you've learned that the founders of Paramount and Fox invented the feature film, that the man who created Universal also created the star system, and that all three, along with the heads of MGM and Warner Bros., were responsible for American movies becoming a multimillion dollar industry that dominated the world. This information has been repeated ad infinitum for nearly a century, but it isn't true.

The fact is that Vitagraph was largely responsible for these developments in American cinema and a good deal more, before any of those other companies ever existed. Unfortunately, if Vitagraph is mentioned at all in the histories, documentaries, and textbooks, it is usually in conjunction with its affiliation in the Motion Picture Patents Company (MPPC), better known as the odious Trust. By virtue of its membership in the MPPC, Vitagraph has been mischaracterized as being the product of unimaginative, shortsighted engineers who produced a primitive form of cinema solely in the pursuit of quick profits that ceased the moment those better-known, more talented and intelligent showmen took over the industry.[1]

Why such fundamental and long-lasting misinformation with regard to Vitagraph's place in the historical record? The answer is essentially twofold. The men who ran Paramount, Fox, Universal, MGM, and Warner Brothers took over the American motion picture industry from Vitagraph and the other pioneers at a time when no widely circulated history of the medium had yet been published. As is the custom of conquerors, they took credit for the accomplishments of their predecessors, and forged myths about themselves that have been accepted at face value and reinforced by subsequent generations. Bolstering their claims is the widespread familiarity with their brands into the twenty-first century. The other reason for the scant information regarding Vitagraph's role in the development of motion pictures is the absence of a comprehensive history of the company.

This is the story of some of the people who contributed to Vitagraph's successes and failures, as well as an account of the business of Vitagraph, drawn from correspondence and business records, trade publications, newspaper and magazine coverage, interviews, and the work of many scrupulous scholars, including Anthony Slide, whose 1976 short history of Vitagraph, *The Big V*, inspired me to want to learn more about the company. In addition, more than three hundred long-forgotten films and nearly four hundred fragments have been screened for this project.

Vitagraph encompasses the birth and development of motion pictures in America. The beginning of the story follows the familiar narrative of impoverished young immigrants who got off the boat with little more than a tenacious drive to pursue the American Dream. It led them to an industry that hadn't even been invented yet.

1

1875–1904

Two English-born Americans founded the Vitagraph Company of America: James Stuart Blackton, born in Sheffield on January 4, 1875, and Albert Edward Smith, born five months later on June 4, 1875, in Faversham. They spent their formative years living 280 kilometers apart and wouldn't meet until they were nineteen years old. By then both had relocated to the other side of the Atlantic in New York City, living within a few miles of each other.

James Blackton's parents divorced within a month or two of his birth. In 1886, Blackton and his mother immigrated to America, eventually settling in Brooklyn. Shortly after arriving in New York, Blackton was apprenticed to a carpenter. His mother remarried and gave birth to a son, William Stuart Adams, in 1892. Shortly after the birth, Blackton's stepfather unexpectedly died. At seventeen James became the sole support for his family as a carpenter. His ambition, however, was to become an artist. The indefatigable Blackton attended art classes at night at New York's tuition-free City College.

In 1888 Albert Smith crossed the Atlantic with his parents, sister, six brothers, and a grandmother, and settled in Brooklyn. Many of the values instilled by Smith's very religious Church of England parents would later inform his business decisions, some of which were uncharacteristic of other movie moguls. Albert was apprenticed to a Manhattan bookbinder, but he yearned for a career in show business.

As a teenager Albert once borrowed eleven dollars from his father to rent a social hall in Flatbush, Brooklyn, where he presented an evening's entertainment. Admittance was twenty-five cents, collected by Smith's father at the door. As soon as he recouped his eleven dollars, Smith Sr. went home. Albert recalled that his parents "cherished individual enterprise in the American style, but in their prim English minds it could not be stretched to include my desire to become an actor." In 1890 the Smith family moved to Santa Barbara, California, leaving fifteen-year-old Albert behind to live with an elderly couple in Flatbush. "Show business was still in my mind, and New York seemed the best place for it."[1]

Because he was financially responsible for his mother, baby brother, and his mother's sister, it is doubtful that James could have afforded the oils, brushes, or canvas necessary to develop into a professional painter. However, charcoal pencils, paper, chalk, and blackboard were within his budget. James learned to draw quickly, specializing in caricatures of celebrities and his patron of the moment. For hundreds of years people with limited means but similar gifts have worked as café or sidewalk artists. Fortunately Blackton, like Smith, found a bigger outlet for his talents: the stage, at the dawn of vaudeville.

When James Blackton and Albert Smith entered show business in the early 1890s, live, family-friendly variety shows were becoming the most popular form of entertainment in America. Prior to that time, variety catered to an adult male audience, characterized by crude jokes, revealing costumes, and bawdy physicality. Singer, showman, and impresario Tony Pastor cleaned up variety and transformed it into an entertainment suitable for everyone. Beginning in 1881, Pastor's Fourteenth Street Theatre in New York City demonstrated to showmen everywhere that variety entertainment "clean as a hound's tooth" could attract men, women, and children. It proved to be a more lucrative aesthetic *and* business model than traditional variety. The showman who most successfully embraced Pastor's approach was B. F. Keith, who popularized the term "vaudeville" to describe the variety shows at his growing chain of theaters.[2]

Albert Smith's original ambition was to become an actor in the style of famed nineteenth-century tragedian Richard Mansfield, "but the early evidences were that a Mansfield was not in the making." Still apprenticing by day as a bookbinder, Smith's focus shifted from the legitimate stage to mastering performing arts that were better suited to both his analytical temperament and to vaudeville. He worked on perfecting voice impressions, ventriloquism, and, especially, magic. At sixteen Smith began getting bookings at Brooklyn-area men's clubs and other organizations.[3]

By 1894 Smith had entered into what would become a lifelong friendship with Ronald Albert Reader, who like Smith and Blackton was English-born, having immigrated to New York by himself as a teenager. The two young men shared a passion for magic, endlessly practicing card tricks for each other until Smith became, by his own admission, "a passably good sleight-of-hand performer." Sometime that year at a boarding-house party in Harlem, Reader introduced Albert Smith to his friend James Blackton. It appears the two hit

Magician Albert E. Smith, *Mahatma* magazine, 1899. Albert E. Smith Papers (Collection 2004), Library Special Collections, Charles E. Young Research Library, UCLA.

it off instantly; for the rest of their lives Blackton called Smith "A.E." and Smith was the only person that Blackton allowed to call him "Jim." They appreciated qualities in the other that they themselves didn't possess. For Smith, it was Blackton's "wonderfully artistic temperament," and Blackton admired Smith's "caution and conservation."[4]

At heart Smith was a serious-minded introvert while Blackton was outgoing and carefree, yet they had a great deal in common. Their parents wanted them to pursue stable blue-collar trades, but these young Americans desired to be part of the unpredictable, exciting world of show business. Albert Smith recognized and accepted his shortcomings as an actor, and James Blackton understood that circumstances prevented him from becoming a professional painter of portraits and seascapes. But neither would be deterred from finding a niche in an industry that would allow them to utilize their creative skills while offering unlimited financial potential. Vaudeville symbolized that "belief in progress, the pursuit of happiness, and the hope for material success basic to the American character." It was a siren call to sons of poor immigrants entering adulthood, fueled with ambition and drive.[5]

Smith, Reader, and Blackton decided to combine their individual talents in order to provide a full, self-contained evening's entertainment and thus presumably attract bigger audiences and remuneration. Smith recalled their first job was entertaining at the grand opening of the YMCA in Prospect Park, Brooklyn. The magic of Smith and Reader, charcoal drawings by Blackton, and recitations by all netted the trio fifteen dollars apiece. Buoyed by their success, they decided to hit the road a week later as the "International Novelty Company." Blackton arranged for them to play north of New York City in a handful of small towns on either side of the Hudson River. The tour proved to be a disaster that included the trio once playing to an empty house and getting shortchanged by several unscrupulous theater operators.[6]

Returning home, they honed their skills. Smith added comedy to his magic act and, with Reader, worked up a mindreading and disappearing cabinet routine. Blackton perfected his rapid patter while drawing caricatures of celebrities and people in the audience. He called these "Chalk Talks" and later, "Lightning Sketches." His presentations proved more lucrative when he switched from chalk on blackboard to charcoal pencil on paper that he could sell to his models in the audience. Inevitably these were local celebrities and neighborhood characters that Blackton would be tipped off about beforehand. The trio renamed themselves the "Royal Entertainers" and achieved better bookings, playing churches and YMCAs, as well as men's and women's clubs. Blackton's advertising copy hailed the "Celebrated Reader, Smith and Blackton Combination" as the "World's Greatest and Most Magnificent Entertainment of Magic, Mirth and Mystery."[7]

One component of Albert Smith's act was shadowgraphy whereby he would contort his hands to form images of faces, animals, and familiar objects in shadow cast by a bright light onto a screen. It is the oldest form of entertainment involving a projected image. Smith produced a barnyard of animals and told shadow stories of characters based on physical exaggeration and stereotype. He likely used burning lime as the light source with which to cast his shadows; that is, unless he could borrow a magic lantern. Magic lanterns were projectors with a self-contained gas light source designed to cast still images from a glass slide through a lens and onto a screen. Magic lantern shows were popular around the world during the Victorian era, and would have a significant influence on future media.[8]

Blackton and Smith both turned twenty in 1895. At that point their ambition was merely to improve sufficiently so they could quit their day jobs and become full-time entertainers. But something unexpected happened that led to monumental change, not only for them personally but also for how the world would come to prefer its entertainment. That June they were walking along Nassau Street in lower Manhattan and came upon a storefront arcade featuring "Thomas Edison's Latest Marvel, the Kinetoscope." It was a new kind of machine encased in a wooden box. After paying a nickel, an individual could watch moving pictures through an eyepiece in the top of the cabinet: a photographic reproduction of movement as seen in life. Like everyone else who peered into a kinetoscope, Smith and Blackton were mesmerized. They were also inspired, wanting to make moving pictures themselves. Perhaps they could supplement their act with this new technology, but project the images like a magic lantern? It would certainly take a long time to save the money necessary to finance such an undertaking. Just as daunting was attaining the knowledge required to accomplish what only the "wizard" Edison, alone, had been able to do. Or so everyone was led to believe.[9]

It was actually William K. L. Dickson, assisted by other Edison technicians, who created a motion picture camera and a self-contained cabinet designed for individual viewing. After a few years of private showings and tweaks, the kinetoscope made its commercial debut in New York City in April 1894. Kinetoscope parlors soon opened in cities across the United States and Europe.[10]

By the time Albert Smith and James Blackton encountered a kinetoscope in 1895, cameras and projectors were already being adapted from it by Englishman Birt Acres, Americans Woodville Latham, Francis Jenkins, and Thomas Armat, the Skladanowsky brothers and Oskar Messter in Germany, and the Lumière brothers of France. Edison never applied for foreign patents on his invention. When he refused to sell a kinetoscope to Robert W. Paul, the Englishman built sixty knockoffs for the European market. By early 1896 Paul also built a projector he called the Theatrograph that was sold throughout the world.

Competition came also from an unexpected source, much closer to home. Having anonymously made at least 125 films for the kinetoscope, and resentful that his employer failed to recognize his contributions to the new medium both publicly and in the patents, William Dickson left Edison. In late 1895 he became a founding partner in the American Mutoscope and Biograph Company, Edison's first serious American rival in the production of motion pictures. At Biograph, Dickson had to invent motion pictures all over again so as not to infringe on *Edison*'s patents.[11] Without access to outside financing as Biograph had, Blackton and Smith would have to wait more than a year before they could afford to become filmmakers.

The top vaudeville theaters in Manhattan in 1896 were Tony Pastor's, Keith's Union Square, Hammerstein's Olympia, Proctor's Twenty-Third Street, and Proctor's Pleasure Palace. After these came Koster & Bial's, which from January through March ended each eight-to-nine-act show with "Living Pictures," an act that consisted of attractive women posing inside an enormous frame in reenactments of well-known paintings. On April 23, 1896, an act debuted at Koster & Bial's that signified a new kind of living picture: "Thomas A. Edison's Latest Marvel: The Vitascope."

Projected films were exceeding kinetoscopes in popularity wherever they were shown. When newspapers reported that agents for F. F. Proctor were in England acquiring a projector and films to show at his New York theaters, Edison purchased a projector from Washington-based Thomas Armat that he had built with ex-partner Francis Jenkins. As part of the deal, Armat allowed Edison to take credit as the inventor of the rechristened Vitascope projector. Adding to the subterfuge, at least one of the films screened at Koster & Bial's wasn't even made by Edison. *Sea Waves* was actually Acres and Paul's *Rough Sea at Dover.* R. W. Paul sent the print and other films to Edison in the hope of buying, selling, or trading product. Instead, Edison kept the films and claimed them as his own. The press and public responded *very* enthusiastically to the Vitascope screenings. However, no one seemed to remember, care, or believe that a year earlier on May 20, 1895, Woodville Latham had projected movies to paying customers in a storefront on lower Broadway in New York.[12]

In an instant the debut of the Edison Vitascope came to be regarded as one of those defining moments that usher in a new era. In his unpublished memoir J. Stuart Blackton stated that he was at Koster & Bial's covering the event for the *New York World.* Albert Smith asserted in his autobiography that his homemade Vitagraph projector made its debut at Tony Pastor's a month *before* the Vitascope had its unveiling. Neither claim is true. Edison wasn't the only one who wanted recognition for things he wasn't really responsible for; it seems to be a shortcoming common to many who work in motion pictures.

What is true is that for most of 1896 Albert Smith was by day a bookbinder for a printer on John Street in lower Manhattan and James Blackton occasionally freelanced as a cartoonist for the *World*. Ronald Reader was by now infrequently appearing with the Royal Entertainers, preferring the financial security afforded by his job with the Royal Insurance Co.[13]

On June 26, 1896, Blackton and Smith performed at a benefit for the *Evening World*'s Sick Baby Fund for which they received a glowing review in that paper. Whether hoping to capitalize on his association with the benefit or inspired by films of British "lightning cartoonist" Tom Merry made by Birt Acres and R. W. Paul that may have been included with the *Rough Sea at Dover* shipment, an Edison production unit made three films of Blackton. They were shot on a Manhattan rooftop, with Blackton wearing evening clothes and making lightning sketches of Edison, William McKinley, and President Grover Cleveland, along with "a life-size picture of a female figure" with rapidly changing expressions. The movies premiered in September at Proctor's vaudeville houses in Manhattan, and were singled out as the best of the films on the bill. *Inventor Edison Sketched By World Artist* was the only one to be held over a second week. It was a heady experience for James Blackton. If, as Albert Smith suggested, his partner had been skeptical of their chances at making good in a nascent industry that didn't yet have a name, by his own admission Blackton was now a believer. Through the remainder of 1896 the Vitascope competed for business at New York vaudeville theaters with the Lumières' Cinematographe, Latham's Eidoloscope, Jenkins's Phantoscope, Paul's Theatrograph, and Herman Casler and W. K. L. Dickson's Biograph, among other projectors. In the meantime Smith and Blackton continued to bide their time.[14]

The year 1897 was a time of major commitments for Smith and Blackton. Early in the year they finally managed to scrape enough money together to obtain their first projector and films. These were all made by the Edison Manufacturing Company but were purchased illegally from the father of a boyhood friend of Smith's who was licensed to sell Edison machines and films only to foreign clients. This coincided with Ronald Reader dropping out of the Royal Entertainers. Now the act would open with Smith performing his magic. While Blackton entertained, Smith would prepare the projector and thread the first of ten movies. The show would conclude with the screening of *The Black Diamond Express*, Edison's remake of a Lumière film. Edison projectionists offered an unadorned presentation of the film, but the Royal Entertainers enhanced the experience. As Smith cranked the projector, the audience would see a train coming toward them. Blackton stood behind the screen simulating train noises, banging on sheets of metal, ringing a bell with a rope attached to one foot, blowing into a train whistle, and pounding a bass drum. Afraid a runaway train was about to run them over, "those in the front rows would either dodge under the seats or go over backwards."[15] Such showmanship would distinguish Vitagraph productions throughout its history from unimaginative competitors interested solely in turning a quick profit.

Smith and Blackton were now earning a living solely as entertainers, though mostly still on the Lyceum and Chautauqua circuits. They took every gig offered, often traveling long distances between shows on their quest to save enough money to become producers of their own moving pictures. One of Smith's appointment calendars, though printed for the year 1896, has pencil notations indicating that he used it instead for 1897—an example of his thrift in the face of poverty. In January alone, they played small-town YMCAs and churches in Pennsylvania, New Jersey, Massachusetts, upstate New York, and Long Island. The only travel options were trains or horse-drawn conveyances. It was a grueling but lucrative month.[16]

When they returned home at the beginning of February 1897, Blackton and Smith took the next step toward becoming filmmakers. Most of the pioneers who made films also built their own cameras and projectors, and exhibited their productions themselves. Since there was still no term in common usage for this new entertainment, most firms coined names that served two functions: they provided their company with a distinctive name that also identified the projectors they made. Vitagraph followed suit. It has been suggested that the name "Vitagraph" was derived from combining the names of two projectors already on the market: the Vitascope and Biograph. Albert Smith provided a different explanation, "We got the name from a dictionary, 'Vita' meaning life, and 'graph,' picture."[17] This occurred at a time when the partners were also making personal commitments. On February 10, 1897, Blackton married Isabelle MacArthur. They met while he was entertaining at her father's church in the Bronx. On May 21, Smith wed May Arthur at her parents' home in Brooklyn. Ronald Reader was one of the ushers; Jim Blackton and his new bride were also in attendance.[18]

In June, J. Stuart Blackton parlayed his celebrity from the Edison film into a weeklong gig making lightning sketches at B. F. Keith's Union Square Theater. Each show at the Union Square concluded with a short program of Biograph

Blackton and Smith's open-air studio on the roof of the Morse Building, 140 Nassau Street, New York, 1903, drawn from memory by J. Stuart Blackton. Albert E. Smith Papers (Collection 2004). Library Special Collections, Charles E. Young Research Library, UCLA.

films. For the remainder of the summer, the Royal Entertainers played resorts and other venues along the New Jersey shore. Blackton returned to Keith's for the last week of September, then it was back on the road with his partner playing the Lyceum circuit in Ohio for the month of November. Smith recalled that the Royal Entertainers earned $2,000 in 1897. Three days before Christmas, Blackton and Smith took another big step in their moving picture business by signing a lease for an office with roof access at ten dollars per month in the Morse Building at 140 Nassau Street in lower Manhattan.[19]

In the two years since their first encounter with a kinetoscope, Albert Smith managed to save $900 to fund Vitagraph's entry into production and exhibition. Blackton was only able to contribute $36 toward the venture, such was the profligacy that characterized him throughout his life. The money was invested in more projectors of various manufacture, including a new model marketed by Edison that also photographed and printed. Using that machine as a guide, Smith was able to build a better, more lightweight camera, and he purchased an excellent secondhand lens. He also hired a mechanic to build apparatus designed to improve projection based on lessons learned on the road. Smith considered his most important inventions to be a device that greatly reduced the flicker from the projector shutter, and an automatic reframing mechanism that compensated for skipped frames caused by film shrinkage and torn sprocket holes.[20]

Vitagraph was purchasing and projecting other producers' product because they hadn't yet shot many films of their own, beyond a Brooklyn street scene, a sidewalk bootblack shining a man's shoes, and a few others. By day Blackton and Smith would shoot "experimental bits of film and learn how to develop these trial negatives." At night the films were projected at clubs in Brooklyn, Manhattan, and the Bronx. By the time Vitagraph entered production in late 1897, interest in motion pictures was waning. Views of city traffic or someone getting a shoeshine captivated the earliest audiences because they offered something never before seen: pictures that moved. But after a year and a half, the novelty of movement for the sake of movement was abating. Some vaudeville theaters like Keith's Union Square eliminated moving pictures from their programs. Those that retained them used films as "chasers," so called because they were positioned as the last act on the bill to chase audiences out of the theater in order to make room for new customers for the next show. It was beginning to look as if Thomas Edison might be right after all about the public quickly tiring of moving pictures.[21]

Blackton and Smith supplemented their Vitagraph income by creating a short-lived subsidiary called the Commercial Advertising Company that made advertisements on magic lantern slides for such clients as Lickmann's Cigar and Photo. The slides would be projected between films while the reels were being changed. Smith and Blackton's first venture presenting movies supplemented with commercials on slides took place atop the roof of a one-story building on 125th Street in Harlem. The exhibition lasted only a week before the police made them shut it down for creating a traffic hazard. A second, more successful effort took place on a vacant lot along the road to the beach and amusement park at Coney Island. Horse-drawn carriages and bicycles would pull onto the property at what was Brooklyn's first, and perhaps only, drive-in theater. In addition to the projected advertisements, Smith and Blackton operated a refreshment stand that more than compensated for the free admission.

The Harlem and Coney Island exhibitions raised Vitagraph's profile in New York, leading to Blackton and Smith being hired to film a scene that was incorporated into the play *The Good Mister Best*, which opened on Broadway on August 23, 1897. The highlight of the play involved the protagonist spying on people throughout his home via a secret surveillance system. The glimpses into each of the rooms represented Vitagraph's contribution; probably the first time motion pictures were utilized on the legitimate stage.[22]

"Remember the *Maine*!" became the rallying cry that swept the nation after the American battleship *Maine* exploded in Havana Harbor on February 15, 1898, killing approximately 250 officers and crewmen. Newspaper tycoons Joseph Pulitzer and William Randolph Hearst insisted that the United States retaliate by driving Spain out of Cuba. Blackton and Smith exploited the situation and in the process produced their first hit film. They built a miniature flagpole and attached a small eighteen-inch Spanish flag to a rope at the top. A similarly sized Stars and Stripes was fastened to the rope below frame. As Smith cranked the camera, Blackton lowered the Spanish flag and hoisted Old Glory to the top as it fluttered in the breeze. The backdrop was a painting of Morro Castle made by Blackton.

Since movies as yet did not include identifying titles, Vitagraph's production was known variously as *Tearing Down the Spanish Flag*, *Old Glory and the Cuban Flag at Colors*, and *Old Glory Over Morro Castle*. Consisting of a single shot and lasting just over thirty seconds, it was an enormous success. Almost every vaudeville theater in the country with movies on the bill closed their show with it, often running the film a second time for audiences demanding an encore.[23]

During the first ten years of projected cinema in America, it was common for Vitagraph and its competition to provide a complete package of films, projector, and projectionist to vaudeville theaters on a weekly basis. Churches, YMCAs, social clubs, and similar venues would rent the package for single showings; carnivals, fairs, and municipalities offering summer park shows had seasonal leases. James Blackton claimed hundreds of prints of *Tearing Down the Spanish Flag* were sold, no doubt an exaggeration. Closer to a hundred copies were sold at the going rate of ten dollars per film, totaling half the money the Royal Entertainers earned for the previous year. This was the first time other producers and exhibitors bought a Vitagraph film with which to supplement *their* programs. Every vaudeville theater that could afford to was adding or reinstating a program of films to satisfy the public mania for war-related moving imagery. Biograph was once again presenting films at Keith's Union Square, while Edison supplied both of Proctor's New York City houses. Smith and Blackton realized that supplying a regular program to vaudeville theaters would result in a steady, more lucrative income.[24]

The success of *Tearing Down the Spanish Flag* inspired the Vitagraph partners to make more films of their own. They started by producing the easiest, least expensive, and most popular films of the moment: war-related actualities (aka documentaries) of troops and battleships leaving for the front and returning home from Cuba. They also made recreations of *The Battle of Manila Bay* and *The Battle of Santiago Bay*, shooting the former in Blackton's bathtub and the latter in their New York office. The vessels consisted of cut-outs from photographs of American and Spanish battleships nailed to pieces of wood floating in water. Blackton blew cigar smoke to simulate cannon fire in *Manila*; his wife did likewise with a cigarette in *Santiago*. Other producers photographed mock battles closer to home. Only cameramen William Paley under license to Edison and Biograph's Billy Bitzer traveled to Cuba to take genuine footage of Spanish–American War activities.[25]

In later years Smith and Blackton both asserted that they, too, photographed the war in Cuba. Blackton claimed that he and Smith traveled from New York to Key West to Cuba via the *New York World* tugboat *Dauntless*. According to Smith, Teddy Roosevelt made room for them aboard a troop ship transporting the Rough Riders from Hoboken to Tampa to Cuba. Blackton said that when they reached Cuba, "we took some pictures of American troops sniping and some patrols reconnoitering," then returned to the States via the *Whitney* shortly before Roosevelt and the Rough Riders landed. Smith devotes eight pages of his autobiography to their adventures in Cuba, including going up San Juan Hill behind Roosevelt and war correspondent Richard Harding Davis.

A program of Vitagraph films shown at Martha's Vineyard on August 3, 1898, states, "We have just received from Mr. Edison's Cuban Representatives at Havana and Key West, Florida, a series of Thrilling Animated Pictures, taken especially for The Edison Vitagraph." According to the Vitagraph check ledger for 1898, the company purchased Paley's Cuban films from an Edison sales agent and some battle reenactments from a Chicago filmmaker. There was only $5.53 in the Vitagraph account after they purchased a projector one week before the Battle of San Juan Hill occurred on July 1, 1898. One week later $25 was deposited into the Vitagraph account. Beyond the physical and financial unlikelihood of a trip to Cuba is the fact that there is no record of any Vitagraph-produced actualities in Cuba ever existing.[26]

The success of *Tearing Down the Spanish Flag* combined with their actualities and the staged productions acquired from other firms resulted in Vitagraph landing their first booking in a New York City vaudeville house. During the weeks of May 7 and May 14, 1898, Smith and Blackton supplied a program of films to the Central Opera House, for which they received a total of $95. It may have been the least of New York's vaudeville theaters, but it was a big step up from Vitagraph's sporadic one-nighters. At the more popular Proctor's, the weekly film program closing the bill was advertised as the "Edison war-graph." But at the end of June, Proctor's Twenty-Third Street was showing Vitagraph's program instead. Proctor's Pleasure Palace followed suit at the beginning of September, billing the "act" simply as the "war-graph." The most plausible explanation for the switch is that Vitagraph was able to supply a package of films, projector, and projectionist at a lower rate than Edison.

Initially, Albert Smith operated the projector at the Twenty-Third Street Theatre, but production and business commitments led him to hire a replacement, J. B. French, a former magician's assistant. Smith had to train French in how to do the job, something he and Blackton would do with virtually every employee over the next decade. This involved every facet of an emerging industry undergoing rapid change, including innovations for which Vitagraph was directly responsible. There was no other way to learn the art and business of moving pictures.[27]

Smith and Blackton's weekly income from Proctor's was $150; but, since the deal guaranteed a new program each week, Vitagraph found itself in immediate need of product. On June 8, 1898, they purchased used films from William T. Rock, who conducted business out of a billiards hall he owned on 125th Street in Harlem. "Pop" Rock was born in Birmingham, England, in 1851. At fourteen, he made the crossing alone to America and joined a circus, before acquiring a Manhattan hotel and interest in a New York electric company. In partnership with tightrope walker Walter Wainright, Rock purchased exclusive rights to the Edison Vitascope projector for the state of Louisiana for $2,500. Their storefront theater on Canal Street in New Orleans opened on July 18, 1896, the first documented venue in America to exclusively project moving pictures. Vitascope Hall seated four hundred and charged ten cents for admission, fifty cents to tour the projection booth.

A streetcar company hired Rock and company to show films at night during the summer at what was then called West End Park on the southern shore of Lake Pontchartrain. Rock supplemented the Edison productions he owned with a substantial quantity of British- and French-made films purchased from Charles Urban of the Warwick Trading Company in London. By the end of the season the partners netted $4,000.

Homesick, Rock parted company with Wainright and returned to New York with three hundred used films, two projectors, "and a lot of diamonds." Rock was a widower with a teenage son and daughter, who may have

William T. "Pop" Rock, far right, outside Vitascope Hall, New Orleans, ca. 1896. *Transactions of the Society of Motion Picture Engineers*, 1925.

been in boarding school while he was in New Orleans. From his Harlem billiards hall Rock dealt primarily in coin-operated record players, newspaper dispensers, and similar devices, collectively called "slot machines." That is, until a man in long coat and high hat, "Jimmie" Blackton, came calling in August 1898.[28]

Blackton came to Rock hoping to swap product. After showing off his large stock of used films, Rock was invited to meet Albert Smith and inspect Vitagraph's operation. Rock was impressed with what the two young men had accomplished in only a year and a half, but recognized that business-wise they were babes in the woods. The Vitagraph partners found forty-seven-year-old Rock imposing. To Albert Smith, he "gave off an appearance of power because of a massive chest, square jaw, keen eyes, deep voice, and an inevitable cigar" tucked in the corner of his unsmiling mouth. Rock also possessed "a poet's ear for profanity." James Blackton remembered Rock wearing "a derby hat on the back of his head, a diamond like a locomotive headlight in the tie," and flashing "a roll of bills big enough to choke a horse." Even more intimidating was the fact that Rock was among the crowd that seemed to know ahead of time the outcome of horse races and prize fights.[29]

Pop Rock recognized the inexperienced Blackton and Smith as easy prey. He contacted Thomas Armat, who was in the midst of trying to assert his patent on the projector he had sold to Edison. Rock suggested that Armat bring suit against Vitagraph for using a modified Vitascope. Armat authorized him to ask for $10,000 in damages, but Rock had a change of heart. He realized there was potentially much more to be gained by becoming a partner in Vitagraph. But first, there was the matter of investigating a lawsuit recently brought against J. Stuart Blackton and Albert E. Smith by the Edison Manufacturing Company.[30]

Thomas Edison's original patent applications "covering the method of taking [moving] pictures and subsequently reproducing or exhibiting the same" were rejected, citing the priority of others' inventions. But the success of the Armat projector at Koster & Bial's proved that motion pictures were more lucrative than Edison had ever imagined. He knew from experience that a patent holder could profit handsomely from a widely used invention, even if it "did not entirely originate with him." Edison's attorneys were thus instructed to file new applications based on the Armat projector; a patent was subsequently granted to Edison on August 31, 1897. That patent was viewed as evidence that Edison alone had invented moving pictures, and justified his desire to control and profit from all subsequent filmmakers.[31]

The May 28, 1898, issue of the *New York Clipper* contained an advertisement that included a warning inspired by the day's popular slogan: "Remember the patent (Edison's). Also that Infringers are Being Proceeded Against Right and Left." Among the "Edison War Films" for sale were *The Transport "Whitney" Leaving Dock* and *Tenth U. S. Infantry.* The following week's *Clipper* contained a Vitagraph ad offering its projectors and "Edison War Films" for sale. That same week salesman George Dutel and two others representing Edison interests called at the Vitagraph office. Dutel was there to pick up prints of *Transport Whitney* and *Tenth U. S. Infantry* that were copied from originals he had provided to Smith and Blackton. Dutel said he intended to secretly sell the copies at a profit, but it was a ruse. He was really there on behalf of Edison to entrap them.

In mid-July, Blackton and Smith were served with subpoenas. Blackton met with one of Edison's attorneys and learned that he and Smith were charged with pirating copyrighted Edison films and using projectors that infringed on his patent. Afraid of going to jail, Blackton signed an agreement promising Vitagraph would stop copying Edison films and cease from using non-Edison projectors. Blackton also agreed to supply negatives of Vitagraph productions for Edison to copy and sell; Blackton and Smith would then receive a royalty from any sales. Vitagraph was forbidden to sell prints of their films to competitors, though they could make prints to supply to their own exhibition clients. As was the case with William Paley during and shortly after the Spanish–American War, Blackton and Smith in effect became Edison licensees. The naive Vitagraph partners signed documents without benefit of counsel. Rather than incur legal fees, they chose to trust verbal assurances of Edison attorneys and staff, even when Edison filed an injunction against them "merely as a formality."[32]

Virtually every filmmaker at the turn of the twentieth century was engaged in making and selling pirated duplicates ("dupes") of films made by competitors. Edison had already brought suit against Siegmund Lubin and the American Mutoscope and Biograph Company, and would continue to do so with every other American moving picture producer in operation during the first dozen years of commercial cinema. Some were driven out of business. Albert Smith understood that he and Blackton were too inexperienced to survive the Edison assault. They lacked the financial means as well as the gumption to challenge the fairness, legality, and hypocrisy that allowed Edison to sell dupes of Vitagraph's *Tearing Down the Spanish Flag* but prevented them from doing likewise with Edison productions. They needed a partner who knew his way around and who could go toe-to-toe against the Edison forces. They wanted Pop Rock as much as Rock wanted a chunk of Vitagraph.[33]

Before entering into the partnership, Rock insisted that they visit William E. Gilmore, vice president and general manager of the Edison Manufacturing Company. Gilmore confirmed that a lawsuit for infringement of Edison copyrights had been brought against Smith and Blackton, but assured Rock that the matter had been satisfactorily "adjusted" and that he "need have no fear" that Vitagraph would suffer any further interference from Edison. Rock was satisfied.

Unlike later motion picture company partnerships, there was no written contract among the Vitagraphers. At the end of September 1898, William T. Rock became president because he was the oldest and most experienced, J. Stuart Blackton was secretary, and Albert E. Smith the treasurer because he was far more responsible with money than Blackton. Despite an utter lack of training in business or financial matters, the triumvirate that ran Vitagraph would thrive for nearly twenty years.[34]

Now that the Edison troubles were seemingly behind them, and with Pop Rock focused on growing the business, Smith and Blackton returned to making films. Except for *Tearing Down the Spanish Flag* and the two homemade naval battles, their efforts had been confined to actualities, documenting military parades and flotillas. Albert Smith finally got around to making the kind of film he had dreamed of when first peering into a kinetoscope, one that would supplement and enhance his magic act. As virtually everyone has discovered who has ever started, stopped, and then restarted a camera photographing from a fixed position, any objects moving within the frame either jump in space or disappear altogether between the two takes when the footage is projected. The title of Smith's first magic film is to the point: *The Vanishing Lady* (1898). Blackton operated the camera while Smith hocused and pocused one of their wives away. Presumably there were no trap doors through which a woman could disappear in the stages of the YMCAs and churches where Smith entertained, but thanks to moving pictures he was able to add this most basic of illusions to his repertoire.[35]

Georges Méliès had made a similar film two years earlier, also titled *The Vanishing Lady.* Albert Smith held the legendary magician in high esteem and in later years would visit Méliès whenever he was in Paris. They had much in common. Both came away from their first exposure to moving pictures anxious to include films in their magic act. This was not an uncommon response within the profession. William Selig of Chicago, like Albert Smith, also abandoned magic to become a producer of moving pictures. These magicians turned filmmakers shared a curiosity to explore and exploit properties and possibilities unique to the new medium. Equipped with his own theater and unencumbered by Edison legal machinations, Méliès was able to give free rein to his formidable creativity. His films became the most popular in the world at the turn of the twentieth century; more than a century later he is the best-known filmmaker of early cinema.[36]

Blackton and Smith followed *The Vanishing Lady* with their first "posed production"; it was also their initial attempt at comedy. *The Burglar on the Roof* is an example of a type of movie that Vitagraph came to excel in: light entertainment rooted in an action-based story. From atop a roof a burglar pries open a skylight, reaches in, and retrieves some clothing; he is quickly set upon by two women, one of them repeatedly swinging a broom at him. Four men come upon the scene and fight with the burglar until he is restrained and carried away. It was staged in a single shot lasting thirty seconds, photographed by Albert Smith from a fixed camera position, with the action centered around the skylight above the Vitagraph office on the roof of the Morse Building. James Blackton authored the story and played the burglar. Their friend Ronald Reader and the building's custodian Mr. Olson portrayed two of the men apprehending the burglar. In later years whenever they told the story, both Blackton and Smith claimed that Mrs. Olson happened upon the scene quite by accident and began "screaming and raining blows down on the heads of the startled actors," unaware that a movie was being made. It is a humorous anecdote, but both of the women play the scene too broadly for it to be true. Altogether seven people take part in the action, even a small dog. Why they were on the roof is never addressed. None of it seemed to matter to Proctor's audiences, where *The Burglar on the Roof* was held over for at least three weeks. Edison copyrighted the film as his own production two months later on December 12, 1898.[37]

Things were looking up for the company. By the end of 1898 Vitagraph had established itself as a producer and exhibitor of moving pictures, nearly doubling its income from the previous year. The Vitagraph partners entered 1899 looking to add to their clientele.

Vitagraph shot three films of boxer James J. Jeffries training for his June 9, 1899, title fight against world heavyweight champion Bob Fitzsimmons. Jeffries's manager, William A. Brady, arranged for Albert Smith to film the actual bout, scheduled to take place at night inside the Coney Island Athletic Club. It would be several years before efficient movie lights would be developed, but Smith devised a way to get a proper exposure using more than one hundred arc lights with thick carbons that required massive amounts of electricity. Unfortunately the plant generating the electricity for the lights suffered a power failure during the first round of the fight, and Smith's film was too underexposed to capture an image. William Brady was livid, especially because his fighter won the championship. Consequently, Biograph was chosen to film Jeffries's title defense in November, once again at Coney Island's Athletic Club using the lighting method devised by Smith.

At the instigation of his employer Thomas Edison, filmmaker James White convinced Smith to secretly film the bout using a small, lightweight camera manufactured in France. They snuck the camera and film into the arena and surreptitiously photographed the fight. The moment the fight ended, Smith was spotted by Brady and Jeffries and ran for his life back to the Vitagraph office. The completed film was leased to a traveling vaudeville show for a full season at a lucrative rate. In his autobiography written more than a half century later, Smith expressed regret for having taken part in the scheme. Ironically Smith's bootleg is the only version of the fight that has survived into the twenty-first century.[38]

Smith and Blackton made at least two "trick" films during 1899, *The Mesmerist and the Country Couple* and *A Visit to a Spiritualist. The Mesmerist and the Country Couple* survives because Edison had the complete film copied onto paper and deposited at the Library of Congress for legal protection, as was the custom until the copyright laws were amended several years later. During the 1950s and 1960s the paper prints were rephotographed onto film stock. In many cases, the image quality of these surviving prints is so soft that it is difficult to accurately identify the players. Such is the case with *The Mesmerist and the Country Couple*, inspired by one of the routines Albert Smith and Ronald Reader performed for their Lyceum engagements, in which one would pretend to hypnotize the other. Smith recalled that in the film he played the mesmerist and Blackton the hayseed victim. *The Mesmerist and the Country Couple* is an early example of a type of film that Vitagraph seemed to do better and produce more often than any other major American studio. It is a motion picture that isn't concerned with following conventions of narrative structure. Instead it explores the possibilities of what film can be. As narrative cinema developed and grew in sophistication, so, too, did Vitagraph's experiments with form and content.[39]

Smith and Blackton played similar roles in *A Visit to a Spiritualist*, which helped promote Smith's other career as a magician on the Lyceum circuit. Blackton recalled that for this film he and his partner directed the cameraman and each other *while* they were being photographed. Such were the exigencies facing two young filmmakers with very limited resources at the dawn of cinema. The events in the film are as haphazard as those in their earlier efforts: a farmer visits the office of a "spiritualist" and when hypnotized sees a handkerchief turn into a large ghost. As before, chairs disappear as he attempts to sit; and, after he removes his hat and coat, they fly back onto his body. Eventually a multitude of "ghosts and hobgoblins" materialize and chase the frightened farmer from the office.[40]

The Mesmerist and the Country Couple and *A Visit to a Spiritualist* were made for the urbanites that constituted the majority of the audience for moving pictures in 1899. These films demonstrated the alleged superiority of sophisticated men of the city over farmers and others from the countryside. Vitagraph wasn't alone in this approach. British filmmaker R. W. Paul's *The Countryman and the Cinematograph* and Edison's remake, *Uncle Josh at the Moving Picture Show* (1902), satirized country folk new to cinema in 1901 who react to the *Black Diamond Express* as urban habitués of cinema did *way back* in 1896 and 1897. Georges Méliès poked fun at French "rubes" in two films that the Edison Company copyrighted and retitled *Uncle Josh and the Spooky Hotel* and *Uncle Josh's Nightmare.* Vitagraph would make plenty of films extolling the virtues of small-town and rural life, but the company became better known for stories that reflected the preoccupations, attitudes, and values of young urban Americans like J. Stuart Blackton and Albert Smith. These films also fed the hopes and dreams of people from small towns and countrysides everywhere who yearned to live in the city. It would prove to be a very successful strategy.

While his partners were busy making actualities and posed films, Pop Rock was lining up new customers for Vitagraph. During the first decade of American moving pictures, a popular seasonal exhibition site was the black tent show. One of many entertainment options available at carnivals, summer resorts, and fairs, black tents provided an inexpensive, self-contained space where moving pictures could be projected day and night for paying audiences. Vitagraph would provide their typical package of projector, projectionist, and films for these venues, and sometimes even the tent. Albert Smith recalled that he and James Blackton personally operated two black tent shows in Richmond, Virginia, for a week during the summer of 1899 and made a small fortune. At Brooklyn's Bergen Beach, the "Respectable Resort for Respectable People," the black tent was dubbed the "Vitagraph Building." The highlight of the Bergen Beach show was a film of a later Jeffries fight that Vitagraph had purchased from Philadelphia producer Siegmund Lubin. Lubin was known as the "Pirate King" because when he wasn't duping other companies' films he was remaking them shot for shot. Or, in the case of the Jeffries fight, restaging it using two look-alike combatants, one of the actors wearing a wig in order to better resemble his counterpart. At one point in the bout the wig was knocked off, but filming continued as he put it back on. No one seemed to care, least of all Lubin, who didn't bother to edit out the mishap. Of all Vitagraph's competitors, the only one "Pop" Rock was genuinely fond of was "Pop" Lubin, whom he had known since 1896.[41]

Another turn-of-the-century Vitagraph client likely secured by Rock was the Kickapoo Indian Medicine Company. The New England–based Kickapoo Company manufactured alcohol-based elixirs, aka "snake oil," that were sold by smooth-talking "professors" making spurious claims about the "medicine's" restorative powers for virtually any and all ailments. Kickapoo put together small troupes of performers that would travel with the professors and a large stock of bottled elixirs throughout the back roads of rural and small-town America. A troupe would arrive at a town or crossroads and, after a crowd gathered, put on a show. A sales pitch for the "medicine" occurred in between performances, a prototype for the radio and TV commercials that would assault later generations. At the end of the show, bottles of the "ancient Indian remedy" would be sold to gullible spectators. Kickapoo employed three or four Vitagraph exhibition units at a time, bringing moving pictures to many people in faraway places for the first time.[42]

At the opposite end of the exhibition spectrum were the Chautauquas, which just a few years earlier had provided Smith and Blackton with their primary source of income. Chautauquas were independently operated Christian summer school camps for adults and families. Rooted in nondenominational Protestant education, worship, and social activism, the Chautauquas also offered classes in science, history, literature, and foreign languages as part of the general uplift movement prominent during the late nineteenth and early twentieth centuries. By 1900 many of the 150 Chautauquas included moving pictures in their programs. Vitagraph exhibitions were especially popular components of the Lexington, Kentucky, Chautauqua Assembly from 1898 to 1900. Lexington's Vitagraph shows included Spanish–American and Boer War actualities and re-creations, trick films, a *Spanish Bullfight*, and panoramas of the Brooklyn Bridge and Rocky Mountains.[43]

Placing their product in black tents, Kickapoo troupes, and Chautauquas was certainly good for Vitagraph, but these were all seasonal venues. Prior to the nickelodeon boom of 1905, the only entertainment able to accommodate moving pictures year-round was vaudeville. Unfortunately for Vitagraph, by the end of 1898 both of Proctor's Manhattan theaters eliminated moving pictures from their programs. But not all was lost. By mid-May 1899 Vitagraph enjoyed limited runs in more than a half dozen vaudeville theaters stretching from Richmond to Montreal. Even better, the company was in the midst of much longer relationships at two Brooklyn vaudeville houses, the Novelty on Driggs Avenue and the Music Hall at Fulton Street and Broadway. As far as the Vitagraph partners were concerned, that still wasn't good enough. They wanted a continuing presence at a Manhattan vaudeville house to give them prestige within the business and with far-flung audiences who were impressed with a New York City residency. The most stable and best-known venue was also the city's oldest. Pop Rock set his sights on landing Tony Pastor's Fourteenth Street Theatre.[44]

Tony Pastor began entertaining professionally in 1846 and more than half a century later was still performing nightly at his Fourteenth Street Theatre, drawing from a vast repertoire of comic songs. The venue was tiny by any standard, containing only three hundred seats: a neighborhood theater. But the neighborhood was the entertainment capital of America. The biggest stars of the era played Pastor's, including Lillian Russell, George M. Cohan, and the comedy team of Weber and Fields. Tony Pastor tried Englishman Birt Acres's Kineopticon, the Lumière brothers' Cinematographe, and Edison moving picture shows at his theater between June 1896 and September 1898. James Blackton said that when Pop Rock approached Tony Pastor in June 1899 about using the Vitagraph service, Pastor agreed to do so not because of the merits of its films but rather as a result of the blandishments of the company's senior partner. Although Pastor could pay no more than $75 per week and used the films mostly as chasers at the end of his otherwise live shows, his theater became Vitagraph's showcase. Tony Pastor's Fourteenth Street Theatre presented Vitagraph films every week for the next nine years. The job required a dependable and trustworthy projectionist; Albert Smith persuaded his old friend Ronald Reader to accept the position.[45]

Vitagraph doubled its net profits for 1899 over the previous year, even though the Edison Company failed to pay royalties on the Vitagraph productions they copyrighted and sold as their own. This was especially galling, given that half of the films sold by Edison in 1898–1899 were actually made by Vitagraph and William Paley. Smith also learned that improvements he made to the Edison projectors he was forced to purchase were adapted for a new projector recently put on the market by Edison, though Smith received no credit or compensation.

In January 1900, Vitagraph threatened to sue the Edison Company to get an accounting of the royalties they were owed. Edison responded by canceling its licensing agreement with Vitagraph, and presented Rock with a copy of the injunction against his younger partners that the Edison attorneys had been holding in abeyance for just such an occasion. It was only then that Blackton and Smith realized one of the documents they had signed in 1898 was a consent decree in which they admitted illegally duping films and infringing on Edison patents. Rock's young partners were terrified at the possibility of going to prison.[46]

Pop Rock's levelheaded maturity saved the company. He talked Smith and Blackton into reorganizing Vitagraph in order to protect the business. The American Vitagraph, Inc. was incorporated on February 15, 1900, with assets totaling $6,000, the valuation of the physical equipment and films owned by the company. As expected, Edison brought suit against them and depositions were taken in April 1900. The Vitagraph partners revealed that in addition to their being coerced into illegally photographing the Jeffries fight, Edison repeatedly instructed them to purchase and make multiple dupes of films produced by Thomas Armat, the Lumière Brothers, and especially Siegmund Lubin; Edison then sold the dupes at a discount. A surviving account ledger corroborates that Vitagraph did indeed do Edison's dirty work, purchasing more than $700 worth of Lubin films during the first eight months of 1899. An agreement was finally reached in October whereby Vitagraph would pay Edison a 10 percent royalty on all future exhibition income. As if that wasn't bad enough, the company also had to provide Edison with prints of films it had made since the beginning of the year and momentarily refrain from producing any more films for sale to Edison or anyone else.[47]

Smith and Blackton applied new techniques to moving pictures that had lasting ramifications. According to Smith, Vitagraph made "the first stop-motion picture with inanimate objects." *The Humpty Dumpty Circus* opens on his young daughter Ethel playing with a set of wooden circus performers and animals. When she departs, the toys begin to move by themselves. Smith explained the "moveable joints enabled us to place [the toys] in balanced positions. It was a tedious process inasmuch as movement could be achieved only by photographing separately each change of position." Smith's reminiscences are the only records of the movie's existence and he is not always reliable. But *The Humpty Dumpty Circus* account seems plausible given Vitagraph's other experiments in stop-motion circa 1900. Considering how new technology is exploited in this film and its uncanny parallels to *Toy Story*, the first computer-generated feature made nearly a century later, it is hoped that a print of *The Humpty Dumpty Circus* will eventually surface.[48]

One Vitagraph experiment in stop-motion dating from 1900 for which a print does survive is *The Enchanted Drawing.* Four years earlier *Inventor Edison Sketched By World Artist* documented an aspect of J. Stuart Blackton's vaudeville act. *The Enchanted Drawing* represents Blackton's first step toward making his drawings cinematic. In the film he draws the face of a man on a large white paper. Blackton then draws a bottle of wine and glass, a top hat and cigar, removes them from the illustration as real three-dimensional objects, and returns each of the items to the paper as two-dimensional drawings. The transformations from two-dimensional drawings to three-dimensional counterparts and back are seamlessly executed via stop-motion cinematography and make this a noteworthy film. But something else about the film had a far more profound and lasting impact on cinema: every time an object is removed from or returned to the illustration, the illustrated man's expressions change from frown to smile and back, becoming *animated.* This movement across two illustrations was the beginning of motion picture animation. Six years of Edison legal maneuverings would impede Blackton before he could resume his experiments in illustrated movement.[49]

Shortly before another Edison-imposed moratorium on production went into effect, Albert Smith shot eight films documenting the aftermath of a hurricane that destroyed Galveston, Texas, on September 8, 1900, and claimed more than six thousand lives. Martial law was imposed, and Smith had to pretend to be an official with a salvage company in order to gain entry into the city. Most of his Galveston footage consists of long, smooth pans. The simplicity and purity of the imagery coupled with the absence of an audio track make for a powerful, unsettling viewing experience. Smith spent eight days in Galveston, his traveling expenses totaling $109.41. The Edison Company sold between seventeen and thirty-five prints of each film, which resulted in Vitagraph receiving $71.40 in royalties. At this stage in the company's history it didn't pay for Vitagraph to make actualities too far from home, even if it had been able to sell them on the open market.[50]

On October 11, 1899, the Boers of the South African Republic and Orange Free State declared war on British newcomers. The Boers were white South Africans descended from settlers of the Dutch East India Company, who were on the verge of losing control of the areas they inhabited to growing numbers of English colonists. Most of the colonization into what is today South Africa and Swaziland was motivated by the discovery of gold and diamond mines. For England, maintaining control of those mines was worth fighting for. In his autobiography, Albert Smith wrote that he and Pop Rock were meeting with John Koster when news of the Boer War reached New York. Koster told them that if Vitagraph would cover the war and "give them first call on the film," then Koster & Bial's account would be theirs.

According to Smith, he consequently sailed for London where he was provided with credentials from the British War Office; he then made the long voyage to Durban on the east coast of South Africa, arriving in early December. There he ran into his friend Richard Harding Davis who was covering the war for the *London Times* and the *New York Times.* Together they spent the next two months documenting the war with camera and pen. When Smith ran out of raw film stock at the end of January, he returned to New York triumphant: "the Boer War netted us Koster and Bial's."

Albert Smith's tale includes witnessing a Boer militia defeating British troops outside the town of Ladysmith, stumbling into the camp of a notorious

Boer guerrilla leader, and having afternoon tea with a Zulu chieftain. But is it true? Vitagraph began including Boer War films in its exhibition service in January 1900, more than a month before Smith could have returned from South Africa with his unprocessed footage. John Koster, of Koster & Bial's, died in 1895; John Jr. briefly ran the theater on at least two occasions after his father's death. But from September 27 through December 9, 1899, before, during, and after the start of the Boer War, William Brady managed Koster & Bial's. Brady was producing the stage show "Around New York in Eighty Minutes," which featured his boxer Jim Jeffries; for one or two weeks Brady included Vitagraph films on the program. Koster & Bial's went through at least seven other managers and format changes before closing for good in July 1901. Any single theater's promise of a long-term contract would not have covered the expense and risk associated with traveling to Africa to photograph the war.

Unlike Albert Smith's trip to Galveston, no records exist regarding business or travel expenses to England or South Africa for 1899 or 1900. Nor is there any documentation in the British War Office pertaining to Albert E. Smith. According to a trade article published in 1925, as soon as the Boers declared war on the UK, "Vitagraph . . . hastily made contracts with European producers which gave Vitagraph the sole right to the pictures made in the South African battlefront." This is borne out by a catalog published by Vitagraph circa April 1900 that lists thirty-four Boer War actualities for sale. Cameramen affiliated with the Warwick Trading Company of London photographed at least twenty-nine of those films. In fact, a photograph on the cover of Albert Smith's autobiography purporting to be the author is actually of Warwick's cameraman, Joseph Rosenthal, "photographing transport wagons during the Boer War." *New York Herald* and *London Mail* correspondent Richard Harding Davis didn't arrive in South Africa until the end of January 1900, about the same time Smith said he left Africa to begin the month-long voyage home. Smith ends his Boer War reminiscence by quoting a letter written to him by Davis describing his experience when the British retook Ladysmith. Except for the opening and closing sentences, the Smith letter is a word-for-word duplicate of a letter Davis wrote to his mother that was reprinted in a book about the legendary war correspondent in 1917, one year after his death.[51]

At the end of 1900 Vitagraph wasn't earning enough to continue paying Edison the 10 percent royalty on its monthly exhibition gross. Blackton's efforts to reach a compromise failed, and Edison canceled their licensing agreement. Vitagraph could only remain in the moving picture business as an exhibitor of other companies' films. Faced with a similar dilemma, Siegmund Lubin relocated his family and business to his native Germany. Thanks largely to the efforts of Pop Rock, Vitagraph had more clients than any other exhibition service in the United States, extending as far west as Michigan and Ohio, and, with the exception of New Orleans, as far south as Washington, DC. But the company required a steady supply of films. Charles Musser has indicated that of the 246 films exhibited by Vitagraph in 1900, 117 were made in England and 66 in France. From 1898 through 1904 Vitagraph acquired nearly fifty of Georges Méliès's Star Film productions from London-based sales agent Charles Urban, who also represented several British filmmakers.[52]

As was the case with virtually every exhibition service at this time, Vitagraph would purchase one original print of a film and then strike as many copies from it as necessary to be shown simultaneously among its regular customers. This practice impacted Méliès more than the others because he wasn't adequately profiting from his films, the most popular in the world.

On March 10, 1902, the circuit court of appeals reversed an earlier decision in a suit Edison brought against Biograph, declaring Thomas Edison's key motion picture patents invalid. The judge stated, "It is obvious that Mr. Edison . . . was not the inventor of the film [and] was not the first inventor of apparatus capable of producing suitable negatives. . . . The predecessors of Edison invented [such] apparatus." He noted that while Edison was undoubtedly the first to utilize equipment and film for commercial success, it "did not entitle him under the patent laws to a monopoly of all camera [or projection] apparatus capable of utilizing the film." The ruling terminated all Edison lawsuits alleging patent infringement. Edison's attorneys scrambled to reinstate the patents based on narrower claims.

Siegmund Lubin consequently returned from Europe to resume production in Philadelphia and sell duplicates of Edison films "at bargain prices," and Chicago-based William Selig more than quadrupled his production output over the previous year. It was only natural, then, that the Vitagraph partners would instruct their attorney, W. R. Baird, to ascertain whether they too could legally resume production. Baird contacted Edison's lawyers for guidance about how to proceed. The Edison position was that the circuit court's decision had no bearing on Vitagraph because of the consent decree and injunction Blackton and Smith had agreed to and, it was claimed, subsequently violated. The charge was based on dupes Vitagraph made of its foreign acquisitions utilizing the same size sprocket holes as films manufactured on Edison equipment. Smith and Blackton were at their wits' end. They subsequently engaged new attorneys and even offered to sell the company to itinerant showman Lyman H. Howe, who turned them down.[53]

Vitagraph's catalog and advertisements for 1903 stated, "we are exhibitors only." But that wasn't true. The company actually produced at least twenty-five films between the autumn of 1900 and summer of 1905. They were made under the radar for use only in the company's exhibition service. Most of the actualities were of limited appeal by design. For example, Vitagraph's film of an Elks' convention in Atlantic City was then shown at individual lodges; footage of President Roosevelt's visit to New Haven in honor of Yale University's two hundredth anniversary was shown only at Sylvester Poli's theater in that town. Scenes of local landmarks and residents were made for Poli theaters in Norwalk and New Britain, Connecticut. These were similar to footage taken at Brooklyn's Brighton Beach one summer afternoon. A tiny article in the *Brooklyn Eagle* was headlined "Did You Bathe at Brighton? If so . . . it will be a pleasurable surprise to many a person seated in the [Orpheum Theater] to suddenly see himself [in] a moving film." Such films might pack a single theater once or twice, but were of no interest anywhere else, akin to watching another family's home movies. They weren't profitable enough to justify the time and expense it took to make them.[54]

In the midst of their five-year moratorium on production, Vitagraph took a huge risk by making a few relatively high-profile fiction films. Kyrle Bellew was a leading matinee idol at the turn of the twentieth century; he played swashbuckling heroes in the kinds of roles that Errol Flynn would later achieve stardom with in the movies. *A Gentleman of France* opened December 30, 1901, and became one of Bellew's most popular successes. The highlight of the play occurred on the stairs of a castle as Bellew's character crossed swords with seven villains trying to prevent him from rescuing a damsel in distress. After closing on Broadway, *A Gentleman of France* continued to play theaters in the Greater New York area.[55]

When Bellew approached Vitagraph in October 1902 about photographing the sword fight so that he could watch and admire himself as others did, it was an offer the partners couldn't refuse. At that point in time, theatrical stars of Bellew's caliber wouldn't have anything to do with the new medium. This was a major coup. Blackton arranged with the play's producers, Liebler and Company, to have the staircase scenery transported from the Newark, New Jersey, theater where the show was currently playing to a nearby minor league baseball park where Bellew and his troupe reenacted the scene under an autumn sun.

After the five-minute-long scene was completed, Bellew asked that a closer shot be taken so he could study his face. According to Smith it was the first time Vitagraph ever made a close-up. "*The Great Sword Combat on the Stairs* from the play 'A Gentleman of France,' posed by Mr. Kyrle Bellew and his company exclusively for the Vitagraph," was highlighted in a catalog the company mailed to potential customers of its exhibition service. It was risky to advertise such a high-profile production, but there doesn't seem to have been any direct backlash from Edison's attorneys. Even so, it would be another three years before Vitagraph would resume production of "posed" films.[56]

Just six months after losing his patents case against Biograph, Thomas Edison was granted a patent reissue on narrower claims. In November 1902, his attorneys filed new suits against Biograph, Selig, Lubin, Méliès, William Paley, Pathé Frères, and Eberhard Schneider. Lacking the means to continue fighting Edison, Schneider dropped out of film production. A few years later when Paley's primary client Proctor sold out to the Keith vaudeville circuit, he could no longer afford to fight the Edison litigation and got out of production to become a freelance cameraman. Since Vitagraph was for the most part abiding by the terms of the consent decree, Edison held off until March 1905 in filing a new suit against the company.[57]

In the meantime Georges Méliès realized that something was amiss regarding the meager profits coming in from America, and in March 1903 sent his brother Gaston to New York to set up an American sales office. But it was too late; interest in Méliès's "trick" films was on the wane. By 1904 the biggest supplier of moving pictures to the United States was Pathé Frères, also of France. Pathé took advantage of the dearth of films being produced in America due to Edison's incessant litigation. When Pathé opened a New York sales office in 1904, Vitagraph purchased thirty of its titles and would have bought more had Pathé not held some back to sell to the competition. For the next half dozen years Pathé released more films in the United States than any other company until it was supplanted by Vitagraph.[58]

In 1903 Vitagraph moved their business office to the Morton Building, just a few doors down Nassau Street from their original office in the Morse Building. The company showed a net profit of $15,860 for 1903. Profits jumped to $25,750 in 1904. Vitagraph reorganized that year as a copartnership owned equally by President William T. Rock, Vice-President and Secretary J. Stuart Blackton, and Treasurer Albert E. Smith. Until the spring of 1916 the business was officially known as the "Vitagraph Company of America."[59]

2

1905–1908

For years, France's contribution to the *invention* of cinema has been overstated. British, American, and German filmmakers designed and constructed the equipment necessary to record and show moving pictures, which the Lumière Brothers and others then made improvements on. Underemphasized, however, is the role of another French company, Pathé Freres, in establishing the *business* of motion pictures. Charles Pathé developed his organization on a massive industrial scale. By 1905 Pathé had established a stock company of actors and directors, and maintained multiple production units at three studio complexes on the outskirts of Paris. Pathé also set up offices in major cities throughout the world from which to sell his product. Pathé provided America with a steady supply of new films at a time when US producers had to devote most of their financial resources to fighting Edison litigation. Vitagraph's exhibition service grew more profitable year by year, thanks in part to a steady supply of new Pathé titles. Inspired by Pathé's success, Rock, Blackton, and Smith decided to significantly expand their business in 1905.[1]

Vitagraph's expansion was slow and methodical. Virtually all American exhibitors included Pathé films in their programs. Vitagraph's success to this point was due largely to Pop Rock's "urbane charm, driving good bargains" with operators of vaudeville theaters and other venues that utilized the company's exhibition service. Rock accomplished much of this outside the office, over drinks. Possessing neither an aptitude nor inclination for business, J. Stuart Blackton relished being the public face of Vitagraph as its artistic director. Thus it fell upon the conscientious and seemingly indefatigable Albert Smith to decide on and execute the policies and operations of the company. Among his many duties, Smith began making annual business trips to Europe in 1903 to open up foreign markets for Vitagraph and scout the competition. Given his firsthand knowledge of the Pathé operation, it was Smith who convinced the others that they needed to forgo rooftop filmmaking and,

Building the Brooklyn studio, 1906. *Nickelodeon*, January 1911.

instead, construct a facility for the year-round production of story-based moving pictures. Having spent half his life in the Flatbush section of Brooklyn, Smith found a parcel of land in that area to establish a "manufacturing plant."[2]

The property in Greenfield (today commonly known as Midwood) was at Locust Avenue and East Fifteenth Street on the southwest edge of Flatbush. Because the neighborhood was far from Manhattan, Vitagraph was able to purchase a 200-by-200-foot lot in August 1905 for approximately $1,000. The land bordered Brooklyn and Brighton Beach elevated railroad tracks near the Elm Avenue rapid transit station, as well as adjacent parcels that could be purchased for future expansion. The dimensions of the company's initial building were approximately 50 by 100 feet. It took thirteen months to complete, at a total cost of $25,000.

A studio took up half of the top floor and was large enough to accommodate at least two sets simultaneously. The ceiling and one wall were made of prismatic glass to diffuse sunlight evenly and, thus, eliminate harsh shadows. Adjacent to the studio were dressing rooms for the men and women, and an office shared by Blackton and Smith. The ground floor contained a darkroom for processing the film, a joining (editing) room, a costume department, and a machine shop where cameras and projectors were constructed. Props and scenic backdrops were built in the carpenter's shop in the basement. Greenfield was not yet powered with electricity, and connecting the facility to the nearest Edison generating station was cost prohibitive. Thus, the basement also contained a diesel 100-horsepower generator operating a dynamo that supplied power. The original chimney was soon replaced with a smokestack towering over the facility on which "V-I-T-A-G-R-A-P-H" was spelled out in vertically inlaid brick. The tallest structure in the neighborhood, it served as a beacon to all who dreamed of working in the movies.

Shortly after the Vitagraph plant was completed in autumn 1906, construction began on a second building of equal dimensions built flush against the first, which doubled the size of the studio. Eighteen adjacent parcels were purchased over the next few years until the plant encompassed three acres that housed four separate studio buildings. Administrative offices, the processing lab, and other departments were eventually housed in their own structures on the lot.[3]

Long after the death of his partners, Albert Smith revealed, "A state of open warfare [existed] between Jim and Pop." Blackton was terrified of Rock, which the senior partner used to his advantage, "drenching Jim with a torrential outpouring of personal abuse." Smith also averred that although "Mr. Rock . . . had no imaginative ability in the dramatic line," it didn't stop him from interfering with creative decisions related to what he believed were excessive costs during the rooftop filmmaking in lower Manhattan. "When we started the studio in Brooklyn . . . we kept the office [for Rock at] 116 Nassau Street New York just to keep him away." For the next ten years, Vitagraph's exhibition business was presided over by Pop Rock in Manhattan, while Smith and Blackton devoted their attention to production and attendant business matters at the Brooklyn complex.[4]

Throughout 1905, Vitagraph's exhibition service continued to be featured on the bills of most of the major vaudeville theaters in the northeast. By 1907, venues dedicated solely to moving pictures, popularly known as nickelodeons, had taken over exhibition. The nickelodeon boom is attributed to Pittsburgh exhibitor Harry Davis, who converted a vacant store into a moving picture theater in June 1905. The price of admission was a nickel. Davis's nickel theater was so successful that he opened other nickelodeons throughout the northeastern United States. Arcade operators and small business entrepreneurs created storefront theaters of their own, with the result that nickelodeons saturated much of the country in less than two years.[5]

Some early film histories recognize William T. Rock's New Orleans theater as the prototypical "store show." However, had Rock tried to expand in 1896 as Davis did nine years later, he would have failed, for it wasn't until 1904–1905 that American movies found their form, substance, and audience. A large segment of the nickelodeon audience consisted of Italian and Jewish immigrants who were attracted to inexpensive visual entertainment that didn't rely on familiarity with the English language. For them, silent cinema was preferable to the language-based entertainment of most vaudeville acts. However, working-class American-born Protestants and Catholics accounted for a much larger portion of the nickelodeon audience than has been reported. Native born or immigrant, it seemed that everyone who patronized nickelodeons preferred films with fictional stories.[6]

In addition to inspiration from Pathé's lucrative business model, Vitagraph was motivated to resume making films of their own following the success that William Selig and Siegmund Lubin had in renewing production in the face of further Edison litigation. The Edison Manufacturing Company's *The Great Train Robbery*, released in December 1903, became the most successful American film during the first dozen years of commercial cinema. The New Jersey Western inspired Lubin to make a shot-by-shot remake near his Philadelphia home, and Selig to begin producing fictional Westerns in the West with real cowboys and Indians. Inspiration for *The Great Train Robbery* came from such British crime and chase films as *Desperate Poaching Affray*, *Daring Daylight Robbery*, and *Trailed by Bloodhounds*, all released earlier in the year. Rather than follow the American trend and make a Western, Vitagraph chose to resume production with a story that was closer to the British model but had an urbane twist.[7]

Given the legal and financial risks associated with the resumption of production, Vitagraph took steps to protect and maximize the return on its investment, choosing a successful existing property to adapt. One year after *The Great Sword Combat on the Stairs*, Kyrle Bellew was back on Broadway in his greatest triumph, *Raffles.* Adapted from two popular novels, *Raffles* and *The Amateur Cracksman*, the play concerns a gentleman burglar who preys on high society and ultimately eludes capture after returning some stolen jewels. Permission was acquired from the play's producer, Theodore Liebler, though Bellew did not appear in the film. Smith and Blackton wanted their *Raffles* to be bigger and better than anything they had ever attempted, signaling the end of single-shot, minute-long films. They hoped to cast professional actors, but neither man was confident of adequately directing them.

What initially seemed a fortuitous coincidence occurred when G. M. Anderson visited the Vitagraph office. Known variously as George, Gilbert, Billy, and Andy, Anderson was born Max Aronson and had a modest background acting in theatrical stock companies before playing three small roles in *The Great Train Robbery*, directed by Edwin S. Porter. Never lacking in chutzpah, Anderson convinced gullible Smith and Blackton that he was the real director of *The Great Train Robbery* and would bring similar success to Vitagraph with a professional cast that he himself would recruit. Filming of *Raffles* occurred in late July to early August 1905, with exteriors staged at real locations, including a bank at Fifth Avenue and Thirty-Fourth Street, one of Manhattan's busiest intersections. Interiors were photographed in front of backdrops on the roof of Vitagraph's Manhattan offices. Capitalizing on the popularity of the novels and play, Blackton and Smith titled their film *Raffles, the Amateur Cracksman* and released it during the first week of September 1905.[8]

Despite a relatively sizable budget and multiple locations, *Raffles, the Amateur Cracksman* is uninspired and confusing cinema. Lacking the compositional clarity and editorial dynamism evident in *The Great Train Robbery*, each scene in *Raffles* is photographed in a single, very wide shot, making it nearly impossible to distinguish individual characters or their relationships with each other. Narrative clarity is further thwarted by the fact that the lead character wears disguises throughout much of the story. Since there are no explanatory intertitles, only those with an intimate knowledge of the novels and/or play could make sense of the film.

With *Raffles, the Amateur Cracksman*, Vitagraph instituted a new policy of offering the film for rent during its first few weeks in release. The popularity of the source material seemed to trump the film's shortcomings, for in its first weeks of release it played such leading vaudeville houses as Tony Pastor's, Hammerstein's Victoria, Chase's Theatre in Washington, DC, and the Steel Pier in Atlantic City. After three weeks Vitagraph sold prints of *Raffles* outright for $126. To everyone's surprise, sales failed to meet expectations, not because of the narrative confusion but due to its length. Maxing out a standard reel at 1,050 feet, *Raffles, the Amateur Cracksman* was as long as *The Great Train Robbery*. But in the nearly two years between the release of the Edison film and *Raffles*, a fundamental shift had occurred in exhibition. Albert Smith recalled that most of the nickelodeon operators who quickly came to dominate exhibition refused to purchase "long" films of fifteen minutes' duration, claiming that "the public would not remain in their seats that long for any single subject." The unspoken truth was that audiences were in the habit of entering nickelodeon theaters not in conjunction with the start time for any given title but rather at their own convenience, and they did not necessarily stay for a complete cycle of very short films. Exhibitors believed that when customers remained in their seats for longer films, it cut down on audience turnover and, thus, hurt ticket sales. Faced with this opposition,

Vitagraph did not release another full-reel production until 1909. Exhibitor prohibition on "long" films also meant that during this period Vitagraph and the other pioneer filmmakers were hamstrung into producing simplistic stories of between five and ten minutes' duration.[9]

Of the dozen moving pictures produced by Vitagraph in the latter part of 1905, *The Escape from Sing Sing*, supervised by Albert Smith, bears the closest resemblance to British crime and chase films. Although the title was cribbed from a popular theatrical melodrama, the film's narrative was inspired by a real event: the escape of two Death Row convicts from Sing Sing Prison. Interior scenes, including the prison breakout, were staged atop the roof of the Morton Building, but the chase was filmed in Bronx Park. Unlike the real prison break, in which the escapees were never caught, the Vitagraph film ends tragically when the young daughter of the principal convict is killed during a shootout between her father and the police. Anderson directed the actors by talking them through the action: "Now when [the prison guard] turns his back to you . . . run down the ladder and jump on him. That's it, come, quick now!" Office workers watching from nearby skyscrapers enthusiastically applauded the performances. Both Smith and Blackton operated cameras simultaneously in order to insure seamless cutting on the action and enhance the dynamism that multiple angles provide.[10]

Later that summer, Vitagraph made *The Servant Girl Problem*, a domestic comedy that the company would remake with slight variations several times over the ensuing years. The story is simple: After a woman fires her clumsy maid, her husband hires the prettiest applicant at an employment agency, but back home he is caught flirting with her. The couple returns to the agency, and this time the wife chooses the homeliest candidate. The new maid turns out to be clumsier than the first and much lazier, forcing the husband to do many of her chores. As with *Raffles*, interiors were photographed on the roof of the Morton Building. The drawbacks of shooting on a stage exposed to the elements are obvious in the kitchen scenes, where the sunlight is harsh and a strong wind inadvertently animates props and apparel.

Heavyset character actor William Shea appeared in drag as the homely maid. Shea was a veteran of the theater, having played alongside such legendary figures as Edwin Booth and Joseph Jefferson. The beloved cornerstone of what became the first American moving picture stock company, Shea was a Vitagraph mainstay for thirteen years. The funniest moment in *The Servant Girl Problem* is a close-up of Shea holding a sign reading: "Her Choice." Earlier in the film, the pretty maid holds a sign reading "His Choice." Paula

Hilburn, known professionally as Paula Dean, played the comely servant. At a time when it was difficult to recruit professional actors for moving pictures, Albert Smith recalled that Dean was the first "persistent applicant for whatever there might be in the way of bit parts." Her close-up resulted in another first: scores of letters and phone calls from male viewers anxious to learn Dean's identity and contact information. Paula Dean's popularity, both with moving picture audiences and within the company, led to her being featured in more Vitagraph productions through the end of 1905.[11]

The last big Vitagraph release for 1905 was *Monsieur Beaucaire*, adapted from a novel by Booth Tarkington. This was another production initiated by Blackton and is the company's earliest surviving film with intertitles. It may also have been Vitagraph's first production with interiors shot on an outdoor stage in Flatbush while the studio was under construction. Exteriors were photographed at an old mansion with marble staircase and stone columns in Brooklyn's Prospect Park. Louis XVI–style costumes and wigs were rented, adding to the authentic mise-en-scène. It was the most opulent Vitagraph effort to date. Unfortunately, *Monsieur Beaucaire* is played out in a handful of tableaux wide-angle shots and lacks the cinematic dynamism of *Escape from Sing Sing*. This is in keeping with the continental model favored by Blackton, both in terms of presentation and story, as opposed to the British aesthetic that Smith preferred. Austrian-born Paul Panzer starred as the dashing Beaucaire. Panzer had played the main convict in *Escape from Sing Sing* and remained with the stock company into 1909. Paula Dean played Beaucaire's lover, Lady Mary, and Blackton was the villainous Duke, willing to kidnap and kill in order to have her. Blackton later admitted that "sundry love scenes with the fair leading lady had more than a little to do with my becoming a member of the cast." His attraction to Paula Dean, hinted at in *The Servant Girl Problem*, mushroomed into an open affair on the set of *Monsieur Beaucaire*.[12]

Blackton's flagrant indiscretion notwithstanding, he and Smith were very careful about conveying propriety in Vitagraph's stories and costuming, and even in the unheard words spoken by the actors on camera. Signs posted around the sets made things clear: "What you say in front of the camera is our business. . . . What you say at home is yours." This sense of responsibility was common among Vitagraph employees. Reflecting on his career shortly before his death, William Shea said, "The Vitagraph firm has been very kind to me. The exhibitors have stood for me during many years before them on the screen, and the public seems to appreciate my efforts to please. I am satisfied—I wouldn't be a Christian if I asked for any more."[13]

Even with all the costs associated with Vitagraph's return to production and the expansion of its facilities, the company still managed to post a net profit of $38,860 for 1905, an increase of more than $13,000 over 1904. Anderson continued to direct and occasionally appear in Vitagraph productions into early 1906, earning about $50 per week. William Shea recalled that featured actors received $5 a day for a six-day workweek. Paul Panzer remembered it as $3 per day; however, every actor in the stock company was expected to build and paint sets and props, for which they earned an additional $14 per week. Occasionally other Vitagraph personnel, such as idle projectionists, were pressed into service as extras. Blackton and Smith were always on set operating the camera and overseeing production while Anderson focused on the performances. During the half year Anderson was in their employ, all three contributed scenarios.[14]

In the first three months of 1906 Vitagraph released thirteen films, mostly comedies along with a few crime and chase films. G. M. Anderson suffered from an inflated sense of his value to the company and insisted on being made a partner; instead he was fired. Albert Smith indicated that Anderson too often delegated his responsibilities to propman Walter Ackerman, whom he also used as a scapegoat when things didn't turn out as planned. Before a replacement was found, the Vitagraph partners took brief sabbaticals. For J. Stuart Blackton, this meant completing his latest efforts to marry illustration with moving pictures.[15]

Blackton's film of a female figure with rapidly changing expressions, made for the Edison Company in 1896, merely documented a component of his vaudeville act. Four years later *The Enchanted Drawing* utilized the same technique that made Albert Smith's stop-motion films possible: by interrupting a shot to make a change to objects in motion and then resuming photography, substitutions and even "unmotivated" movement in time and space occurred in the shot when it was projected. Blackton would momentarily halt filming to substitute two-dimensional drawings for three-dimensional objects, and change the expressions on his hand-drawn characters. Progressing from these early endeavors, Blackton's *Humorous Phases of Funny Faces*, released in April of 1906, is undeniably, unmistakably motion picture animation. The advertising copy he wrote for the film proclaims its significance: "Absolutely different from any film ever made." It is probably the only time Blackton didn't exaggerate.[16]

The opening card of *Humorous Phases of Funny Faces* consists of bits of line that come together to form recognizable letters spelling out the title. In the first segment Blackton's hand is visible drawing the face of an old man on a blackboard. The head of a woman materializes alongside him. Eyeglasses appear on the man, his eyes move in the direction of the woman, he smiles and winks. The woman smiles and winks back. The man sprouts hair, and a cigar appears in the corner of his mouth. Its smoke drifts over and obscures the woman. A top hat appears on the man's head. He wiggles his eyebrows, Groucho-style, before Blackton's hand returns to erase the characters from the blackboard. The second segment opens on an empty blackboard as a heavyset man in profile takes form in chalk. He flips his umbrella and doffs his hat. The movements of the arm, umbrella, and hat are made with black paper cutouts outlined in white, giving the appearance of being hand-drawn. The third segment starts on a swirl made by an eraser. The action moves in reverse, "un-erasing" the faces of a man and woman facing each other in profile until the chalk lines defining them disappear. The final segment opens on a circus clown already drawn in chalk on the blackboard. Attentive viewing reveals that when his arms, legs, hat, magic wand, dog, and hoop move, they, too, are paper cutouts. At the climax of the film the cutouts are seamlessly replaced by chalk drawings, enabling the hand of the otherwise unseen Blackton to completely erase the figure.

As the first animated motion picture, *Humorous Phases of Funny Faces* introduces a new form of cinematic expression and incorporates other properties unique to the medium. Albert Smith recalled that his partner began working on *Humorous Phases* in 1904, two years before the release of the finished product. Prints of the three-minute-long film sold for $27.60.[17]

Blackton's next hand-drawn animated film, *Lightning Sketches*, was released in 1907. It is more than twice as long as *Humorous Phases* and abandons chalk and blackboard for a return to charcoal on paper. The film opens with Blackton at an easel sketching the Vitagraph logo: an eagle on a crest. When the drawing is completed, Blackton steps out of frame and the eagle flaps its wings. In the second segment, Blackton reenters the frame accompanied by a bald man with prominent nose, whom he sketches in profile. When finished, Blackton hands his model a cigar, lights it, and they exit the frame. The man's caricature then smokes its cigar. Blackton returns and writes "Coon" and "Cohen" on blank paper, then draws caricatures of a black man and Jew from the letters of those words. Other segments include a boat sailing across the water; a clown riding atop an elephant; Blackton applying tonic to the drawing of a bald-headed man who then sprouts hair on his head and face; a bottle pouring its contents into a glass, followed by a spray of seltzer;

and a small man using his top hat as a step stool to kiss a taller, curvy Gibson Girl. The print of *Lightning Sketches* at the British Film Institute, which seems to be the most complete extant, ends as Blackton uses scissors to cut paper rectangles, suggesting there may have been at least one more segment to the original film.

Frenchman Émile Cohl has often been cited as the originator of motion picture animation. However, his first film, *Fantasmagorie* (1908), is an unmistakable homage to Blackton's method, style, and characters. Cohl could not have made his film had Blackton not shown the way. Other historians claim animation began with Winsor McCay. McCay called on Blackton in 1909 seeking advice and assistance in how to bring the characters from his newspaper comic strip *Little Nemo in Slumberland* to cinematic life. Blackton provided the production facilities and technical expertise necessary to make McCay's dream a reality. When it was completed in 1911, Vitagraph distributed the film, titled *Winsor McCay*, throughout the world.

Vitagraph's resumption of the production of story films in May 1906 necessitated the hiring of a replacement for Anderson, William V. Ranous. Recruited via an advertisement in a theatrical newspaper, Ranous had been a veteran of the stage since 1874. The stigma of moving pictures, seen as cheap entertainment for immigrants and the working class, deterred top-rank stage actors and directors from working in the new medium. Thus it was mutually advantageous to employ second-tier veterans like Ranous and other newcomers such as D. W. Griffith. These men were more than actors and directors; they also functioned as writers, drawing from a vast repertoire of plays they could adapt to moving pictures. Ranous et al. also hired stock company veterans they had previously worked with.

As production increased, directors, cameramen, and writers were added to the staff, personally trained by the partners. Smith and Blackton were each responsible for half of Vitagraph's productions, functioning as supervising producers for the films made by their individual units. According to Smith, this resulted in a friendly rivalry "between the two 'camps' . . . to produce better pictures in shorter time." Virtually every other American production company would follow Vitagraph's organizational structure, which has come to be known as the "studio system." Unfortunately, the origin of the studio system has been erroneously attributed to later producers who merely copied the Vitagraph model, which itself was inspired by Pathé.[18]

The fifteen Vitagraph productions released during the latter half of 1906 reflect a variety of genres and reveal developments in cinematic technique.

The 100 to 1 Shot is the story of a rural family on the verge of losing their home who are able to pay the mortgage thanks to a winning bet on a horse race. The domestic scenes that bookend the story are photographed in wide shot in harsh sunlight without close-ups or explanatory intertitles, which makes it impossible to discern relationships within the group. However, a pawnshop exterior and most of the racetrack scenes were photographed in genuine locations, with the protagonist placed close to the camera as an actual race is in progress. With his winnings, the man hires a car and driver to rush home. In one shot, the car drives toward and past a stationary camera; in another, the camera pans with the car. These are intercut with the landlord and police arriving to make an arrest. Parallel editing of simultaneous actions occurring in two different locations that ultimately converge in a race to the rescue was rarely utilized in the pre-Griffith era. *The 100 to 1 Shot* represents a medium in transition, straddling the artificial theatricality of the movies' first decade and elements of framing, location shooting, and editing that are inherently cinematic.[19]

And the Villain Still Pursued Her; or, The Author's Dream is an outrageous comedy that by later standards is crudely made. It tells the story of an impoverished playwright who falls asleep at his desk and dreams of being the hero in his own three-character play. The narrative satirizes a type of entertainment that moving pictures were on the verge of supplanting: theatrical melodrama. This film is another of J. Stuart Blackton's whimsical explorations into what cinema could be and do. *And the Villain Still Pursued Her* subverts real-world cause and effect in ways that only cinema is capable of. The film also satirizes an entertainment form that was in decline due in large part to the staleness of its conventions.

Another comedy nightmare released in 1906, *The Dream of a Rarebit Fiend*, made by Edwin S. Porter for the Edison Manufacturing Company, sported some excellent special effects but otherwise seems ordinary when compared with Blackton's imaginative film. In *And the Villain Still Pursued Her*, the playwright's manuscript materializes on the wall of his flat simply because it can. The same is true of a reversed leap back onto a roof. Cinema alone offered the possibility of visualizing stream of consciousness and mimicking dream worlds. That is what *And the Villain Still Pursued Her* offers: a glimpse into surreal possibilities that are distinctly cinematic.

The final Vitagraph release for 1906 was also the first of what became an annual tradition of Christmas movies. *A Mid-Winter's Night Dream, or, Little Joe's Luck*, like most of the subsequent Christmas films, was an Albert Smith

British Christmas advertisement, *Pictures and the Picturegoer*, December 1915.

production. After begging on the street, a homeless boy falls asleep in the snow on the steps of a church and dreams of being taken in by a wealthy family with four young daughters. After dinner, the father, dressed as Santa Claus, comes down the chimney with presents. Little Joe receives stuffed animals and toy circus performers. The mother puts the children to bed. As Joe sleeps, his Teddy bear and circus toys come alive, performing on his bedside table. The scene dissolves back to Little Joe asleep on the steps of the church. A kindhearted policeman takes pity on the homeless boy and brings him home to celebrate Christmas.

A Mid-Winter's Night Dream was shot in Vitagraph's newly opened Flatbush studio. Absent is the harsh, unfiltered light and shadow that plagued the company's earlier productions. Daytime interiors are evenly lit and even flattering to the actors in a way that audiences have since come to expect from American movies. The nighttime lighting and realistic range of shadows in the children's bedroom are very impressive. Shooting within the confines of an enclosed studio meant that the camera now had to be closer to the action than had been the norm. In the studio, Smith and Blackton staged the action precisely nine feet from the camera. These medium close-ups, framing the top of the head to the knees, resulted in tighter compositions and greater narrative clarity. Unlike wide shots that mimicked the theater experience, this arrangement placed the viewer in the midst of the action. Vitagraph's new approach to cinematography was a radical break with tradition and was eventually adopted everywhere; in Europe it was known as the "American foreground" or "plan américain." It was now easier to identify individual characters and discern their relationships with each other; it was also easier to discern the actors' expressions, which had radical consequences on performance in cinema. Compact compositions also heightened movement within the frame, accentuating the essential property of *motion* pictures.

The most memorable sequence in *A Mid-Winter's Night Dream* is Little Joe's dream within the dream of his stuffed animals and circus toys coming to life. Adding to the believability of the toys' sudden vitalism is the sophisticated construction of the shots. The boy is established in his own bed across from the girls in the bedroom as the light is turned off. A medium shot provides a closer view of the toys atop the nightstand next to the bed. This is followed by a close-up of the boy falling asleep, the camera then panning to the toys coming to life, then back to the sleeping boy, all seemingly uninterrupted within the same shot. Although we only have Albert Smith's assertion of the existence of the earlier *Humpty Dumpty Circus*, the smooth execution in *Little Joe* is evidence that this wasn't Vitagraph's first attempt at animating toys through stop-action. *A Mid-Winter's Night Dream* is also noteworthy as a Christmas parable that inspires its audience to respond compassionately to the hungry and homeless, especially children in need.[20]

Completion of the Flatbush studio brought a more controlled environment in which to film, an increase in production, and the opportunity to achieve effects that were virtually impossible on open-air stages. Audiences couldn't help but notice marked improvement in production design and overall aesthetics. Coinciding with the opening of the studio, the company added to its burgeoning stock company and doubled its pay rate to ten dollars per day for principal actors and five dollars for bit players. A manuscript department was established; readers were employed to evaluate submissions. For the first few years the company was paying five to ten dollars for scenarios written by freelancers.[21]

In addition to adapting Pathé's business model, Vitagraph went into business with the French company as copartners in the American moving picture industry's first trade publication, *Views and Films Index*, launched on April 25, 1906. The few periodicals then devoted to the entertainment industry each had their own focus, such as *Variety* (vaudeville), *Billboard* (circus and carnival), and the *New York Dramatic Mirror* (theater). Blackton, Smith, and Rock, along with Charles Pathé, understood that the dissemination of information regarding technology, production, distribution, and exhibition would benefit the entire industry. The initial reluctance of the competition to take out advertisements for their own films actually benefited Vitagraph and Pathé by reinforcing their status as industry leaders. Within six weeks, readership for *Views and Films Index* reached nearly four thousand, corresponding to the number of nickelodeons and vaudeville theaters then exhibiting motion pictures. In March 1907, *Moving Picture World* began publication; in time it would supplant and absorb the retitled *Film Index*.[22]

In 1906 Vitagraph continued to sell prints of its films to individual exhibitors. For those who preferred renting, the company instituted a rental service that was managed by Pop Rock from his Nassau Street office. The going rate for most in the American industry was twelve cents per foot of film; thus a five-hundred-foot, half-reel production sold for sixty dollars. This fixed-rate system held, no matter what the actual cost of a production might be. Lubin tended to keep costs low to maximize profit, counting on a steady clientele that didn't seem to care much about originality or quality. Vitagraph and Selig, on the other hand, believed that investing more time, effort, and money into making exceptional productions would result in greater sales and would more than compensate for the higher costs. This philosophy is at least partially responsible for the longevity and profitability of these two companies. In spite of Vitagraph's substantial expenses, the company's net profit for 1906 was $120,749, more than the combined profits for the first nine years of its existence.[23]

By 1906–1907, Pathé films were earning more money in the United States than in France. Pathé maximized its profits by eliminating the middleman and setting up its own distribution offices in the United States and throughout the world. Inspired yet again by Pathé's success, Vitagraph resolved to similarly expand its business in America and beyond.[24]

Although Vitagraph had made the successful transition from exhibition service back into production, its clientele was still for the most part confined to the northeastern quadrant of the United States. Through 1906, Chicago-based George Kleine acted as sales agent for Vitagraph, filling orders for much of the rest of the country. The problem was that Kleine took a significant commission and represented a number of other American and European producers competing for the same business. The Miles Brothers of San Francisco functioned in a similar capacity as rental agents for Vitagraph in the West. Smith, Blackton, and Rock agreed it was time to open up a satellite office in Chicago to sell their product. Smith prevailed over the objections of Rock in placing the old man's son, John B. "Johnnie" Rock, in charge of the Chicago office. Pop thought his son too timid to handle the responsibility, but with Smith's encouragement the younger Rock proved to be more than capable and utterly loyal to the company. The Chicago headquarters, located at 109 Randolph Street, opened at the end of October 1906 and did "tremendous business" selling films to regional distributors (aka exchanges) who, in turn, rented them to nickelodeons in the territories they served.[25]

Sometime after Vitagraph resumed production in late 1905, Pop Rock made a deal with London-based Charles Urban to sell Vitagraph films outside the United States. It was a reciprocal arrangement whereby Vitagraph would, in turn, represent Urban Trading Company productions in the United States. Vitagraph was told that Urban sold nine hundred prints of *Escape from Sing Sing*, from which they received little or no royalties. The figure was a gross exaggeration, but Smith, Blackton, and Rock realized that Urban had been cheating them just as he had Georges Méliès. Now that the Chicago facility was open, Albert Smith convinced his partners that the time had come for Vitagraph to open its own foreign distribution and sales offices in England and France.[26]

Albert Smith arrived in London on January 28, 1907, and in little more than five days he established a London office in Cecil Court on Charing Cross Road. As had been the case in the selection of Johnnie Rock to preside over the Chicago office, Albert valued loyalty and honesty as highly as administrative skills. Thus, his genial older brother "Uncle" George Smith was installed as general manager of the London office, a position he would hold for the next eighteen years. The London branch was initially responsible for sales of Vitagraph films in Great Britain, Germany, China, Japan, and all of the

British colonies. On February 2 Albert crossed the channel to France and rendezvoused with old friend Ronald Reader, whom he talked into leaving New York to head the Paris office located at 15 rue Sainte Cecile. The territory originally covered by the Paris sales office included all of Europe that was not handled by the London branch, as well as South America. Later in the year Smith entered into an agreement with Ambrosio Film to act as Vitagraph's exclusive sales agent for Italy.

Although Biograph had established a short-lived London studio and sales office in 1897 and Lubin had opened a sales office in Germany in 1899, Vitagraph's London and Paris offices were permanent and far more successful, quickly making it the first American producer with significant international sales. William Selig soon followed suit. Audiences around the world quickly preferred Vitagraph and Selig productions above all others, establishing an American motion picture dominance throughout much of the world that continues to this day.[27]

Shortly after opening the Paris office, Vitagraph launched an aggressive advertising campaign to promote its latest effects film, *The Haunted Hotel*. Known as *L'hôtel hanté* in France, the film is set at an inn where a traveler played by William Ranous encounters ghosts, a toy clown, and other objects that come to life, as well as a giant ogre. Effects are accomplished via cutouts, invisible wires, stop-motion, dissolves, substitutions involving miniatures and full-scale props, and double exposures; flashes of lightning and a face that materializes on the front of the inn are executed via hand-drawn animation. The highlight of *The Haunted Hotel* is a scene in which breakfast is served to the traveler. After the innkeeper departs, the film cuts to a close-up of the tabletop. A knife rises and cuts several slices from a loaf of bread. A dish rolls into view, and the slices rearrange themselves before stacking onto the plate. A coffee pot pours its contents into a mug, and a spoon stirs in sugar. A toy clown emerges from a pitcher and pours milk into the coffee. The clown pauses to smoke a pipe before climbing back into the pitcher. The camera then pans left to show the traveler seated at the table staring in wonder, as if everything occurred in real time within the same shot. More than a century later, this is still a very effective sequence. *Haunted Hotel* was a collaboration of Blackton and Smith that incorporated effects developed by each for previous films. The story was inspired by Cecil Hepworth's 1904 British production, *The Bewitched Traveler*.

L'hôtel hanté was an international sensation with sales of over 150 prints in Europe. It became the best-selling American film in France, playing the largest theaters in Paris for extended runs. French filmmakers were initially unable to figure out the frame-by-frame method Vitagraph used to give life to inanimate objects and drawings. The French called the effect "le mouvement américain" in honor of Vitagraph. The Vitagraph eagle, whether perched on a shield decorated with the Stars and Stripes or atop a globe, was becoming as recognizable a logo as the Pathé rooster.[28]

Beginning in May 1907, Vitagraph was releasing a new film each week; by August the output had doubled. No other American producer came close. Albert Smith's appointment calendar for 1907 lists scores of titles and notes for several stories, most of which were never made. However, one outline became the basis for one of Vitagraph's most important productions of the year. *The Mill Girl, A Story of Factory Life*, released on September 28, is a drama about a pretty factory worker harassed and assaulted by her foreman. In terms of both form and content, it is a relatively mature production. *The Mill Girl* adheres to most of Smith's original notes, utilizing interiors and exteriors of a real factory. Home, tavern, and factory interiors shot inside the Flatbush studio were all designed to give the impression of authenticity. Thus, for virtually every moment of the film, the audience believes in the visual reality of the story they are witnessing. The plot was all too real for many young women entering the workforce in the industrial era.[29]

Eileen Bowser's detailed analysis of *The Mill Girl* notes that while the story is rooted in simple theatrical melodrama, "showing basic emotions, lots of action, and spectacle," the filmmaking itself is sophisticated for 1907, containing thirty-one shots, "a very high number for its 700-foot length." Unlike so many other dramas of the era that are either confusing or overwhelmed by too many explanatory title cards, *The Mill Girl*'s plot and characters are easy to follow because the shot compositions and juxtapositions visually convey the story, necessitating a sole intertitle. As Bowser and Jon Gartenberg have noted, entrances and exits in *The Mill Girl* are most frequently staged on a diagonal to the coaxial frame, providing a greater sense of depth and three-dimensionality to the compositions, as well as linking shots where directional continuity is maintained. Not only does this construction aid in understanding the story and lead the spectator's gaze to the most important elements within a given composition but it also allows for a more aesthetically pleasing experience. *The Mill Girl*, like *The 100 to 1 Shot*, contains scenes of simultaneous action occurring in different locations that build suspense and ultimately converge, culminating in a race to the rescue via parallel editing that is considered the most "carefully articulated" of any surviving film from 1907, and from which would emerge D. W. Griffith's signature editorial style. The complex construction of *The Mill Girl* was successful because Albert Smith trusted the growing sophistication of the audience for which it was made. It serves as a prime example of Vitagraph developing fundamental cinematic language in the pre-Griffith era.[30]

The other major Vitagraph release for 1907 was *Francesca di Rimini; or, The Two Brothers.* Supervised by J. Stuart Blackton and directed by William V. Ranous, the film is bereft of the creative and innovative flourishes one might have expected from Vitagraph. *Francesca di Rimini* was originally written as a passage in Dante's *Divine Comedy*. The production is little more than filmed theater, staged as *tableaux* style mostly in front of painted backdrops and photographed in wide angle just as *Raffles*, *Monsieur Beaucaire*, and Blackton's earliest efforts had been. Close to filling an entire thousand-foot reel, the film consists of only thirteen shots. *Francesca* contains several intertitles; the first, though excessive, is absolutely vital for anyone not already familiar with the story: a love triangle between a hunchbacked nobleman, his beautiful bride, and handsome brother that ends with the cuckold killing the unrepentant lovers and then committing suicide.

Despite its regressive style, *Francesca di Rimini* is important as J. Stuart Blackton's initial attempt to reach beyond Vitagraph's working-class and immigrant audiences. America was experiencing a Dante renaissance at the turn of the twentieth century, especially among middle- and upper-middle-class women. This was the audience Blackton aspired to reach with this film. Not only would it expand Vitagraph's viewership, it couldn't hurt the social-climbing Blackton's desire to gain entrée into a society closed to the world he had been born into. The strategy turned out well for Blackton, Vitagraph, and the American moving picture industry in general, but at a price. Blackton poured far more of the company's financial and material resources into similar productions without any noticeable increase in receipts. These films were more heavily promoted than other Vitagraph offerings and attracted patrons who had previously avoided moving pictures, but they did not have the support of Vitagraph's core audience.[31]

Florence Turner played the role of the unfaithful wife in *Francesca di Rimini*, as well as the title character in *The Mill Girl*. She was twenty-two years old when she began working for Vitagraph in May 1907. Turner was living in nearby Sheepshead Bay with her mother and grandmother and, like them, had a modest stage career. Initially engaged by director William Ranous on a freelance basis, Turner showed an enthusiasm and talent for playing anything, both leads and supporting roles. Her youthful appearance and dark features photographed well, and she was "very clever in every way, shape and form." After five months, Albert Smith engaged Turner as the first actress in an American moving picture company to receive a weekly salary. In keeping with the propriety observed at the Flatbush studio, she was always addressed as "Miss Turner" by coworkers and her employers.

The widespread popularity of Vitagraph, coupled with her own formidable talent, made Florence Turner the first American movie star, the idol of women and young girls throughout the world; but during her first three years in the movies, fans knew her only as the uncredited "Vitagraph Girl." As a salaried player, Turner was expected to help out wherever needed. She served as company accountant and cashier, doling out pay envelopes to each of the players. Turner also sewed canvas for backdrops that she would help Paul Panzer and William Shea tack onto the frames they built.[32]

Two months after Florence Turner joined the company, twenty-one-year-old Florence Lawrence began working for Vitagraph on a freelance basis. Her moving picture experience was limited to the Edison Company's production of *Daniel Boone*, released earlier in 1907. Florence Lawrence's light complexion and blondish hair made her better suited than Florence Turner to play an Irish peasant girl opposite William Shea in *The Shaughraun*, which she recalled as her Vitagraph debut, codirected by Blackton and Smith. She played the title character in the Civil War drama *The Despatch Rider* directed by Albert Smith and appeared in a half dozen more Vitagraph productions through mid-1908, starring in *Romeo and Juliet* and *The Viking's Daughter*. When fledgling director D. W. Griffith began to build a stock company at Biograph, he gave assistant Harry Solter the task of recruiting Florence Turner with the inducement of a higher salary. But Solter had been in love with Florence Lawrence dating from when they worked together at Vitagraph. Solter returned to Griffith with Lawrence instead, claiming he was unable to locate Turner. Griffith recognized Florence Lawrence at once; he complimented her work in *The Despatch Rider* and offered her the position intended for Turner. Lawrence accepted, and the public came to know Griffith's first leading lady as the "Biograph Girl." Florence Turner, the Vitagraph Girl, and Florence Lawrence, the Biograph Girl, have been confusing filmgoers ever since.[33]

During Albert Smith's month-long trip to London and Paris early in 1908, Pop Rock wrote that Vitagraph was now supplying at least one print of every production to each of the 118 film distributors in America, which translated into minimum monthly fees of $1,200 per exchange. Since many exchanges purchased multiple prints of some titles, Vitagraph was grossing far in excess of the $141,600 monthly minimum. However, the company was also accruing significant expenses, such as the $33,750 it paid Eastman Kodak each month for raw film stock. The company was using two cameras to simultaneously photograph every shot of every production. One negative would be used to print positive copies for the American market and then shipped to a French lab from which to print copies. The other negative would be sent to London along with ten positive prints of every subject for the British market. This changed when Vitagraph camera engineer Reggie Lyons designed a double-lens camera that utilized two rolls of negative simultaneously, eliminating the need for a second camera and cameraman.

Because France maintained reciprocal trade agreements with many countries, Albert Smith purchased an old estate in the Paris suburb of Courbevoie, which was converted into a processing plant from which prints would be struck for the international market. Films were often reedited to satisfy public tastes and censor prohibitions in the regions served. Based on his knowledge of the continental markets, Ronald Reader advised his friend to find ways of getting more acrobats into comedy films and to cut down on depictions of smoking, handshaking, and religion. Albert Smith also assigned the Paris office the responsibility of translating intertitles into French, German, Spanish, Italian, Russian, Swedish, Norwegian, Dutch, and Portuguese.[34]

During the decade that Vitagraph was the undisputed leader of moving picture production in the United States, Ronald Reader and George Smith were doing at least twice the amount of business in the international market. The Vitagraph partners treated foreign earnings as profit, which they split evenly. Domestic earnings were used to pay company expenses and fund expansion.[35]

In the summer of 1908, on the same day his divorce was granted from first wife, Isabelle, J. Stuart Blackton married Paula Hilburn in Reno, Nevada. The films Blackton was making at the time reflect the dichotomy between his artistic sensibilities and the social aspirations he shared with his new bride.[36]

In *The Thieving Hand*, released February 1, 1908, a wealthy man takes pity on a one-armed pencil seller and buys him an artificial limb; but the phony limb has a life of its own, picking the pockets of various pedestrians until a policeman apprehends and incarcerates the unfortunate pencil seller. Inside a shared jail cell the thieving hand returns to its original owner, a hardened criminal. *The Thieving Hand* is a product of Blackton's dark sense of humor and utilizes stop-motion substitutions between an artificial limb and a real arm. Six prints were included in Ronald Reader's first sale to South America, more than any of the other titles in the shipment.[37]

Vitagraph produced films from eleven of William Shakespeare's most popular plays between 1908 and 1912, making seven in 1908 alone. It isn't difficult to imagine the result: actors gesticulate in togas or medieval garb, alternating with a profusion of lengthy intertitles. London's leading trade paper applauded Vitagraph's first effort, *Macbeth*, noting "the masterly way" in which such cinematic devices as double exposures were utilized. But not everyone approved. Chicago's police censor considered the film "worse than the bloodiest melodrama" and ordered the deletion of two violent scenes. The censor explained, "The stabbing in the play is not predominant. But in the picture show it is the feature. . . . You see the dagger enter and come out and see the blood flow. . . . Shakespeare is art, but . . . not [as] adapted . . . for the 5-cent style of art."

Several months after the release of *Macbeth*, *Romeo and Juliet*, and *Othello*, *Moving Picture World* judged the productions "as good as any that could have been made," given the limitations in technology and abbreviated lengths imposed by the nickelodeon operators. Audience response was also noted: "The three films have all been successful and are still in demand by the moving picture theatres in good neighborhoods catering to a grade of patrons perhaps a little above the average." This gets to the raison d'être for why J. Stuart Blackton initiated these productions in the first place. While Shakespeare on film might not hold as much interest for Vitagraph's core audience as did the contemporary comedies and melodramas to which they were accustomed, Blackton believed such films would appeal to social-climbing immigrants like himself who craved respectability. He also hoped they might attract middle-class audiences that heretofore had avoided the fledgling medium. However, *Julius Caesar*, the company's sixth Shakespeare production, was panned by the critics. *MPW* admitted that "none of these plays without a lecture are more than a bewildering mass of moving figures to the majority of the patrons of electric theaters." Vitagraph consequently furnished nickelodeons with printed lectures that could be read aloud simultaneously with the films; the result was more an educational experience than entertainment.[38]

While Vitagraph's production and distribution organization were based on the Pathé model, another key to the company's success appears to have been of its own design. Like most production companies able to sustain popularity and profitability over an extended period of time, Vitagraph adhered to the vaudeville aesthetic of engaging in an array of genres with mass appeal. The company sometimes took this approach a step further by producing both favorable and critical variations on the same theme, as is evident in some of its 1908 productions.

More than a decade before women achieved the vote, Vitagraph satirized *The Female Politician* as someone who resorts to physical violence and bribes in order to gain votes from reluctant men, while her henpecked husband does the housework and cares for the baby. A newspaper cartoon ridiculing the couple brings the woman to her senses and she returns home. On the other hand, *An Auto Heroine* is celebrated as the only person capable of driving a speedy new automobile to victory in the big race at Brooklyn's Brighton Beach.[39]

Salome; or, The Dance of the Seven Veils was inspired not by the Biblical account of the young woman responsible for the beheading of John the Baptist, but rather was made to capitalize on the "Salome craze" then in vogue following the scandalous production of the Richard Strauss opera at New York's Metropolitan Opera House in 1907. A scene in which Florence Turner as Salome exposes her breasts to John the Baptist is one of the few instances of nudity in a Vitagraph production. Far more common were films like *A Child's Prayer* with its reverent depiction of heartfelt supplication. A wealthy couple overhears a destitute little match seller pray for help for her sick mother. The couple surprises them with an abundance of groceries and money for medicine.[40]

Levitsky's Insurance Policy; or, When Thief Meets Thief features a scheming Jewish merchant who intends to burn his store in order to collect on the fire insurance, but a thief breaks in, steals his money, and activates an alarm. Firemen arrive and, failing to find flames, turn their hose on the merchant. *Leah, the Forsaken* was adapted from a nineteenth-century play by Augustin Daly. It is the story of secret love between a persecuted Jewish girl and a Catholic boy from a prominent family. Through the treachery of an apostate Jew, they suspect each other of being unfaithful, and the boy consequently marries a Catholic girl. Years later, the former lovers briefly reunite to expose the machinations of the apostate, after which the title character collapses in death. Twice in the story, Catholic villagers stone Jews for no other reason than that they are Jewish. It is doubtful that such a story would have held much appeal for Catholics, but Vitagraph made this film for its Jewish audience, just as it would make other films with appeal primarily to Catholics.[41]

The most peculiar Vitagraph production of 1908 also marked the only time in the company's history that it made a film set in the distant future. *The*

Air-Ship, or, One Hundred Years Hence may have been the first American moving picture to posit a future world, specifically, America in the year 2008. The comedy's focus is on air travel. None of the vehicles bear any resemblance to the Wright Brothers' biplane that captured the world's attention just a few years earlier, but the variety of flying machines on display correspond to an economic caste system: "The poorer people fly with ordinary wings which can be purchased for a small sum, while others have air-cycles and the richest have large and handsome air-ships."[42]

The company was now releasing four mostly half-reel films per week; thus, at least four individual self-contained production units were working simultaneously. As of November 1908 Vitagraph had a staff of two hundred full-time employees, including painters, machinists, costumers, carpenters, lab technicians, editors, and sundry other specialized workers. Vitagraph also employed several young women to evaluate the thousands of scripts submitted in-house and from the public.[43]

A key indication of the importance of nickelodeons to the fortunes of Vitagraph is the decline of vaudeville as an exhibition site for the company. The year 1908 marked the end of Vitagraph's unbroken nine-year run at Tony Pastor's Fourteenth Street Theatre in Manhattan. Failing health, competition from a proliferation of new vaudeville theaters and nickelodeons along Fourteenth Street, and an increase in rent spelled the end for Pastor. Vitagraph picked up the lease and during the summer ran continuous programs of its films Mondays through Saturdays from 1:00 p.m. until 11:00 p.m. It was the first time Vitagraph ever possessed its own theater. Six years later Vitagraph would again lease a theater, albeit with more significant consequences.[44]

Vitagraph was noted for its lavish productions as well as the fast pace that characterized the content and structure of its stories, "so that the interest of the onlookers will never sag." This was especially evident in "films conveying the dynamism that was closely associated with urban life." By comparison, the Selig Polyscope Company was in the midst of establishing the essential characteristics of the Western, which every other producer would eventually adopt; Siegmund Lubin continued to imitate successful films of other producers; Edwin S. Porter was no longer the innovator he had been for the Edison Company and would soon move on; and D. W. Griffith was beginning his legendary residency at Biograph. Two other production companies were in their second year of operation. Kalem was a partnership between former Biograph employees Samuel Long and Frank Marion, with distributor George Kleine. Chicago exchange operator George Spoor and actor-director G. M. Anderson were the partners in Essanay, initially producing rough-hewn imitations of films Anderson had worked on during his brief associations with Vitagraph and Selig.[45]

On March 5, 1907, the courts ruled that Thomas Edison's patents covered the cameras in use by all of the American production companies except for Biograph, which utilized a significantly different design of its own manufacture. Emboldened by the victory and well aware that his company alone could never fill the growing demand for moving pictures, Thomas Edison floated an idea whereby producers working in the United States would pay him a licensing fee for every foot of film they shot in order to remain in business. Vitagraph was adamant that they would "not submit to any arrangement whatever." Consequently, Edison's attorneys were instructed to lean on the courts to render decisions on the individual infringement suits still pending against Vitagraph, Selig, Lubin, Pathé, and Méliès that had been filed between 1902 and 1906.[46]

Seven months later on October 24, 1907, Judge Christian Kohlsaat of the United States Circuit Court in Chicago ruled in favor of Vitagraph, not in the case brought by Edison but in a suit filed against an exchange that was making and selling illegal dupes of Vitagraph films. There was no time to savor the victory, for on that same day Judge Kohlsaat ruled against the Selig Polyscope Company for infringing on Thomas Edison's camera patents. A week later Col. Selig was served with an injunction forbidding him from "making, using or selling any moving picture machine containing and embodying" the patents held by Edison. Panic ensued. According to J. Stuart Blackton, it was only a matter of time before every other American producer would succumb to the same fate as Selig, liable for damages covering years of past infringement and facing the possibility of a prison sentence. Blackton traveled to Chicago to meet with Selig, George Kleine of Kalem, George Spoor of Essanay, and Arthur White, Edison's Chicago manager. Blackton and the others huffed, puffed, and bluffed for the benefit of White, but ultimately conceded that they were now willing to capitulate and become permanent Edison licensees.[47]

Albert Smith described the situation as being "betwixt the devil and the deep sea; it was either a case of fighting again and running the risk of being put out of business, or accept the license and pay tribute." At the end of January 1908, Edison's lawyers met with Rock, Blackton, Col. Selig, and Gaston Méliès in Vitagraph's business office in lower Manhattan and read over the proposed licensing agreement. Pathé, still the major supplier of films in the United States, and George Eastman, who at the time held a monopoly on the manufacture of raw film stock, had already signed the contract. Such was the respect for Pathé, that Vitagraph and the others added their signatures to the agreement without the benefit of legal counsel. What they didn't know was that Pathé had secretly agreed to the terms because it barred all other foreign producers from doing business in the United States. Vitagraph and the others were assured that as soon as Lubin, Kalem, and Biograph signed on, all their legal troubles would end. The expectations for peace within the industry were dashed, however, when Biograph refused to become an Edison licensee.[48]

Unlike the other producers, Biograph had no reason to knuckle under to Edison's extortion since the courts upheld the legality of its patents. Instead of prospering, mismanagement and recent defections of key personnel resulted in Biograph being in default of interest payments on a $200,000 loan from the Empire Trust Company. Bank officer Jeremiah J. Kennedy was assigned to liquidate the company. The pugnacious Kennedy instead saw enormous potential and took command of the operations of Biograph, the first time an American bank controlled a moving picture company. George Kleine realized that under the Edison agreement his distribution business would collapse because he would be prevented from importing films made by foreign producers; thus, he allied himself with Biograph. In order for Kalem to become an Edison licensee, it was necessary for Long and Marion to purchase Kleine's stake in the company since he was now persona non grata with Edison. Consequently, every company then making moving pictures in the United States, with the exception of Biograph, became an Edison licensee. Vitagraph and the others were assured that Edison's patents prevented anyone else from producing or exhibiting motion pictures in the United States.[49]

Under the terms of the licensing agreement, the seven other production companies paid Thomas Edison a royalty of half a cent for every foot of film they purchased, reportedly totaling $200,000 at the end of the first year. In return, all suits against the franchisees were canceled, and Edison would prevent any would-be producers from entering the field. Each of the companies leased their films at regular intervals to a limited number of licensed exchanges, collectively known as the Film Service Association (FSA), for a finite period of time. The FSA in turn rented the films to licensed exhibitors at a fixed rate, after which the prints would be returned to the manufacturers and destroyed. The reason for this was that the six thousand nickelodeons then in operation had been in the habit of projecting films until they were so scratched and torn as to be unwatchable, incurring the wrath of audiences and adding to the

MPPC members, December 18, 1908. Front row, left to right: Frank L. Dyer, Siegmund Lubin, William T. "Pop" Rock, Thomas A. Edison, J. Stuart Blackton, Jeremiah J. Kennedy, George Kleine, George K. Spoor. Second row: Frank J. Marion, Samuel Long, Col. William Selig, Albert E. Smith, Jacques A. Berst, Henry N. Marvin, Ferdinand W. Singhi, Peter Huber. Author's collection.

disdain held by many toward the medium. The FSA also required that the nickelodeons it supplied meet safety standards and that their projectionists be trained and certified as a safeguard against another tragedy such as the one in Boyertown, Pennsylvania, in which a fire in an opera house sparked by a projector claimed the lives of 171 people. In addition, the producers pledged not to indulge in the kind of excessively violent or sexually charged content that characterized some of the European imports.[50]

The Edison forces began warning that anyone found infringing on any aspect of the licensing agreement would be prosecuted and driven out of the business. J. J. Kennedy was trying to woo exchanges and exhibitors into aligning themselves with Biograph by offering lower rental rates. To make matters worse, Biograph sued Vitagraph and other Edison licensees for violating some of *their* patents.[51]

Edison finally blinked and agreed to an even split of the royalties from the licensees, which Biograph had insisted on all along. The armistice was signed on December 18, 1908. Tweaks were made to the year-old arrangement and a new organization was formed, the Motion Picture Patents Company (MPPC). Once again the licensees grudgingly signed on in order to stay in business, with the new rules taking effect January 1, 1909. At its core, the MPPC was a holding company for sixteen patents that covered virtually every piece of equipment involved in the photography and projection of motion pictures, though not all of the patents were controlled by Edison and Biograph. Five belonged to Albert Smith, including his framing device and nonflicker shutter. Smith assigned his patents to the MPPC in return for an unspecified cash payment and royalties he split evenly with his two partners. For the fiscal year ending June 20, 1911, this amounted to only $5,693. Vitagraph collected a much larger royalty on its share of the two-dollar weekly fee charged to every exhibitor affiliated with the MPPC, initially $150,000 per year.[52]

For Vitagraph, Selig, and Lubin, the Motion Picture Patents Company was a necessary evil built on a sham. Many if not most of the Edison patents were either purchased or stolen from the rightful inventors, and Biograph's key patent in the MPPC, the Latham Loop, had been purchased during its war with Edison. While it is true that Edison and Biograph were the first two commercially successful makers of motion pictures in the United States, Lubin, Selig, and Vitagraph were quick to establish themselves as successful competitors by 1898. For having done so, each of those companies over the next ten years suffered an unrelenting barrage of litigation, harassment, and intimidation from attorneys and private detectives working on behalf of Edison, with the goal of either putting them out of business or taking a substantial cut of their profits. Ironically, by the time the MPPC was established Vitagraph and Selig had emerged as the leaders of the American motion picture industry as a result of the innovations they developed regarding the business and content of their films. Lubin prospered because he copied those models. The same is true of every successful production company that followed. And yet the MPPC was instrumental in insuring the legacy of Vitagraph and the survival of the American motion picture industry by organizing production, distribution, and exhibition into a stable, profitable business. As Robert Jack Anderson has noted, the MPPC "removed price as a consideration for the exhibitor by establishing a uniform rental rate for all licensed film. . . . For the first time, what differentiated a Selig from a Biograph and from a Vitagraph was the quality of the individual film." After more than ten years, Vitagraph could comfortably anticipate substantial long-term growth and profit.[53]

3

1909–1913

During 1909, Vitagraph embraced a new strategy for uplifting and expanding its audience. Reducing its Shakespeare output to only two films for the entire year, the company chose instead to focus its "high art" efforts on classic literature and biblical and other historical subjects, releasing at least two such films per month.

While honeymooning in late 1908, the Blacktons made perfunctory visits to Vitagraph's London and Paris offices. The newlyweds then plunged into a month-long crash course in French culture, studying and embracing the mores and etiquette of high society. Evenings were spent attending the theater and movies. During the day, museums, art galleries, and historic sites in and around Paris were scoured, fueled by J. Stuart's mania for Napoleon. He made sketches and took photographs of the emperor's homes, furnishings, and apparel, and bought prints of classic paintings depicting major events in the life of Bonaparte. He also purchased a bronze bust of the emperor to sit atop the desk in his Brooklyn office.[1]

After returning home, Paula Blackton began to host soirées that were attended by socially prominent Brooklynites. Up to this time, Vitagraph's Flatbush facility was referred to variously as "the plant," "the yard," or "the factory." The new Mrs. Blackton convinced her husband that henceforth the term "studio" should be used to the exclusion of all others, the lasting contribution to American motion pictures of a social-climbing Francophile.

Immediately J. Stuart Blackton plunged into production of a Napoleon biopic, the most ambitious and costly film yet undertaken by an American producer. Authentic reproductions of Napoleon's furniture were acquired, and Vitagraph's wood and metal shops built other decorations and props based on Blackton's photographs and sketches. Cast in the lead was noted stage actor William Humphrey, who had played Napoleon on Broadway. Julia Swayne, the second woman put on weekly salary at Vitagraph, played

William Humphrey and Julia Swayne in *Incidents in the Life of Napoleon and Josephine* (1909). *Cine-Journal*, May 29–June 4, 1909.

the Empress Josephine. At least fifty extras were used in scenes as soldiers and members of Napoleon and Josephine's inner circle.

In a challenge to the nickelodeon animus toward full-reel thousand-foot productions, Blackton made his film two full reels long. He circumvented the financial and exhibition obstacles to long movies by releasing his epic as two self-contained stories in single reels on consecutive weeks during April 1909. The first, *Incidents in the Life of Napoleon and Josephine*, focused on the emperor's relationship with his first wife; the second reel, *Napoleon—The Man of Destiny*, was mostly an overview of his military exploits.[2]

Blackton chose not to present Bonaparte through a cause and effect narrative. Rather, he mimicked as precisely as possible the poses and compositions of Napoleon in the paintings of David, Gros, Delaroche, and others. Thus, most scenes resemble Living Pictures, the kind of live entertainment that recreated famous artwork, which had been supplanted by the movies. Blackton's tableaux vivants freeze time, at least for several moments. When movement occurs, it often consists of processions of sumptuously costumed extras. With few exceptions, each scene consists of an excessively long static shot lasting up to two minutes. In most cases the framing was much wider than anything Vitagraph had ever attempted, motivated by the desire to fully reproduce the familiar paintings.

The wide shots were achieved thanks to the new studios that Vitagraph had built in the fall of 1908, so large they were able to accommodate battle scenes. Commentators marveled at the depth of many of the compositions, in which simultaneous actions occurred along different horizontal planes within the same frame.

Napoleon and Josephine uses intertitles to announce and identify its tableaux, while in *Man of Destiny* many titles are superimposed over shots of Napoleon in his study. This is because the episodes in *Man of Destiny* are structured as a series of flashbacks, externalizing the ruminations of the emperor in exile. The structure for *Napoleon and Josephine* is even more radical; the scenes are presented as a series of flash-forwards that enable Josephine to glimpse her future, beginning with a double exposure in which she sees herself on a throne. In spite of these innovative framing devices, the films are intelligible only to audiences already familiar with the historical Napoleon, the paintings, or theatrical treatments. Contemporary criticism, however, was directed instead toward exhibitors who refused to run both reels together or book the films for more than one day at their nickelodeons.[3]

The most ambitious and profitable Vitagraph production of 1909 was *The Life of Moses*, in five reels. Rev. Madison C. Peters was recruited to help adapt the story, serve as technical consultant, and, more importantly, confer ecclesiastic approval on the project. Peters was a celebrity clergyman, whose Chautauqua circuit lectures included "The Divine Mission of Fun" and "The Jew as Patriot." Peters was publicized as the producer (aka director) of the films, though in reality *The Life of Moses* was directed by Charles Kent. Born in London in 1852, Kent began acting in 1875 shortly before he moved to America, where he supported Edwin Booth in *Hamlet* and *Macbeth*. Kent was a versatile character actor who, by his own account, played virtually every kind of role until he lost his voice in 1906. The following year he joined Vitagraph as an actor, occasional writer, and director. It is likely that Kent's primary responsibility as the director of *Moses* was in working with the actors, while Blackton supervised camera placement and framing. Many of the scenes consist of a single wide shot, though there are a few cuts within scenes to closer views. Despite Charles Kent's years of theatrical experience, or perhaps because of them, there is nothing subtle about any of the performances. However, the production did benefit from beautiful tinting, especially the red of the holy fire and the blue during the night of Passover.[4]

The Life of Moses was the most successful of Blackton's "high art" productions. The films reached far beyond Vitagraph's regular nickelodeon audience to include exhibitions in churches and synagogues around the world, where all five reels were usually shown together. For at least fifteen years, *The Life of Moses* was a perennial holiday favorite during the Passover and Easter season.[5]

Of Vitagraph's two 1909 Shakespeare productions, the first, a confusing *King Lear*, was a failure with audiences. The other, *A Midsummer Night's Dream*, is one of Blackton's great achievements. In comparison with the artificiality that plagued his previous efforts, only genuine settings were utilized for Shakespeare's great fantasy. Albert Smith recalled that most of the picture was shot in a forest at the south end of Flatbush. "The scenes [by the lake] were posed at the old Gravesend water works, [and the setting] with the fountain and stone columns [that bookends the film] was the Ocean Avenue entrance to Prospect Park." As directed by Charles Kent, the typically hamfisted, self-conscious performance style of William Ranous is entirely appropriate for his role as Bottom, the amateur actor transformed for a time into an ass. As Puck, boyish Gladys Hulette appears to be having the time of her life, setting the tone for the entire movie. The transformations are well executed, and the special effects employed for Puck taking off in flight from a meadow to obtain the magic love herb, soaring across the globe and back, are brilliant in conception and execution. *A Midsummer Night's Dream* isn't filmed theater; it is cinema. After eight tries, Blackton and company finally got Shakespeare right.[6]

Of all the effects-based fantasy and experimental films produced by Vitagraph, its most successful effort by any measure is *Princess Nicotine*, released in the summer of 1909. The film bears certain similarities to *The Haunted Hotel*; a full-sized Paul Panzer is taunted and charmed by two tiny fairies, the smaller "Princess" of the title played by thirteen-year-old Gladys Hulette of *Midsummer Night's Dream*. Smith recalled, "We put all the tricks we knew into this one." The concept was Blackton's, possibly inspired by a 1905 Biograph film, *A Pipe Dream*, in which a tiny man materializes out of the cigarette smoke a woman blows into her hand.

Princess Nicotine's elaborate effects were the product of Albert Smith's engineering expertise. In the film, Hulette sabotages Panzer's efforts to smoke his pipe by, among other things, hiding in the bowl amidst the tobacco and setting all of his matches ablaze. Pixilation is used to show rose petals detaching from a stem and reforming into a cigar. Double exposure was used to show the fairy taunting the smoker from inside a wine bottle, which he smashes with a hammer. Scenes in which the human-sized smoker appears in

Princess Nicotine (1909) production still signed by Paul Panzer: "My dear Albert, You made me what I am today. God Bless You. Paul W. Panzer, 1903–1954." Albert E. Smith Papers (Collection 2004). Library Special Collections, Charles E. Young Research Library, UCLA.

the same shot next to the two-inch-tall fairy on the table were accomplished by placing Hulette on a platform alongside the camera lens out of frame, her image reflected in a mirror blended into the black background behind Panzer and the full-sized table. Her tiny reflection appears to place her standing atop the table among Panzer's smoking accessories. The depth of the new studio and electric lighting made the effect possible, producing sharply defined imagery. High-angle views of Hulette in close-up among large-scale props are shown as though from Panzer's point of view via a magnifying glass to get a closer look at her. In 1912 the first instructional book on how to make motion pictures referred to *Princess Nicotine* as "one of the finest trick films ever made in the United States." That evaluation remains just as true more than a century later.[7]

In 1909 the leading trade papers on both sides of the Atlantic agreed that "the Vitagraph Company and the Biograph Company represent the top notch of American manufacturers." Albert Smith recalled that the end of Edison litigation enabled Vitagraph to improve and expand "at such a rapid rate that we caught up with and passed" the European producers. Eileen Bowser has noted, "In 1907 60 percent of the subjects released on the American market were of foreign origin, but by the last six months of 1909, foreign productions represented less than 50 percent of films released and the percentage was declining." American stories and characters were becoming as popular with international audiences as they were at home.[8]

In the year following the formation of the Film Service Association, many exchanges continued to cheat producers and nickelodeon operators by giving the best films and rates to their own theaters or friends, as well as to those who would pay extra for the privilege. In addition, many exhibitors secretly subleased films to competing nickelodeons and pocketed the rental fee *they* charged, a practice known as "bicycling." The MPPC's solution to these problems was to require each exchange to purchase $2,500 worth of film per month and to require nickelodeons to use patented projectors built by member companies and pay a weekly royalty fee of $2.00 to the MPPC. The new rules came with a warning: "Infringers . . . will be vigorously prosecuted." The admonition also covered licensed theaters showing unlicensed films and vice versa. According to MPPC statistics, as of May 1909 there were eight thousand theaters in the United States, six thousand of which were licensed. The Edison and Biograph forces controlling the MPPC assumed that every nickelodeon owner would obey the law and capitulate to its terms, just as every producer had. But for two thousand nickelodeon operators, profit potential far outweighed the risks of not joining the MPPC.[9]

Behind the scenes, all was not well within the Patents Company. Edison's representatives had promised the licensees that because it controlled the key patents on motion picture equipment, no entity outside of the MPPC could legally produce or exhibit movies in the United States. As further protection, Edison made an arrangement with Eastman Kodak whereby it would sell 35-mm raw stock only to MPPC licensees. However, barely a month after the MPPC began operation, George Eastman arranged to sell raw stock to "all of the important French, English, Italian and German [production] houses." Soon some of those companies began selling the raw film they had purchased from Eastman to aspiring American producers operating in defiance of the courts and the Patents Company.[10]

An early supporter of the MPPC was exchange operator Carl Laemmle; a former clothing store manager who entered the industry as a nickelodeon operator in 1906, he soon moved into the distribution end of the business. One of the keys to Laemmle's success was his incessant self-promotion in the trades. He urged exhibitors to become MPPC licensees because he had, using a racist epithet to justify his position. Two months later in April 1909, Laemmle took out a full-page ad announcing he had quit the Patents Company and joined the "independents," offering two reasons for his defection: his support for nickelodeon operators who refused to pay the $2.00 weekly projector royalty, and his claim that he could provide better films for his clients than what the licensees were producing. Laemmle and a few other exchanges began importing films from British, Italian, Scandinavian, and French producers shut out by the MPPC. The only American production company at the time of Laemmle's announcement that was not affiliated with the Patents Company was Centaur, which had made two or three Westerns in New Jersey. A month later the New York Motion Picture Company entered production under the name "Bison," also making New Jersey Westerns. In June 1909 Laemmle announced that he, too, was going into motion picture production.[11]

In the months leading up to his first release, Laemmle mounted a relentless campaign in the press against the MPPC, referring to it as the "Trust" in an effort to demonize the organization and its licensees and, thus, woo exhibitors to his own seven exchanges. As Robert Jack Anderson has noted in his analysis of the MPPC, "From the 1890's to 1916, the term trust was synonymous with corporate greed and the maladies associated with America's 'free enterprise system' being dominated by big business." When the MPPC was formed, *Moving Picture World* noted, "The new company is not a 'trust' in the conventional meaning of the term; nor is it a monopoly. It is a combination . . . carried out in a perfectly legitimate way." But soon even *MPW* was referring to the Patents Company as the "Trust," so ubiquitous was use of the term by nonlicensed exchanges and exhibitors, who called themselves "independents." "Trust" connoted evildoers; "independents" were "brave" and "heroic." Few have ever bothered to look beyond the labels to learn that the licensees, including Vitagraph, reluctantly joined the MPPC only after the courts had decided against them, while independent newcomers such as Laemmle openly flouted the law.

It has been claimed that Laemmle "obviously [tried] to distinguish his films from those of the Edison Trust. . . . Making better movies was good business, but it was also a way of legitimizing the film industry itself and the men who ran it." The truth is that Laemmle was clueless about what constituted a "better" movie, let alone how to make one. His solution was to lure Pop Rock's son-in-law Doc Willat away from Vitagraph to organize a production company for him. Tony Gaudio, who managed the Vitagraph developing laboratory, jumped ship to build a lab for Laemmle. Vitagraph actor-director William V. Ranous joined Laemmle at the higher salary of $100 per week. It appears that Ranous, in turn, convinced Gladys Hulette to accompany him in the new venture. Laemmle's first production, *Hiawatha*, was released in October 1909, advertised as having been shot on location "in the land of the Dacotahs" but it was actually made in New Jersey. Although Ranous had been held in high esteem at Vitagraph and Hulette's Puck and Princess Nicotine continue to enchant more than a century later, their portrayals as American Indians in *Hiawatha* are embarrassingly bad. Cheaply made and crudely produced, *Hiawatha* set the tone for the productions that followed. Instead of "making better movies," Laemmle was actually making quickie knockoffs with talent from Vitagraph and other licensees. Few remained with "Uncle Carl" for any length of time. Laemmle named his production arm the Independent Moving Picture Company, usually abbreviated as "IMP." Accompanying IMP advertisements was the company logo: the devil holding a pitchfork.[12]

Edison attorneys working on behalf of the MPPC brought suit against Centaur, Bison, and IMP; but the courts were in no hurry to render judgment, which allowed Laemmle and the others to make motion pictures without having to pay financial tribute to Edison. The licensees were furious at this turn of events, yet they held a banquet at New York's Plaza Hotel on December 20, 1909, to pay a different kind of tribute to Thomas Edison: celebrating the one-year anniversary of the formation of the MPPC. As much as the licensees bitterly resented the harassment, litigation, and extortion conducted by Edison, they all recognized they were, nonetheless, personally acquainted with the most famous man in the world, widely regarded as one of the most influential men in history. The MPPC banquet honoring Thomas Edison became an annual event throughout most of that organization's existence.[13]

Within days of the Edison banquet, Vitagraph held its annual Christmas party, bringing together management and labor to celebrate the holiday and acknowledge the contributions of all. As was the custom, every employee received a "fat turkey" to take home for Christmas dinner and a cash bonus handed out by the partners. On the evening of January 8, 1910, the company hosted a much bigger party for its staff. One of the studios was converted into a banquet hall where two hundred employees were served dinner as an orchestra played softly in the background. After dinner the space was converted into a ballroom for late night dancing, while the party moved into three adjacent studios that opened onto each other to form an enormous theater. An audience of six hundred employees, spouses, and guests watched a "home talent" vaudeville show that was bookended by screenings of a few old and new Vitagraph productions. In between, live performances included Smith and Blackton recreating their old magic and lightning sketch routines, William Shea and actor-director Van Dyke Brooke in an Irish comedy act, and propman turned actor Walter Ackerman performing Hebrew dialect comedy. Another highlight was a sketch by Vitagraph's leading actors, Florence Turner and Maurice Costello.[14]

Florence Turner had been the company's principal star for two years, known throughout the world as the "Vitagraph Girl." Although she had been paired with every actor in the growing stock company, Turner hadn't developed on-screen rapport with any of them until Maurice Costello joined Vitagraph. Maurice George Costello was born in Pittsburgh on Washington's Birthday in 1877. He began acting professionally at age twenty and worked for a succession of traveling stock companies. In 1902 he married Brooklynite Mae Altschuh, who gave birth to daughters Dolores and Helen. Between theatrical engagements in 1907, Maurice Costello visited his friend Van Dyke Brooke at the Vitagraph studio to inquire about work that paid $5 per day. At the time theatrical managers were threatening to blacklist actors who appeared in moving pictures, but Costello didn't care. He realized that movies offered greater earning potential than the stage and, more importantly, would allow him to get off the road and remain at home in Brooklyn with his family. Asked once what interested him most, he replied, "Loving Dolores and Helen Costello." Albert Smith quickly recognized Costello's talent as well as the effect the handsome actor had on the studio's female employees, and put him on salary as a leading man. Nearly half a century after his Vitagraph debut, "Handsome Maurice Costello" was remembered as "the first matinee idol of the screen, and to a generation . . . the perfect male."[15]

When informed that as a salaried player he would be expected to help construct and paint sets for the films he appeared in, Maurice Costello replied, "I am an actor. An actor does not build sets." Albert Smith agreed, acknowledging the "moral basis" of Costello's stance. This "revolutionary" moment inaugurated a new policy at Vitagraph and was quickly adopted by the other American production companies. It led to the employment of specialized craftsmen and improvement in overall production design. Smith admired Costello for being "very particular about what he did . . . about his position in the company and before the public. He and I were very good friends. I liked him a lot." Female audiences were so captivated by Costello's "grand profile, curly hair and dimple" that Blackton returned to the nine-foot-line rule, realizing that "it was [in] the scenes nearest to the camera that Costello's personality was most evident." Costello was one of the few veterans of theatrical melodrama to adopt a more realistic, understated performance style when the camera was close, though he occasionally reverted to a broader technique in wider shots. Making the individual prominent in the frame also resulted in greater character development, which in turn made for more compelling stories.[16]

Costello played the enchanted lover Lysander in *A Midsummer Night's Dream*, though six-year-old Dolores and three-year-old Helen garnered at least as much attention playing two adorable fairies. During his first few years in the movies, when actors worked in anonymity, Vitagraph received hundreds of letters each week addressed to "Dimples." Before 1910 was over, Maurice Costello would begin receiving fan mail addressed to him by name.[17]

Vitagraph grew at a dizzying pace in 1910, more than doubling its profit from the previous year. In mid-February, the company increased its production output to three full-reel films per week, releasing on Tuesdays, Fridays, and Saturdays. There were now thirty salaried actors in the Vitagraph stock company and seven directors. The success of the company was palpable. One visitor to the Brooklyn plant noted the "esprit d'corps" that existed among employees, each seeming "to feel that upon him or her depended the success of Vitagraph pictures, [an attribute] essential to the . . . expansion of any large business." Also impressive were the large number of young women employed by the company who were provided with the opportunity "to earn a good living, free from many objectionable features of factory life."[18]

Among the more discreet expressions of Vitagraph largesse in 1910 was its financial support of Méliès. In 1908 Georges produced the equivalent of a film per week, but he released only eight films in all of 1909 and in 1910 didn't release any at all, such was the public's abrupt lack of interest in his trick films that had once captivated the world. Acting on his brother's behalf, Gaston applied for an MPPC license in 1909. That the Méliès brothers were granted one indicates how insignificant a threat they posed to Pathé or the other licensees. That fall Gaston produced a few films at a Brooklyn studio that Smith and Blackton helped him acquire, each owning a quarter interest in his American production company. Vitagraph actress Edith Storey was

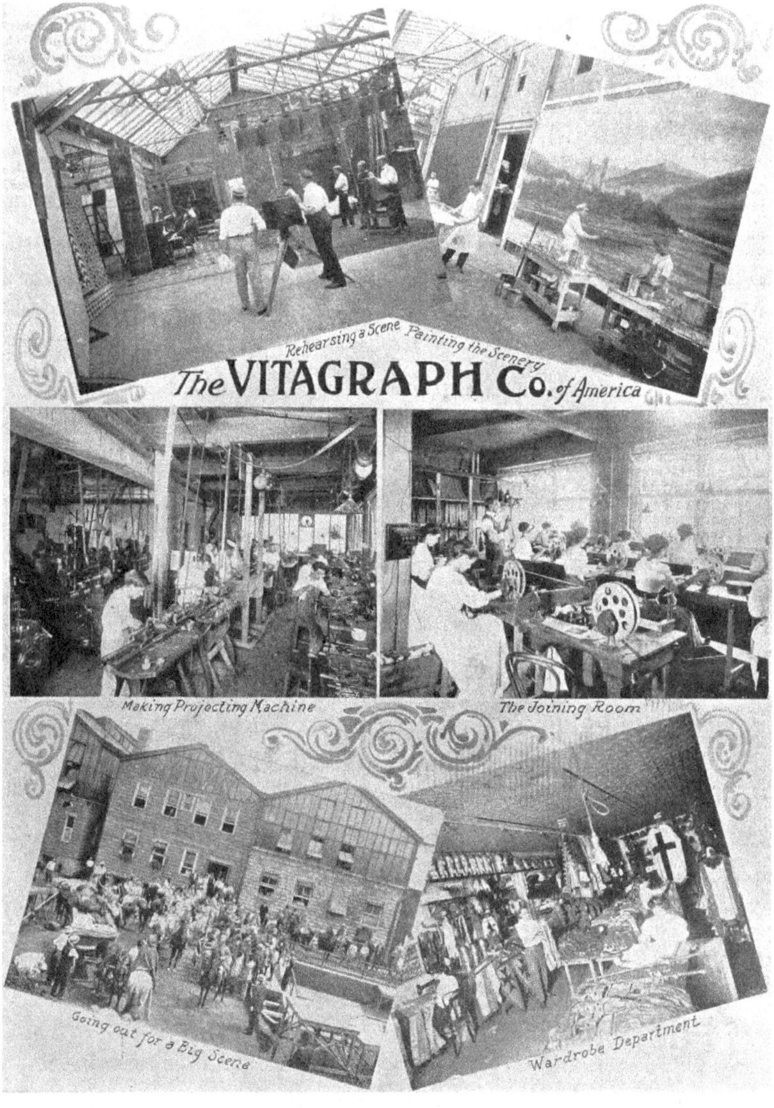

Working at the Brooklyn studio in 1912. *Moving Picture World*, June 8, 1912.

loaned to Gaston Méliès when he hit the road to make Westerns in Texas and California. The partners thought that by aiding Gaston they were also helping his brother. Unbeknownst to them, Georges never received a dividend from his brother nor, for that matter, did Vitagraph. The company did, however, control the foreign rights to Gaston Méliès's productions for countries outside the United States and France.[19]

The Film Service Association held its fifth semiannual convention in New York City at the end of January 1910. It was a heady experience for nickelodeon operators traveling from far-flung towns and cities across America. William T. Rock was the star of virtually every exhibitor convention he ever attended. To nickelodeon operators, Rock was the ultimate success story. He entered the business at the dawn of commercial cinema as one of them, the first to exhibit movies in the state of Louisiana. Before almost anyone else, Rock recognized the advantages of the projected image over an individual viewing experience. As the head of Vitagraph's New York exchange, Rock dealt personally with individual exhibitors on a daily basis. He knew his customers by name, and the conventions gave thousands of showmen an opportunity to rub elbows with this legendary figure with the outsized personality. The goodwill and loyalty that Rock generated through his comradery with conventioneers was as important to the success of Vitagraph as was the entertainment value, promotion, and distribution of its films. Unfortunately, the greed of the men in charge of the MPPC and those who desired to supplant them was about to undo the short-lived peace and prosperity that Vitagraph, Selig, and Lubin had worked so long and diligently to attain.[20]

After having taken over Biograph, former bank executive Jeremiah J. Kennedy was instrumental in negotiating the terms of its membership in the MPPC, which included Kennedy becoming treasurer. Early in 1910 he convinced his Edison counterparts that the MPPC should take over the distribution of its members' films to reap even greater profits and control. In order to accomplish this, the FSA was dissolved and the General Film Company formed to acquire most of the exchanges licensed to do business with the MPPC. From April 1910 to the end of 1911, General Film purchased fifty-seven exchanges for $2,243,000 in cash and approximately $794,000 in preferred stock. There are many reasons why Blackton and Smith wouldn't have been happy with the new arrangement, not least of which was that it meant having to give up their exchanges, which in turn meant that Pop Rock now had a lot of time on his hands. They decided to keep Rock's office in lower Manhattan to prevent him from meddling in studio affairs. Of the exchanges that didn't join General Film, one licensed exchangeman held out for a bigger payoff. Approximately forty formerly licensed exchanges either weren't purchased due to overlap with competitors serving the same regions or were canceled for breaking FSA or General Film rules. The formation and policies of General Film would eventually prove to be a significant factor in the dominance of the American motion picture industry as well as the demise of the MPPC licensees.[21]

$2.00 PER YEAR 20 CENTS PER COPY

THE NICKELODEON

Vol. I CHICAGO, APRIL, 1909 No. 4

W. T. Rock, President of The Vitagraph Company of America.

PUBLISHED MONTHLY BY
ELECTRICITY MAGAZINE CORPORATION
MONADNOCK BUILDING, CHICAGO

William T. "Pop" Rock, the idol of nickelodeon operators. *Nickelodeon*, April 1909.

Before 1910 American motion picture producers chose not to publicize the names of the members of their stock companies. Until then, audiences were attracted to a company's brand, knowing they could expect lush historical and snappy contemporary productions from Vitagraph, better Westerns from Selig, and the best acting and dynamic editing from Biograph.

In the autumn of 1909 "Biograph Girl" Florence Lawrence joined IMP at a much higher salary than she had been receiving. Former Vitagraph colleague William V. Ranous directed her IMP debut. Although she starred in several productions for the new company, the public still referred to Lawrence as the "Biograph Girl." It obviously rankled Carl Laemmle, because after four months he anonymously tipped off the press that the "Biograph Girl" had been run over by a streetcar and killed. A few weeks later an advertisement appeared in *Moving Picture World* in which Laemmle claimed the report of Lawrence's death was a lie, concocted by "enemies of the 'Imp.'" The ad included her name and photograph, and referred to Lawrence as the "Imp Girl."

Contrary to popular film lore, this was not the first time a salaried player of an American production company received credit. Advertisements appearing a few weeks earlier prominently listed Hobart Bosworth in a Selig Polyscope Company production. At the same time, the trades were being inundated with requests to know the names of the "Vitagraph Girl" and "Dimples." Vitagraph realized that Florence Turner and Maurice Costello had become bigger drawing cards than the company itself and began to promote them and other leading players by name. This occurred simultaneously with Laemmle's promotion of Florence Lawrence. However, Pathé once again led everyone else by promoting its star comedian Max Linder several months earlier.[22]

With the signing of Florence Lawrence, Carl Laemmle once again disrupted the ethics and harmony that had taken the pioneer producers so long to achieve. Making matters worse, he continued to open nonlicensed exchanges and mounted a vicious, expensive campaign against the MPPC in the trade press while failing to pay long overdue bills to licensees for past film rentals. Contrary to the myths attached to "Uncle Carl" Laemmle, of whom it has been claimed that "even competitors testified to [his] basic decency," among the licensed production companies he was one of the most despised men in the industry, along with Biograph's J. J. Kennedy and the Edison Company's William Gilmore and Frank Dyer, the men who ran the MPPC.[23]

The Edison forces continued to pursue patent infringement as they always had by means of intimidation and litigation. Carl Laemmle's authorized biographer claimed he endured 289 legal actions from the MPPC, a figure often repeated without ever having been verified. In 1911 the IMP players spent a few weeks in Cuba, allegedly "to avoid Trust persecution," though Robert Jack Anderson has noted that when Laemmle *was* served with an injunction it was at his New York office, the address listed in the telephone directory. Edison did, however, utilize detectives to track down and compile evidence against infringers. Fred Balshofer, director of New York Motion Picture Company's Bison films, devoted several pages of his autobiography to colorful tales concerning MPPC detective Joseph F. McCoy. Balshofer charged McCoy with "persistent spying and harassment," yet on the few occasions when they actually crossed paths it was Balshofer who intimidated and threatened the detective. Director Allan Dwan, who worked for the unlicensed American Film Company in Southern California, claimed that "gangsters" hired by the Patents Company nearly burned down Universal's New York facilities and shot "two or three people," though no corroborating testimony, newspaper, or trade accounts exist. Dwan said his cast and crew "all wore sidearms . . . and watched for snipers while we worked," adding, "Sometimes our cameras got hit." Dwan boasted that the harassment ended only after he beat an MPPC detective in a shooting contest and "my well-armed cowboys" escorted the loser onto a train heading back East.[24]

For more than a decade Vitagraph had to contend with Edison's unrelenting assault. All attacks by Edison detectives and his legal team on production companies formed after the creation of the Patents Company pale by comparison. And yet a majority of historians have never bothered to investigate early cinema for themselves, which has led to the surmise that Vitagraph and the other licensees were willing participants in "Edison's cabal." The fact is that detective McCoy began working for the Edison Manufacturing Company in 1903 to spy on and collect patent infringement evidence against Vitagraph, Selig, Lubin, and Biograph. The utter lack of evidence regarding MPPC violence against unlicensed companies has not prevented historians from accepting at face value and embellishing the exaggerated claims made by so-called independents, resulting in "one of the most persistent myths in American motion picture history." Neal Gabler recklessly utilizes the phrase "Trust persecution" to bolster the "gravity" of Carl Laemmle's claim of being in a "fight for my life" against the "Trust bulls." Ironically, the only documented case of bullets ever being fired at a motion picture company during this period occurred in 1912, when gunmen *acting on behalf of Laemmle* attempted to take possession of the New York Motion Picture Company's offices and Bison studio headquarters during Carl Laemmle's hostile takeover of the newly formed Universal Film Exchange (soon to be renamed Universal Pictures). Sadly, it appears there was one genuine tragic consequence of the so-called Patents War. It occurred in January 1900 when Smith and Blackton learned that the Edison Company had filed an injunction against them and they were being threatened with prison and the loss of their business. Albert Smith testified in court that "I know that I was so worried, and it worried my wife, and we had a little baby at that time and it killed that baby."[25]

Mindful of the growing hostility toward the movies, Vitagraph continued to produce films suitable for family audiences. In 1910 a review of *Nellie's Farm* was titled, "A Reply to Some Enemies of the Motion Picture." *Nellie's Farm* tells the story of a poor boy living in a city tenement that gets to spend part of the summer on a farm thanks to New York's Fresh Air Fund. He returns home with souvenirs of the farm for a neighborhood friend whose disabilities prevented her from making the trip. The earliest movie critics weren't skittish when it came to recognizing that motion pictures influence the values and behavior of its audience. Singling out *Nellie's Farm* as an example of Vitagraph "doing [its] best to create a demand for moral and educational pictures," one reviewer recommended that the film "be shown in every school and known all over the world as the correct illustration of the great commandment: 'Love thy neighbor as thyself.'" It wasn't enough.

J. Stuart Blackton felt compelled to address opposition to moving pictures in an article for the *New York Telegraph.* It provides a glimpse into Blackton the artist when he asks, "When is a film not a film?" and reveals his pragmatism as a movie mogul with his sardonic response: only when "narrow-minded . . . iconoclastic . . . censors" say so. He argues that suggestive violence occurring offscreen is far more effective and less objectionable than blatant displays of brutality in the "Silent Drama." Thirty years later Maurice Costello concurred, recalling that Vitagraph "always made pictures with good morals to them. . . . I had youngsters of my own and I always wanted to feel that a whole family could see my pictures. . . . Virtue was always rewarded . . . and the wages of sin was, unfailingly, death. . . . You never heard any foul language on the sets in those days [nor] off-color stories."[26]

In 1909 Albert Smith hired commercial advertising pioneer Sam Spedon as Vitagraph's first full-time advertising and publicity manager. Initial responsibilities included writing a synopsis and advertising copy for each Vitagraph production. Exhibitors and the public appreciated the material written by Spedon for its accuracy and restraint, especially when compared to competitors such as Laemmle who claimed that each new production was the greatest ever made and who sometimes deceived the public by describing scenes that weren't even in the films. Spedon's promotional efforts on behalf of

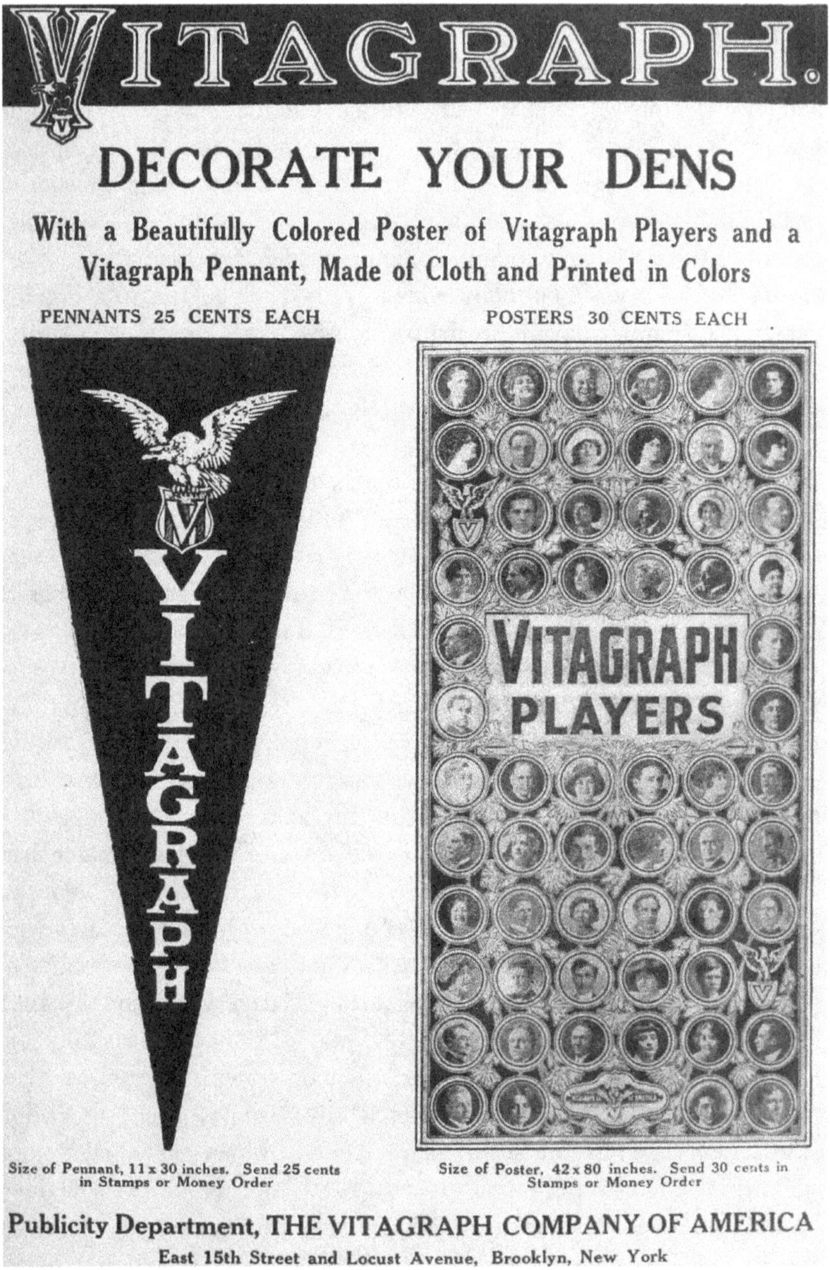

Sam Spedon promotes the studio and its stars. *Motion Picture Story Magazine*, December 1913.

Vitagraph would have a lasting effect on the public's understanding of and relationship with motion picture actors.[27]

In March 1910 Sam Spedon wrote an article that was reprinted in three trade papers in which he referred to leading moving picture players as "Gods and Goddesses," such was the adoration expressed in letters to Vitagraph by their worshipful admirers. By April, Vitagraph improved on Kalem's lead by supplying theaters with poster-sized photographic portraits of individual players. Soon those images became available to the public in the form of picture postcards. Even more significant, that month saw Vitagraph's first public appearance of what Sam Spedon dubbed "a motion picture star." He arranged for Florence Turner to appear at a Brooklyn "moving picture parlor" in conjunction with the debut of a song commissioned by the company, "The Vitagraph Girl." After the audience sang along to piano accompaniment with the lyrics projected on the screen, Spedon introduced Turner as the "ordinary girl with extraordinary abilities." The applause was "deafening" as Turner walked onto the stage and "responded in a very naïve and fetching little speech." At the same time Carl Laemmle had Florence Lawrence appear at a St. Louis nickelodeon to dispel the rumors of her death that he himself had started.

Spedon continued to send Florence Turner to other theaters in the Greater New York area on what became known as "Vitagraph Nights." An open-roof theater in Brooklyn, the Airdome, drew thirteen hundred fans to a Florence Turner appearance. A reporter who witnessed the "good-natured, shoving, jostling mob" that filled half the street, hoping to get inside an already packed Jersey City theater to see Turner in person, called the experience an "enlightening illustration, or demonstration, of the hold the moving picture itself has on the people." Sam Spedon also arranged for newspapers and magazines to interview Florence Turner; one of them printed the "astonishing" admission that in the three years since joining Vitagraph, she had received about three thousand marriage proposals in the mail.[28]

Of all Vitagraph's promotional efforts in 1910, the one that Florence Turner found most satisfying occurred in conjunction with a film she appeared in opposite James J. Corbett. Filmed in May and released on June 15, *How Championships Are Won and Lost* was made to cash in on the frenzy sweeping the country surrounding the upcoming Johnson–Jeffries heavyweight bout. The second half of the full-reel film showed Corbett with boxer Tom Kennedy in the ring, reenacting "famous 'knockout' blows" from memorable fights of the past, including Corbett's own defeat of the legendary John L. Sullivan for the heavyweight championship. The film ended with Corbett demonstrating Jack Johnson's fighting style and Kennedy mimicking Jim Jeffries's approach. The first half of *How Championships Are Won and Lost* was a fictional comedy, in which Corbett invites frail Florence Turner to his "physical culture studio" (gymnasium), where she is shown exercises she can do at home "as an aid to health, strength, grace and beauty." A month later a more robust Turner returns to the gym for a boxing lesson from Corbett and knocks him out, among the earliest of the cinematic female empowerment fantasies. Of much more importance to Florence Turner was Vitagraph's decision for the actress to play herself in the film: a movie star whose celebrity is akin to that of the ex-heavyweight champ. This resulted in the first on-screen credit for a Vitagraph stock company player. Years later, Turner recalled, "I can still remember my great interest and pleasure at seeing my name seemingly jump out from the little screen in the projection room at Vitagraph when Mr. Blackton surprised me with it." With this film, Florence Turner became the first Vitagraph player known by name everywhere that movies were shown.[29]

In November 1910 Sam Spedon began arranging Vitagraph Night appearances for Maurice Costello. The first filled Brooklyn's Fulton Auditorium with sixteen hundred fans, with three hundred more unable to get in. A few days later Costello enjoyed a similar reception at the Park Row Theatre in lower Manhattan. Typically on such occasions, three single-reel Vitagraph films would be shown, followed by Spedon taking the stage to talk about some of the qualities that made Vitagraph movies the best. Spedon would then introduce Costello, who would regale the audience with anecdotes about his experiences making movies. Costello participated in personal appearances at every opportunity over the next four years because they paid even better than his Vitagraph salary, enabling him to provide a comfortable life for his family.[30]

As the company's biggest stars, Florence Turner and Maurice Costello were the only actors to have their own dressing rooms. However, there was one performer that joined Vitagraph in 1910 who became as popular as Costello and Turner from her very first appearance but never had a dressing room because she didn't need one: Jean the Vitagraph Dog. Jean's owner and trainer, Larry Trimble, was an aspiring writer who visited the Vitagraph studio to write a magazine article about how movies are made. He became so intrigued with the process of filmmaking that he talked his way into a writer's position starting at $15 a week. Trimble soon learned that an Albert Smith production was about to be abandoned because the Pomeranian dog hired for the film was unable to perform on cue. The next day Trimble brought his collie Jean to the studio, and a star was born. Jean initially earned $10 a week more than her trainer, until Trimble became a director at Florence Turner's behest. There had been a few other movie dogs prior to Jean, but she appears to have been the first canine to star in multiple films over the course of several years. Titles were usually self-explanatory, such as *Jean, the Match-Maker*, *Playmates*, and *Jean Rescues*. Nearly everyone in the stock company appeared with Jean during her four years at Vitagraph. In 1910 young Helen Hayes made her film debut as the juvenile lead opposite the canine star decades before she earned the sobriquet, the "First Lady of the American Theater."[31]

At an MPPC meeting in the autumn of 1910, J. Stuart Blackton convinced his fellow licensees to publish the first magazine targeting the moviegoing public. The magazine would consist of synopses of upcoming films, written in short-story form and illustrated with production stills. It was believed that those who read the stories would then be enticed to see the films for themselves. Blackton spent three months cobbling together the debut issue of *Motion Picture Story Magazine*. Eugene V. Brewster took over editorial responsibilities beginning with the second issue. Brewster was a well-connected lawyer, writer, and artist, and is visible in the Blackton-directed live action prologue to Winsor McCay's *Little Nemo* film as the man holding a copy of *Motion Picture Story Magazine*. Within a year, the focus of the magazine shifted from stories to stars, and its name was shortened to *Motion Picture*. Maurice Costello was voted by its readers as the most popular movie star in America in the first such contest ever held. By 1914 circulation reached 250,000 and spawned a plethora of similar fan magazines around the world.[32]

Long before exhibitor rental fees or paid admissions were tabulated as indicators of an individual film or company's popularity, a key measurement of success was in the number of movies a firm produced. At the end of June 1911, Vitagraph became the first American producer to release four full-reel films per week.[33]

In 1911 Florence Turner scored her greatest triumph as both writer and actress in the one-reel film *Jealousy*. While no prints are known to have survived, the written record and some production stills are worth noting. At the time it was made, virtually every movie contained intertitles to convey or clarify information about plot and character, but they were deliberately omitted from *Jealousy*. Turner appeared alone in the film, except for the arms of a man and woman that are occasionally extended into view through a closed

Florence Turner in *Jealousy* (1911). *Moving Picture World*, August 12, 1911.

curtain. The action is confined to a room ornately decorated with exotic feathers and animal pelts, with Turner clothed in a fanciful gown and jewelry, all of which suggest a harem setting in keeping with the film's prerelease title, *A Discarded Favorite*. The curtains surround the perimeter of a slightly raised and carpeted platform in the midst of the room, presumably shielding from view the bed of a sheik. Florence Turner gave a tour de force performance as a spurned lover consumed with jealousy, conveying "alternate flashes of uncontrollable anger and the equally dark depths of despair" as she contemplates her former life within and present reality outside the curtained bedchamber. Her inner torment builds, climaxing with the plunging of a dagger through the curtains and then into her breast. One critic summed up the overall effect as "a transmutation of life into pictorial art."[34]

Maurice Costello regarded his performance as Sidney Carton in Vitagraph's 1911 three-reel production of *A Tale of Two Cities* as "my masterpiece." Charles Kent played Dr. Manette; he is also listed as the director on the opening title card, though some sources credit former Vitagraph Napoleon William Humphrey as director. The all-star cast included Florence Turner in a blonde wig as Lucie Manette and Leo Delaney, who bore a resemblance to Costello, as Carton's doppelganger Charles Darnay. William Shea and newcomers Lillian Walker and James Morrison were featured in prominent supporting roles. Virtually every interior setting in the film appears authentic, along with the French Revolution–era costumes. Even though most of the scenes were shot inside the company's glass studios, electric lights were utilized to highlight leading players in crowd scenes and create the shadowy room where the villain is murdered in his sleep. The nine-foot-line rule was adhered to, but most of the action is staged perpendicular to the camera, inadvertently stressing the two-dimensionality of the medium.

Maurice Costello's performance as the self-sacrificing hero is clearly the highlight of the film. When forlorn Sidney Carton devises his plan to replace Darnay in the Bastille, Costello moves closer to the camera to allow the audience to better see his subtle changes of expression. *A Tale of Two Cities* became Vitagraph's most popular release of 1911, enjoying its greatest success in England, where one hundred prints were purchased. Ignoring the pleas of Vitagraph and the American trade press to release all three reels of *A Tale of Two Cities* as a single unified attraction, General Film's Frank Dyer and Jeremiah Kennedy insisted on maintaining their policy of releasing each reel on separate days. In cities and towns containing multiple General Film licensees, this meant that one theater contracted to show Vitagraph films on Tuesdays could only exhibit the first reel, while another theater with a Friday contract showed reel two, and still another theater contracted for Saturday releases exhibited the third reel. Consequently, Vitagraph advised theaters to wait until all three reels could be exhibited together following the film's initial run. In such cases, the film was promoted as a special "feature" with a higher admission price charged, usually ten cents instead of five. According to published accounts, the strategy proved lucrative for all involved.[35]

Part of the success of *A Tale of Two Cities* was attributed to the built-in appeal of Dickens's beloved novel and the film's fidelity to a long-running theatrical adaptation from which it took its structure. In addition, a star was born in the final moments of the film. The pretty seamstress who rides in the tumbrel with Carton and kisses him as he ascends the steps to the guillotine, as played by teenager Norma Talmadge, captured more attention than did the performance of Florence Turner. It earned Talmadge her first on-screen credit. Until then she had only appeared in a handful of nondescript parts. In the fall of 1910 Norma Talmadge was a fifteen-year-old student attending Brooklyn's Erasmus Hall High School and dreaming of her idol Florence Turner. Talmadge was among the first generation of fans that made the movies their religion, describing her adoration of Turner in analogous terms: "I would rather have touched the hem of her skirt than to have shaken hands

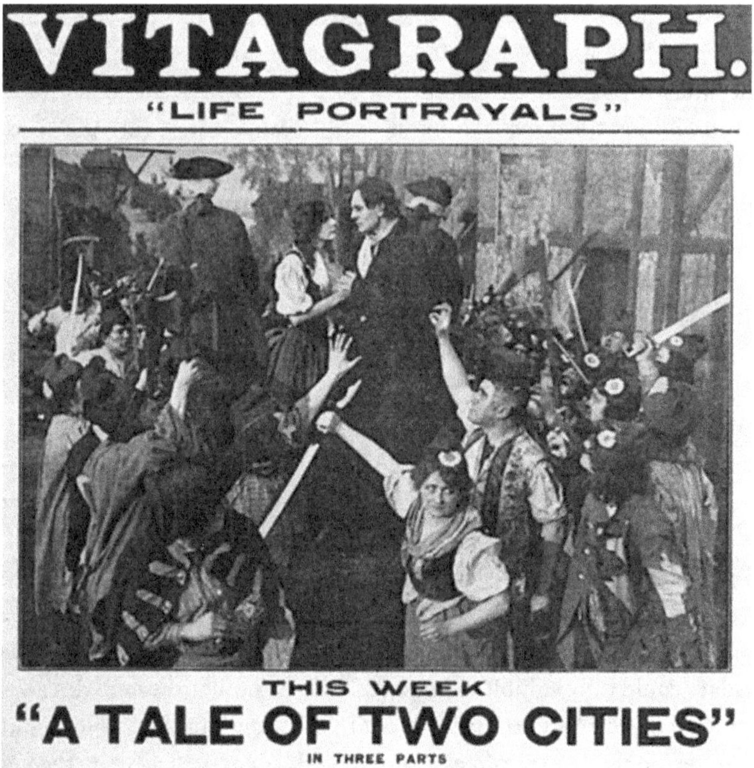

Maurice Costello and Norma Talmadge in *A Tale of Two Cities* (1911). *Film Index*, February 25, 1911.

with Saint Peter." Talmadge applied for extra work at the nearby Vitagraph studio and made her debut in a film about a mischievous horse, in which only the back of her head was visible. Her brief appearance in *A Tale of Two Cities* required little more than an expression of innocence from the pretty teen. Over the next four years, Talmadge learned how to act on the job, playing every kind of role. Although Albert Smith was "very, very fond of Norma," he once confided that it wasn't easy finding directors willing to work with her. "They said she was so dumb" that getting an acceptable performance from her required more time and effort than most were willing to endure. Clarence Brown, who fifteen years later directed one of her biggest successes, considered Talmadge "the greatest pantomist that ever drew breath. She was a natural comic." Her old colleagues at Vitagraph knew better.[36]

While the careers of Norma Talmadge and other members of the Vitagraph stock company were ascending, Florence Turner suffered an emotional and physical collapse. Having averaged a film per week for the past four and a half years, she worked only sporadically during the final months of 1911 and the first half of 1912, spending part of that time recuperating on a ranch in California. When strength permitted, Turner made a handful of appearances in West Coast vaudeville while still on the Vitagraph payroll.[37]

The Battle Hymn of the Republic may be Vitagraph's best-known production from 1911, not because anyone has actually seen the film since its release, but rather due to Vachel Lindsay's passionate appreciation of the film written for *The Art of the Moving Picture*, originally published in 1915. Lindsay considered *Battle Hymn* one of "the two most significant photoplays I have ever encountered." Three stories are woven through the movie: (1) a recreation of historical events that occurred during the American Civil War, focused on the lack of men joining the Union Army until "The Battle Hymn of the Republic" was written and utilized as a recruiting tool, (2) a fictional story about an elderly woman whose husband was killed fighting for the Union Army and her reluctance to allow their son to enlist until after she hears the song, and (3) an allegory inspired by Julia Ward Howe's lyrics as commentary on the consequences of human behavior through the ages. Accompanying the lyrics printed on-screen are recognizable historical figures marching toward the camera, a variety of Biblical scenes, and angels materializing in the sky blowing trumpets. For Lindsay, *Battle Hymn* illustrated "ritualistic birth, death, and resurrection," and he urged that "every student of American Art should see this film." He was not alone in his praise. The review in *Motography*, typical of the trade's response, declared, "The effect is like that of poetry, elevated and impressive . . . an artistic achievement."

Maurice Costello appeared in the allegorical scenes as Jesus. The principal roles went to Mary Maurice as the Civil War widow and Julia Swayne as Julia Ward Howe. White-haired Mary Maurice was born in 1844 and had a long career on the stage. She joined Vitagraph in 1910 and played the mother to virtually every member of the stock company until her death in 1918. Julia Swayne was often cast as the long-suffering wife or mother in hundreds of films for Vitagraph through early 1919. A few months after playing Julia Ward Howe, she starred as the title character in another historical drama, *Lady Godiva*, based on the Tennyson poem. Swayne made the famous bareback ride through Coventry wearing a long wig and a somber expression. Noticeably absent are the painted backdrops that marred the reality of many an earlier exterior scene; instead, an eleventh-century village was constructed on the backlot. With the success of *Lady Godiva*, Julia Swayne began to receive on-screen credit for her roles. According to Albert Smith it was only then that she changed her name to the better-remembered Julia Swayne Gordon.[38]

In 1909 Adele DeGarde became the first youngster to officially join the Vitagraph stock company, after having spent a year working as a freelancer for D. W. Griffith at Biograph. *The Voiceless Message*, produced in 1911, is her best surviving film. DeGarde plays an orphan whom a childless couple decides to adopt after learning she is a deaf mute. The little girl and her parents are unable to communicate until the couple learns to sign. The parents' ability to do so saves their lives when the wife silently signals to her husband that an armed burglar in hiding is holding a gun on her. DeGarde's signing is believable, and there is a noticeable lack of the cloying sentimentality that mars so many kid-centered dramas. The film was directed by William Ranous, back at Vitagraph after having been fired by Carl Laemmle.[39]

Child actor Kenneth Casey also joined the Vitagraph stock company in 1909. Three years later he costarred in *Father and Son*, one of many Vitagraph films that challenged social conventions rooted in racism. Casey plays an orphan whose foster father, Sang Lee (played by American Indian actor Eagle Eye), is the proprietor of a Chinese laundry. A woman from the Children's Aid Society objects to the interracial adoption and has Casey placed in an orphanage, but a judge overrules her and allows father and son to remain together. Twenty years later, the son, now played by Earle Williams, learns that his fiancée's mother will allow them to marry only if he abandons his Chinese foster father, but Williams refuses. His fiancée's father, the judge who allowed him to remain with Sang Lee, overrules his wife and gives his blessing to the marriage after hearing the young man's heartfelt defense of his loving dad. *Father and Son* is an example of a movingly effective story about love and prejudice that makes its point without resorting to the kind of didactic exhortations that are so prominent in movies of late.[40]

Over the years Vitagraph employed several other child actors. The best among the boys was Paul Kelly, who joined the company in 1911 after having worked on the stage. Like DeGarde and Casey, Kelly was born in 1899, but unlike them he portrayed a different type of kid. In one of his first films, *Jimmie's Job*, the Brooklyn-born Kelly plays the kind of brash, street-smart office boy endemic to American cities in the new century. He is late to work after shooting craps on the corner with other boys, smokes cigarettes in the office when the boss isn't around, and flirts with a pretty secretary who responds with good-natured teasing. Feigning illness so he can attend a baseball game, Jimmie demonstrates his true mettle when he foils a purse snatching while en route to the stadium. The boss encounters Jimmie at the ballpark and fires him, but just as quickly hires him back; the woman he protected from the purse snatcher turns out to be the boss's fiancée. Jimmie is a mischievous boy with a heart of gold and, as played by Kelly, is utterly believable.[41]

On October 24, 1910, a middle-aged journeyman actor with thirty years' experience on the stage arrived at Vitagraph inquiring about work. John Bunny was born in New York City in 1863, played in minstrel shows, Shakespeare, comic opera, melodrama, and vaudeville, and he had recently appeared on Broadway supporting comedian Lew Fields. With his Falstaffian physique and ingratiating smile, Bunny was hired to star in *Jack Fat and Jim Slim at Coney Island*, in which he and rotund character actress Kate Price double date with a thin couple at the seaside resort. In the background of virtually every shot, bystanders laugh at the antics of Bunny, just as nickelodeon audiences responded to the finished film. Albert Smith immediately hired John Bunny at a salary of $40 a week to join the Vitagraph stock company.

During his first year at Vitagraph, Bunny had supporting roles in big productions such as *A Tale of Two Cities* and more modest efforts like *Davy Jones in the South Seas*, in which William Shea played the leading role. Unlike Shea, whose broad playing was best served in small doses, Bunny played most everything straight. More often than not he was the everyman to whom funny things happened, with the comedy often punctuated by his expressive consternation or self-deprecating bemusement. It became obvious to everyone that Vitagraph had a new comedic star. An indication of Bunny's rapid rise to stardom is his prominence in the live-action prologue of Winsor McCay's *Little Nemo* film, released only four months after his motion picture debut.

Audiences seemed to enjoy Bunny most in domestic comedies opposite Flora Finch. Tall and painfully thin with a hawkish face, Finch provided a funnier visual contrast to Bunny than roly-poly Kate Price. Whether antagonistic or flirtatious, Finch proved the perfect foil. While half of Bunny's movies were made without Finch, she became so closely associated with him that audiences had trouble accepting her paired with anyone else. In *The Subduing of Mrs. Nag*, produced in 1911, Mabel Normand plays Bunny's pretty secretary that jealous wife Finch forces him to fire. Normand returns disguised as Bunny's new male secretary whom Finch giddily flirts with. When Bunny walks in on them he forbids his wife from further visits to the office, enabling Normand to resume her normal appearance and cozy relationship with him. Less than a year after entering the movies, it was reported that John Bunny was "rapidly becoming the most famous comedian the world has ever known," while Mabel Normand moved on to stardom with the newly formed Keystone Company.[42]

The mushrooming of new production companies like Keystone made it clear that assurances the MPPC would limit the American motion picture industry to its licensees and put an end to litigation were anything but true. During 1911 independent production companies began to outnumber the licensed producers. That year the Patents Company spent more than $100,000 in litigation fees. Adding insult to injury, the Latham loop patent was overthrown in a decision brought against the MPPC by IMP. It was beginning to seem as if there were two sets of rules, one that constricted the law-abiding licensees and the other that overturned those rules in favor of newer companies operating *independent* of the law.[43]

During the year and a half that General Film purchased most of the major film exchanges in the United States, the only holdout was the Greater New York Film Rental Company owned by William Fox. When the FSA overhauled distribution from sales to the short-term rental of prints, Fox disregarded the rules and kept every film sent to his exchange. For years afterward he leased those prints to exhibitors and kept the rental fees for himself. At the end of 1908, Fox's "rental library" totaled over three thousand reels; he possessed at least twice that number by 1911. Rather than take horribly scratched prints out of circulation, Fox continued to rent them until the films could no longer run through a projector. Needless to say, Fox was not popular with the MPPC hierarchy or its licensees. Under the circumstances, it is surprising that Fox was offered the going rate (either $75,000 or $89,000 depending on the source) for his exchanges, but he held out for more. Albert Smith, who during the summer of 1911 was appointed to the MPPC's executive board, attempted to mediate a compromise, urging J. J. Kennedy to pay Fox the $100,000 he was willing to settle for, but Kennedy refused and decided to cancel Fox's license. Lawsuits and countersuits were filed, with the courts finally ruling in favor of the MPPC.

Just when it seemed the situation had been resolved, the United States Department of Justice intervened and in 1912 brought suit against the MPPC–General Film combination for being in violation of the Sherman Antitrust Act. Fox secretly bankrolled the government's case. Ironically, the government chose not to sue Carl Laemmle of IMP and Adam Kessell and Charles Baumann of NYMP, who had banded together within weeks of the announcement of the formation of General Film to form the Motion Picture Distributing and Sales Company. Their plan was to control the distribution of all independent firms in the United States and to cancel the license of any exhibitor found to be in violation of *their* rules. Other companies would follow, controlling the three principal branches of the motion picture industry—production, distribution, and exhibition—yet more than three decades would pass before the courts got around to ruling on them.[44]

For the year 1911, Vitagraph paid its stock company of actors $106,000, staff writers received $9,945, cameramen earned nearly $8,800, and the combined salaries of the carpenters, painters, propmen, scenic department, costumers, custodial staff, restroom attendants, and chauffeurs totaled $34,384. Factory expenses were more than $1,155,000, with nearly half that figure coming from the cost of purchasing and processing film. Each of the partners earned nearly $300,000 in salaries, royalties, and dividends; 1912 would prove to be even better.[45]

Not long after Vitagraph began promoting its players, it discovered that the public was also curious about the process of making motion pictures. The central characters of 1912's *A Vitagraph Romance* are struggling newlyweds and the bride's disapproving father. The couple runs into friends working on a film shoot on location, which leads to an interview with J. Stuart Blackton in his office. He hires the couple to act in a film that the woman's father ends up seeing in a nickelodeon. Outraged, he calls on Blackton, Smith, and Rock at the Vitagraph offices. The partners mollify the man, convincing him that his daughter and son-in-law are working in an honorable profession. The film concludes with a happy reunion between the man and the young couple inside one of the glass-roofed studios.[46]

A Vitagraph Romance was written and directed by James Young. He joined the company early in 1912 with actress wife Clara Kimball. She accepted a starting salary of $25 per week, but her husband insisted that he always be paid more. Full-figured with large expressive eyes, Clara Kimball Young became an instant hit with movie audiences. James Young was assigned to write and direct an increasing number of his wife's films. Fortunately he was a good director, with an eye for composition, as well as a light touch and sense of pacing. Unlike other directors at the time, Young often cut between shots within the same setting. His excessive salary eventually caused trouble within the company when other writers and directors learned how much he

Clara Kimball Young. *Motion Picture Story Magazine*, March 1912.

was making. Although there were never any written contracts, Blackton and Smith had agreed to James Young's terms and, unlike later producers, their word was inviolable.

James Morrison costarred opposite Clara Kimball Young in *A Vitagraph Romance*. Born in 1888, Morrison received training in theatrical pantomime at New York's American Academy of Dramatic Arts. Shortly before *A Tale of Two Cities* went into production, Morrison was hired by J. Stuart Blackton. Initially Morrison would gather with fellow newcomers Norma Talmadge, Lillian Walker, and Earle Williams on Saturdays; they would tentatively open their pay envelopes to see if they had received a dreaded "blue ticket" indicating their services would no longer be required. Fortunately all continued with Vitagraph for several years, with baby-faced Morrison forever typecast as a young man in his late teens and early twenties, which he performed to perfection well into his mid-thirties.

Florence Turner appears at the end of *A Vitagraph Romance* as the star of the film within the film playing opposite Clara Kimball Young. Although no one realized it at the time, the scene represents a passing of the torch between Vitagraph's longtime leading actress and the woman who would take her place, though Young's reign would last only a couple of years. *A Vitagraph Romance* is even more noteworthy for its shots of Vitagraph crews engaged in production inside glass-enclosed studios, on the backlot, and on location. The film is also important for the sequence featuring J. Stuart Blackton, Albert Smith, Pop Rock, and unbilled Sam Spedon. *A Vitagraph Romance* was one of the first movies about movies, creating a boilerplate of sorts for subsequent behind-the-scenes films that disingenuously suggest the ease with which aspiring writers and actors could find success in the industry.[47]

Visitors to Vitagraph's Brooklyn studio in 1912 were struck by the "happy-family atmosphere, which is so abundant that it seems to spill over the walls." Albert Smith was different, "one of those undemonstrative sort of men who are difficult to understand, even by their most intimate companions," though when it came to the business of Vitagraph he "spoke with the unhesitating directness of a man who knew what he was talking about." J. Stuart Blackton, on the other hand, was described as a "man of brains" and a "solid contributor to the evolution of the new art." As Vitagraph prospered, Smith became more aloof at the office, a no-nonsense businessman committed to the health and management of the company. Blackton was much more personable; it was important to him to be well liked and regarded as a brilliant artist.

Blackton and wife, Paula, yearned for acceptance into high society. Toward this end, he embraced a pastime of the wealthy: yachting. According to his daughter Marian, his accumulation of steam-powered yachts and speedboats, which before World War I numbered fifteen, were tangible proof of her nouveau riche father's wealth. While Blackton was winning races and joining the most exclusive clubs, Paula, arrayed in diamonds, played hostess

Commodore Blackton in 1912. Library of Congress, Prints and Photographs Division, NYWT&S Collection, LC-USZ62-115740.

aboard their yachts and at home to captains of industry and their wives, donating freely to everyone's pet charities. Their efforts resulted in Blackton being elected Commodore of the Atlantic Yacht Club in 1912. Although his tenure lasted but a few years, for the rest of his life Blackton insisted that friends, acquaintances, employees, and even his own family address him as "Commodore." It seems that everyone did, except for Smith and Rock.[48]

While the Blacktons entertained, Albert Smith created a unit in 1911 to make Westerns in the American West. Writer-director Rollin S. Sturgeon established a temporary base of operations at a small house near the beach at Santa Monica, California. The Harvard-educated Sturgeon initially joined the scenario department and was soon named editor of that department prior to becoming director of the Western unit. Albert Smith visited the troupe in June 1912 and purchased a much larger house with a barn one block from the beach to serve as the unit's new headquarters. An outdoor stage was constructed on the property, on which to shoot interior scenes, though most production occurred amidst the natural splendor of the nearby Santa Monica Mountains.[49]

Rollin Sturgeon made some of Vitagraph's finest films during his five years as the principal director of the West Coast unit. His Westerns are notable for their stunning outdoor compositions and sense of scale that place man amidst exotic landscapes, with relatively high horizon lines splitting the

Lined up for the Oklahoma Land Rush, *How States Are Made* (1912), directed by Rollin Sturgeon. *Moving Picture World*, February 17, 1912.

horizontal plane; he also obtained understated, believable performances from his casts. In 1912 Sturgeon directed *How States Are Made*, the first film to recreate the Oklahoma land rush. The story bears similarities to William S. Hart's better-known *Tumbleweeds*, released in 1925; the films include nearly identical shots of prairie schooners and men on horseback at the starting line fading into the horizon. Unlike the later film's dynamically edited race among the pioneers to stake their claim, Sturgeon chose a very different way to convey the rush across the empty landscape. A vast grassy plain in the foreground is framed in the back by a tall barren hill. Tiny figures begin to appear on the ridge of the hill in silhouette until the entire crest becomes filled with people on horseback. Each of the riders gallops down the hill and toward the camera. The framing encompasses an enormous expanse of land, and the action is covered in a single take that lasts several minutes. The viewer is challenged to make sense of the initial empty space, the indiscernible images that begin to appear on the ridge, and the ensuing race down the hill and across the plain, with scores of galloping horses moving at varying speeds. The shot contains a kind of dynamism that became extremely rare in American action sequences following the dynamic editing that D. W. Griffith perfected a few years later in *The Birth of a Nation*. The unadorned documentary quality of the sequence led one critic to wonder if a motion picture camera had in fact been on hand in 1889 to capture the real Oklahoma land rush.[50]

With the addition of a weekly Western, Vitagraph became the only American production company releasing five one-reel films per week beginning in March 1912. At the end of September the company added a sixth single-reel movie to its weekly program. By comparison, Selig and Edison, the company's closest competitors, both began releasing five films per week in September, and Pathé's American subsidiary made four films each week, in addition to three weekly releases from its Paris studio.[51]

General Film distributed product to six thousand licensed theaters that on average changed their programs twice a week. Vitagraph was second only to Pathé in the amount of footage sold through General Film for 1911, but in 1912 it would overtake Pathé for good. As for the overseas market, Vitagraph did twice the amount of business that it did in the United States. Edison's London representative as much as confirmed this to Frank Dyer, writing, "The Vitagraph Company has the reputation for doing excellent work and their films are considered second to none here so far as quality is concerned."[52]

There are several reasons why Vitagraph was so popular outside of America. The company had better distribution than any of its competition except for Pathé. More important was the widespread preference for the kinds of films Vitagraph made and the popularity of its stars. Robert Youngson's documentary compilations, such as *Days of Thrills and Laughter*, and Walter Kerr's seminal text, *The Silent Clowns*, helped focus the study and celebration of early screen comedy on the frenzied physicality of slapstick. However, during the many years that it was the world's number one production company, Vitagraph specialized in making situation comedies. Almost from the moment he joined the company, John Bunny became the most famous motion picture comedian on the planet.

In *Mr. Bolter's Infatuation*, John Bunny is a naive man from a small town who pursues impish showgirl Lillian Walker to the city; she deliberately misleads him into a series of misadventures. Whether conveying the lovesick longings of an innocent, the confusion of a fish out of water, or the anger of someone who has had his pocket picked, Bunny is utterly sincere throughout. His performance was hailed as a "masterpiece." *Mr. Bolter's Infatuation* may be a fairer gauge of John Bunny's talent than some of his more widely circulated films. Bunny's costar was Lillian Walker. Like several of Vitagraph's leading ladies, Walker had attended Brooklyn's Erasmus Hall High School.

Mr. Bolter's Infatuation (1912), Lillian Walker, Rosemary Theby, and fourteen-year-old Moe Howard (?). Frame capture.

She personified the curvaceous, blonde Gibson Girl then in vogue, but it was Walker's vivacious personality and dimpled smile that made her a star of light comedy and an attractive counterpart to John Bunny. There is a scene in *Mr. Bolter's Infatuation* in which Bunny gives a message to a callboy working backstage at the theater to give to Walker. The impertinent thirteen-year-old enters the women's dressing room without knocking and smokes a cigarette while waiting for Walker to write a response for him to deliver back to Bunny. In his autobiography, Brooklyn-born Moe Howard of the Three Stooges devotes an entire chapter to his work as a child actor in Vitagraph movies. He credits Maurice Costello with giving him his big break, and recalls working with John Bunny and "Vitagraph glamour girl" Lillian Walker, who requested him for one of her movies. The unbilled actor playing the messenger boy in *Mr. Bolter's Infatuation* appears to be young Moe Howard.[53]

John Bunny was so valuable to Vitagraph that Albert Smith indulged his dream of starring in Charles Dickens's *Pickwick Papers*, "one of the most widely read of all works of English literature." Smith also agreed with Bunny to make *Pickwick* as authentic as possible by allowing him to film it at locations in England that inspired Dickens, not far from where Smith himself was born. Six months were spent in preparation, which included Bunny shooting two movies per week instead of the usual one in order to maintain the regular release schedule of "Bunnygraphs" while he was away. It was a grueling pace for the obese, middle-aged actor, but one he obviously felt was

John Bunny as Pickwick, 1912. Frame capture.

worth the sacrifice. To keep costs down, the smallest possible crew accompanied Bunny to England: director Larry Trimble and cameraman Arthur Ross, with Bunny's son George assisting. They departed New York on May 25, 1912. Aboard ship a short comedy was improvised, *Bunny All at Sea*, costarring the ship's captain, boatswain, and several passengers.

As soon as their ship docked, Bunny and company learned the Derby was about to occur at Epsom Downs. They quickly cobbled together a story in which Bunny plays a poor fruit and vegetable vendor at the world-famous horse race. Bunny was accustomed to being recognized and mobbed by fans wherever he went in his native New York, but he was unprepared for the ovation he received the moment he arrived, unannounced, at Epsom Downs. *Bunny at the Derby* contains excellent documentary footage of the race and spectators to authenticate the fictional story, as well as scores of excited fans visible in the background of many of the shots that Bunny appears in as the poor costermonger.[54]

John Bunny resembled Pickwick as originally illustrated by Robert Seymour, Robert W. Buss, and Hablot K. ("Phiz") Browne. In London, when he set about to cast the movie, Bunny selected his costars based as much on the resemblance to their illustrated counterparts as on their acting ability. Bunny and Trimble were also meticulous about securing costumes that resembled Dickens's precise descriptions, some dating to the 1820s when the story is set. Exterior locations were secured in and around Kent in southeast England, as well as buildings and roads referenced or alluded to by Dickens.

The production was also fortunate to secure the original stagecoach that traveled the Kent circuit during the mid-nineteenth century.

Larry Trimble rented studio space for interior scenes from British film pioneer Cecil Hepworth at Walton-on-Thames. It was an inspired choice. Hepworth began his moving picture career as an itinerant exhibitor at about the same time as Blackton and Smith, moved into production in 1898, and, like Vitagraph, outlasted all of his original competitors. Hepworth's collie became the movies' first canine star in *Rescued by Rover*. Of much more importance to the *Pickwick* production was the fact that in 1912 Hepworth himself produced a fifty-minute adaptation of Dickens's *Oliver Twist*, the first British multireel feature. Hepworth's commitment to realism rivaled Vitagraph's; thanks to his staff, the interior scenes for *Pickwick*, including an impressively paneled dining room, have fooled some commentators into believing they were made inside historic buildings in Rochester.

Given the expense and commitment of time that shooting a period story in England entailed, it is surprising that Bunny and company made only three one-reel episodes from *The Pickwick Papers*. *The Adventure of the Honorable Event*, a faithful condensation of the first three chapters of the novel, was released as a two-reeler paired with *The Adventure of the Westgate Seminary*, culled mostly from chapter sixteen. The third film, *The Adventure of the Shooting Party*, encompasses chapter nineteen. When production on the three *Pickwicks* wrapped, Bunny and company visited Ireland to make a handful of actualities and fictional films, then vacationed in Paris and Germany. As the first credited American movie star to visit Europe, Bunny discovered that his popularity spanned much of the world. In Paris they called him "Monsieur Cinema" and in Berlin Bunny was known as "Herr Kintop." Bunny also learned that in Russia he was billed as "Pockson."

The troupe returned to New York on September 7, 1912, after being away for more than three months. John Bunny told reporters that his dream was to return to England "and complete the picture version" of *The Pickwick Papers*. For all the publicity the expedition generated on both sides of the Atlantic, Vitagraph didn't release the first two films until the end of February 1913, and *The Adventure of the Shooting Party* wasn't released until the following September. The films received excellent reviews, with one critic noting that Bunny's performance in *Hunting Party* "pleased the audience greatly." He seemed "made for the part so perfect is he in it."

When he left the United States Bunny was earning $200 per week. He cabled from London that an English producer, probably Hepworth, offered him much more to remain in London and make movies for him. Smith countered by tripling Bunny's salary, which the comedian agreed to, making him the highest salaried actor in motion pictures at the time. Decades later J. Stuart Blackton charged that "the trip spoiled him." Bunny "was a jolly, kindly, simple, elderly actor when he went away. . . . But he returned with delusions of grandeur and was never the same again." The delayed release of the *Pickwick*s and minimal publicity may thus have been a punitive response by Vitagraph toward an actor who had attained a much better sense of his financial value to the company. Blackton may have grown to dislike Bunny, as did Flora Finch and Larry Trimble, but others at Vitagraph thought otherwise. For instance, John Bunny was among the first motion picture celebrities to champion both the industry and the lot of his fellow actors as leader of the Screen Club, the "First Social Organization in the Moving Picture Industry."[55]

Also prominent in the affairs of the Screen Club was Maurice Costello. As the movies' first credited leading man, Costello's popularity exceeded Bunny's in America. His celebrity brought far greater fame and a higher standard of living than he had earned from the stage, though it had its drawbacks. As was the case with Florence Turner, Costello received staggering amounts of fan mail, most coming from infatuated young women who were particularly aggressive in pursuing him. In 1912 he starred in *The Picture Idol*, a humorous example of art imitating life, in which Clara Kimball Young plays a high school girl with an all-consuming crush on "Vitagraph's Maurice Costello." Her father conspires with Costello to disillusion the impressionable girl by bringing her to the actor's home. Costello introduces her to four neighborhood ragamuffins posing as his children and an office boy in drag pretending to be his wife. Young returns home, disgusted, and tears up the photos of her former idol that adorned her bedroom walls. Clara Kimball Young is gamely naive but too old to pass for a high school girl. Maurice Costello, on the other hand, is clearly having great fun lampooning his status as a matinee idol. Everything came full circle when Sam Spedon advised exhibitors to advertise *The Picture Idol* by placing a large portrait of Costello on a board outside the theater and adding the caption: "A Feature for the Ladies."[56]

Director Van Dyke Brooke was Costello's oldest friend and "most severe critic." Two of Brooke's most successful 1912 productions starred Costello's daughters. In *Lulu's Doctor*, six-year-old Helen plays Lulu, an orphan raised by aunt Clara Kimball Young. When the leg on her doll breaks, a neighborhood policeman directs Lulu to nearby doctor Maurice Costello. After bandaging the doll, the doctor is reunited with his former fiancée, Lulu's aunt. Helen gives

Helen and Dolores Costello, ca. 1912. *New Movie Magazine*, January 1931.

an unaffected performance, especially in a scene in which she sings with abandon while helping in the kitchen. The kiss between real-life father and daughter after the doll is repaired is genuinely tender. A critic observed that while Vitagraph didn't promote Helen Costello as it did their other child stars, her "naturalness" and "delightful naïveté stamp her as second to none among small children who have achieved fame on the screen."

In *Ida's Christmas*, nine-year-old Dolores is the title character, whose unemployed father can't afford to buy her the five-dollar doll she wants for Christmas. While running an errand for her mother, Ida notices a man unwittingly drop his wallet on the sidewalk. Ida returns it to him and he rewards her with a five-dollar bill; Ida then rushes to the doll store. Once there, she realizes that the money would be better spent on groceries and other necessities. Ida returns home and tearfully hands over the bill while describing how she got it. John Bunny, sporting a white beard, shows up with the coveted doll, a Christmas tree, and other presents for the family. The film is deliberately constructed to allow the gifts to come either from a wealthy woman who learned of the family's hardship and Ida's desire, or directly from Santa Claus himself. Like her sister, Dolores Costello was an utterly believable child actress. This is especially evident in the scene where she looks at the money in the man's wallet and momentarily contemplates keeping it. Costello is so convincing in her brief contemplation that the outcome could have gone either way. The quality of the Costello sisters' performances transcended stories, roles, and directors, suggesting the guiding influence of father Maurice.[57]

Nineteen-year-old Hazel Neason wrote *Ida's Christmas*. She joined Vitagraph as an actress in mid-1911 and played the attractive secretary in *Jimmie's Job* opposite Paul Kelly. Neason abruptly moved to Kalem early in 1912 but continued writing for Vitagraph under a pen name. A profile in *Motion Picture Story Magazine* described her as "ambitious" and noted that her smartly furnished apartment overlooking the Hudson River was strewn with American Beauty roses. The flowers and possibly the apartment itself were gifts from Albert Smith. Upon his divorce from first wife, May, Smith and Hazel Neason married in January 1913.[58]

Christmas 1912 and the New Year was a happy time for almost everyone connected with Vitagraph. The company had been depositing $1,000 each month into an account to be shared among the Brooklyn, London, and Paris employees as a Christmas bonus, but when the holiday came it was learned that Vitagraph's partners had added $12,000 of their own money to the fund. In addition, each employee received the traditional Christmas turkey. Blackton, Smith, and Rock could afford to be generous. Net profits for 1912 reached $925,000, Vitagraph's best year yet.[59]

Several of Vitagraph's key personnel didn't participate in the annual Christmas celebration because they were circling the globe making movies. The troupe consisted of Maurice Costello, his wife and daughters, James and Clara Kimball Young, Mr. and Mrs. William V. Ranous, writer Eugene Mullin, cameraman Harry Keepers, and Albert Smith's brother William "Stephen" Smith, who served as business manager. Albert Smith recalled that the trip came about after Van Dyke Brooke tipped him off that a new production company was intent on luring Maurice Costello away from Vitagraph.

In mid-December, the "Vitagraph Globe Trotters" sailed from San Francisco to Hawaii aboard a Japanese steamer, spent four weeks in Yokohama making two actualities and two dramas, and toured Tokyo and Nagasaki before continuing on to Shanghai and Hong Kong to make more movies. The troupe next visited Singapore, staying just long enough to shoot an actuality about street dancers. The Globe Trotters' next stop was Rangoon, Burma, where they filmed an adaptation of Rudyard Kipling's *Mandalay*, starring Clara Kimball Young and Maurice Costello.

The troupe crossed the Indian Ocean to Calcutta, where they produced a travelogue and *The Hindoo Charm*, part of which was filmed at a rajah's palace. After struggling with the oppressive heat and humidity of Calcutta, the Globe Trotters traveled by train across India for sixty hours to Bombay. Over three days in Bombay, the climax was filmed to *On Their Wedding Eve*, a story about quarreling lovers that contained scenes photographed in some of the countries previously visited. It was the first American narrative to utilize multiple international locations, but like most of the Globe Trotters' productions it hasn't survived.

From Bombay, the Vitagraph troupe took a steamer to Port Said, and from there traveled by rail to Egypt. The Globe Trotters spent more than two weeks shooting in Cairo, Luxor, and the Temple of Karnack. The troupe then traveled by steamship to Brindisi, Italy. While traveling across the seas, the Globe Trotters made at least three shipboard movies, including *The Joys of a Jealous Wife*, costarring Mae Costello, who also wrote the script. She "plays very realistically and effectively a jealous wife," a woman who won't allow her husband to leave her sight for a moment. *Moving Picture World* noted that the film "comes too precious near being a tragedy to be wholly comic." Later events would confirm that the movie did indeed mirror aspects of the Costellos' real-life relationship.

The Vitagraph Globe Trotters' favorite city was Rome. More than sixty years later, Dolores Costello recalled that the Italians "went mad" for her father, mobbing him and tossing "gardenias and violets at him." It was in Rome that Maurice Costello discovered that he was even more popular in Europe than America. The troupe photographed interior scenes for many of the films they had shot location footage for earlier in their travels, using the studios of Società Italiana Cines.

The Globe Trotters moved on to Venice, where they made their final films, including *The Lonely Princess*. Clara Kimball Young plays a young woman who lives in a cloistered palace until she locks eyes with Maurice Costello, a vacationing American touring the canals via gondola. *The Lonely Princess* is the best of the Globe Trotters' films that survive, thanks in large

Maurice Costello in Yokohama, Japan, and at the Great Sphinx in Giza, Egypt, 1913. *Moving Picture World*, April 12, 1913, *Motography*, October 4, 1913.

part to Maurice Costello's direction. Many of the traveling shots were made with the camera mounted at the bow of a gondola facing Costello seated midboat. This provides movement within the frame, allows for background views of such iconic structures as the Bridge of Sighs, and gives Costello prominence as he reacts to Young with appropriately subtle expression. These are complemented by low-angle point-of-view shots from gondola to balcony and high-angle shots of the gondola, with precise eye-line matches.

The troupe visited Paris before returning home, arriving in New York on June 3, 1913. They circled the globe in 175 days, making eighteen comedies and dramas, and almost as many travelogues. Nearly twenty years later at the pinnacle of her career as a movie star, Dolores Costello recalled that for her and sister Helen, the trip was "the biggest thrill of our lives."[60]

The success of the Globe Trotters' expedition and the earlier John Bunny London venture emboldened Florence Turner and Larry Trimble to take the biggest gamble of their lives. In early 1913 they resigned from Vitagraph to form their own London-based production company, Turner Films, Ltd.[61]

Simultaneous with Florence Turner's departure from Vitagraph, it was reported that John Bunny would headline the bill at Hammerstein's Victoria for the week beginning January 20, 1913. He was paid $1,000 for a thirteen-minute act. Bunny was allowed to appear at Hammerstein's (which at the turn of the century had been one of Vitagraph's most important clients) because the evening performances didn't interfere with his filmmaking activities during the day. Vitagraph even provided a clever opening to Bunny's act, filming him oversleeping at home. "Late for his act at the theatre he partially dresses, makes a dash for a taxi and finished dressing in that. As the film ends, the lights go up and Bunny steps through [a slit in the screen onto the stage] still buttoning on his collar." Bunny was such a hit that he was held over for a second week, earning an additional $1,000. The experience proved so successful that Bunny periodically interspersed vaudeville appearances with his motion picture career for the rest of his life.[62]

As popular as John Bunny was, there were those like the Blacktons who professed a preference for more "refined" comedy. In 1913 Vitagraph acquired such a comedian in Sidney Drew. Born in 1864, Drew hailed from a prominent theatrical family. His mother was "one of America's foremost comediennes" of the mid-nineteenth century, and for fifty years brother John was the American theater's most popular and critically acclaimed player of drawing room comedy. Sidney followed them into the theater as a light comedian, playing alongside his wife Gladys Rankin, also from a leading theatrical family. In 1896 Mr. and Mrs. Sidney Drew were among the first theatrical stars to enter vaudeville, presumably because the money was better. For fifteen years they headlined in one-act plays. In 1911 Sidney Drew made one film each for Kalem and the nonlicensed Champion Company. Two years later the Drews, along with their adult son Sidney Rankin Drew, joined Vitagraph. The move was motivated in part by Mrs. Drew's declining health. She no longer performed but continued to "punch up" her husband's scripts and write originals as she had done in vaudeville under the pen name George Cameron.

Sidney Drew's first big success at Vitagraph was the two-reel comedy *A Regiment of Two*, written by playwright Anthony E. Wills. The story concerns two men who tell their wives they've joined the Army Reserve, but it is a canard to provide them with an excuse to go out at night once a week to get drunk and visit "tango parlors." When it is reported that the real regiment has been called to one month of active duty in Panama, their ruse grows more complicated, with tearful goodbyes and letters mailed from Panama on their behalf. Critics noted that even though it was "an old farce motive," thanks to

Vitagraph directors on staff in 1913. *Screen Club Annual*, 1913, Margaret Herrick Library, Academy of Motion Picture Arts and Sciences.

the performances of Drew and Harry Morey, "the going out and coming home of these two . . . fills the house with laughter."[63]

Coinciding with an increase in the production of comedies at Vitagraph's Brooklyn studio was the decision in March 1913 to add a second producing unit to the studio in Santa Monica, charged with making comedies and occasional dramas; by August a third unit was added. During the summer Albert Smith oversaw the construction of new facilities at 1438 Second Street in Santa Monica to house three studios for the Western company. A year later he installed brother William Stephen Smith to oversee day-to-day operations.[64]

Rollin Sturgeon continued to focus on Western dramas. *The Courage of the Commonplace*, made in the summer of 1913, is his masterpiece, an unflinchingly realistic story about the hardships suffered by a poor farm family in the contemporary American West. The movie stars Mary Charleson who, unlike other Erasmus Hall classmates at Vitagraph, did not possess the kind of beauty commonly associated with leading ladies. Hers was a plain, everywoman type of attractiveness rooted in the integrity of her character.

She was the perfect choice to play the "family drudge," the oldest daughter who has inherited the responsibilities of a mother too worn out by a lifetime of unrelenting toil to carry on. Charleson's character, also named Mary, has never had the chance to develop friendships. She dreams of attending Fine Arts School, of having a boyfriend and girlfriends; and she saves pennies, nickels, and dimes toward that goal. Mary learns she has been granted a partial scholarship, but the following day her father's plow horse dies. Without a replacement the family won't survive. Mary sacrifices her tuition money for the purchase of a strong young horse, putting an end to her dreams and facing the prospect of a bleak future. *The Courage of the Commonplace* was accurately promoted by Vitagraph as "The unknown sacrifice of those who practice self-denial for others, strongly and impressively set forth." *MPW*'s critic echoed the sentiments of many in declaring, "There is nothing in particular to recommend it as entertainment." Albert Smith, on the other hand, recognized Mary Charleson's extraordinary talent and had her transferred to the Brooklyn studio, where for the next year she frequently starred opposite Maurice Costello.[65]

In August 1913, Albert Smith reported that Vitagraph was regularly making between nine and ten productions per week. This meant that the company was employing at least ten cameramen on a full-time basis. With the exception of Biograph's Billy Bitzer, precious little is known about any cameramen prior to the founding of the American Society of Cinematographers in 1919, which helped institute the crediting of its members. Blackton and Smith photographed most of the early Vitagraph productions but eventually delegated the responsibility to others, including Blackton's half brother William Stuart Adams and Smith's nephew Steve, who eventually became chief cameraman for Vitagraph's Western studio after serving an apprenticeship in the Brooklyn developing lab.[66]

Some of the most celebrated cinematographers of the twentieth century were trained at Vitagraph. After learning the principles of still photography at his father's portrait studio in Italy, Tony Gaudio immigrated to the United States and was placed in charge of Vitagraph's processing laboratory from 1908 to 1910. Gaudio later received an Academy Award for his cinematography in *Anthony Adverse* (1936), though his work at Warner Brothers for *Little Caesar* (1930), *High Sierra* (1941), and *The Letter* (1941) became far more influential. Milton Krasner began his career in 1919 as a teenager working in Vitagraph's developing lab and was soon promoted to assistant cameraman. He would later receive an Academy Award for *Three Coins in the Fountain*

(1954), but is better known for photographing such black-and-white classics as *The Woman in the Window* (1944), *Scarlet Street* (1945), and *The Set-Up* (1949). Italian immigrant Nick Musuraca worked as Commodore Blackton's chauffeur before joining Vitagraph in 1913. Musuraca was a projectionist, cutter, and assistant director before Blackton made him a "first cameraman" in the late teens. After Vitagraph, Musuraca was under contract to RKO for most of that studio's existence, where he photographed such groundbreaking films as *The Stranger on the Third Floor* (1940), *Cat People* (1942), and *Out of the Past* (1947). He received his only Academy Award nomination for *I Remember Mama* (1948).[67]

The influential, better-known work of Gaudio, Krasner, and Musuraca shares certain visual motifs that complement narratives of crime, betrayal, and horror populated by characters plagued by lust, greed, and doubt. These films emphasize shadowy interiors and nighttime exteriors that serve to heighten the potential for physical violence and reflect the inner anxieties of the characters. Two-shots are sometimes composed in a way that enable one character to be bathed in light while another is partially hidden in shadow. This approach to black-and-white cinematography dominated by chiaroscuro lighting is *the* key stylistic visual element of what has since come to be known as *film noir*. The similarities in lighting and composition applied to particular types of narrative common to Gaudio, Krasner, and Musuraca in the maturity of their careers weren't really of their own invention. Nor did they originate with French poetic realist filmmakers of the 1930s or German Expressionists in the post–World War I era. Rather, that aesthetic evolved over time with key components developed in similarly themed films made during their apprenticeship at Vitagraph.[68]

One of the chief goals Vitagraph had in building its first indoor studio was to provide for evenly lit sets, where every element in a frame would be easily identifiable. This was the prevailing aesthetic dominating the American film industry for more than a dozen years. The addition of electric lights was originally intended to insure such uniformity. That approach began to change around 1911 in films like *Proving His Love or the Ruse of a Beautiful Woman*, in which an attractive actress tests the sincerity of her suitors by wearing makeup that gives the impression she has been disfigured in an accident. She is cloaked in darkness as each of her callers, bathed in light, recoils at the sight of her. Her true love, thinking she has rejected him, backs away into a darkened doorway until she pulls him back into the light and they embrace. There can be no doubt that Vitagraph was at the forefront of a sophisticated approach to cinematography that included elements that have since come to be associated with film noir. Circumstantial evidence suggests that Blackton's brother, William Stuart Adams, was a key figure in the development of dramatic lighting at Vitagraph.[69]

In 1913 a director emerged after years of preparation to become the preeminent filmmaker at Vitagraph. Ralph Ince was born in Boston in 1887 into a theatrical family. He received formal training as a graphic artist during his early teens and worked as a commercial illustrator for newspapers and magazines; he then switched careers to acting, playing with some of the leading theatrical companies of the era. At the age of twenty, Ince fell in love with Lucy Stuart when they were both in the choir of the Episcopal Church of Sheepshead Bay, Brooklyn. Determined to settle down and get married, Ince found work as a propman, "scenery shifter," and bit player at Vitagraph's Flatbush studio. Florence Lawrence recalled that Ince "would stand for hours watching the directors and actors at their work, never saying a single word." Four years later, he finally attracted notice as a motion picture actor with his portrayal of Abraham Lincoln in *Battle Hymn of the Republic.*

A few months before the release of *Battle Hymn,* Ince appeared uncredited as one of Winsor McCay's tuxedo-clad companions in the live-action prologue of his *Little Nemo* film. Only a handful of people then, as now, could identify Ralph Ince by sight or name. Why, then, was he included instead of a more recognizable player such as Maurice Costello? Because it turns out that Ince assisted his friend McCay with the making of *Little Nemo.* Exactly what part or how much of *Little Nemo* he may have animated will probably never be known. Of much more importance to the career of Ralph Ince and the development of cinema was the decision by Vitagraph in mid-1912 to promote this quiet, thoughtful man of many talents "into the ranks of photoplay directors."[70]

Shortly after he began directing it became apparent that Ralph Ince hadn't spent the previous five years merely "watching" other directors and actors, but had also been analyzing their choices. He identified those elements that were peculiarly cinematic and went on to utilize them himself, along with several ideas of his own. Ince was an early adherent of shot/reverse shot construction. In its simplest form, a shot is taken of a character gazing at something, followed by a shot of the object of the gaze, culminating in a return to the character reacting to what was just seen. Robert Spadoni has noted that this technique shifted cinema's emphasis from mise-en-scène to character. Eileen Bowser observed that by the time Ince made *Red and White*

Production still from *Winsor McCay* (aka *Little Nemo*, 1911). Left to right: unknown, George McManus, Ralph Ince, Winsor McCay, John Bunny, Eugene V. Brewster. *Film Index*, April 8, 1911.

Roses, released in March 1913, he added shots that represented the point of view of a third-person narrator to a shot/reverse shot sequence between two characters. She calls it "a more modern scene dissection [that] marks a significant shift" in the way scenes are filmed and understood.

Red and White Roses features a predatory "vamp" hired by an unscrupulous politician to lure his married opponent into an illicit affair in order to discredit him. When the vamp, played by Julia Swayne Gordon, meets with the crooked politician in her apartment, she is smoking a cigarette while lying belly down atop a tiger skin rug, the tiger's head prominent in the foreground. Gordon is edge lit against a dark background, the statue of a female nude visible behind her in the shadows. Barry Salt has recognized that this approach of sculpting Gordon with light to set her in sharper relief against a darker background visually complements the development of character-centered cinema. Ince also demonstrates sophistication in the variety of compositional choices and editing strategies that best suit the moment. The vamp and her prey are neighbors, enabling her to spy on and then communicate with him from their windows. The windows provide smaller frames within the bigger frame of the movie itself, giving an aesthetic balance to the overall composition but, more importantly, focusing on and isolating vamp and prey within their own private worlds. Ince utilizes a deep focus shot that encompasses both windows at the moment the vamp makes contact with her prey. This shot is a portent of their physical and emotional union. Ralph Ince's principal cinematographer was William Stuart Adams.[71]

Twelve days after the release of *Red and White Roses* came another two-reel production from Ralph Ince, *The Strength of Men*, that couldn't have been more different in story or execution. The love triangle at the heart of the narrative is utterly predictable. What makes the film noteworthy are the exotic locations and Ince's direction. The story, set in "the rugged north," resulted in Ince shooting all of the exteriors in mountain forests, lakes, and rivers in upper New York State. The shot compositions are stunning, reflecting his training as an artist. Ince knows just where to stage his action and place his camera for maximum effect. He exalts the hero with a low-angle shot that makes him appear as tall as the treetops. A canoe race between the two suitors is covered in static shots that reflect the tranquility of the water, and later via tracking shots as the canoes enter white-water rapids. A high-angle shot looks down on the canoers as they come upon a raging forest fire dropping flaming trees and branches all around them. It is a spectacular, genuinely exciting sequence, all the more impressive because the rapids, fire, and danger are real. After the inevitable fistfight amidst the raging fire, the combatants emerge from a thick cloud of smoke. Barry Salt has pointed out that the cinematography in *The Strength of Men* resulted in the first known reference to camera angles in an American movie critique. Salt also notes that up to this point D. W. Griffith's "large-scale scenery" was merely decorative, whereas in *The Strength of Men* the "giant landscape is much more part of the action. . . . There just isn't anything else comparable, in all these respects, in any film made up to the beginning of 1913." By the end of the year Ince was utilizing even more camera setups, including close-ups that were inserted "at the emotional peak of the scene." Salt's thorough analysis has led him to conclude that Ralph Ince is "the first master of mainstream continuity cinema, or 'classical cinema,' or whatever one wants to call the standard form of cinema." The claims made by and on behalf of his more famous brother Thomas Ince "as the man who created the American system of studio production . . . seem feeble" by comparison.[72]

Shortly after he commenced directing in the summer of 1912, Ralph Ince was assigned *Her Choice*, a comedic updating of *Cinderella* that included among the supporting characters a teenage girl who is "outrageously selfish and snobbish." He hired for the role his wife's attractive younger sister Anna

Anita Stewart in *The Wood Violet* (1912). *Motion Picture Story Magazine*, June 1914.

Stuart, who by her own admission was "selfish at times [thinking] only of my own pleasures." Anna was born in 1895 and, like the Talmadge sisters, Lillian Walker, and Mary Charleson, attended Erasmus Hall High School. During her first six months at Vitagraph she was variously billed as Anne Stewart, Anna Stewart, and Anita Stuart, before settling on Anita Stewart. After she had played a number of supporting roles, Ralph Ince came across a story about a "child of nature" written by Beta Breuil that he believed Anita, with her carefree personality and exceptional beauty, would be perfect for. In *The Wood Violet* Anita plays a girl who lives with her father in a cabin cloistered deep in the forest, spending her days communing with nature. She marries a visitor from the city and moves into his home, but when she misses her old life they return to live with her father. The wispy story resulted in Vitagraph deciding not to promote *The Wood Violet*. It is one of those movies that the public found on its own and turned into an enormous success, especially in

Europe. Overnight, Anita Stewart became a star. It is unfortunate that no print of the film is known to have survived. Surviving stills shows Anita Stewart clad in shapeless burlap bags roughly sewn together, making her sudden stardom all the more remarkable. Ince and Stewart worked under the supervision of Smith. Their rivals within the company were James and Clara Kimball Young, supervised by Blackton.[73]

Late in life Albert Smith declared, "I think we had the cleanest studio of any one of them from the stories that I heard [of] young girls trying to get into the business [that] had to give up to the director. . . . There was none of that in our studio." He averred that "Blackton was just as particular about those things as I was." While this may have been true, the fact remains that both men left their first wives to marry Vitagraph starlets. Smith wrote that Pop Rock "approved heartily of every girl interviewed for casting in our pictures [but] his was a deep, gentle, sympathetic sense of responsibility, and entirely platonic." However, Smith also recalled that Rock "believed every woman had a price." Rock's cynicism toward women appears to have been motivated by the actions of his second wife, which resulted in a public scandal. In 1900 Rock married a burlesque actress he had seen on a Coney Island stage. He eventually learned that she had been unfaithful during their marriage and that her lover was the father of the baby she gave birth to in 1905. The woman received $2,000 in a divorce settlement in 1907. By 1913 Rock's ex-wife had married her lover but tried to have her divorce from Rock overturned in order to have her son named as his heir. Rock testified that the couple planned to kill him if the court were to decide in their favor. The presiding judge dismissed the suit, castigating Rock's former wife and new husband in the process.[74]

In March 1913, Commodore Blackton sailed for Naples on a painter's grand tour of Europe. Albert Smith had already been in London and Paris for a month on a working vacation at the time of Blackton's departure. In the meantime, Pop Rock managed affairs from out of the Brooklyn studio until Smith returned in April. The Commodore arrived back home at the end of May in order to preside at the season's opening of the Atlantic Yacht Club. By then Blackton had acquiesced to his wife's demand that they move into "a big estate on Long Island, where the Best People have their homes." The Blacktons acquired Harbourwood, a 116-acre beachfront estate in Oyster Bay. The property included a casino on the beach for dancing, a golf course, tennis courts, greenhouses, stables, and their own dairy. Even more impressive were the neighbors: the Tiffanys on one side and Theodore Roosevelt on the other.

Aerial view of Vitagraph's Brooklyn studio, ca. 1915. *Motion Picture News*, August 19, 1922.

Over the next decade, Blackton's work ethic was challenged by an equally strong desire to play amongst the smart set.[75]

As Vitagraph was the world's most successful producer of movies, its scenario department received between seventy-five and one hundred scripts in the mail every day from established and aspiring writers. Marguerite Bertsch and another female reader were employed at the Brooklyn studio to pass judgment on each day's submissions. Those that were deemed worthy were forwarded to department head Beta Breuil. Stories that met with Mrs. Breuil's approval were submitted to Smith and Blackton, who alone had the authority to green-light a script for production and determine a purchase price, which varied from project to project. Those selected would then be returned to the scenario department to be adapted by Mrs. Breuil or another staff writer to conform to the aesthetic long established by the two partners. Thomas Ince and/or Irving Thalberg are usually credited with devising a management system that put the producer in charge of production, but years earlier Smith and Blackton were supervising a "studio system" of skilled laborers, many if not most of whom they had personally trained.[76]

During the summer of 1913, W. Stephen Bush wrote a series of articles analyzing the state of the motion picture industry in Italy, England, and France, following extended visits to each of those countries. "Italy is a poor market for the sale of American films with one notable exception. The films of the Vitagraph Company are very popular here. The agent of the Vitagraph is selling as many films as the best of the native producers." Among the French, Bush observed, "With the notable exception of the Vitagraph films, which seem to lead American films in Europe almost everywhere, there is comparatively little sale of American-made films in France. . . . Bunny and

Costello are great favorites with Parisians." By this time Vitagraph had sales agents in Berlin, Barcelona, Milan, Budapest, Buenos Aires, Rio de Janeiro, South Africa, and Australia.

The growing success of Vitagraph in Europe resulted in the company constructing a much larger processing factory in Gennevilliers, having outgrown the plant in the Paris suburb of Courbevoie. In July, George Smith moved Vitagraph's London office to 31–33 Charing Cross Road. London's leading trade paper noted that the offices boasted a liveried doorman, a screening room that could accommodate one hundred people, and a fireproof vault to store the supply of upcoming releases. Such plush offices suggested that Vitagraph "productions [were] of an equally high-class nature."[77]

Vitagraph made more movies in 1913 than any other company in the world, producing 245 reels of dramas, 18 reels of miscellaneous subjects, and 138 reels of comedies, which were significantly more than the 105 reels made by the second largest comedy producer, Keystone, which *only* made comedies. To outsiders it must have seemed as though Vitagraph had become one of the wealthiest corporations on the planet. However, in testimony given in connection with William Fox's lawsuit against the MPPC, Albert Smith admitted that "the Vitagraph Company's [domestic] business is less profitable than it was before" the formation of General Film. In fact, all of the licensees showed a proportionate decrease in profits for 1913 compared with 1912 and 1911, due in part to "heavy overhead and operating expenses." The greatest expense was the legal costs incurred by Edison's attorneys, who dictated General Film policy while defending it in lawsuits brought by Fox, Laemmle, and others. Those fees were supposed to be paid from Edison's 60 percent cut of the General Film royalties, but in reality were taken from profits that rightfully belonged to the licensees. Thus for 1913 Vitagraph netted only $65,747 from General Film, while the company's international business operating outside the jurisdiction of General yielded a profit of $1,050,599. As had been the case in the previous half dozen years, Vitagraph was doing twice the amount of foreign business—while renting at half the price—as it did domestically. This suggests that for 1913 the company lost at least one million dollars as a consequence of MPPC chicanery and incompetence.[78]

Denied its full domestic profit, Vitagraph still managed to become the first American motion picture company to net one million dollars in a single year. Pop Rock's share was $243,920.66; Albert Smith's, $237,593.47; and Commodore Blackton's, $229,970.55. At Christmas, Rock celebrated his good fortune by gifting his two partners and best friend Pop Lubin each with a 540-piece solid gold dinner set. On Boxing Day 1913, Vitagraph and the other licensees received what must have seemed at the time to be the ultimate Christmas present when William Fox's civil suit against the MPPC was dismissed by the New York state court of appeals, affirming a lower court's ruling that the MPPC did not constitute illegal restraint of trade. The ruling did not bode well for the government's antitrust suit against the Patents Company. For the moment it appeared that the assertion of Edison's attorneys that the MPPC would prevail over the unlicensed producers was finally coming true. Vitagraph had every reason to expect significantly greater profitability and influence for 1914 and beyond.[79]

4

1914–1918

Beginning in January 1914, Vitagraph altered its weekly release schedule so that two of the six productions were now two reels in length. This was in addition to the three-reel feature films the company had been making periodically since May 1912, when General Film initiated a separate service to distribute three-thousand-foot films intact. These contained more complex stories and characters, as well as richer production design, and thus were more expensive to make than single- and two-reel productions.

Despite the ongoing efforts of Vitagraph and Selig to expand the complexity and length of their films, most nickelodeon operators remained steadfast in their opposition to longer movies. This finally began to change after distributor George Kleine imported the eight-reel Italian epic *Quo Vadis?* in April 1913. At two hours, *Quo Vadis?* was too long as far as General Film and America's exhibitors were concerned. Kleine had to book the film into legitimate theaters in major cities around the country and ended up making a fortune.[1]

William Selig was the first American producer inspired by the success of *Quo Vadis?* to produce a nine-reel feature, *The Spoilers*, but it sat on the shelf for seven months while he lined up playhouses and distributors. On the heels of *The Spoilers*, Vitagraph produced its first eight-reel feature, *The Christian*, adapted from a best-selling novel and stage play. Liebler and Co., whom supervising producer Blackton had dealt with years earlier on the Kyrle Bellew and *Raffles* films, controlled the theatrical rights and became a coproducer responsible for distributing *The Christian* to legitimate theaters. The movie opened in March 1914 to mixed reviews, and Liebler consequently sold its interest outright to a few distributors who were only able to book *The Christian* in a limited number of theaters.[2]

Having learned from its unprofitable venture into coproduction, Vitagraph embarked on a different approach to feature film production and exhibition that had far more lasting consequences. Entering 1914, the company announced that it would supplement its regular production of one- and two-reelers with films consisting of four or more reels, the length to be determined by each individual story. These longer productions were marketed as "Broadway Star Features" because they enjoyed premiere engagements at a theater on the corner of Forty-Fourth Street and Broadway in New York's Times Square. Formerly a thousand-seat legit house known as the Criterion, it was redecorated in the French Renaissance style favored by the Blacktons, altered to accommodate the projection of motion pictures, and renamed the Vitagraph Theatre. Then as now, touring companies of theatrical plays and musicals were often advertised to the public as "direct from Broadway." Vitagraph's partners hoped that a similar allure would benefit these longer films and convince exhibitors that audiences would pay higher admission prices to see features that cost more to lease because they were more expensive to produce.

During the two years that Vitagraph leased the theater, it established a policy that remained in effect for most of the twentieth century: exclusive first-runs in major cities for movies of particular merit prior to their release into general exhibition. Another innovation was the installation of a $30,000 Wurlitzer organ that offered a wide range of orchestral-like instrumentation and sound effects to accompany the films. As an exhibitor Vitagraph had come a long way from vacant lot and tent shows at Coney Island in 1897, to the three-month lease of Tony Pastor's Theatre in the summer of 1908, to now operating its own "ornate and chic" theater on Broadway.[3]

The feature that opened the Vitagraph Theatre on February 7, 1914, was *A Million Bid*, a four-reel drama supervised by Albert Smith, directed by Ralph Ince, and starring Anita Stewart, Julia Swayne Gordon as her scheming mother, and perennial villain Harry Morey. It was adapted from the play *Agnes*, written by Gladys Rankin Drew (under her pen name George Cameron), though neither she nor husband Sidney was in the movie; in fact, Mrs. Drew died shortly before the premiere.

Opening night was a gala affair with such socialites as Diamond Jim Brady in attendance. Following the feature was a live performance in silent pantomime, *The Honeymooners*, written and directed by Blackton and starring John Bunny, Mary Charleson, and James Morrison. The one-act comedy, for which Bunny received compensation far in excess of his regular salary, was performed at every evening show during the two-month-long run of *A Million Bid*. Bunny and company took thirteen curtain calls on opening night. Concluding the program was the three-reel comedy *Goodness Gracious, or Movies As They Shouldn't Be*, written and produced by Blackton, starring Sidney Drew and Clara Kimball Young, and directed by James Young.

Vitagraph Theatre, February 1914. *Motion Picture Magazine*, April 1914.

Goodness Gracious satirized the type of theatrical melodrama that Vitagraph was at the forefront of supplanting, and was one of Blackton's triumphs. The highlight of the film occurs when Drew, as Kimball's college student boyfriend in letter sweater, tosses her out an open window to evade a gang of villains, then races down the stairs to catch her outside before she hits the pavement. Just as funny was casting Sidney Drew as a "brave youth"; in reality, he was fifty years old and the toll of heavy drinking gave him the appearance of being twice his age.[4]

Surprisingly, Vitagraph entered into the production of longer features and the lease on the theater without having arranged for a wider distribution mechanism for those films. Smith, Blackton, and Rock were confident that their features would prove so popular that a distribution network would emerge. Vitagraph's exhibitors worried that the company was about to embark on the acquisition of its own chain of theaters and threatened to cease showing its films until assurances were made to the contrary. Admission prices at the Vitagraph ranged from twenty-five cents to one dollar; because of the high rental fee, the theater operated at a loss of approximately $500 per week. This undoubtedly influenced the partners' decision not to acquire additional theaters.

Within weeks of the debut of the Vitagraph Theatre, Selig's *The Spoilers* opened the Strand, the first theater specifically constructed to show movies in Times Square. Carl Laemmle then rented the nearby Republic Theatre to present a two-reel comedy, longer feature, and one-act play starring Universal's leading player. The year 1914 marked the advent of the long feature and spelled the end of the nickelodeon era.[5]

The Vitagraph Theatre showed only Vitagraph films and changed programs only when attendance began to wane. After two months *A Million Bid* gave way to *Mr. Barnes of New York*, a six-reel drama starring and codirected by Maurice Costello. *Mr. Barnes* was a critical and commercial success. Two weeks into the run, General Film announced it would open a separate feature department to distribute films four reels or longer in length. By the end of the year, such features became so ubiquitous that three-reel films were incorporated into General's regular weekly program of shorts.[6]

In addition to his Vitagraph Theatre performances, John Bunny starred in twenty-eight films for Vitagraph in 1914, twenty-two of them opposite Flora Finch. Of their surviving films from that year, the baseball comedy *Hearts and Diamonds* is significant for containing shots of Bunny and Finch seated among a grandstand full of spectators intercut with actual game footage of the Dodgers in action at Ebbets Field during that ballpark's second year of existence. John Bunny received excellent notices for his performance in *The Old Fire Horse and the New Fire Chief*, which provided him with a role in which he demonstrated his versatility in comic and dramatic situations. The movie, now lost, was cowritten by Bunny's costar Kate Price four years after they made their movie debuts opposite each other in *Jack Fat and Jim Slim at Coney Island*. Price's role as the New Fire Chief is similar to others she played at the time, such as *Officer Kate*; these roles depict suffragettes who enter the workforce in positions of authority for which they are unqualified, with disastrous consequences.

As former child actors Kenneth Casey, Adele DeGarde, Paul Kelly, and the Costello sisters took sabbaticals from the movies during adolescence, Vitagraph found an even bigger star in Bobby Connelly. Connelly made his debut with Kalem in 1912 at the age of three before joining Vitagraph the following year. Shortly before his fifth birthday in the spring of 1914, Connelly attained sufficient popularity to merit an interview in *Moving Picture World*. He comes across as bored and uncooperative, not in the manner of other children his age but rather as a jaded veteran of scores of movies. His ever-present stage mother kept him on a tight leash, exercising "perfect control over his emotions," which included the shedding of genuine tears "upon demand." In sharp contrast to his real-life ennui, much of Connelly's early screen work appears impressively unaffected.

While Bobby Connelly played in support of virtually every adult star on the lot, 1914 marked the beginning of a four-year run in which he starred in his own series of one-reelers, the first twenty as "Sonny Jim," a naive, good-hearted though often mischievous boy from an upper-middle-class family. The best of the surviving Sonny Jims, *An Easter "Lily,"* is not a traditional Easter story but rather a contemporary parable of the unconditional Christ-like love a white boy has for a black girl, set against a backdrop of institutionalized racial prejudice. The film opens with Sonny Jim becoming friends with Lily (played by Ada Utley), the daughter of one of the African American servants working for his family. Sonny Jim is excited to receive a new suit to wear on the upcoming holiday. Upon learning that the only garment Lily has is the ragged dress she wears every day, Sonny Jim gives her a new lace dress that was purchased for one of his cousins. He then insists on bringing her to church on Easter Sunday. The sole surviving print of the film ends abruptly as Sonny Jim leads Lily by the hand down the aisle toward his family's pew as the adults react in angry dismay and laughter. The missing finale involved Sonny Jim's family back home presenting Lily with a new gingham dress.

Ada Utley and Bobby Connelly prepare to enter the church in *An Easter "Lily"* (1914). Frame capture.

An Easter "Lily" is particularly scathing in exploiting the holiest day in the Christian calendar to draw attention to color lines within society at large as well as in the church. Sonny Jim is too young and innocent to be aware of the prejudices of his family. Connelly's performance mirrors the single-mindedness of Sonny Jim, focused entirely on bringing happiness to his friend. Ada Utley's awareness of the camera and offscreen direction complements Lily's consciousness of the racial boundaries she is afraid to cross.

The success of *An Easter "Lily"* resulted in Bobby Connelly and Ada Utley being reteamed for at least three more Sonny Jims. However, those films are coarse by comparison, lacking the poignancy and social criticism so prominent in *Easter "Lily."* The final film of the series was *The Faith of Sonny Jim*, Vitagraph's Christmas release for 1915, featuring white and black Santa Clauses serving segregated constituencies. Vitagraph's occasional inclusion of African American characters in its contemporary dramas represents an acknowledgment of minorities that was virtually nonexistent among the companies that later came to dominate Hollywood.[7]

Shortly after the release of *An Easter "Lily,"* Vitagraph sent a troupe of players and technicians to St. Augustine, Florida, to produce a five-reel feature focusing on a different group of social outcasts. *A Florida Enchantment* was based on a controversial novel and play by prolific author Archibald Clavering Gunter, who also wrote *Mr. Barnes of New York*. Although director Sidney Drew received top billing in the cast, second-billed Edith Storey is the real star of *A Florida Enchantment*. Believing that flirtatious fiancé Drew has been unfaithful to her, Storey swallows a seed that "reverses the nature of all men and women." Anatomically Storey remains a woman but is now imbued with an overwhelming sexual desire for other women. Mannish in her comportment, she flirts with and kisses virtually every woman she comes into contact with. Eventually Storey dresses as a man and adopts a male persona in order to openly pursue and cohabit with a woman she is particularly attracted to. Drew mistakenly believes that this "man" has killed his fiancée, until Storey reveals her true identity and convinces him to also ingest a seed. Drew's behavior changes abruptly; he begins to flirt with other men but is angrily rebuffed. Inspired by Storey's cross-dressing, Drew changes into women's clothes. However, his attempted subterfuge fails, and he is chased by an angry mob. The film ends with Storey waking in her original attire and telling Drew about her dream, clutching the seeds in her hand.

Although never referred to as lesbian or gay within the intertitles, Storey and Drew are clearly regarded as such by the other characters in the film. *Variety* noted in its review of the film that several people in the audience walked out less than halfway into the story, and declared "The picture should never have been put out." *A Florida Enchantment* only ran for a month at the Vitagraph Theatre. Sidney Drew plays his character with gross exaggeration such that the audience never believes for a moment that he could actually be gay. Edith Storey's performance, on the other hand, is so utterly convincing in her attraction to other women that one can't help wondering if she may in fact have shared a similar orientation with the character she played, the hallmark of a great performance. It was probably the first time Americans witnessed a frank depiction of lesbian desire in a mainstream movie.

A Florida Enchantment went into production three months after the passing of Gladys Rankin Drew. For more than two decades Sidney Drew and his late wife were billed on the legitimate stage and in vaudeville as "Mr. and Mrs. Sidney Drew." Cast as the principal object of Edith Storey's desire

Sidney Drew looks on as Edith Storey kisses Jane Morrow in *A Florida Enchantment* (1914). Frame capture.

was Jane Morrow, making her acting debut. Prior to this, Morrow, whose real name was Lucile McVey, was briefly employed by Vitagraph as a script editor. Soon after returning from the Florida shoot, Sidney Drew and Morrow married. She quit the scenario department to become her husband's new costar and script doctor, billed as "Mrs. Sidney Drew."

The Professional Scapegoat is a better showcase for Sidney Drew's exceptional talent. In the film he is hired by a large department store to take the blame when dissatisfied customers complain about incompetent salespeople, ill-fitting garments and shoes, etc. In each case, the store manager proceeds to fire Drew in front of the complainants only to rehire him once the now-placated customers have left the premises. Drew's initial shock at being fired, followed by his desperate plea for reinstatement, is masterfully executed. In the movie's hilarious coda, Drew is now married to one of the store's saleswomen. When their small son breaks a china cup, he pleads for mercy in the same manner as the elder Drew. *The Professional Scapegoat* is the kind of situation comedy Vitagraph did better than anybody else at a time when Mack Sennett's style of slapstick ruled the movies. It is impossible to imagine any other comedian performing the role as effectively as Sidney Drew.

Drew scored a different kind of triumph in 1914 when he starred in a one-act play presented at the Vitagraph Theatre during the month of December. *What the Moon Saw* was written by his adult son, Sidney Rankin Drew, who himself was gaining recognition as an actor after costarring in *Mr.*

Sidney Drew in *The Professional Scapegoat* (1914). *Photoplay*, December 1914.

Barnes of New York. With *What the Moon Saw*, S. Rankin Drew was also following in the footsteps of his late mother, writing the playlet as a starring vehicle for his father. *What the Moon Saw* received excellent notices, though it turned out to be the last one-act play ever presented at the Vitagraph Theatre. The reason for the change in policy was the result of an unforeseen economic downturn that was beyond the control of anyone.[8]

During the first half of 1914, Vitagraph was on pace to far exceed the record-setting one million dollars in profit it had attained during 1913. For the year ending March 30, 1914, American movies were exported at a rate of nearly twenty-four times the number of foreign films imported into the country. By then, British filmmakers were supplying only about 15 percent of the movies viewed in the United Kingdom.

The assassination of Austria's Archduke Ferdinand in Sarajevo was of no consequence to Vitagraph or the rest of the world; that is, until Austria attacked Belgrade on July 28, Germany declared war on Russia and France four days later, and Britain joined France and Belgium in declaring war on Germany on August 5. In his autobiography, Albert Smith recalled that the outbreak of the First World War killed Vitagraph's foreign market literally "overnight." When war was declared, the entire male workforce at Vitagraph's processing factory outside of Paris were drafted into the French army. The company eventually donated the entire facility to the French government to use for the duration of the war. Business in Great Britain declined significantly, with much of the male population mobilized for the war effort. There was also difficulty transporting new product across the Atlantic given the threat of U-boat attacks and the British blockade that enveloped the United Kingdom and Ireland. This led to Vitagraph's New York office making a greater effort to expand international sales in Latin America and Asia, having already enjoyed great success in Brazil, Chile, and the Philippines.[9]

In March 1914 when an unexpected blizzard hit Flatbush, Clara Kimball Young opened up her home less than a hundred yards from the studio to shelter stranded Vitagraphers and preside over an impromptu party until the storm subsided. It was the kind of selfless act that endeared Young to her coworkers and reinforced the feeling of a Vitagraph family. That summer the Vitagraph Theatre premiered the six-reel feature *My Official Wife*, starring Clara Kimball Young, directed by husband James, and produced by Commodore Blackton. Set in contemporary Czarist Russia, it was based on one of Archibald Clavering Gunter's more popular novels and was adapted by Marguerite Bertsch. Young's performance "placed [her] in the front rank of artistes." *My Official Wife* and *Goodness Gracious* were such big hits that Young was voted the most popular actress of 1914 in *Motion Picture Story Magazine*'s annual contest, garnering five thousand more votes than her nearest competitor, Mary Pickford.[10]

In September 1914, former jeweler turned producer Lewis J. Selznick lured Clara Kimball Young away from Vitagraph with a salary that "was far beyond anything [Vitagraph] could pay at this time," ten times the amount Selznick agreed to pay her husband. Selznick was not a creative producer, as were Blackton and Smith, but rather a deal maker who financed his movies with bank loans and other investors' money. Blackton recalled that "this . . . marked the beginning of a raid on Vitagraph's . . . stars [by] new producers [who] boosted salaries from hundreds into thousands. Contracts became necessary in place of the handshake and the given word."[11]

Despite the crippling effects of the World War on its international business, Vitagraph managed to net over $900,000 for 1914, only $115,000 less than it had for the previous year. On Christmas Eve, Smith and Blackton continued the custom of handing out a turkey and bonus to each of the Brooklyn facility's several hundred employees. Although there were now seventy production companies in the United States, Vitagraph remained the biggest producer of motion pictures in the world.[12]

As the war continued to wreak havoc with Vitagraph's profitability, the company nonetheless remained committed to expanding its operations, especially in Los Angeles. This was spurred in part by the success of *Captain Alvarez* (1915), a six-reel feature (now lost) about an American mercenary involved in a South American revolution, which was the first West Coast production to play the Vitagraph Theatre. *Alvarez* was an enormous hit thanks to Rollin Sturgeon's direction and Marguerite Bertsch's adaptation of the novel on which it was based. William Desmond Taylor as the dashing Alvarez became an overnight star, yet Vitagraph fired the libertine actor-director less than a month before the film's release. Twenty-two-year-old Myrtle Gonzalez, who played the ingenue in *Captain Alvarez*, was the first in a long line of exceptionally attractive actresses employed at the western Vitagraph studio. Another pretty newcomer, Margaret Gibson, appeared in more than fifty movies for Vitagraph between 1913 and 1915, including four opposite William Desmond Taylor.[13]

At mid-1915 Vitagraph had eighteen production units working at the Brooklyn hub and three others at its Santa Monica studio. Albert Smith's younger brother Dave was charged with directing two- and three-reel films, while Sturgeon focused his efforts on longer features; Steve Smith, the son of studio manager W. S. Smith, photographed his uncle Dave's films. Establishing its West Coast operation in Santa Monica was a mistake from the start because of the heavy fog that frequently rolled in from the ocean. After nearly four years Albert Smith acquired eleven acres in East Hollywood on which to relocate the Western unit. The entrance to the Hollywood studio was at the corner of Prospect Avenue and Talmadge Street, a few blocks from the D. W. Griffith studios. The new Vitagraph studio's phone number was HOllywood 2.[14]

Smith was furious with General Film's inadequate, cost-prohibitive distribution of Vitagraph's longer features, few of which returned a profit. In April 1915 he recruited Lubin, Selig, and Essanay to form a new distribution firm, known by the initials VLSE, to handle all of their films of four or more reels in length. Every month each company was to furnish VLSE with twenty to fifty prints of a new feature. In return for managing and paying all of the expenses associated with the operation, Vitagraph received 30 percent of the sales of the other companies' films. Unlike General Film, which operated on a quota system, and such burgeoning distributors as Paramount, which forced customers to purchase bad films along with the good, VLSE president Smith had so much confidence in the product of Vitagraph and his partners that each film was sold individually on its own merits on the open market without any strings attached. The strategy worked; within its first six months VLSE established sales offices in nineteen cities across North America, its day-to-day operations managed in New York by Vitagraph attorney Walter Irwin. Further distinguishing VLSE from other feature film distributors was the fact that Smith earmarked 20 percent of the first quarter's profits for the company's two hundred employees, a policy that continued unabated as more offices and staff were added.[15]

The first Vitagraph feature released by VLSE was an Albert Smith production, *The Juggernaut*, an uninspired melodrama notable for a climactic train wreck. Even though *The Juggernaut* was Vitagraph's third highest grossing movie of 1915, a few days before its premiere the company released a far more interesting one-reeler made by the same team of Ralph Ince, Anita Stewart, and Earle Williams, *His Phantom Sweetheart*. Williams's original screenplay concerns a bachelor's one-night stand with an exceptionally beautiful and aggressive woman that has terrifying consequences for both, revealed to be a nightmare in the denouement. Ince's appropriately creepy direction builds desire through shot/reverse shot editing, accentuates movement via tight frames, and stages the action in Stewart's apartment within pools of light and shadow. As Barry Salt has noted, "Among films made at other studios in 1915 that might be compared with Ralph Ince's work, there is nothing . . . which is so far advanced."[16]

Born in 1880, Earle Williams toured the country with theatrical stock companies for ten years before joining Vitagraph in 1911. Blessed with dark good looks and a strong profile, he played opposite virtually every leading lady at Vitagraph before teaming with Anita Stewart in 1914. For the next two years Williams and Stewart were exclusively paired in Ralph Ince productions. Williams claimed an aversion to being recognized in public but was the first American screen actor to pen an autobiography. Throughout his career he spurned more lucrative offers from new studios and maintained his closest friendships with fellow Vitagraphers.[17]

On March 9, 1915, Ralph Ince and a company of players that included Anita Stewart, Earle Williams, and Paul Scardon (playing the principal villain) left New York to begin location photography in Georgia and North Carolina on the serial *The Goddess*. By the time the first two-reel chapter of *The Goddess* premiered at the Vitagraph Theatre on May 10, 1915, seven episodes had been completed. Each chapter debuted in weekly installments at the Vitagraph Theatre over a span of fifteen weeks prior to its nationwide release by General Film. Following in the footsteps of Col. Selig's marketing innovations for *The Adventures of Kathlyn*, Vitagraph arranged for the Hearst Newspaper Syndicate to publish weekly synopses accompanied by

The most popular screen couple in the world. *Motion Picture News*, May 8, 1915.

production stills of *The Goddess* that corresponded to the release of each chapter, with a book later compiled from those same materials.[18]

All told, *The Goddess* was in production for about five months, with most of it shot in the New York area. Early one morning Ince, Stewart, and a large crew assembled during rush hour at Pennsylvania Station. A throng of two thousand commuters willingly took part in the scene, "following every one of [Ince's] natural, friendly-voice suggestions" to accompany Stewart through the cavernous train depot. In his autobiography King Vidor recalled a similar encounter when he was in New York struggling to sell his first homemade films to distributors. Urged by his wife to send friends back in Texas an encouraging message, he telegrammed: "prospects look good. saw anita stewart and earl [*sic*] williams on the street today," implying this "passing acquaintance with success" somehow boded well for him.[19]

In 1915 General Film was selling, on average, slightly more than thirty-eight prints of each one-to-three-reel film made by Vitagraph, about a third more than its nearest competitor. A year earlier Pathé's American distribution arm, Eclectic, ordered 147 prints for the first episode of *The Perils of Pauline*. General Film requested an unprecedented 1,000 prints of the first chapter of *The Goddess*, with 100 distributed in Manhattan and 150 to Chicago theaters alone, such was its faith in the serial and its stars. Given the extraordinary number of prints in circulation, it is surprising that not a single copy of any chapter of *The Goddess* is known to have survived into the present.

At the time, Anita Stewart and Earle Williams were the most popular screen couple in the world, with salaries that reflected their drawing power at the box office. Earle Williams was paid $26,000 per year, and Anita Stewart earned twice that amount. As the highest paid star at Vitagraph, her $1,000 weekly salary was supplemented with 5 percent of the net profits of the movies in which she appeared. When she starred in *The Wood Violet*, Stewart's salary had been $25 per week. According to Albert Smith, the screenplay of *The Goddess* was tailored to the stars' established screen personas to insure success with their devoted fans. *The Goddess* cost $167,000 to produce and grossed twice that amount in America.[20]

While Albert Smith was overseeing production of *The Goddess*, J. Stuart Blackton was supervising the biggest, highest-grossing movie of *his* career, *The Battle Cry of Peace*. The project began when Hudson Maxim, a well-known author and inventor of explosives, sent Blackton a copy of his latest book, *Defenseless America*, in which he argued for the buildup of American military personnel and armaments as a precaution against invasion by a "foreign foe," which he deemed "inevitable and imminent" given the wars then raging across Europe and Asia. Maxim was one of the first in an endless line of authors to send their book to a producer in the hope of having it turned into a movie, and among the few whose dream became a reality.

Blackton spent three days and nights writing a scenario that incorporated Maxim's facts, figures, and arguments into a three-part fictional story centered around two New York families. In part one, a young man attending an "amply sub-titled" lecture by Hudson Maxim imagines defenseless New York City and Washington, DC, landmarks destroyed by enemy forces attacking on land, by sea, and in the air. The second section contains the bulk of the dramatic narrative, as the young man fails to dissuade his fiancée's father from aligning himself with a pacifist movement, whose leader is secretly working on behalf of the enemy. Virtually all of the principal characters die during the invasion of New York, with the young man's fiancée and her sister killed by their mother as lustful enemy soldiers prepare to ravage them. The final part of the story is allegory: Columbia is "crushed, bleeding and trampled by a merciless foe" and then resurrected by the spirits of Washington, Lincoln, and Grant as a wave of patriotism sweeps the country.

Upon completing the scenario, Blackton called on his neighbor Theodore Roosevelt. As the leading proponent of the preparedness movement and American intervention in the Great War, the former president's endorsement was of vital importance to the success of *The Battle Cry of Peace*. Roosevelt also happened to be Blackton's idol, no doubt the reason why he purchased the estate next door. To a poor, fatherless immigrant who put his faith in the American Dream and became a millionaire in the process, approval from the president was the ultimate validation. Roosevelt purportedly became so enthusiastic that he suggested a coda be added wherein military leaders, government officials, and a prominent theologian speak to the audience via a profusion of intertitles, which Blackton heartily agreed to.

The Battle Cry of Peace went into production a week later. Twenty-five hundred marines were placed at Blackton's disposal, and he personally directed them in mock battles over a period of two weeks. Despite Blackton's public pronouncements to the contrary, he confided to his daughter that the enemy "Ruritanian" soldiers were deliberately cast from "actors and extras of German descent," costumed in uniforms similar to those worn by the German army in order to "scare the hell" out of complacent, smug pacifists. Blackton later boasted, "*The Battle Cry of Peace* . . . was the very first motion picture to be used as actual propaganda . . . for the United States to enter the war [in defiance of the policy of] Mr. Wilson [who] was arguing for neutrality and peace."

Wilfrid North, whose experience was mostly confined to directing John Bunny and Lillian Walker comedies, directed *Battle Cry*'s dramatic scenes. With the exception of theatrical veteran Charles Richman, who was making his motion picture debut as the ill-fated fiancé, the rest of the cast was filled with such Vitagraph stalwarts as James Morrison and Mary Maurice. Commodore Blackton wanted Anita Stewart to play opposite Richman, but

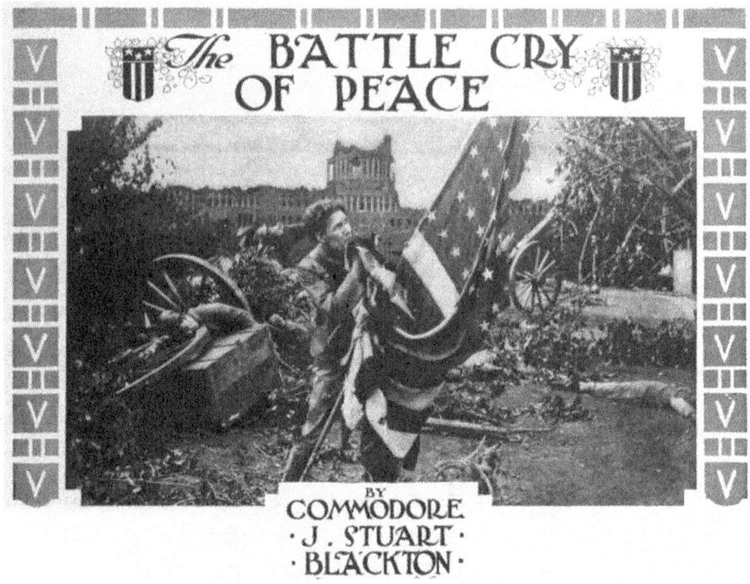

The Battle Cry of Peace (1915). *Motion Picture Classic*, January 1916.

The Goddess was still in production so Albert Smith prevailed on him to instead cast Norma Talmadge.

Production on *Battle Cry* wrapped in late July 1915. A ten-reel version was screened for the press just a few weeks later, but it was shortened by two reels for its official premiere on September 9 for an audience of political, theatrical, and society luminaries at the Vitagraph Theatre. A twenty-five-piece orchestra accompanied the film for its twice-daily screenings through the end of its three-month run. Samuel "Roxy" Rothapfel was engaged to create "stage effects" that included a hidden chorus giving voice to on-screen mobs, as well as a woman emitting a blood-curdling scream at a particularly suspenseful moment. It wasn't all that different from Blackton's behind-the-screen accompaniment to *The Black Diamond Express* nearly twenty years earlier. In his remarks to the opening night audience, Blackton announced that while making *The Battle Cry of Peace* he became a citizen of the United States. He also donated most of his yachts and speedboats to the Navy.

Critical response was divided in the extreme. *Moving Picture World* called *Battle Cry* "more significant" than *Quo Vadis*, *Cabiria*, and *The Birth of a Nation*, because it dealt with a contemporary issue "as personal as an alarm of fire shouted through the night." *Billboard* was just as effusive, regarding

Battle Cry as the "greatest achievement yet recorded in motion pictures." Others weren't so kind. The *New York Times* echoed the sentiment expressed by many, referring to the film as a "sometimes lurid argument [for preparedness made] by bludgeon strokes [that despite its] large scale . . . represents no advance in the motion picture art." For someone who craved social and artistic acceptance as desperately as Blackton did, the comments of Harvard's chair of psychology, Hugo Munsterberg, whom he had personally escorted on a tour of Vitagraph's Brooklyn studio earlier in the year, must have been particularly devastating. Munsterberg castigated *The Battle Cry of Peace* as "esthetically intolerable" due to its "complete disregard for the fundamental principle of art, the demand for unity."

However, even those most critical of the film were impressed with the special effects, about which only production stills and written descriptions survive: shells bursting over Times Square at night; aerial views of a squadron of planes flying over lower Manhattan; the Woolworth Building aflame; New York's Municipal Building and the Capitol in Washington, DC, in ruins. Many of the effects were achieved via glass shots designed by longtime Blackton assistant William P. S. Earle. Unfortunately, it is impossible to give *Battle Cry* a fair assessment because only two heavily truncated prints, totaling less than a reel in length, are known to survive.

Comparisons between *The Battle Cry of Peace* and *The Birth of a Nation* weren't confined to aesthetic considerations. The *New York Sun* predicted *Battle Cry* was "likely to rival *Birth* in popularity." *The Birth of a Nation* opened in New York City at the Liberty Theater in March 1915, where it remained through the beginning of 1916. Admission prices ranged from twenty-five cents to two dollars, the same amount charged for *Battle Cry* at the nearby Vitagraph Theatre. Outside of New York, distribution of *The Battle Cry of Peace* was handled by VLSE, which, early on, placed the film in legitimate theaters that could seat twenty-five hundred to four thousand, in ten cities including Philadelphia and San Francisco. Most of those engagements averaged six to seven weeks. *Battle Cry* did not encounter the degree of censorship that Griffith's film did; however, the Pennsylvania State Board of Censors insisted on the removal of the scene of the mother shooting her two daughters. The manager of Pittsburgh's Pitt Theatre circumvented this by stopping the film and staging the missing scene with live actors in front of the screen, which the Board was powerless to prevent.

The Birth of a Nation became the highest-grossing movie of the silent era; estimates of its gross earnings range from $5 million to $60 million.

Blackton always claimed that *Battle Cry* grossed over a million dollars. However, internal company documents reveal that after more than one and a half years in release, the film actually earned a profit of $231,721, against production expenses of $36,372.[21]

Norma Talmadge had been averaging two to three short films each month. *The Battle Cry of Peace* was by far the highest profile project she appeared in since *A Tale of Two Cities*. During the production, Vitagraph learned that she would be leaving the company as soon as her work on *Battle Cry* wrapped. Like virtually everyone else that jumped ship, Talmadge had been promised a much larger salary and the opportunity to star in "big pictures" for a company that had never before made a movie. Her career didn't really take off until she later joined Lewis Selznick's stable under the personal management of future husband, Joseph Schenck.[22]

As frustrating as it was to lose pretty starlets that the company had patiently groomed for stardom, Vitagraph never seemed to have any difficulty in replacing them. Unfortunately the company suffered a far more tragic, irreparable loss in 1915. During the summer of 1914 John Bunny prevailed upon Smith, Blackton, and Rock to allow him to take a leave of absence so that he could tour the world as the star of a live stage extravaganza called *Bunny in Funny Land*. Vitagraph provided Bunny with a print of one of his movies, which was projected during a *Funny Land* costume and scenery change, as well as the film of Bunny oversleeping and hurrying to the theater that had opened his vaudeville act in January 1913.

The outbreak of war in Europe confined the tour of *Bunny in Funny Land* to the United States, where it opened in Baltimore on September 9. The show played major cities throughout the East and Midwest before closing in March 1915. Critics reacted in the extreme, either loving or hating the show; there is equally conflicting data concerning *Funny Land*'s overall profitability. Late in the run, a newspaper profile of Bunny noted, "The great comedian was plainly tired."

Back in New York, John Bunny made plans to resume making movies at the Brooklyn studio. However, he spent the next few weeks in bed, exhausted and plagued with kidney trouble, and passed away on April 26, 1915. More than fifteen hundred people attended Bunny's funeral, among them theatrical luminaries and representatives of rival studios. Virtually all of Bunny's costars were in attendance, including Flora Finch, Kate Price, Lillian Walker, Earle Williams, Anita Stewart, and Edith Storey. His pallbearers included Pop Rock, Sam Spedon, and Maurice Costello.

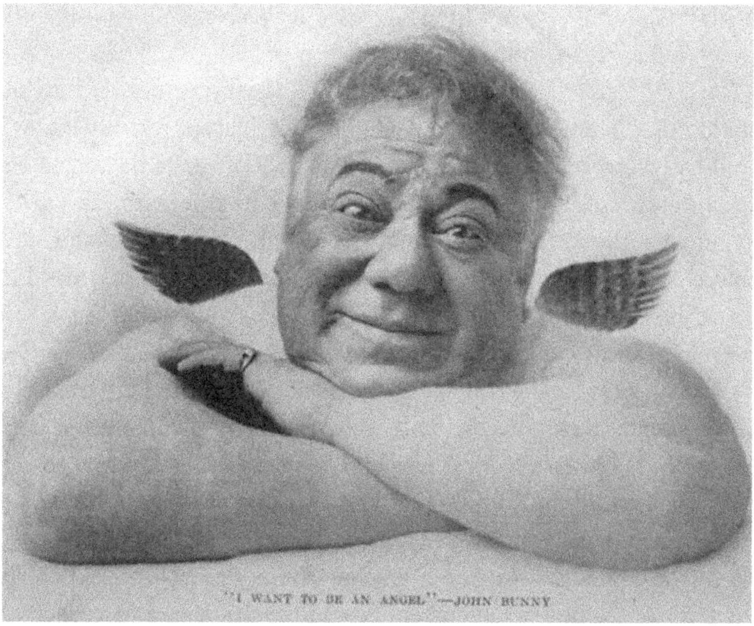

John Bunny. *Motion Picture Magazine*, November 1914.

Eulogies poured in from around the globe. The *New York World*: "Millions of persons no doubt will mourn the loss of John Bunny to whom the death of a Prince or Prime Minister would be a matter of indifference." London's *Kinematograph and Lantern Weekly*: "In point of fact he must have been the best known man in the world." *Motion Picture News*: "His face was as enthusiastically received in England, France, Australia, Germany, South Africa, or India as it was in America. In Italy he was an especial favorite. . . . He has undoubtedly made more persons laugh than has any other player." *Moving Picture World* expressed the opinion of most, declaring that Bunny was ideally suited for silent cinema because "The range of his facial expression was altogether wonderful, and when the emotion of the moment had told its story in his features there was nothing left for the words to do."

John Bunny was the first international motion picture star to die at the height of his popularity. Acknowledging that "Bunny's present fame is beyond dispute," the London *Star* wondered whether he, or any motion picture star for that matter, would enjoy "posthumous fame" given the inevitable changes in fashion and technology to come. Britain's *Bioscope* more confidently asserted that John Bunny's "genial humor" would prove timeless, delighting "our grandchildren" who will thus have no reason to "doubt . . . the critical sagacity of their grandfathers."

Not long before his death, *MPW* took this sentiment a step further in declaring that "John Bunny, pioneer and picture player pre-eminent," will be prominently featured in the histories of the medium yet to be written. *Punch* echoed this belief, noting, "For years [Bunny] had been the favourite big funny-man of the pictures, and though he has left countless imitators there is no successor, while his greatest rival in publicity and popularity, Max Linder, the reckless and debonair, fights for France." The truth is that at the time of his passing Bunny (and Linder's) popularity was being eclipsed by Charlie Chaplin, whose entry into the movies was barely a year old. After more than a century, Chaplin remains the most recognizable motion picture actor of all time, and Max Linder's work has recently enjoyed a much-deserved renaissance. Today John Bunny is all but forgotten, omitted from most histories of the cinema. His surviving films are wildly uneven, as is true of virtually every other movie comedian. But at his best John Bunny provokes as much laughter as many of the better-remembered comedy legends that succeeded him.[23]

Vitagraph and the other pioneer American movie producers received bad news of a different sort that autumn. On October 1, 1915, a federal judge ruled in favor of the government in its antitrust suit filed on behalf of William Fox against the MPPC. The MPPC and General Film were found in violation of the Sherman Antitrust Act for attempting to monopolize the production and distribution of motion pictures and were ordered to disband. The decision has forever since been hailed as a triumph for William Fox in bringing down the MPPC; although, as far as Vitagraph and the actual historical record are concerned, the court established a double standard by punishing the pioneers while turning a blind eye for more than thirty years to similar activities engaged in by subsequent producers. Besides being responsible for legal fees and court costs, the licensees also faced the possibility of having to pay triple damages to William Fox. MPPC attorneys appealed the decision and quickly settled out of court with Fox for $350,000, more than three times what Albert Smith originally negotiated for the sale of Fox's exchange before it was rejected by J. J. Kennedy.[24]

In the spring of 1915 Commodore Blackton revealed that Vitagraph employed twelve hundred people on its regular payroll, which included approximately two hundred actors, twenty-five directors, and twenty-five salaried cameramen, averaging $70,000 in weekly operating expenses. But at the beginning of December, the company announced it was cutting twenty-two actors and three directors from its staff. Two weeks later Vitagraph cut back its number of regular weekly releases to ten reels consisting of three single-reel comedies and two dramas, one in three reels and the other four.[25]

Vitagraph suffered one more high-profile loss at the end of 1915, when four days before Christmas the *Brooklyn Eagle* reported that Maurice Costello was "no longer connected" with the company. Prior to the Globetrotters' 1913 trip around the world, Maurice Costello was, in the words of Albert Smith, "a pretty good fellow," who handled his status as the movies' first matinee idol with "modesty, charm and intelligence." His wife, Mae, on the other hand, resented the attention lavished on him by other women. Her lone scenario, *The Joys of a Jealous Wife*, was a not so thinly veiled expression of her profound rage. Love letters and propositions arrived at the studio in bushel baskets on a daily basis. Women and teenage girls showed up at their home a few blocks from the studio. By July 1915 the situation had become so intolerable that Costello moved his family to a remote twelve-acre waterfront estate.

Whether as a means of coping with his own insecurities or to escape his wife's incessant harping, Costello drank heavily. One day Mrs. Costello called the police after he struck her. Newspapers carried the story, and angry moviegoers threatened to withdraw their patronage from theaters that continued to show his films. Smith and Blackton consequently fired their biggest star at a time when Costello received twice as many votes as his nearest competitor as the movies' top international male star in a poll conducted by a British fan magazine. *Photoplay* lamented, "Vitagraph without Maurice Costello won't seem like the same old place."[26]

Vitagraph's profit plunged from $902,321.63 in 1914 to $152,761.48 for 1915. Albert Smith attributed the decline "to the war and partially . . . to the fact that we invested a large amount of our earnings during 1915 to feature films." Another significant drain on the company's bottom line was the start-up costs for VLSE. Given the enormity of its operations, it is safe to assume that Vitagraph had been incurring the largest overhead expenses of any American studio for ten years.[27]

Early in 1916 Albert Smith expressed the opinion that, after D. W. Griffith, Ralph Ince and Rollin Sturgeon were the best directors in the world. In order to keep Ince in the fold Vitagraph converted a former hunting lodge near his home in Bay Shore, Long Island, into a self-contained studio "with floor space enough to permit deep sets," opening the facility during Christmas week 1915. Before the end of January, Anita Stewart phoned Albert Smith, "angry, nervous and hysterical [declaring that] she would not work with her brother-in-law any longer because he did not give her what she regarded as proper prominence in the pictures" they made. From then on Stewart worked with other directors at the Brooklyn studio. Ince replaced her with his wife, known professionally as Lucille Lee Stewart, Anita's big sister.[28]

Other changes were taking place behind the scenes. Mrs. Beta Breuil, who ran the scenario department for several years, left Vitagraph to take a similar position at the beginning of 1916 with short-lived Mirror Films. Another veteran of the department, Marguerite Bertsch, earned the chance to direct her original screenplay, *The Devil's Prize*. The box office failure of that five-reel feature appears to have resulted in Bertsch's subsequent departure from the company. Colonel Jasper Ewing Brady, brother of writer Rev. Cyrus Townsend Brady and an author in his own right, succeeded Mrs. Breuil as manager of the scenario department.[29]

Vitagraph added a short-lived component to its business when it partnered with William Randolph Hearst at the beginning of 1916 to produce a twice-weekly newsreel. This came on the heels of Hearst's nearly two-year association with Col. Selig in a similar venture, upon which the *Hearst-Vitagraph News Pictorial* was patterned. It was an expensive undertaking: Vitagraph maintained a team of salaried cameramen and stringers throughout the United States and in several world capitals; a new building was constructed on the Brooklyn lot devoted solely to processing, editing, and printing the voluminous footage; and each exhibitor was allowed to name his own purchase price for the service. One-third of each single-reel *Hearst-Vitagraph News Pictorial* contained an animated cartoon based on a comic strip published in Hearst newspapers. For most of the run, Tom Powers's stylish *Phables* alternated with George Herriman's subversive *Krazy Kat and Ignatz Mouse*, made at the Hearst animation studio in Manhattan. J. Stuart Blackton, the inventor of the animated cartoon, had no connection with these efforts. Six months into the venture, Vitagraph backed out after losing $27,000.[30]

Commodore Blackton spearheaded efforts to form a Motion Picture Board of Trade in the autumn of 1915. The Board of Trade was an effort to unite the industry in common goals, such as lobbying against federal censorship of the movies and providing a mechanism whereby disputes between members could be resolved through arbitration rather than in the courts. That latter aspect backfired when the Board of Trade unanimously ruled that no illegal enticement occurred when Metro Pictures signed Mr. and Mrs. Sidney Drew away from Vitagraph in January 1916. Blackton was the Board of Trade's first president; this, coming on the heels of his widely promoted

The Battle Cry of Peace, suggested to the uninitiated that he was *the* leader of the motion picture industry.

On January 27, 1916, the Motion Picture Board of Trade held a dinner in the grand ballroom of New York's Biltmore Hotel. The gala served as the movies' first large-scale exercise in self-congratulation and heralded the motion picture industry as a power to be reckoned with. Led by toastmaster Blackton, the highlight of the evening was principal speaker President Woodrow Wilson. Just two weeks earlier at congressional hearings for a proposed Federal Censorship Bill, Blackton and other representatives of the industry were greeted with a barrage of accusations and complaints from politicians, clergy, and little old ladies. The participation of the president at the Board of Trade's dinner conferred on the business a respectability desperately craved by everyone associated with it, especially the pioneer filmmakers who had weathered more political, legal, cultural, and institutional resistance than would be the case for anyone following in their wake.[31]

At the beginning of the year a New York newspaper reported that Vitagraph was about to be sold to a group of "Wall Street men" that included William Randolph Hearst. Sam Spedon quickly issued a statement denying the rumor. Whether a coincidence or not, Benjamin B. Hampton called on Albert Smith the following month in February 1916 with a proposition. Hampton, vice president in charge of advertising at the American Tobacco Company, told Smith that he represented a consortium of "men of substantial means," including the president of American Tobacco, top executives at the investment firms of Guaranty Trust and Hornblower & Weeks, and financier Thomas Fortune Ryan, all of whom were interested in consolidating the leading motion picture companies into a single entity, with Vitagraph as the cornerstone of the new organization. According to Hampton the financiers planned to invest millions of dollars in the enterprise, paying Vitagraph $750,000 in cash and $25 million in stock. At the time Vitagraph owned $3,713,600.89 in tangible assets.

As appealing as the proposition was, Smith and Blackton remained ambivalent until the latter part of March when Hampton revealed he had just negotiated a contract with Mary Pickford that would bring her aboard the "New" Vitagraph at a weekly salary variously reported as $4,000 and $7,000. Pickford had been a favorite with movie fans since 1909 when she began working for D. W. Griffith at Biograph. At the beginning of 1913 she starred on Broadway in *A Good Little Devil*, and later that year she made a movie version of the play for fledgling producer Adolph Zukor. A former furrier and investor in nickelodeons, Zukor named his company Famous Players. He believed that literal duplications of stage hits starring the original casts were the most sophisticated and lucrative form of motion picture entertainment. Zukor's debut as a producer was actually as an importer of a 1912 French production, *Queen Elizabeth*, starring theatrical legend Sarah Bernhardt. American audiences were both bored by the film's tableaux-style presentation and amused at Bernhardt's broad performance style. Undeterred, Zukor adapted the same approach to his own productions. He may have been the last producer in the world to realize that filmed theater was painfully uncinematic and anathema to movie audiences; after completing *A Good Little Devil* he waited a year before releasing it. In 1914 Zukor released *Tess of the Storm Country*, which according to Kevin Brownlow was the film that made Mary Pickford "the most popular actress in America." While no reliable financial records exist for Famous Players during this period, it is generally accepted that Zukor's company supplanted Vitagraph as the most profitable producer of motion pictures in 1916. Thus the signing of Mary Pickford would be a boon to the fortunes of Vitagraph and would profoundly undermine its rival. In fact Hampton promised Smith that Zukor would be bought out and what remained of Famous Players absorbed as a subsidiary of the "New" Vitagraph.

Hampton's scheme to consolidate the motion picture industry began with a comprehensive reorganization of Vitagraph, which took nearly two months to effect. The new corporation, christened "Greater Vitagraph," was signed into existence on May 17, 1916. As before, Smith, Blackton, and Rock held equal shares of stock in the new company but were now joined by others, including Percival Hill, president of American Tobacco. Benjamin Hampton was added to the board of directors in place of William T. Rock. More significantly, Albert Smith was now president of Vitagraph, enabling him to focus solely on the business affairs of the company, and Commodore Blackton became vice president and producing director in chief, supervising all productions. Smith looked forward to unburdening some of his responsibilities onto new colleagues with proven track records in the upper echelons of big business. Blackton saw the promised infusion of cash as an opportunity to expand the budgets and scope of his films.

Pop Rock had muscled his way into the presidency and saved Vitagraph from extinction at the turn of the century, but was pushed out of Greater Vitagraph by wealthier, more powerful players. Though heartbroken the pragmatic Rock didn't fight it, receiving generous compensation for his departure. He did, however, express the hope of someday producing a significant movie of his own.

While the ink was still drying on the reorganization papers, Hampton announced that he had canceled the Mary Pickford contract "because of some unpleasantness" he had had with his American Tobacco Company boss, Percival Hill. The truth was that Pickford wanted compensation comparable to Charlie Chaplin's new contract with Mutual, which paid him $10,000 a week. Hampton told Albert Smith it was up to him to negotiate new terms. Smith met with Pickford and her attorney, and offered a salary identical to Chaplin's plus profit participation. It was all for naught: Pickford's attorney informed Smith that his client would be staying with Zukor after all. Pop Rock told his protégé, "Al, you was framed for a sucker," convinced the only reason Pickford had dickered with him was to gain leverage in her negotiations with Zukor. Years later Mary Pickford admitted as much in her autobiography without ever referring to Vitagraph by name.

About a month after the formation of Greater Vitagraph, it was announced that Pop Rock had taken ill. Although the extent of the illness was downplayed in the press, it was serious enough for John Rock and his wife to make a hurried trip from Chicago. Pop never recovered. On the morning of July 27, 1916, Albert Smith was called to his mentor's bedside and found Rock with his familiar ill-smelling cigar tucked in the corner of his mouth. An hour later he was dead at age sixty-two from a combination of heart disease and diabetes. Funeral services were held at Rock's Brooklyn home, with Smith and Blackton among the pallbearers. Virtually all of the old-time Vitagraphers attended, including William Shea, Charles Kent, and Sam Spedon, as well as former employees Maurice Costello and Larry Trimble, and Ira Lowry on behalf of his father-in-law Siegmund Lubin, whose own health was in decline. Rock was eulogized as *the* pioneer showman of motion pictures and a shrewd businessman who left an estate valued at between four and five million dollars.

Soon after Rock was laid to rest, Vitagraph closed the Nassau Street office he had occupied since 1903. Coinciding with this, Benjamin Hampton claimed that Rock's son-in-law Doc Willat, who had long been associated with independent producers, was eager to sell his wife's stock in Greater Vitagraph because it was "practically worthless." The allegation was not entirely without merit. Publicly the company was touting the "New and Greater Vitagraph with a capital of $25,000,000," but by midsummer the only infusion of cash the company had received was a million-dollar loan from

Rock, Smith, and Blackton in *A Vitagraph Romance. Moving Picture World*, July 6, 1912.

Guaranty Trust, secured by notes in anticipation of the private investments promised by Hampton. It was a risky if not reckless move for a company that netted only $150,000 for the previous year.

Until 1916 Vitagraph had been privately owned and entirely self-financed. Albert Smith had always managed the company's business operations, though by his own admission he sought the advice of Pop Rock on every significant decision. Now, not only had Benjamin Hampton steered the reorganized company into debt and pushed Rock out but he had also become Smith's primary advisor by fanning the flames of greed and ambition backed by extravagant promises that would prove too good to be true.

Hampton intended that Vitagraph buy out most of its original competitors, but despite their financial woes Lubin, Selig, and Essanay were unwilling to sell their companies for less than $1.5 million apiece. For more than a year Albert Smith had been frustrated that his VLSE partners were habitually late in delivering feature films once a month to exhibitors as contracted, especially in light of Vitagraph's ability to produce a five-reel feature each week. Smith soon realized it was mutually beneficial to all concerned for Vitagraph to simply purchase its partners' interests in VLSE and acquire ownership of the distribution company, though it necessitated an additional loan of $250,000 from Irving Trust. All were amenable; Selig and Essanay reportedly each received $50,000 in cash. Vitagraph ended up purchasing not only Lubin's share of VLSE but also that company's library of films, manuscripts, and scenarios, for $100,000 cash and a token amount of VLSE stock.

On August 21, 1916, Benjamin Hampton, who a month earlier had negotiated an annual salary for himself of $12,000 for services rendered on behalf of Vitagraph, informed Albert Smith that the financiers he represented had decided not to invest in the company after all. As galling as this turn of events was, Vitagraph's full ownership of VLSE to distribute its features would turn out to be one of the wisest decisions Albert Smith ever made. At the time Vitagraph took full possession in September 1916, VLSE operated twenty-three sales offices throughout North America and had doubled its staff to nearly four hundred employees. Dividends were paid on a quarterly basis to all, from custodians to branch managers. Soon VLSE would distribute all Vitagraph productions in North America.[32]

While Vitagraph was undergoing major upheavals in the United States, modifications to its overseas business were more measured. Even though its processing lab had been temporarily turned over to the French government, Ronald Reader continued to sell prints from the Paris office to a dwindling number of continental distributors, until he was recalled to the United States for safety's sake in October 1916 and was put in charge of the Brooklyn plant. That spring, a subsidiary company, the Vitagraph Film Hiring Service, was created to rent features to British distributors, enabling Vitagraph to keep 75 percent of box office receipts. Vitagraph Ltd. continued to sell short films to distributors who, in turn, rented them to exhibitors.[33]

With the war in Europe now in its third year, it became vital for the company to open new foreign markets. Commencing in 1916, Vitagraph films were distributed throughout Spain and Argentina. This coincided with the publication of *Cine Mundial*, the Spanish-language version of *Moving Picture World*. Although it occasionally reprinted translations of articles that also appeared in *MPW*, *Cine Mundial* consisted mostly of original reporting focused on the motion picture business in Latin America. The cover of the debut issue featured a map of the Americas alongside a photograph of Anita Stewart, "'Estrella' [star] popular de la Vitagraph." The April issue featured an overview of Vitagraph, complete with photos of Blackton, Smith, and Rock, as well as an article on John Bunny and Max Linder; in August, Maurice Costello was profiled. Such emphasis on business and talent long associated with Vitagraph reflects the dominance of the company in Latin America, especially compared with the lack of similar coverage for other US studios.[34]

Back home, Vitagraph's Los Angeles productions continued to grow in both scope and sophistication. The first studio at the new Hollywood plant consisted of a large open-air stage on which interior scenes were photographed for productions primarily made far from home amidst natural settings. The most successful such release for 1916 was the eight-reel feature *God's Country and the Woman*, adapted from a story by prolific writer James Oliver Curwood and directed by Rollin S. Sturgeon. The rugged, snowy exteriors for *God's Country* were filmed at Big Bear during the first two weeks of January 1916, with William Duncan and Nell Shipman in the leading roles. After making a living for several years as a physical trainer, Duncan entered motion pictures in 1911 as an actor, writer, and director of Westerns for Selig Polyscope; in mid-1914, he moved to Vitagraph, where his popularity continued to grow. Born in 1892 Nell Shipman began acting with theatrical stock companies at the age of thirteen, and wrote magazine articles, screenplays, and a book prior to making her movie debut in *God's Country and the Woman*. Critics praised the direction and the story, as well as Shipman's star-making performance. Unfortunately no print of the film is known to have survived.[35]

In April 1916 Vitagraph's Los Angeles unit was engaged in making a motion picture unlike any other produced by a major American studio. *The Yellow Girl* represents the last of the company's bold experiments in cinematic expression, but unlike earlier efforts it was bereft of any input from Blackton or Smith. *The Yellow Girl* was written and directed by Edgar Keller, who began working with Rollin Sturgeon late in 1915. Keller, "an artist of repute," had trained at the Chicago Art Institute and the Art Leagues of San Francisco and New York and had exhibited at the Panama Pacific Exposition. He was also a founding member of the Los Angeles Modern Art Society.

For *The Yellow Girl*, Keller applied tenets of the Italian Futurist movement to the traditional romantic comedy structure of boy meets girl, boy loses girl, boy gets girl. A "Manifesto of Futurist Cinema," published in Italy and France in 1916, declared the motion picture to be an inherently "autonomous art," which should eschew the traditions of "literary theatre" to instead "fulfill the evolution of painting [by] detach[ing] itself from reality [in order to] become . . . impressionistic, synthetic, dynamic." Keller thus designed *The Yellow Girl* "to get away from the film idea of following the stage's footsteps" by implementing "a romantic rather than a practical background," romantic

Corinne Griffith and Webster Campbell in Edgar Keller's *The Yellow Girl* (1916). *Motion Picture Magazine*, September 1916.

in the sense of utilizing visual motifs that express subjective emotional qualities and freedom of form. The most obvious manifestation of this approach is in the film's highly stylized scenery and props that evoke suggestion rather than reality, and the "futuristic" costumes designed by Keller's wife. Leafless trees and formless shrubs are painted as light-colored abstractions onto black backdrops; black-and-white tiled floors complement the checkered and striped geometric patterns of the apparel; furniture and props are similarly unique in their construction. At a time when virtually all motion pictures had begun using genuine outdoor locations, all of *The Yellow Girl*'s exteriors were deliberately staged inside the studio in order to create a singularly subjective visual experience. This approach prefigures the German Expressionism of *The Cabinet of Dr. Caligari* (1920), which would have a more lasting impact on world cinema.

Although *The Yellow Girl*'s narrative seems utterly conventional in comparison with the visuals, it contains elements that are in fact subtly subversive. The title itself is a euphemism for "prostitute" that would have been unknown to general audiences. The story concerns a struggling young artist and his best friend who attend a bizarre theatrical performance in which an actress portrays a character called the "Yellow Girl." The artist convinces the actress to model for him, which causes his innocent girlfriend to think he is having an affair with the more-worldly woman until the misunderstanding is inevitably resolved.

Twenty-two-year-old Corinne Griffith played the ingenue in *Yellow Girl*. Griffith joined Vitagraph in October 1915 after winning a Santa Monica beauty contest at which Rollin Sturgeon was a judge. Although she had never before acted, years of experience had taught Albert Smith that "it was fine if [aspiring actresses] could act but beauty was the principal requisite. We could school them in the art of the dramatic as practiced in the guileless film medium of that day." Of all the attractive young women to ever work for Vitagraph, Corinne Griffith was the most beautiful of them all. When she started, Griffith earned $10 for two days' work; by the time she left the company nearly eight years later she had become the company's reigning star, earning $3,000 per week.

The Yellow Girl marked the film debut of Florence Vidor, who played Griffith's best friend. Her husband, King Vidor, made his first script sale to Vitagraph earlier that year. With aspirations of becoming a director, he worked as an extra at Vitagraph as often as possible in order to observe how movies were made. As for Edgar Keller, as soon as *The Yellow Girl* wrapped he made only one more "decorative playlet" for Vitagraph before his career as a filmmaker came to an abrupt end. It would appear that *The Yellow Girl* was too radical for 1916 audiences, as was the case with D. W. Griffith's masterpiece, *Intolerance*.[36]

At the time of the release of *The Yellow Girl* Vitagraph was making sweeping changes intended to cut costs and maximize profits. Most of these decisions have the earmarks of Benjamin Hampton's growing influence on company affairs and his ignorance of fundamental aspects unique to the motion picture industry. For several years Vitagraph's Los Angeles unit enjoyed a degree of autonomy, with Rollin Sturgeon and W. S. Smith free to initiate many productions without prior approval from New York. Now *all* scenarios produced at the Hollywood studio would be preselected by Smith and Blackton. For the time being, the Los Angeles operation was reduced to a single producing unit. Longtime scenario editor Doris Schroeder was let go. Sturgeon was recalled to New York, where he was told he would henceforth be assigned a scenario each month to direct as a five-reel feature at the Brooklyn studio on a relatively modest budget. This did not sit well with Sturgeon, who had enjoyed the freedom to make features as he saw fit, virtually all of them popular and critical successes. Sturgeon believed that his track record entitled him to a percentage of the gross to supplement his weekly salary of $450. After arguing with Smith and Blackton, he was released from his contract. It was a colossal mistake for both parties. Sturgeon joined Flying "A" in Santa Barbara and later Universal but never enjoyed the success he had achieved at Vitagraph.[37]

Hampton's reorganization of Vitagraph had other ramifications. In August, after seven years of groundbreaking service, Sam Spedon, "the dean of publicity," was terminated, along with such longtime players as Flora Finch and Kate Price. James Morrison quit Vitagraph because of Hampton, whom he referred to disdainfully as an "efficiency expert." According to Morrison, Hampton gave newcomers with no marquee value top billing over established players, and even employed two people to straighten used nails in order to save money. Over the next eight years Morrison would periodically return to Vitagraph but only on a freelance basis.

In November, after ten years with the company, Ralph Ince decided to become an independent director-producer. He leased the Bay Shore studio and declared that "pleasant relations" existed between him and his former employers. As Barry Salt has noted, talented as Ince was, "nothing he did thereafter was as striking as his achievements at Vitagraph." Within the span of two months, Vitagraph had lost its two best filmmakers.[38]

Vitagraph spent considerable time and money investing in its star players, losing many to fledgling producers, who may have doubled their salary but churned out inferior product. Thus in 1915 and 1916 the company began putting their most valuable talent under contract, including Anita Stewart, Earle Williams, Edith Storey, Lillian Walker, Harry Morey, and Antonio Moreno. Born in Madrid in 1886, Moreno worked for Biograph and Mutual before joining Vitagraph in mid-1914. He attained star status opposite skinny-dipping Edith Storey in *The Island of Regeneration*, after which they were frequently paired together.[39]

Vitagraph held a Beefsteak Dinner for more than one hundred of its Brooklyn employees on March 18, 1916. None of the attendees could have guessed that this "vivacious gathering" would mark the end of happy times for the Vitagraph family. Within the next few months Benjamin Hampton was in, Pop Rock was dead, and many longtime Vitagraphers were out. As Hampton exerted more influence and power, the studio went from being a place where the employees' security was taken for granted in the pursuit of utilizing their creative talents, to becoming an indifferent, incompetently run factory where the only thing that seemed to matter was maximizing profit. The last vestige of the old Vitagraph, at least during Hampton's brief tenure with the company, occurred on December 23, 1916, when the hundreds of workers still employed at the Brooklyn studio received their Christmas turkey.[40]

In 1917 Vitagraph inaugurated a new release schedule tied to the production of features centered on their biggest stars, following the strategy that Famous Players, Fox, and other newcomers were employing. A "Blue Ribbon" feature starring Anita Stewart, Earle Williams, Lillian Walker, the teams of Edith Storey and Antonio Moreno, Alice Joyce and Harry Morey, and Peggy Hyland and Marc McDermott would be released each week in rotation over a six-week span.

As a way of supplementing their decrease in titles, Greater Vitagraph reissued *My Official Wife* in November 1916, only two years after its original release. Incurring expenses of $9,000 for new prints and advertising, the company still netted $11,000. Buoyed by the modest success, Vitagraph began reissuing its older features in April 1917 at weekly intervals, starting with *A Million Bid* and *Captain Alvarez*, spruced up with new intertitles and tighter editing. Two months later, short comedies starring John Bunny and Sidney Drew were added to the weekly rerelease schedule.

By March, four directors and forty actors were producing a total of two one-reel comedies and one serial episode every week, and one five-reel feature each month at Vitagraph's Los Angeles studio. They also averaged four longer features per year. The Brooklyn studio employed seven directors, each with their own units "under the personal supervision of Mr. Blackton." Albert Smith's brother Victor and Ronald Reader were in charge of the facility, while Blackton's chief aide William P. S. Earle was elevated to production manager. To those outside the company, it appeared that Vitagraph was beginning to regain its equilibrium, but behind the scenes massive upheavals continued that would have significant consequences.[41]

Early in the year Albert Smith notified John Prentiss of Hornblower & Weeks that because the bankers and other alleged investors had failed to honor their promises to Greater Vitagraph, he intended to resign from the company rather than face the prospect of repaying $1,250,000 in bank loans that otherwise he never would have agreed to. Prentiss convinced Smith not to quit and had him meet with a representative of Guaranty Trust who, in turn, talked Smith into allowing a Mr. Davenport of the Finance & Trading Company to look over the company's books. This resulted in a comprehensive report on the company's current state of affairs. It revealed that Vitagraph's net profit for 1916 was only $103,531.68, significantly less than what Albert Smith claimed in his autobiography and down a third from 1915. Failing to take into account the devastating effects of the war in Europe and competition from new producers who enjoyed far greater support from *their* banks, Davenport charged that Vitagraph's severe economic downturn could "only be attributed" to Smith and Blackton's "lack of experience in financial matters." The statement is somewhat true, given the fact that the partners allowed Hampton and his associates into Vitagraph based solely on what turned out to be hollow promises.

The report was also critical of Vitagraph's "extravagant expenditures," especially the "excessive" salaries of at least $500 per week paid to its five most popular stars, which was actually much less than what the newer competitors were paying former Vitagraph players. Although Vitagraph had employed twenty-two directors and a significantly larger stock company of actors just six months earlier, Davenport recommended still further cuts in salaries and personnel. The report bluntly stated, "Messrs. Smith and Blackton . . . should [no longer] be called upon to perform duties [of an] administrative or an executive character," and concluded that "unless arrangements are made in the very near future for an able and experienced business man to act as chief executive of the Company, it is our opinion that a Receiver should be applied for to conserve the assets of the Company."

As the report was being compiled, Benjamin Hampton told Albert Smith that his friend, General Frank H. Hitchcock, former postmaster general of the United States, with close ties to the DuPont fortune, was "interested in and desires to invest millions into the motion picture business," beginning with an initial investment of $250,000 in Vitagraph. Smith received this news on the eve of departing for California to visit his father, who had just suffered a stroke. He thus gave Hampton, Prentiss, and one or two others the power to negotiate a deal with General Hitchcock in his absence. The moment Smith left town Davenport began to institute changes at Vitagraph to which Blackton uncomprehendingly acquiesced. Vitagraph's cashiers were replaced with two of Davenport's associates from the Finance & Trading Company. Davenport made a contract with Hitchcock that gave him thousands of shares of stock for no financial consideration and appointed him Vitagraph's chairman of the board "with full power to control and operate the company's business." Davenport also finagled himself onto the executive committee as a financial director of Vitagraph. He and Hitchcock conducted meetings alone "at which they voted large expenditures of the company's money for the Finance & Trading Company and other items." Aided by Hampton, they fired or drove away half of the remaining stock company, including Edith Storey, Lillian Walker, and Antonio Moreno. Walter Irwin was forced to step down as Vitagraph's attorney under threat of the company filing for bankruptcy, though he continued as head of VLSE. The coup was carried out over March and April 1917.

How could it have happened? From the very beginning, James Blackton relinquished his responsibilities regarding the business of Vitagraph to Albert Smith, but he appears to have lost confidence in his partner. At the onset of the coup he didn't care who controlled the company, focusing his attention instead on producing a follow-up to *The Battle Cry of Peace*. As for Smith, two doctors warned him that due to the stress building up over the past year he was on the verge of a complete physical and emotional collapse and thus needed a long vacation from Vitagraph. Confiding the diagnosis to Prentiss, Smith was assured that Hitchcock would invest in and keep an eye on the company until he returned. Prentiss, Davenport, and Hitchcock then used the opportunity to seize control. Smith further erred by not getting away sooner, for he ended up suffering a nervous breakdown on the second day of his train ride west. He managed to reach Santa Barbara safely only "through the kindness and assistance of the railroad company." It took two months for Smith to recuperate in California, during which time he was kept in the dark about the machinations back in New York. A few days before he departed for the train ride back to New York, Smith received a telegram from Blackton relating some of the dismissals made by the new administration, which he ominously referred to as the "iron claw."

Albert Smith returned to New York on May 2 to find Vitagraph "being operated by individuals who . . . had no rights on the premises whatsoever." Fully recovered from his breakdown, Smith dug in his heels and fought to regain control of the company. He charged that the election of the new directors and executive committee was illegal, that Irwin and Blackton had been forced to resign as Vitagraph counsel and board member, respectively, under threats and duress, and that the payments made to the Finance & Trading Company were invalid. The loss of half of the stars around which their feature program for 1917 had been built resulted in a corresponding loss of half of the company's feature revenue, down to $27,000 per week.

On June 14, a proper board of directors meeting was held with Smith reelected president and Blackton reclaiming his position on the board. At the behest of the banks, General Hitchcock was elected chairman of the board, serving merely as a figurehead and staying away from management of the company in return for a monthly salary of $2,000 and 1,500,000 shares of stock. Somehow Hitchcock remained Vitagraph's chief counsel, at least for a while. By July Albert Smith was able to extricate Davenport and his Finance & Trading Company cohorts from Vitagraph, at which time he wrote Prentiss, "I regret very much having gone to the bankers with my troubles last December. I realize now that I should have kept matters in my own hands, as honesty is not the best policy when it comes to dealing with Wall Street."[42]

Smith expressed similar sentiments to Hampton, writing, "I look back on the events of the past fifteen months with the deepest regret." In the midst of meddling with Vitagraph Benjamin Hampton was elected president of General Film in November 1916 even though many considered him inherently dishonest. Some voted for him precisely for that reason, believing it "takes a crook to make some money out of the picture business." Smith supported Hampton's brief tenure at General Film in the hope that he could recover the $153,000 it owed Vitagraph. It appears Hampton was successful in recouping a third of that debt before he resigned as president on April 9, 2017. The following day, the Supreme Court upheld the decision against the MPPC and General Film, effectively putting an end to both organizations. Hampton reinvented himself as an independent producer, though he somehow managed to retain a small stock interest and membership on the board at Vitagraph.[43]

While Albert Smith was contending with Hampton, Davenport, and Hitchcock amidst the restructuring debacle, J. Stuart Blackton was focused on producing *The Battle Cry of War*. The film wasn't so much a sequel as it was a reimagining of *The Battle Cry of Peace*, about the successful repelling of an enemy invasion thanks to America heeding the call for preparedness. Blackton structured his story around the heroics of two young women, one a spy for the American cause and the other an "American Joan of Arc," who is seemingly executed by the invading army because of her success in military recruitment. For the leading role of the American spy, Blackton cast Alice Joyce, formerly Kalem's leading actress, who had been in retirement. Joyce signed a contract for $20,800 to star in *Battle Cry of War* and two other features, after which she negotiated new terms paying her $31,200 to appear in seven Vitagraph features during 1917. The supporting cast of *The Battle Cry* included such Vitagraph stalwarts as James Morrison, Mary Maurice, and Bobby Connelly. During postproduction the film was retitled *Womanhood, the Glory of a Nation*, pandering to its target audience. As with *Battle Cry of Peace*, reviews for *Womanhood* were mixed, but the movie couldn't have been released at a more propitious time: five days after its New York premiere, the United States declared war on Germany and entered World War I. Initially ninety-four prints of *Womanhood* were placed in general release in the United States, with an additional fifty-two prints added in June. It is therefore surprising that no copies of *Womanhood* are known to have survived into the present.[44]

During the first week of July 1917, just as Albert Smith was beginning to regain control of Vitagraph and restore order, J. Stuart Blackton announced that he was leaving the company to make films for Paramount. According to Marian Blackton, "success and affluence" had caused her father and Smith to drift apart. Differences of opinion regarding studio policy, the rivalry between their producing units, and the inability of their wives to get along were additional factors in undermining "the camaraderie of the early days." In announcing the split, *Billboard* noted that the friction between the partners had lately been "rampant." As difficult as their relationship had become, Blackton had not been looking to leave Vitagraph. Rather, he was deliberately wooed away by Adolph Zukor.

Paramount Pictures Corporation was formed in 1914 by former nickelodeon operator-turned-distributor William Wadsworth Hodkinson as a consolidation of a dozen smaller exchanges. From the beginning, Paramount only distributed features in excess of three reels, including those made by Zukor's Famous Players Company. "In a well-orchestrated putsch" involving secret stock purchases and other manipulations, Zukor wrested control of Paramount from Hodkinson and, a year later, in 1917 installed himself as president. Blackton's contract with Paramount guaranteed him an annual salary comparable to what he had been making at Vitagraph, plus $400,000 in financing for the production of four "high class motion pictures," similar to the budgets for contemporaneous Cecil B. DeMille Paramount productions. In addition,

Blackton would receive slightly more than half the gross profit. Zukor could afford to offer such extravagant terms because Paramount engaged in block booking, whereby an exhibitor who wanted Mary Pickford features was forced to accept all of the films the company distributed, regardless of merit. Although he was prevented from making movies for anyone else, Blackton was allowed to "retain his duties and responsibilities as a stockholder and member of the board of directors of the Vitagraph Company of America." This last condition was the real motivation behind Zukor luring Blackton to Paramount: it was a divide and conquer strategy intended to cripple Vitagraph and enable him, potentially, to acquire Blackton's stock in order to take control of the company. Blackton didn't have a clue; Smith, emerging from the attempted coup orchestrated by Hampton and company, knew better.

Blackton's adult daughter Marian was shocked when he signed with Zukor because her father was an anti-Semite, something only his family was aware of. Blackton's own vanity overpowered any hidden prejudices that would have kept him from joining Paramount. A few months earlier, he declared that he had outgrown his enthusiasm for "trick" films, preferring now such "highbrow" considerations as "the problem of screen metaphysics" with regard to plot and character. Blackton yearned to be acclaimed as a great artist. As a producer he was limited to facilitating and tweaking the work of others. Zukor shrewdly appealed directly to his ego. Blackton built a small studio in Brooklyn and directed three features adapted from novels by Sir Gilbert Parker. When all three "artistic productions" flopped at the box office, Paramount canceled his contract. By then, Zukor no longer required any pretense in his quest to ruin Vitagraph.[45]

In reporting J. Stuart Blackton's departure from Vitagraph, many in the press wondered how the company could survive. After all, "It was Mr. Blackton who personally directed all of the big Vita. productions and supervised all other pictures turned out." In a major policy statement, Smith acknowledged that while *The Battle Cry of Peace* and *Womanhood* successfully served the cause of preparedness for which they were made, Vitagraph would now produce "pictures that will take the minds of the people off the war and their troubles, make them laugh, and in that way, make them happy . . . clean stories with a light atmosphere and a laugh lurking here and there." During the summer, production was increased to twice its normal rate in order to compensate for the downturn in product and loss of stock company that occurred during the spring coup. By September the company was back on track with a regular production and release schedule.

S. Rankin Drew. *Moving Picture World*, February 26, 1916.

Around this time Vitagraph began to acquire the film library and processing laboratory of the Kalem studio for $100,000. Unlike the similar purchase of the Lubin library, the company was to make its money back from perennial Easter and Christmas rentals of *From the Manger to the Cross*, Kalem's acclaimed six-reel life of Christ filmed in Egypt and Palestine in 1912.[46]

In March 1917 Vitagraph discontinued shipping negatives across the Atlantic for fear of the potentially devastating effects of a German U-boat attack. The company had no qualms about shipping less flammable positive prints to London and Paris, though the cost of doing so significantly cut into profits. After Benjamin Hampton forced Smith's brother Victor to resign as the Brooklyn studio cashier, he enlisted in the army. He wasn't the first Vitagrapher to go to war.[47]

S. Rankin Drew starred in thirty-seven shorts and features at Vitagraph, but preferred directing. He emphasized visual composition and "giving the players feasible dramatic lines to speak. . . . If it is colloquial enough to be spoken naturally, it is reflected in their faces and expression and thereby helps the action." Drew's approach to the aesthetics and craft of cinema, as well as the poetry in his private letters, reveals a young man of exceptional artistic sensibility. S. Rankin Drew's directing career flourished at Vitagraph, while his father and stepmother were making movies for Metro.

When her contract with Vitagraph was renewed in February 1916, Anita Stewart and Albert Smith agreed that henceforth she would appear in productions especially written for her and directed by S. Rankin Drew. Drew directed seven features in 1916, three for Stewart in which he also played the male lead. Drew's friend Frank Morgan made his motion picture debut in the Stewart films more than thirty years before playing the title role in *The Wizard of Oz*. The trio's last movie, *The Girl Philippa*, commenced production early in the summer but didn't wrap until the end of October; a freak windstorm decimated a French village constructed on the Brooklyn backlot, which had to be rebuilt, and Stewart contracted typhoid fever, which confined her to bed for all of August and September.

The Girl Philippa was adapted by S. Rankin Drew from a story by Robert W. Chambers that was serialized in *Cosmopolitan Magazine*. A Balkan princess (Stewart), kidnapped as a baby, is now working in the café of a French inn that is "a hotbed of spies" at the outbreak of World War I. The princess and a smitten American artist (Drew) engage in intrigue and battles with agents and soldiers of the Central Powers. Intertwined with scenes of romance are action sequences: in one, an English spy (Morgan) is in a moving automobile with an armed motorcyclist in pursuit who shoots at him and shatters the car window; in another, the artist and princess slide down a rope from the upper story of the inn as it is besieged by machine guns and battering ram; the heroes also dodge an aerial bombardment on their French village; and street barricades are destroyed by hand grenades and Molotov cocktails.

Samuel "Roxy" Rothapfel, manager of New York's Rialto Theatre, entered into an agreement whereby all of Vitagraph's "Blue Ribbon" features would receive their premiere engagements at the Rialto during 1917, beginning with *The Girl Philippa* on New Year's Eve. Rothapfel paid $3,500 for the two-week engagement, which broke the Rialto's box office record, necessitating the addition of morning screenings to accommodate demand. *Philippa* didn't enter wide release in the United States until the last week of January 1917; by

July its rentals totaled $147,328, netting the company $103,130 which was divided evenly with William Randolph Hearst's Star Company as compensation for a massive advertising campaign in his newspapers. *Philippa* enjoyed similar success in London a year later. It was the first film under Anita Stewart's new contract, in which her profit participation was raised to 10 percent on top of her weekly salary of $1,000.

Ordinarily the success of *The Girl Philippa* would have prompted additional Drew–Stewart productions, but immediately after the film wrapped S. Rankin Drew resigned from Vitagraph. According to Albert Smith, Drew had fallen "deeply in love with Anita Stewart, but his affections were not reciprocated" and by the end of the shoot the two were quarreling. Drew immediately joined Metro, for whom he directed one film. Stewart insisted that Vitagraph staff writer Marguerite Bertsch direct her next film, *The Glory of Yolanda*, which appears to have been a major disappointment for all concerned. When Stewart renewed her contract with Vitagraph in January 1917, she told Smith that "Mr. Rankin Drew was the best director she had had and at her request [Smith] agreed to employ him [for her next film], although Mr. Drew then wanted a salary of $500 a week." Stewart also insisted that newcomer Rudolph Cameron be cast as her leading man. Early in the shoot Drew learned that Cameron was engaged to Stewart, and was unable to suppress his jealousy. Stewart consequently had Drew fired, which resulted in Albert Smith negotiating a $1,200 settlement with the director.

Anxious to involve himself with something of greater significance, Drew traveled to France in May 1917. After several months in training with the Foreign Legion he joined the Spad Escadrille as a pilot in March 1918. On May 19, 1918, while on patrol 15 kilometers into German territory, Drew shot down his first German airplane, but was immediately attacked by two others and crashed to his death. The Germans who killed Drew buried him where he landed and placed a wooden cross atop his grave made from the struts of his airplane. His body was later moved to a cemetery in Montdidier, France, and the cross was presented to American Legion Post 340, which was named in his honor. The Legion, in turn, placed a bronze plaque honoring Drew in New York's Central Park, where it remains to this day. According to his stepmother, S. Rankin Drew was the first American actor killed in action in World War I.

By all accounts Sidney Drew was a broken man following the death of his only son and best friend. In 1919 the elder Drew suffered a complete emotional and physical breakdown while appearing with his wife in a play in

Detroit and within days died at his home in New York City. At present none of the films directed by Sidney Rankin Drew are known to have survived. Written descriptions and the critical reception his work received lead one to hope that long-forgotten prints will someday emerge from public or private archives.[48]

In spite of the significant travails experienced by Vitagraph in 1917, the company still managed to release about 275 movies for the year and more than double its net profit from 1916. Expansion during 1918 was more modestly confined to the Hollywood operations, including the construction of an additional studio, new dressing rooms, and offices. During the summer of 1918 Earle Williams was transferred from the Brooklyn studio to Los Angeles, and when Antonio Moreno rejoined Vitagraph to star in serials, he, too, was now based out of Hollywood. The company's other serial unit led by director-star William Duncan was also headquartered in Los Angeles. On the other hand, Corinne Griffith was relocated to the Brooklyn studio, home to the company's top female stars.[49]

On February 1, 1917, Vitagraph entered into a six-year contract with publisher Doubleday Page & Company and the heirs of author William Sidney Porter to adapt his O. Henry stories into two-reel shorts and a few longer features. Initially, the films were "personally supervised by J. Stuart Blackton, for twenty years the dominant genius of the photoplay and . . . responsible for more big, world-wide photoplay successes than any other one producer." After Blackton left, Albert Smith became the presiding genius supervising the O. Henrys. Unfortunately, only two of the ninety-four O. Henry films produced by Vitagraph are known to survive. *A Philistine in Bohemia* (1920) contains beautifully photographed New York City locations such as Union Square Park and adjacent Fourteenth Street, and Washington Square Park, as well as shots of a Jewish street vendor and inside an Italian barbershop. Throughout 1918 the O. Henry shorts alternated every other week with a series of low-budget two-reel *Wolfville Tales* adapted from the popular Western fiction of author Alfred H. Lewis. The *Wolfville*s were produced at the Hollywood studio. More than half starred pretty Margaret Gibson, who after two years away from Vitagraph, playing for other studios, returned with a new name, Patricia Palmer.[50]

Vitagraph earned its biggest returns from the five-reel features it released every week during 1918, averaging a net profit of $35,000 per film. The principal feature stars that year were Alice Joyce, Earle Williams, Corinne Griffith, Harry Morey, Gladys Leslie, and Nell Shipman. After directing forty shorts and

New England exhibitors visit Vitagraph's Brooklyn studio, November 15, 1911. Front row, left to right: Louis B. Mayer (in black derby), Albert Smith, Pop Rock, J. Stuart Blackton. *Moving Picture World*, December 2, 1911.

one serial, Albert Smith's older brother Dave graduated to directing features in 1918, beginning with *Baree, Son of Kazan*. The success of *Baree* solidified David Smith's position as successor to Rollin Sturgeon, and inspired its star Nell Shipman to leave Vitagraph to form a production company of her own.[51]

The loss of Nell Shipman wasn't nearly as damaging to Vitagraph as was the defection of its biggest star, Anita Stewart, to nascent producer Louis B. Mayer. Mayer's motion picture career began in 1907 when he opened his first nickelodeon. In November 1911 Vitagraph hosted fifty-eight New England exhibitors for a tour of the Brooklyn studio. Mayer made a point of standing alongside Albert Smith in the group photo taken to commemorate the occasion. As was the case with Carl Laemmle, Adolph Zukor, and Lewis Selznick, he aspired to become the next Vitagraph. Mayer moved into distribution when he acquired the New England rights to D. W. Griffith's *Birth of a Nation*, agreeing to a fifty-fifty split from his share of the box office receipts. However, Mayer never paid any of the percentage, pocketing between $250,000 and $500,000. That fortune served as the foundation for his move into producing. He set his sights on acquiring Anita Stewart as the cornerstone upon which to build Louis B. Mayer Productions.

Stewart succumbed to Mayer's blandishments and stopped working during the summer of 1917 while he negotiated a three-year deal with her husband, Rudolph Cameron, that paid $80,000 per film and an unspecified percentage of the profits for her first six films, with an option for six more at $100,000 each plus percentage. There was only one problem: Anita Stewart was still under contract to Vitagraph.

Albert Smith was furious and sued Mayer for inducing Anita Stewart to break her contract. He was also chagrined that Mayer would reap the benefits from the extensive advertising campaign promoting Stewart in *The Girl Philippa* that cost Vitagraph over $50,000 to William Randolph Hearst. In April 1918 the New York Supreme Court upheld the decision of the lower courts in favor of Vitagraph, adding that the company could extend Stewart's contract for each day she missed due to her work stoppage—twenty-six weeks in all—establishing the legal precedent that enabled studios like MGM to keep a firm grip on their contract players. Vitagraph promptly sued Louis B. Mayer for $250,000 in damages and won. Anita Stewart returned to Vitagraph in May for a feature directed by Wilfrid North. Shortly after that film wrapped in July, Mayer reached a settlement with Vitagraph, purportedly paying $75,000 to secure Stewart's services a month before her contract was to expire. Mayer promptly rented a studio at Vitagraph's Brooklyn facility to film his first Anita Stewart feature and then relocated to Los Angeles. As popular as Stewart was with movie audiences, she had become too temperamental and erratic for Albert Smith to deal with anymore. The way things ended, it appears he was relieved to have Louis Mayer pay him to take her off his hands. Once again, Vitagraph already had someone under contract to take the place of a departing diva, Corinne Griffith, who would soon exceed Stewart in popularity. Other replacements didn't work out as well.[52]

On the day that John Bunny departed for England in 1912, Vitagraph hired likable Hugh McGowan, a 380-pound Brooklyn undertaker with no prior acting experience, as his temporary replacement. Renamed Hughie (aka Hughey) Mack, he played leads and supporting roles, often opposite Flora Finch and Kate Price. Mack's performance style was much broader than Bunny's and his persona less defined; thus, his popularity never came close to that of John Bunny or Keystone's Fatty Arbuckle, whom he more closely resembled. At the beginning of 1916 writer-director Larry Semon was assigned to invigorate the Hughie Mack films. In the process, Semon single-handedly redefined the approach to comedy at Vitagraph.[53]

Larry Semon was born in a trunk and spent half his childhood assisting his magician father. By his mid-twenties, Semon achieved acclaim as a newspaper cartoonist with the *New York Sun*. Unlike other artists whose subjects tended to be inactive, Semon specialized in drawing sports figures, animals, and objects in motion. J. Stuart Blackton hired him during the latter part of 1915 to direct and write in partnership with C. Graham Baker, a former cartoonist on the *Brooklyn Eagle*. From the very beginning, the kinetic sensibility that characterized Semon's newspaper illustrations infused his film work. For instance, in *The Man from Egypt* (1916), Hughie Mack and his girlfriend leap from the roof of one building into the window of another at least one hundred feet away. "Semon brought the surreal gags and anarchistic spirit of comic strips to [Vitagraph] and sophisticated comedy went out the window."

During 1916 and 1917 the Larry Semon unit moved back and forth between Brooklyn and Hollywood, settling in Los Angeles for good in 1918. By then, Mack and Vitagraph had parted ways and Semon was starring in his own films, which he continued to direct and cowrite. Semon quickly became one of Vitagraph's most popular stars, earning $14,300, far more than the $2,080 to $6,500 annual salaries the company's other top comedians were making. Semon's most frequent on-screen persona was a mischievous oaf dressed in baggy overalls with the bib and pants legs hitched excessively high. The whiteface makeup he wore accentuated his hatchet face and long hooked nose. Historian Steve Massa has described the overall effect as "a slapstick version of Nosferatu." Visitors to the set couldn't distinguish Semon from his stuntmen, who wore similar makeup and pointy papier-mâché noses.

As a director, Semon's action is relentless, staged and edited at a frenzied pace that leaves audiences no time to consider the gaping holes in his plots. Semon's productions are marked by massive destruction; virtually any room he enters is wrecked to pieces, cars and houses are exploded, and every actor is assaulted. His comedies contain more stunt work than those made by any of the other major comedians working during the latter silent era.

Larry Semon made three films with Stan Laurel in 1918. In *Huns and Hyphens*, restaurant customer Laurel is the recipient of waiter Semon's pranks and mishaps, though he is absent from the best gag in the movie, in which the bartender slings beer across the room and Semon catches the liquid in an empty mug with a flourish. The trick was achieved by reversing the film, one of director Semon's favorite devices. Laurel was again one of many supporting players in *Bears and Bad Men*. However, in his final film with Semon, *Frauds and Frenzies*, Stan Laurel attained costar status as they play a pair of escaped prisoners. Historian Rob Stone has noted that *Frauds and Frenzies* presents Laurel and Semon as a comedy team, portending Laurel's later work with Oliver Hardy. Larry Semon was becoming as popular as Vitagraph's top feature stars, but he didn't know it—yet.[54]

Overhauling its style of comedy from character-driven sitcoms to slapstick and supplementing its release schedule to include a new serial chapter every week were two of the ways in which Vitagraph adapted to popular tastes in order to stay afloat. In addition, Vitagraph compensated for some of the sharp decline in exports to Europe by entering into agreements with emerging international distributors that supplied its films to exhibitors throughout Spain, Cuba, Puerto Rico, Argentina, Peru, Bolivia, Ecuador, Uruguay, Paraguay, and Mexico.

Vitagraph's long run as the industry leader in profitability and innovation was clearly over, but at least the company was still in business. The same could no longer be said of its earliest competitors. Shortly before the dismantling of Lubin in 1916, Biograph became the first of the original five production companies to go out of business. Two years later the Edison Company sold its studio and facilities. The Selig Polyscope Company released its final feature at the end of 1917 before closing shop, although Col. Selig carried on for several years as an independent producer. Broncho Billy Anderson left Essanay in 1916, two years before partner George K. Spoor shut down for good. Pathé, hit hardest of all by the war in Europe, resisted the production of features for so long that it became "somewhat marginalized." In 1918 Charles Pathé announced that filmmaking "was no longer profitable" and within two years suspended production, selling off his assets, including his name. Only Vitagraph remained of the original signatories to the MPPC, alone among the pioneers who began at the dawn of the American motion picture industry.[55]

The Vitagraph family was hit by more personal losses in 1918. At the end of April, Mary Maurice, "the grand old lady of the films," died at age seventy-four. In early November William Shea died, the longest tenured member of Vitagraph's original 1905 stock company. Shea had been a regular in the final series of Bobby Connelly films. Connelly left Vitagraph at the beginning of 1918 to work on a Sidney Drew comedy at Metro. Four years later he died of acute bronchitis at the age of thirteen.[56]

The exodus of talent during 1918 culminated in early December when Walter Irwin, general manager and treasurer of VLSE, announced his resignation. Irwin had done such an excellent job in organizing the day-to-day operations of VLSE that the distribution company continued to thrive after his departure. The reason he gave for leaving Vitagraph was "differences of opinion on matters of business policy." More specifically, Irwin had grown tired of the relentless efforts of Benjamin Hampton and General Hitchcock to gain control of the company. So had Albert Smith.

During the trial in Vitagraph's lawsuit against Louis B. Mayer, Albert Smith learned that Benjamin Hampton had told Rudolph Cameron that he had Smith's permission to secure Anita Stewart "for another proposition," presumably either as the linchpin to Hampton's own production company or selling her to the highest bidder. It wasn't the end of Hampton's machinations. In the spring of 1918 Smith discovered that Hampton had been appealing to Vitagraph's creditors and stockholders to allow him and General Hitchcock to take control of the company once and for all. Smith reminded the bank and other preferred stockholders that he alone had gotten Vitagraph back on its feet and was paying off its debts without assistance of any kind from Hampton or Hitchcock, neither of whom ever invested a penny in the company. Still, Smith was reconciled to surrendering control of the company to Hampton if that's what the bankers wanted, but only on the condition of being "bought out at a fair price." In the end, those having a financial stake in Vitagraph realized that their investments were safer with Albert Smith remaining at the helm. It spelled the end of Benjamin Hampton's meddling in the affairs of Vitagraph and led to Hitchcock's departure the following year.[57]

In September 1918 Vitagraph announced that for the coming year it would continue releasing a new "Blue Ribbon" feature film each week. The company's biggest stars, Earle Williams and Alice Joyce, would each appear in eight films, with Harry T. Morey, Corinne Griffith, Gladys Leslie, and newcomer Bessie Love starring in nine productions apiece. With the palace intrigue finally eradicated, Vitagraph was on stable footing for the first time in two years, but this was short-lived. By October the influenza pandemic that had been spreading throughout the world resulted in movie theaters closing across Texas, Indiana, the Carolinas, Iowa, Boston, Chicago, Atlanta, Louisville, Cincinnati, and Minneapolis for fear of contagion. All Los Angeles studios were ordered to suspend operations in mid-October. Several prominent Vitagraphers were "touched" by the influenza, with most recovering. Former Vitagraph player Myrtle Gonzalez wasn't as fortunate. The pretty twenty-seven-year-old died of heart disease exacerbated by the Spanish flu on October 22.[58]

Vitagraph's Hollywood studio reopened on November 11, the day World War I came to an end. During the final year of the war Albert Smith was able to surmount its crippling effects on the business of Vitagraph, emerge victorious from the final showdown with Hampton and Hitchcock, survive the defection of Blackton, and pay off the entire $250,000 loan from Irving National Bank, $125,000 of its obligation to the Guaranty Trust Company, and nearly $125,000 in related debt to Lubin, Eastman Kodak, and sundry others. Unfortunately, the temporary closure of the Hollywood studio and movie theaters around the world resulted in losses to the company of approximately $290,000, necessitating a new loan of $100,000 from Guaranty Trust. As a result, Vitagraph's profit for 1918 was a paltry $19,297.71. There can be little doubt that the company's strength and financial position at the end of the war would have been far more robust had Albert Smith not succumbed to the greed for money and power proffered by Benjamin Hampton. As Vitagraph teetered on the brink of collapse, Smith had only himself to blame.[59]

5

1919–1925

Albert Smith didn't waste any time in charting a course for Vitagraph in 1919. On the day after New Year's he convened a three-day meeting attended by all the VLSE branch managers and studio administrators, including former Paris head Ronald Reader and John Quinn, who took over management of VLSE following the departure of Walter Irwin. Many attendees were no doubt surprised when Commodore Blackton showed up at the opening night banquet. While he retained a sizable financial stake in Vitagraph, he no longer had any influence over its operations because he was still making films away from the company. On the final day of the convention Vitagraph released Blackton's *The Common Cause.* Despite the fact that the film was the fourth highest grossing Vitagraph release of 1919, it was the only independently made Blackton production to be distributed by the company.

Prior to leaving Vitagraph, Blackton had been advocating that the company radically reduce its output to twelve big-budgeted "special" features per year. Smith was unwilling to take the risk, arguing that the company would never be able to survive the box office failure of more than a few such productions. Blackton didn't understand that Vitagraph's weekly two-reel comedies and serial chapters were yielding consistently high profit margins that offset losses incurred by underperforming features. Smith thus adopted a more moderate approach, one that retained the weekly release of a short comedy, serial, and five-reel feature, but was now supplemented with the production of a half dozen much longer features over the course of the year. He informed the branch managers that each five-reeler would henceforth be sold separately on its own merits, no longer as part of a yearly package tied to an individual star. By March, Smith's strategy was yielding $40,000 in average weekly earnings for the five-reel features, a 30 percent increase over 1918.

In February 1919 George Randolph Chester was appointed editor in chief of Vitagraph's scenario department, replacing Eugene Mullin, who had held that position for two years. Chester earned his reputation as a writer of short stories, which were published in leading magazines of the era. The exploits of his most popular character, a con artist named Get-Rich-Quick Wallingford, were published in book form in 1907. As editor in chief, he supervised the writing staff and helped select short stories and novels for Vitagraph to acquire. Chester, in collaboration with his second wife, also rewrote the title cards for a half dozen Anita Stewart features reissued in 1919. Sales of those films were comparable to many of Vitagraph's new releases, yielding nearly pure profit for the company.

In March, Albert Smith organized a family reunion at his father and sister's home in Santa Barbara. It was the first time since 1886 that all of the Smith family was together. Five of Albert's six brothers were employees of Vitagraph: George, head of the London office; Victor, returning home from the war in Europe to assist the New York operations; W.S., Los Angeles studio chief; Dave, now the company's chief director on the West Coast; and J.P., Vitagraph's representative in Australia. Albert Smith's wife, Hazel, and their children accompanied him on the trip.

Smith spent two months in California and focused most of his attention on improving the Hollywood facilities. Additional glass-roofed and covered stages, dressing rooms, and a processing lab were built. In November the company purchased nine acres bordering the property, which expanded the complex to twenty acres in all. A "mammoth pool, large enough to accommodate a number of small boats," was constructed at the foot of the barren hills that abutted the eastern back end of the lot. The most impressive addition was the 175-foot-long city street set. The set contained five distinct buildings three stories high, constructed of brick, between two of which was an alley; there was also a bisecting street at the end of the block. The unadorned set was utilized for virtually every Vitagraph comedy and was redressed for use in dramatic features.

During 1919 seven full-time units were based at the Hollywood studio: the William Duncan and Antonio Moreno serial companies, the comedy units of Larry Semon, Montgomery and Rock, and Jimmy Aubrey, and the companies that made Bessie Love and Earle Williams features. Four units operated at the Brooklyn studio, making features that starred Alice Joyce, Harry T. Morey, Gladys Leslie, and Corinne Griffith. The Griffith unit also utilized the Bay Shore studio originally built for Ralph Ince.

When Albert Smith returned from his California sojourn to New York, he entered into negotiations to lease the Rialto Theatre in Times Square but was thwarted by Adolph Zukor, who turned it into a first-run house for

Paramount productions. The best Smith could do was make deals with smaller theaters, such as the Bunny in Upper Manhattan and the Palace in downtown Los Angeles, which booked a majority of Vitagraph product.[1]

During the summer of 1919 Albert Smith learned that someone in Barcelona was attempting to trademark the name "Vitagraph," which if successful would have ended his distribution of films to the Spanish market. A leading trademark attorney was hired to resolve the matter in Spain and conduct trademark searches in every other country that exhibited Vitagraph films. The investigation revealed that a trademark for "Vitagraph" as a motion picture concern was registered in France on June 26, 1896, approximately eight months before Smith and Blackton coined the term in New York. Everyone was perplexed, unaware that in 1896 and 1897 a French magic lantern company manufactured a projector that it named the Vitagraphe. Further complicating the matter was a British photographic firm, Chard, that had acquired one of the French projectors at the end of 1896 and renamed it Chard's Vitagraph. Chard produced about ten of its own films during 1897 and 1898.[2]

Now that the Great War was over, new distribution agreements were made to exhibit Vitagraph movies in Guatemala and San Salvador. Presumably it was J. P. Smith who negotiated another deal that granted Australasian Films Ltd. exclusive distribution of Vitagraph productions in Australia, New Zealand, Burma, Ceylon, Straits Settlements, Federated Malay States, Siam, Dutch East Indies, and China. Australasian and other emergent distributors significantly extended Vitagraph's reach into new markets and even countries where the company had long enjoyed success, such as Japan and India.

After the family reunion, George Smith returned to his base of operations on Charing Cross Road in London. In August he scored the biggest coup of his career when he negotiated the purchase of a major distribution firm that supplied eight hundred theaters in the north of England. The acquisition meant that Vitagraph films were now exhibited in every principal city in the British Isles, including Wales and Scotland, similar in range and effectiveness to VLSE in North America.

Ronald Reader, recalled to Brooklyn for the duration of the war, returned to France in June 1919 to supervise relocation of the Paris headquarters to Rue de l'Evêche and establish new branches throughout the country, as well as in Belgium and Algiers. Reader reported that the serials of William Duncan and Antonio Moreno were especially popular in Paris, as were the features of Corinne Griffith and Alice Joyce.[3]

Alice Joyce became Vitagraph's most popular feature player in 1919. It has been suggested that part of her success can be attributed to a quiet dignity that infused her characters with nobility. Her productions also benefited from John Quinn's new sales approach that stressed heavy billboard advertising. The first Joyce feature to earn over $100,000 in rentals, *The Lion and the Mouse*, was adapted from a popular play that Lubin acquired in 1914. It appears to have been the only Lubin asset purchased by Vitagraph of any real value. The Alice Joyce version was so highly acclaimed that Adolph Zukor overcame his hostility against Vitagraph to allow it to be booked into the Rialto Theatre for its initial New York engagement.[4]

The Cambric Mask, Joyce's least successful film of 1919, is nonetheless her most interesting Vitagraph production. She plays the fiancée of a man who has been abducted by the White Riders for refusing to sell his land to the group's leader. Joyce dons a white robe and hood to infiltrate the group and rescue her beau moments before he is to be burned alive. The term "White Riders" was a euphemism for the Ku Klux Klan. The brutality of that group and Joyce's heroic actions in opposition to it stand in stark contrast to the Mary Pickford vehicle *Heart o' the Hills* released eight months later, in which "America's Sweetheart" is a member of the "Night Riders," portrayed as the heroes of her community. Maurice Costello played Alice Joyce's lover in *The Cambric Mask*. It marked his third film with Vitagraph and second pairing with Joyce since he returned to the company at the end of 1918. Costello had been absent from motion pictures for nearly three years. In all, he appeared in five features released by Vitagraph in 1919, playing love interests and villains.[5]

Vitagraph's most successful serial of 1919, *Smashing Barriers*, starring William Duncan and future wife Edith Johnson, earned $494,036 in exhibitor rentals. Taking into account that the serial was fifteen chapters long, with each installment two reels in length, *Smashing Barriers* outperformed a comparable number of Alice Joyce features in terms of total footage. Even more impressive, rental fees for second runs in small-town theaters (for which figures are available) reveal that Joyce features including *The Cambric Mask* commanded $30 per day, whereas each *Smashing Barriers* chapter rented for $5 per day. Assuming that similar pricing ratios existed for large cities and first runs, more people paid to see Vitagraph movie serials than features in 1919.

Noted author and theologian Dr. Cyrus Townsend Brady and Albert Smith wrote *Smashing Barriers*. Brady received $2,000 plus a royalty of 5 percent of gross receipts of North American rentals up to $100,000, and 10

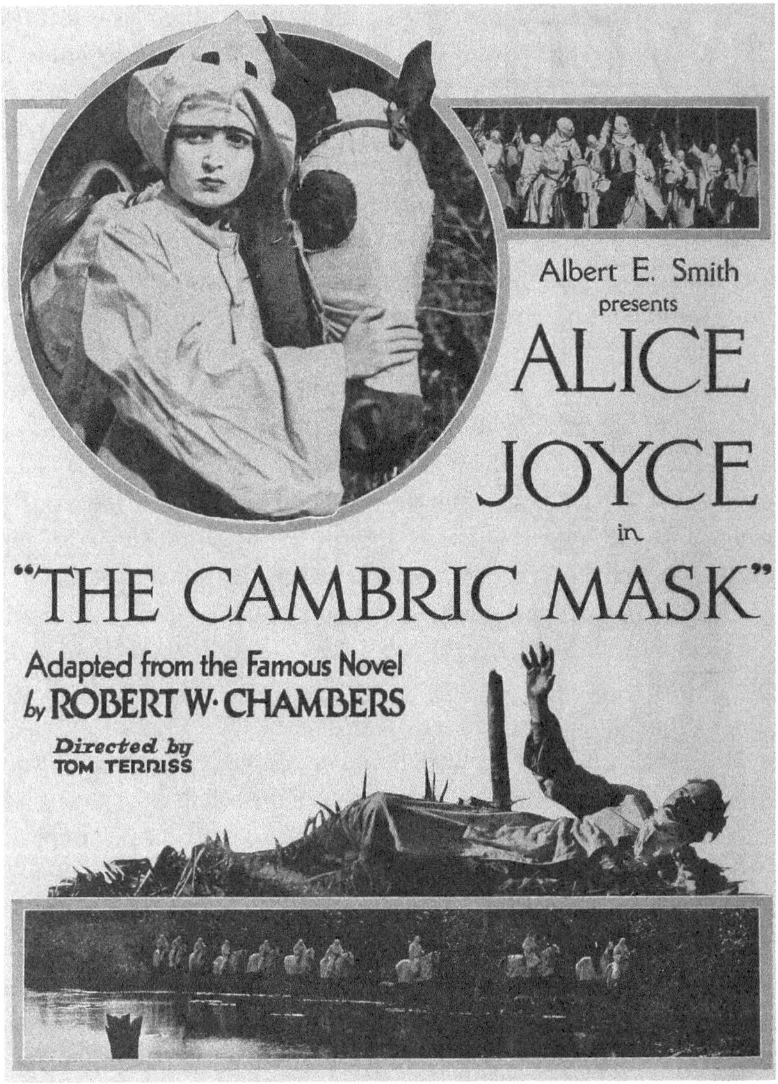

Alice Joyce and Maurice Costello in *The Cambric Mask* (1919). *Motion Picture News*, April 5, 1919.

percent thereafter. Smith and Brady collaborated on all of the post-*Goddess* Vitagraph serials except for 1917's *The Fighting Trail*, which Brady cowrote with Blackton. The Vitagraph serials emphasized rugged action in scenic outdoor settings; this was as much a financial consideration as an aesthetic choice and was not without consequences. In episode eight of *Smashing Barriers*, a speeding car was to plunge off a pier into the ocean. A platform

William Duncan. *Cine-Mundial*, November 1922.

was nailed to the dock in order to contain the three cameras covering the action and the fifteen-member crew, but too much weight caused the platform to collapse, plunging the crew and cameras into the water. During production of the Antonio Moreno serial *Perils of Thunder Mountain*, actor and assistant director Jack Pierce suffered serious burns when he became tangled in wires atop a cabin that had been set afire. The incident likely influenced Pierce's decision to shift gears and pursue a career as a motion picture makeup artist at Universal, where he became legendary for creating the classic visage for the Frankenstein monster, the Mummy, and Wolfman, among others.

The success of *Smashing Barriers* led Albert Smith to have it cut down and reissued as a feature in 1923. The feature, in turn, was edited down to nine minutes for release on the home movie market in 1932, which is now the only surviving footage from the 450-minute original. What remains are scenes taken at a logging camp and in the nearby forests ringing Huntington Lake in the Sierra Nevada Mountains. Highlights include a runaway wagon (supposedly with Johnson in it) plunging off a cliff into the lake, followed by Duncan diving more than fifty feet from the top of a dam into the lake to save her; later the two rappel above the forest from a mountain shack down to the lake below. Lost are such scenes as Duncan riding a log down a flume, and the "human chain of men" that rescue Johnson from a rock ledge.[6]

After getting the boot from Paramount, J. Stuart Blackton was forced to sell his Long Island estate and what remained of his fleet. Bereft of studio financing and a steady income, he had to raise money for his independent productions from private investors. During this time genuine hostility developed between Smith and Blackton. The Commodore had every right to be galled that Smith had allowed predatory outsiders with no experience in motion pictures into the company. Smith felt utterly betrayed by and was jealous of his old friend, whom the press continued to extol. The resentments were ameliorated by the renewed growth of Vitagraph in 1919. With Smith completely on his own for the first time to manage company affairs, there was a spike in profits: $235,028.

In a Christmas letter to Smith, Cyrus Townsend Brady expressed happiness that "there is [now] peace between you and Blackton, your oldest friend." Brady, an ordained Episcopal priest, had been confidant to Blackton and Smith for four or five years. Several months earlier Smith and Brady had experienced their own falling out because Smith had taken on a new writing partner for the serials and Brady further resented George Randolph Chester's treatment of him. Fortunately Smith and Brady chose to forgive and forget. As expressed by Brady, "The Christian spirit therein appeals to me at this Christmas-tide. Insofar as I am concerned, the regrettable incident that caused the severance of our relations is as if it had not been." Three weeks later Brady was stricken with pneumonia and died.[7]

Average net billings for the first three months of 1920 for Vitagraph features increased to $44,000, with overall weekly net billings averaging $114,000 during the same period. However, profitability was down because overhead expenses were also increasing. For the week ending March 26, 1920, extras were paid $892, special actors not under contract received $1,759, the Brooklyn payroll was $17,717, and payroll for the Hollywood staff was $34,947. In addition, $1,590 was paid for scenarios, and executive salaries for the week totaled $3,125.[8]

During the first three months of 1920, the company entered into 3,110 contracts with North American exhibitors for Larry Semon productions. By contrast, there were 2,875 contracts for Alice Joyce films and 2,735 for those of Earle Williams, the company's most popular feature players. Through the end of March, Vitagraph was averaging over $52,000 in net profit on each Semon film. For the week ending April 24, 1920, the company shipped sixty-seven prints of Semon's two-reel comedy *School Days*, compared with fifty-three prints of the latest Alice Joyce release and fifty-one of Corinne Griffith's newest feature.

Larry Semon always prioritized the individual gag over a coherent story. Thus, his films aren't built around a plot, per se, but rather contain sequences of cause-and-effect sight gags that build on each other, such as the classroom fight at the start of *School Days* that culminates in Semon getting caned. Unlike earlier Semon films such as *Bathing Beauties and Big Boobs* (1918) and *His Home Sweet Home* (1919) that take place in a single location over a relatively short period of time, *School Days* jumps ahead in time and space to show Semon and a rival as adults working on a farm, still vying for the affection of a former classmate. The mayhem builds until Semon awakens from his dream of adulthood, seated once again at his desk in the schoolroom.

Most of the gags in *School Days* are products of Semon's fertile imagination, but the atypical bookending of the classroom scenes and the leap forward in time are most likely contributions of his new twenty-one-year-old cowriter and codirector Norman Taurog. Taurog brought more structure to Semon's clothesline of gags as well as a more polished look to the productions. Semon certainly needed help. He was burnt out, dropping from a film per week in 1916 to making only a dozen in 1919. He was also beginning to repeat gags from his previous films. Ironically, as his output declined his popularity grew. By 1920 critics were hailing Semon as Charlie Chaplin's "only equal." His popularity was not confined to North America, either. Just as John Bunny was given different names in other languages, Semon was known as Ridolini in Italy, Jaimito in the Spanish-speaking world, and Zigoto in France.

As an incentive toward greater productivity, Albert Smith renegotiated a contract with Semon at the end of 1919 that paid him $3.6 million over the

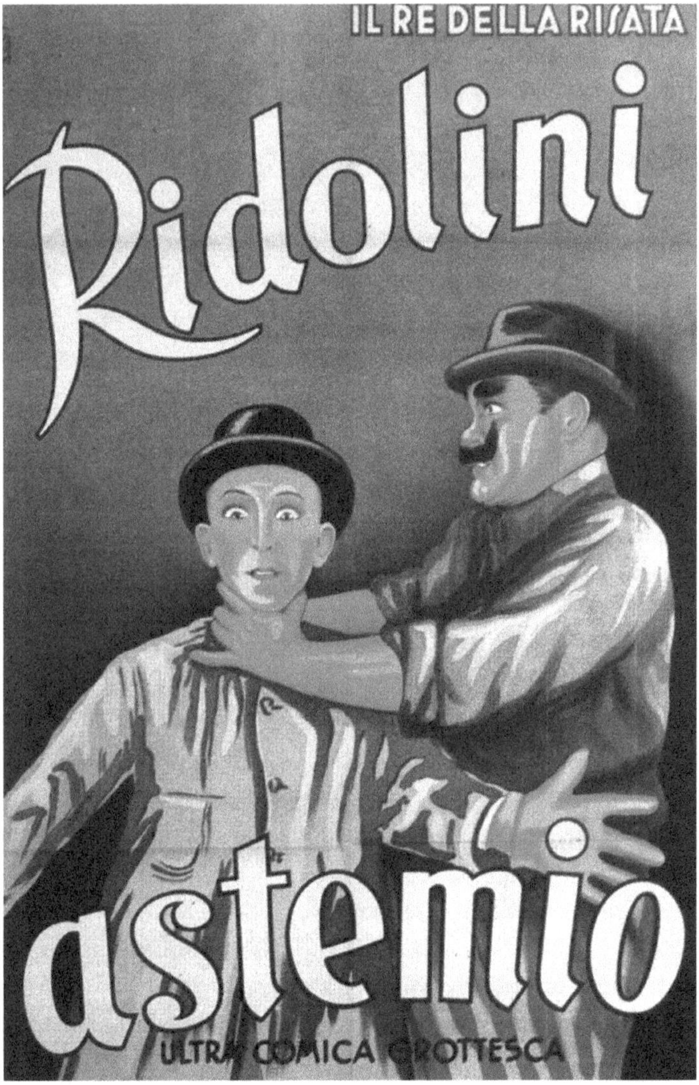

Larry "Ridolini" Semon in *Trouble Brewing* (1924), costarring Oliver Hardy. Author's collection.

next three years. No one at Vitagraph was earning anywhere near that amount, and among comedians only Chaplin was making more. There was, however, a catch. Actually two. First, Vitagraph expected Semon to deliver twelve two-reel films per year over the length of the contract. And second, Semon was to finance those films out of his own pocket. This condition was meant to reinvigorate Semon's work ethic and insure that Vitagraph would not be responsible for any production cost overruns. Unfortunately Semon worked at an even slower pace, producing only six movies during 1920. In September Vitagraph sued him for breach of contract. The company believed that he was recklessly wasting time and money. For example he paid Taurog, who had previously directed only two or three shorts, a starting salary of $750 per week. Semon countersued for one million dollars and his production unit ground to a halt.

Vitagraph could ill afford to lose Ridolini, Jaimito, Zigoto, or Larry Semon. In the meantime, the company stepped up production from several other comedians under contract to supply a steady stream of lower-budgeted slapstick. Chief among them was Jimmy Aubrey. Like Charlie Chaplin and Stan Laurel, Aubrey had been a member of Fred Karno's legendary music hall troupe before entering motion pictures in 1915. He joined Vitagraph a year later, and was initially teamed with Hughie Mack in one-reelers written and directed by Larry Semon. Aubrey was away from the company for most of 1918, but returned at the end of the year in two-reel comedies opposite another "hefty heavy," Oliver "Babe" Hardy. Hardy began his movie career with Lubin in Jacksonville, Florida, in 1914 and played with at least a half dozen other companies before being paired with Aubrey at Vitagraph.

One of Aubrey and Hardy's best surviving films from 1920 is *The Backyard*. Aubrey is in love with a pretty street urchin, introduced in the film roughhousing with four much younger playmates, one white and three black, a scene that would have been forbidden during Hollywood's "Golden Age." Hardy is the urchin's mean-tempered keeper, the kind of role that Eric Campbell and Mack Swain played opposite Charlie Chaplin. A neighbor drags Aubrey, disguised as a policeman, to the girl's apartment to arrest the bully. The entire police force chases after Aubrey, culminating in Hardy tossing each of them out of a second-story window. Back on the street Hardy prepares to pounce on Aubrey but is run over by a car. Aubrey is a forgettable clown, especially alongside Hardy, who commands attention. The production values are impressive for a low-budget film; and, like virtually every other Vitagraph comedy made during the Semon era, it moves at a lightning pace.

The other comedy mainstays at Vitagraph during this period were the team of Earl Montgomery and Joseph Simbert, who both started out as stuntmen. After a year they decided to quit doing stunts for others, wrote a script, and convinced Albert Smith to give them their own series. Simbert changed his name to Rock so that they could be billed as Montgomery and Rock, a takeoff on the famous musical comedy team of Montgomery and Stone. With

Aubrey, Montgomery and Rock, and reissues of Hughie Mack shorts written and directed by Semon, Vitagraph was able to release a Big V Comedy every week for four years. The second-run rental rate for single-day showings of Big V Comedies in small towns during 1919 was $1.00 per film. In order to distinguish their product from the others, Montgomery and Rock engaged in death-defying stunts, often putting their lives on the line for the sake of a laugh.

Montgomery and Rock seemed to bring out the worst in each other. By the autumn of 1919 they were no longer taking direction and had embarked on a work slowdown, setting a bad example for everyone else on the Hollywood lot. Albert Smith decided to break up the team in order to maintain a steady output of Big V Comedies during the impasse with Semon and instill a healthier sense of competition between the two malcontents. *Footprints*, starring and written by Joe Rock, is a terrific two-reeler made right after the breakup in 1920. Rock plays an aspiring detective hired to find a reluctant bride who is kidnapped by a former suitor on the day of her wedding. The movie contains the sort of adventurous explorations of cinema that Vitagraph had previously engaged in. For instance, during the abduction, as the villain's gang carries the bride out of her house there's a quick time-lapse dissolve to everyone now seated in the getaway car parked in front. The victim is then brought to the gang's hideout, the room next to the detective's second-floor office, constructed as a giant two-story set with the front wall removed. After reading his instruction manual the detective enters a walk-in wall safe, and exits wearing a change of clothing and false beard. A car chase between the detective and villain is covered in a beautifully photographed tracking shot. The chase moves to the roof of a building, where the detective avoids capture at the last moment by grabbing onto a rope dangling from a passing biplane. There are tracking shots, taken from the air, of the plane in flight and the gang in pursuit in an automobile below. The detective drops a bomb onto the car and it explodes, causing the occupants to fly onto various nearby rooftops via reverse slow motion. The pilot is revealed to be the villain, and he throws the detective out of the plane. Rock drops through the air, falling through a skylight above his office, and pops out of the wall safe with the bride on his arm. Two days before *Footprints* was released, it was reported that Joe Rock had left Vitagraph to form his own production company. *Footprints* bears many similarities to Buster Keaton's *Sherlock Jr.*, but was made four years earlier.[9]

As inexpensive as the Aubrey and the Montgomery and Rock comedies were to produce and exhibit, none were big box office draws. Vitagraph learned this firsthand when yet another Smith relative was tasked in September

1920 with visiting every exhibitor in Manhattan from Fort Washington to Greenwich Village. A few managers believed that Vitagraph needed to develop newer and stronger stars, while the St. Marks Theatre prominently displayed photographs of nine Vitagraph players in its lobby. VLSE was considered the best-managed exchange; it treated the exhibitor fairly, unlike Paramount, which many exhibitors cited as the worst. Larry Semon was by far the most popular Vitagraph star. Alice Joyce was second, but more exhibitors spoke of how quickly Corinne Griffith was gaining in popularity. William Duncan's serials were preferred in several theaters; in others, Antonio Moreno's serials and some of the reissued features were laughed off the screen.[10]

Three times as many prints were ordered for William Duncan's 1920 *Silent Avenger* serial as for *The Invisible Hand*, the Antonio Moreno serial that preceded it. Duncan was easy to work with, stayed within his budgets, and didn't ask for a higher salary when he prevailed on Albert Smith to allow him to direct his own movies. Moreno, on the other hand, was temperamental and unreliable. He was docked three weeks' salary after abruptly taking off on vacation during the summer of 1919. When he returned to the Hollywood studio he walked off the set and refused to work until he was paid for the time he was away. A year later Moreno threatened to leave the company in the midst of yet another production unless he received a new contract at better terms. Once again the ploy worked.

James B. French, who had been with Smith and Blackton since the Nassau Street days, briefly jumped ship in 1920 to join Famous Players-Lasky. The worst defection of all, as far as Albert Smith was concerned, occurred when his youngest brother, Victor, took a sabbatical from Vitagraph to become studio manager of Famous Players' Long Island City facility. Victor didn't have the courtesy or courage to tell his brother in person, preferring instead to send a telegram.[11]

Albert Smith experienced a far more painful loss at the beginning of the year. On January 24, 1920, the same day that his friend Cyrus Townsend Brady died, Smith's wife, the former Hazel Neason, passed away just two days after contracting pneumonia. Widower Smith was left to raise their young son and daughter. Before the year was out he remarried, once again wedding a Vitagraph starlet. Lucille O'Hare entered motion pictures at Vitagraph's Brooklyn studio in 1917. Adopting the screen name Jean Paige, she was cast in several of the O. Henry two-reelers. Because they were inexpensively made, the O. Henry shorts served as training ground for new talent. After a year Paige graduated to supporting roles in features.

During the summer of 1920 Jean Paige relocated to Vitagraph's Hollywood studio. Albert Smith made at least two extended trips to California in late summer and early autumn, bringing his children along on the second visit. The trip coincided with the production of *Black Beauty*, his pre-wedding gift to Paige and her first starring role in a special feature. As soon as production wrapped, Smith, who was forty-five, Paige, his children, and "a retinue of servants and large contingent of cinema celebrities" traveled in private railroad cars to the home of the twenty-five-year-old bride's parents in Paris, Illinois, for the December wedding.[12]

One week into 1921 Vitagraph announced that the previous year had been the company's biggest, with a 32 percent increase in business over 1919. Like the claims made by virtually every other motion picture producer in the history of the medium regarding finances, it was a lie. The company produced a third fewer movies in 1920 than 1919, with the same percentage also applying to reissues. The total net income for 1920 was $192,659.31, representing an 18 percent *decrease* from 1919.[13]

The Smiths didn't have a honeymoon, at least not right away. After the wedding Albert Smith continued on to New York, carrying the negative of *Black Beauty* with him, such were his priorities. Through mid-January 1921 he supervised the editing of the film at the Brooklyn studio. Smith had learned the value of the massive print ad promotions that Paramount, Fox, and so many of the newer producers had profited from. In November before *Black Beauty* was finished, the company ordered *lots* of posters: seven thousand one-sheets, three thousand three-sheets, two thousand six-sheets, and two thousand twenty-four-sheets. More than six thousand production stills and publicity photos were shipped to exhibitors along with the film.

Vitagraph paid £500 to the British publisher and copyright owner for the motion picture rights to Anna Sewell's beloved 1877 novel. By 1920 *Black Beauty* had become the fifth-best-selling book of all time written in the English language. Mr. and Mrs. George Randolph Chester spent several months on the adaptation, a difficult task given the fact that the title character, and narrator of the story, is a horse who goes through twenty-five owners. The Chesters did a masterful job of eliminating most of the owners and adding a parallel story that focused on Black Beauty's human keepers. The film story alternates between the horse's first-person point of view narration and an omniscient narration to convey information about the owners that the horse doesn't have access to. To help viewers distinguish between the narrators, title cards were designed in two different styles: Black Beauty's narration

Jean Paige and James Morrison in *Black Beauty* (1921). Seaver Center for Western History Research, Los Angeles County Museum of Natural History.

was placed within an ornamental frame and illustrated with the horse's face, and titles for the "indoor story" were printed in Victorian-era typeface to mimic pages from the book.

Dave Smith directed *Black Beauty.* Filming began in July 1920, and many of the exteriors were shot in Santa Barbara. According to James Morrison, who played the love interest opposite Jean Paige, the climactic chase was filmed in Griffith Park using stunt riders. Interiors were staged throughout November at the Hollywood studio, and the stable scenes were photographed on the backlot.

Reginald E. Lyons, a forgotten pillar of cinematography, photographed *Black Beauty.* Lyons entered the industry constructing equipment in Vitagraph's camera department in 1910, and advanced to cameraman in 1913. During the war, as official photographer for the Seventy-Ninth Division of the American Expeditionary Forces, Lyons was gassed three times and spent eleven months in the hospital. He returned to work in May 1919, rejoining the Montgomery and Rock unit in Hollywood. Lyons was freelancing away from Vitagraph when he got the call to shoot *Black Beauty*.

Upon its release *Black Beauty* was seven reels in length, and contained 477 individual shots. Today only three reels from the feature are known to have survived. A thirty-five-minute abridgment made for the home market in December 1929 is the only version currently available to the public. It reveals Reggie Lyons's cinematography and Dave Smith's direction to be of the highest order. The leading players are always edge lit in close-up and medium shots. Exposures are perfectly balanced between interior settings and real world exteriors viewed through windows. Stunning tracking shots enhance the multitude of angles during the climactic chase between hero and villain. *Black Beauty*'s most memorable sequence is the fire inside the brick stable. It is as effectively disturbing today as it was one hundred years ago because human actors and horses are seen running through flames and narrowly missing burning hay falling from the loft.

Black Beauty was the first film that six-year-old Ingmar Bergman ever saw when it played the Sture Cinema in Stockholm in 1924. Fifty years later he could still vividly recall the fire sequence that had excited and disturbed him as a child. Contemporary critics were just as enthralled. "Artistically and photographically the entire production is a masterpiece" containing "scenes of exceptional beauty [and] dramatic climaxes." *Black Beauty* had the unenviable task of following Charlie Chaplin's *The Kid* into New York's Strand Theatre on February 20, 1921, where it was favorably compared as "another of the best pictures of the season." *Black Beauty* smashed all records at the Capitol Theatre in Hartford, Connecticut. That had to have been especially gratifying for Albert Smith and the theater's owner, Samuel Poli, one of Vitagraph's earliest clients, who began booking its films into his vaudeville theaters in 1899.

Black Beauty earned $407,000 in exhibitor rentals. It would have made even more had it not been for the Eskay Harris (EH) Feature Film Co. Vitagraph began promoting *Black Beauty* at least as early as August 1920, more than three months before production wrapped and five months before the film was released. Someone at EH, a bottom of the barrel distributor of old fairy tale movies, remembered that one of the last movies made by the Edison Company, *Your Obedient Servant*, was a knockoff of *Black Beauty*. EH acquired a print of the 1917 film and gave it a new title. On December 22, 1920, an EH advertisement appeared on the back page of a leading trade magazine: "Warning, Anyone showing a motion picture entitled 'Black Beauty' without our permission does so at their own risk. We control the motion picture rights and title of the name of 'black beauty' and will prosecute any infringement to the full extent of the law." This came three weeks after Vitagraph began plastering New York City with enormous twenty-four-sheet posters advertising *its* production of *Black Beauty.* EH rushed the faux *Black Beauty* into theaters at the beginning of January 1921 ahead of the Vitagraph release.

Vitagraph appealed to the Federal Trade Commission for help, charging that the EH film was made to deliberately deceive the public into thinking it was the Vitagraph production and thus reap the benefits from its massive advertising campaign, that EH deliberately refrained from informing the public that their movie was in fact an older Edison film released under another name, and that EH falsely claimed ownership of the copyright to make a film of *Black Beauty*, "such acts and practices constitut[ing] unfair competition within the intent and meaning of Section 5 of the Federal Trade Commission Act." Two years later the FTC handed down its decision, affirming Vitagraph's claims and banning EH from distributing or exhibiting its *Black Beauty* movie. *Variety* noted that for Vitagraph, the ruling was nothing more than a "moral victory" because EH "almost wholly reaped all commercial benefits from its production for the two years the action was being adjudicated." There was no opportunity for Vitagraph to sue EH for financial damages because Congress failed to provide such a mechanism when creating the FTC in 1914. Unfortunately it wouldn't be the last time Vitagraph would encounter such blatant and nefarious appropriation of its product.[14]

In the afterglow of *Black Beauty*'s successful rollout, Albert Smith gave up his townhouse on Riverside Drive in Manhattan and purchased the three-thousand-acre Rancho San Bernardino in northern San Diego County, about nine miles west of Escondido and two and a half miles east of the Pacific Ocean. He paid $150,000. There were twenty buildings on the property, along with citrus groves, purebred Hereford cattle, and other livestock. However, the family spent most of their time at their Hollywood home a few blocks from the Chaplin studio. Jean Paige all but retired from the screen in order to raise her young stepchildren and engage in charitable work and other social activities befitting the wife of a motion picture mogul.[15]

In 1921 Vitagraph's Brooklyn studio was down to producing the features of its three most prominent female stars, veteran Alice Joyce, newcomer

Corinne Griffith in *Moral Fibre* (1921). Author's collection.

Alice Calhoun, and glamour queen Corinne Griffith. By then Griffith had become the movies' paragon of haute couture. The leading fan magazine, *Photoplay*, declared her to be one of the eight most beautiful women in Hollywood. By then attention was being focused almost as much on what she *didn't* wear.

Corinne Griffith received excellent notices for her work as twin sisters in *The Broadway Bubble*, imbuing each of the characters with distinctive personalities. She was "principally responsible" for the movie being made because it provided her with the opportunity to show off her dancing skills, which were photographed on the stage of the George M. Cohan Theatre. But the highlight of *Broadway Bubble* was Corinne Griffith in her sunken bath. One critic likened it to "a DeMille bathroom scene that for sheer sparkling audacity has never been approached by Gloria Swanson or anybody else." The success of *The Broadway Bubble* enabled Griffith to have more authority in selecting her subsequent productions. The 1921 film *What's Your Reputation Worth?* is said to have contained a scene in which Griffith wore "a gown made almost entirely of pearls." Later in the year she performed a

Salome dance in *The Single Track* that climaxed with her clad in a feather-trimmed bra and G-string. An eyewitness to the filming reported that through it all Miss Griffith managed to maintain "her aloof dignity." Such scenes were always tasteful in their execution. Unlike other beautiful women in the movies, Corinne Griffith possessed a mix of innocence and "Southern indifference" that made her all the more alluring.[16]

C. Graham Baker wrote *The Broadway Bubble*, *What's Your Reputation Worth?*, and *The Single Track*, in addition to *Smashing Barriers*; he also co-wrote many of the Larry Semon comedies. Given the variety and track record of his success, Baker was chosen to replace George Randolph Chester as editor in chief of Vitagraph's scenario department, following the latter's abrupt departure in late November 1921. Baker also wrote for Alice Joyce, who made only four features for Vitagraph in 1921, each earning less than $100,000. Joyce blamed her decline on the quality of the stories she had been given. This may have been somewhat true, though it appears that she herself was responsible for selecting at least one of those vehicles, *Cousin Kate*, for which she insisted that Vitagraph hire a female writer and director. At the end of the year Alice Joyce chose not to renew her contract with Vitagraph.[17]

Larry Semon returned to Vitagraph as soon as the impasse of 1920 was resolved. Semon's first two productions for 1921, *The Sportsman* and *The Hick*, were made at breakneck speed. These and Semon's four other two-reel shorts released in 1921 all earned over $100,000 apiece in exhibitor rentals, making him Vitagraph's most popular star. By then Semon and his films were often described as "human cartoons." The designation is apropos given the fact that he approached comedy from a cartoonist's perspective and was credited with creating the "illustrated scenario," aka storyboard, an extension of his work in newspaper comic strips.

Early in the year Oliver Hardy got the axe from jealous Jimmy Aubrey and quickly became a member of the Semon unit, playing his nemesis. Babe Hardy was an excellent comic villain long before he played the innocent oaf with Stan Laurel.

The Bellhop was photographed by Hans Koenekamp who, like Babe Hardy, became a permanent member of the Semon troupe in 1921. Koenekamp started with Keystone in 1913 and photographed Charlie Chaplin's first movie. Joining Vitagraph in 1917, he shot almost all of Semon's post-1920 comedies. He believed that effective silent comedy depended, in part, "upon the ability of the artist at the camera to get freak effects, stunt stuff and make the camera do tricks." One of Semon's trademarks was sliding

Larry Semon. *Who's Who on the Screen*, 1920.

to a halt during a chase just before turning a corner. Koenekamp achieved this by reducing "his cranking speed to a slow turn just as Semon threw his feet out, braked, and then vanished around the corner."

Larry Semon believed, "A comedy is only as funny as its gags. The comic is of secondary importance." Buster Keaton observed that "Chaplin, Lloyd and [I] couldn't make two-reelers as packed with laughs as Larry's [but] when an audience got half a block from the theatre, after being convulsed by Semon's whamios, they couldn't have told you what they had laughed at." Keaton attributed this to the fact that Semon's gags were too far-fetched, having no basis in reality. Just as important, only superficial concessions were made to explain the behavior of Semon's characters. Nor was there ever any consideration of ingratiating himself with the audience. Semon, like his legion of fans, enjoyed the gag for the sake of the gag.[18]

In late 1921, Commodore Blackton and Johnnie Rock empowered Albert Smith as their voting trustee with regard to Vitagraph's financial matters. It was an enormous risk, given how Smith's previous bungling in the Hampton affair had nearly ruined the company. He regained their trust by guiding Vitagraph to another year of profitability. However, the numbers continued to sink. The company's net profit for 1921 was $106,490.58, a drop of more than 45 percent from the previous year. Industry leader Famous Players-Lasky (Paramount) reported a net profit for 1921 of $4,695,499. Adolph Zukor would see to it that the disparity grew much worse.[19]

The Smiths finally went on their long-delayed honeymoon during the summer of 1922, spending six weeks touring England and France. It was workaholic Albert's first trip abroad since before the war, so naturally much of his time was spent in Vitagraph's branch offices, conferring with brother George in London and trusted friend Ronald Reader, who returned to Paris earlier in the year. There is no record of the honeymooners visiting the Blacktons while in England.[20]

With the exception of *The Common Cause*, Commodore Blackton's post-Vitagraph career had been a disappointment; when his distribution contract with Pathé ended, tea magnate and yachtsman Sir Thomas Lipton came to his rescue by providing partial financing for three features produced in England. The first was his most notable. *The Glorious Adventure* starred Lady Diana Manners, an attractive British socialite who caused a scandal among some of the peerage for appearing in a movie. Blackton hired Victor McLaglen to play the villain, the future Oscar winner's first high-profile role. Looking a bit like Keith Moon in a Beatles' wig, McLaglen steals the movie from the wooden Lady Diana. The highlight of the historical drama is a recreation of the 1666 Great Fire of London, which required an enormous outdoor set to be built and subsequently burned. The Blacktons didn't stint on anything while hobnobbing with the aristocracy, but what really drove up the cost was the fact that *The Glorious Adventure* was the first feature to be photographed in color. Prizma Color was a forerunner of the two-strip Technicolor process; the cost for two prints alone was nearly $5,000. Lady Diana and color cinematography were enough of a novelty to make *The Glorious Adventure* a huge hit in the United Kingdom. Despite a massive advertising campaign, the movie failed to catch on in the United States, where it was distributed by a subsidiary of United Artists. Neither of Blackton's subsequent British productions could find an American distributor.[21]

Back in the States, Vitagraph continued to lose ground, producing only twenty-seven films in 1922, its comedies no longer released on a regular basis. The company produced only three Jimmy Aubrey two-reelers that year. One exhibitor expressed the prevailing sentiment, calling *The Chicken Parade* "a good slapstick picture which would have been twice as good if Aubrey hadn't been in it." Perhaps as an antidote to Aubrey, Vitagraph welcomed comic stage actor Edward Everett Horton into the fold, albeit briefly. He made his motion picture debut in *Too Much Business*, about "a young man who . . . starts out in business for himself—as the director of a hotel for babies." Future serial director Ford Beebe adapted the screenplay from an Earl Derr Biggers story. Jimmy Aubrey's former director Jess Robbins helmed all three of the movies Horton made for Vitagraph in 1922. All are presumed lost, which is unfortunate in light of *Photoplay*'s critique of *Too Much Business*: "A Laughter barrage [starring] Edward Horton (who has moments of being delightfully reminiscent of Sidney Drew)."[22]

The Sawmill, starring Larry Semon, cowritten and codirected with Norman Taurog, was released on New Year's Day, 1922. Ordinarily Semon had thirty-two people in his stock company; for *The Sawmill* the cast, crew, and day laborers numbered one hundred, including chefs imported from the Alexandria Hotel, the top hostelry in Los Angeles. That's because at Semon's insistence the movie was shot at Hume Lake in Sequoia National Forest, 250 miles away from the Hollywood studio. A small village was constructed to house the troupe, along with a working sawmill complete with log flumes, on which several of the gags were staged. Semon took three months to film the two-reel short, far longer than most features. Gone were the days of shooting a reel per week. Albert Smith was apoplectic, but *Moving Picture World* hailed it as Semon's best comedy.

Larry Semon's third release of 1922, *A Pair of Kings*, while not necessarily his funniest effort, contains the best-constructed story of his many surviving films. It is essentially a variation on *The Prisoner of Zenda*, with a malicious king embroiled in a palace coup trading places with his doppelganger: a happy idiot newly arrived in the country. Aide-de-camp Babe Hardy leads the unending assassination attempts. The scenes in which Semon appears as both characters within the same shot are convincing, and the moment where the king tosses his coat to the happy idiot is masterfully executed.

According to those who worked with Semon, his on-screen persona as a smiling simpleton abruptly dissolved the moment the camera stopped rolling. When he wasn't performing, Semon was "a terrible, pitiable and most unhappy man . . . sullen [and] suspicious." Norman Taurog described Semon as "not a nice guy." Shortly after *A Pair of Kings* was released in the summer of 1922, Taurog left Semon to direct comedies at smaller production companies. During the sound era, Taurog won an Academy Award, and enjoyed long associations with Dean Martin and Jerry Lewis, and Elvis Presley.

Albert Smith also reached his breaking point. Fed up with profligate spending and interminable production delays, Smith discharged the Semon unit. Semon, in turn, told the press he was shopping for a new producer. Vitagraph had promised exhibitors twelve Larry Semon films per year under the terms of the current three-year contract, but the comedian had only completed fourteen halfway through the final year. Once again lawsuits were filed but this time Albert Smith capitulated, realizing that he needed their top-selling commodity a lot more than Semon needed Vitagraph. The parties settled on a new contract whereby Semon would produce, at his own expense, ten two-reel comedies for the company, each film to be completed within six to eight weeks. Vitagraph, in turn, would purchase the negatives for each of the first five films for $45,000 and the remainder for $50,000 each. Semon was in the driver's seat and Albert Smith knew it. He could no longer afford *not* to acquiesce to the overruns and delays caused by his temperamental star.[23]

With Alice Joyce in retirement and Alice Calhoun transferred to the West Coast, Corinne Griffith was the only star still making movies at the Brooklyn studio in 1922. Griffith's sole surviving film from that year has two different titles: *A Virgin's Sacrifice* and *A Woman's Sacrifice*, retitled for communities that prohibited use of the word "virgin." At least one exhibitor recognized it as a remake of Vitagraph's 1916 feature *God's Country and the Woman. A Virgin's Sacrifice* provides Griffith with a different kind of story where fashions are not a consideration: a compelling mystery set in a remote area of northern Canada. Griffith's husband, Webster Campbell, was the director, guiding her to an excellent performance and composing stunning shots of the snow-covered wilderness. Scenes were staged amidst genuine snowfall, there is an exciting dogsled chase leading up to the climax, and a lodge becomes fully engulfed in fire at night. The movie is just as entertaining today as it was one hundred years ago.

Corinne Griffith followed *A Virgin's Sacrifice* with one more movie produced in Brooklyn. She was then summoned to the Hollywood studio but took her time in making the trip. When Griffith finally did show up she told Albert Smith that she wanted to buy out her contract so that she could sign with another studio. Smith offered to set Griffith up with her own production company, as long as she released through Vitagraph. She rejected the offer and sat out the remaining six months of her contract, then set up her own company releasing through First National.[24]

As devastating as the departure of Corinne Griffith was to Vitagraph, her negotiations with Albert Smith had been civil, and the two remained on friendly terms for the rest of their lives. Antonio Moreno's exit from Vitagraph was more acrimonious. In January 1922 Smith told Moreno that he had been selected to play the male lead in a remake of *The Shaughraun*. Moreno refused after learning that Alice Calhoun's mother had arranged top billing for her daughter. He argued, "She's not known as well as I am, it would belittle me to play opposite her." It wasn't the first time Moreno had done this. In 1921 he refused to appear in William Duncan and Earle Williams movies because he wouldn't receive lead billing. After years of putting up with Moreno's inflated sense of his box office value, Albert Smith had had enough. His latest refusal was tantamount to walking out on his contract. He was given a day's notice to vacate the Hollywood studio. Moreno immediately filed suit against Vitagraph for $127,000 and the next day began working for Goldwyn in a Colleen Moore film. The Moreno suit dragged on for over a year until his lawyers put a lien on the Hollywood studio, which resulted in the actor accepting a cash settlement from Vitagraph of $22,500.[25]

The Moreno lawsuit was trifling compared to one brought by Vitagraph later in 1922. Two years earlier the company had announced plans to produce *The Son of Wallingford*, based on a serialized story that Mr. and Mrs. George Randolph Chester were writing for *Collier's* magazine. In February 1921 the trades reported that Albert Smith and Mr. Chester were en route to Hollywood to make *The Son of Wallingford*. In April, Chester brought suit against Adolph Zukor's Famous Players Company after learning they were producing a film based on his *Get-Rich-Quick Wallingford* stories. Judge Julius Mayer, an acquaintance of Zukor's, refused Chester's request for an enjoinment on the dubious grounds that preventing Famous Players from releasing their film would harm them more than it would the author. Articles then began appearing in the trades stating that *Get-Rich-Quick Wallingford* was "adapted from the original stage success by George M. Cohan." The articles failed to note that the Cohan play was adapted from short stories written by Chester.

Vitagraph's *Son of Wallingford* opened to mostly excellent reviews on October 30, 1921, but despite a massive prerelease advertising campaign, Albert Smith confided to his brother, "We are finding it very difficult to sell the picture." Most of the country's top theaters wouldn't book it. On the other hand, *Get-Rich-Quick Wallingford* opened on December 4 simultaneously at two of Broadway's premiere movie palaces, the Rialto and the Rivoli, both controlled by Adolph Zukor.

The same thing happened a few weeks later when Paramount released Zukor's production of *The Little Minister* on Christmas Day and Vitagraph followed with its own *Little Minister* nearly a month later on January 22, 1922. This time around it was Vitagraph who owned the motion picture rights to a popular play adapted from J. M. Barrie's novel, while Paramount owned the movie rights to the book itself. As had been the case with the competing *Black Beauty* and *Wallingford* productions, the two *Little Minister* movies created confusion with the public. Even though critics and the public expressed a preference for the Vitagraph version, VLSE had trouble booking it and some reviews were actually defamatory in denouncing the film. Once again, only Paramount's *Little Minister* was booked into the big theaters.

The Son of Wallingford netted $209,622 in exhibitor rentals and *The Little Minister* just $100,409. Based on the reception and advertising associated with similar past productions, Vitagraph had every reason to expect the films to have been booked into far more theaters and to have earned twice as much as they did. Something was amiss. Albert Smith discovered that the *Boston Evening Transcript*'s review of *The Little Minister* stated that the movie was a rerelease of Vitagraph's 1913 three-reel production starring Clara Kimball Young, a movie "poor beyond the ordinary." It charged that the company had since relinquished the motion picture rights it had regarding the original book and that the raison d'être for the rerelease was to take advantage of the advertising campaign mounted for the Paramount version. Someone had supplied the newspaper with these mendacities and it wasn't Vitagraph. As if that wasn't damaging enough, Vitagraph came into possession of an advertising circular distributed to every exhibitor in Boston (and presumably the rest of the country) that reproduced the *Evening Transcript* review with additional copy written by Paramount's sales department reinforcing the misinformation. Vitagraph contacted the *Evening Transcript* and demanded a retraction, which the newspaper complied with and also published in the trades.

Soon came the discovery that Paramount was involved in a much more sinister scheme that extended far beyond merely discrediting *The Little*

Minister. Famous Players' sales manager Sidney R. Kent was Adolph Zukor's most trusted lieutenant. Inseparable, the two traveled cross-country and to Europe together plotting how to increase the profitability and dominance of Paramount at the expense of its rivals. Cunning as he was, Sidney Kent didn't make a move without the boss's approval. Someone in Paramount's Denver office forwarded to Vitagraph a copy of a January 31, 1922, letter written by Kent to Denver branch manager M. S. Wilson, in which Wilson was instructed "to kick out every Vitagraph account you can find, irrespective of the terms you may have to make, just so you . . . get them out of the way." Vitagraph also received a copy of Wilson's consequent letter to his salesmen, telling them to offer Paramount's *Little Minister* to exhibitors at any price they wished to pay, even gratis if need be. "Please do not permit anyone to read this communication and work quietly on this subject, but get the results." John Quinn of VLSE learned that branch managers in Cleveland and Omaha received and complied with the same missive. It is reasonable to assume that all of Paramount's regional managers did as well.

Albert Smith began to consider this information in terms of the bigger picture. Vitagraph was instrumental in demonstrating to the rest of the industry the value of Broadway first-runs for top features during its two-year lease of the Criterion/Vitagraph Theatre. From 1914 to 1918 the company enjoyed unrestricted access to the movie palaces that subsequently sprang up in major cities across North America. These first-run exhibitions reportedly accounted for as much as 50 percent of a feature film's revenue. In 1919 Adolph Zukor prevailed upon Otto Kahn of Kuhn, Loeb and Company to arrange a $10 million stock offering of Paramount Famous-Lasky Corporation preferred shares to finance theater construction and acquisition on a massive scale. At the end of 1922 Paramount controlled 442 theaters in North America, including three of the five movie palaces in Times Square. Zukor engaged in block booking, which extended not only to the theaters he owned outright or held controlling interests in but also to the hundreds if not thousands of other theaters throughout North America that carried his product, to the exclusion of all others. It is quite possible that not a single Vitagraph production had been booked into any theater showing Paramount movies since *The Cambric Mask* in 1919. Coinciding with Zukor's efforts to curtail the exhibition of Vitagraph movies was the ongoing raiding of its personnel that extended beyond Albert Smith's partner, brother, key actors, directors, and writers, to include a production designer, editor, electrician, and mechanics.

As far as Albert Smith and John Quinn were concerned, Paramount was engaging in illegal restraint of trade. Vitagraph attorney William Seabury agreed but warned that joining a suit that had recently been filed by the Federal Trade Commission against Famous Players or suing the company on its own would "incur their everlasting enmity" and ultimately prove too expensive to pursue. Seabury suggested that Vitagraph instead go directly to Paramount with the evidence and, under threat of contacting the FTC, insist that it publicly declare it would cease such activities. It appears that such a meeting did occur sometime in late April 1922 but to no avail.

Seemingly out of the blue, Guaranty Trust notified Albert Smith a few weeks later that he had until September 1 to significantly pay down the million-dollar debt still owed by Vitagraph or the bank would foreclose. Then on August 1 came news that Guaranty found a party willing to pay off half the debt and invest "$2,000,000 new money into the business" via a foreclosure sale. The purchasers were offering Smith $100,000 cash if he would deliver Blackton's and Johnnie Rock's shares in the company "for a song." Smith learned that a member of the purchasing group was associated with Otto Kahn, who had only recently arranged for Guaranty Trust to open a $1,000,000 line of credit for Paramount.

Immediately Smith contacted Blackton, who was still in England. It was clear to both that the purchasing party was "our old friends the Famous Players, in sheep's clothing," and that Adolph Zukor was motivated by some private prejudice to "Smash Vitagraph." The partners rejected the offer, taking solace in Vitagraph's solvency, certain that the company would achieve better terms in a voluntary bankruptcy if it ever came to that. On November 1, 1922, Guaranty Trust Company of New York sued Vitagraph for $947,000 in unpaid notes. With their backs against the wall, there seemed to A. E. and Jim to be only one course of action for them to take. Even their cautious attorney William Seabury agreed.

On November 28, 1922, Vitagraph filed a Bill of Complaint in the United States District Court for the Southern District of New York charging Famous Players-Lasky Corporation, Adolph Zukor, et al. with violation of the Clayton Antitrust Act of 1914. The suit spelled out in detail all of the illegal and unethical activity engaged in by Paramount that Vitagraph had confronted it with back in April. It also showed a correlation between Paramount's malicious actions and Vitagraph's decline in gross revenue during the postwar years as it was being squeezed out of theaters. Vitagraph characterized itself as an "independent" in the suit. By controlling production, distribution, and exhibition, Paramount engaged in a true monopoly, far worse than what the MPPC had been convicted of. Vitagraph sought $6 million in damages.

News of the suit rocked the industry. At the time, a poll was being conducted involving over one hundred of the leading producers, distributors, and exhibitors to determine who was the most important man in the industry. The winner, by a landslide, was Adolph Zukor. No one had the courage to take on the Czar or publicly support the only man that did, Albert Smith. Adolph Zukor did not respond, at least publicly, to the charges; he was said to be away on business with Sidney Kent.

On December 4, 1922, six days after the lawsuit was filed, a mysterious fire destroyed Vitagraph's Bayshore studio originally built for Ralph Ince. William Seabury had warned there might be repercussions. Similar fates befell exhibitors unwilling to accept yearlong contracts for expensive Paramount product sight unseen, and especially theater owners unwilling to sell Zukor their business. His strong-arm thugs were dubbed the "wrecking crew" and the "dynamite gang" for good reason.

In June 1923, more than six months after the lawsuit was filed, Paramount's treasurer reached out to Albert Smith and Commodore Blackton with an offer. If they dropped the suit, Paramount would run every feature film made by Vitagraph at either the Rialto or Rivoli. Smith and Blackton acquiesced. They could no longer afford to wait on the court. Between the lockout by Paramount, mounting legal fees, loss of feature stars, and accelerated payments to Guaranty Trust to forestall a forced foreclosure, Vitagraph was in the red for $500,415 by the end of 1922. Paramount appears to have sweetened the deal by paying Vitagraph a settlement of at least $100,000. Smith and Blackton also agreed to Paramount's odd request that Motion Picture Producers and Distributors of America (MPPDA) president Will Hays publicly receive credit for brokering the deal, when all he did was ask Vitagraph to drop the suit for the sake of Paramount and the industry. The contract with Paramount guaranteeing feature film exhibition at the Rivoli and Rialto was for one year. The day it expired Paramount did not allow a single Vitagraph feature to ever again be exhibited at either of those theaters, or any of the others it controlled.[26]

Lest there be any thought that Smith and Blackton were deluding themselves into thinking that Adolph Zukor was out to "Smash Vitagraph," much of the foundation for the FTC's case against Paramount was based on documentation it possessed regarding Zukor's "systematic efforts . . . to put the Vitagraph Company out of business." More importantly, six of the ten features produced and released by Vitagraph in 1923 during the Paramount moratorium *significantly* outperformed *Son of Wallingford* and *The Little Minister.* In fact the new features and shorts produced and released by Vitagraph in 1923 netted over $2,600,000. Unfortunately, overhead expenses, legal fees, and the accelerated payment schedule to Guaranty Trust reduced overall profits to a relatively trivial amount by the end of the year.

The biggest event at Vitagraph during 1923 was the return of J. Stuart Blackton into the fold. If Adolph Zukor facilitated Blackton's departure and the subsequent rift that developed between the partners, he was also inadvertently responsible for their reunion, as Smith and Blackton came together to oppose the man intent on destroying the company they had devoted their lives to building. A. E. and Jim must have been aware of how much each needed the other. Most of Blackton's efforts as an independent producer-director failed miserably on both sides of the Atlantic. The high-living Blacktons no longer had a steady income, and now that Vitagraph was operating in the red there were no year-end dividends to draw from. There was really nowhere else for Blackton to go but back to Vitagraph. The prodigal was welcomed with open arms. Albert Smith's brother, affectionately known as "Uncle Dave" around the lot, had been the company's only salaried director in 1922, having made six features. Albert intended to produce a dozen "specials" in 1923 and needed another director with the same work ethic, artistry, and loyalty as his brother. Jim Blackton was the perfect—and really only—choice.

Blackton titled his first production back at Vitagraph *On the Banks of the Wabash,* trading on the popular song written by Paul Dresser in 1897. Even though the plot as outlined by Blackton had virtually nothing in common with the song's lyrics, Vitagraph paid the song's publisher $8,000 for use of the title. A steam-powered riverboat was acquired for the movie and figured prominently in the spectacular climax, rescuing the victims of a small-town flood and then catching fire. The town and flood are utterly convincing, belying the film's $75,478 budget. *On the Banks of the Wabash* netted $209,037 in exhibitor rentals, less than any of the other Vitagraph "Specials" of 1923. It is unfortunate because the shortened version of *Wabash* is far better than most of the other surviving home market condensations from Vitagraph's latter years.[27]

As Vitagraph continued making fewer movies, Albert Smith could no longer afford to maintain weekly salaried players, preferring instead to hire freelancers on a per picture basis. Earle Williams's contract expired, and he spent the rest of his career freelancing at various studios. *Photoplay* noted

J. Stuart Blackton and Albert Smith at Vitagraph's Hollywood studio gate, 1925. Marc Wanamaker/Bison Archives.

that Williams was "the last to leave the old nest from which most of our great stars first tried their wings." Alice Calhoun, who was earning a weekly salary of $433, still had two years remaining on her contract and consequently became the busiest player on the Vitagraph lot in 1923.[28]

Larry Semon continued to pack fans into neighborhood theaters. According to the December 1923 issue of *Cine Mundial*, Semon received the highest weekly salary of any actor in Hollywood, though three actresses earned more. Despite his popularity, everyone began to notice that Semon was repeating gags and even plots from earlier movies. Under his contract with Vitagraph, which wasn't set to expire until September, Semon owed the company a two-reel comedy and a feature. Albert Smith ended up settling for two rural-themed two-reel comedies costarring Babe Hardy, *Horseshoes* and *Trouble Brewing*, which weren't released until 1924. With that, Vitagraph's most popular comedian of the postwar era was gone.[29]

Financially unable to renew contracts, sign new talent, or produce as many features as he hoped, Albert Smith began slashing expenses. The Hollywood studio was shut down and most of the staff laid off for six weeks, from late November 1923 through early January 1924, until sufficient rental fees were collected to resume operations. Long gone were the Christmas bonus checks, turkey giveaways, and company parties.

In the meantime, Jim Blackton prepared to move his family west. He confided, "I think I have been happier in my work during the past six months, since I came back home to Vitagraph, than at any time during the six years I was away." Blackton's glee was no doubt buoyed by the news that while Vitagraph continued paying down the million-dollar loan from Guaranty Trust, the company still managed to turn a modest profit of $39,544.38 for 1923. The optimistic mood at Vitagraph stood in stark contrast to the passing in September of Pop Rock's friend and fellow moving picture pioneer Siegmund Lubin, who died penniless at the age of seventy-two.[30]

Vitagraph produced only ten features in 1924 and distributed five others made by small independent producers. Even in its condensed home movie form, Blackton's production of *The Beloved Brute* remains thoroughly enjoyable thanks to the performance of its charismatic star, Victor McLaglen. Vitagraph purchased the screen rights to the recently published novel for $5,000 and paid for McLaglen's passage to America. He earned approximately $2,700 for the five-week shoot. If not for McLaglen, *Beloved Brute* would be a forgettable Western. He plays a circus wrestler challenging all comers. It is an example of art imitating life; the actor did just that and even boxed prior to entering the movies. McLaglen appeared in several British films following his turn in *The Glorious Adventure*, but with *The Beloved Brute* a Hollywood star was born. Vitagraph needed the family-friendly crowd-pleaser following the disputation surrounding one of Blackton's earlier 1924 efforts.[31]

If *The Battle Cry of Peace* was Vitagraph's most controversial production, then *Between Friends* was its most scandalous. It was a remake of a 1918 feature, *The Woman Between Friends*, which in turn was adapted from a novel by Robert W. Chambers, author of *The Girl Philippa* and *The Cambric Mask.* The story concerns a man who secretly has an affair with his best friend's wife; she commits suicide after he tires of her. When the best friend, a sculptor, hires a model to pose for him, the unfaithful friend attempts to woo her, too. The sculptor learns the truth about his friend's betrayal and compels him via mental telepathy to commit suicide to atone for causing the death of his wife. Alice Joyce played the model in the 1918 film directed by Tom Terriss; Alice Calhoun was the model in Blackton's 1924 version.

From the start, Alice Calhoun was determined to become and remain a movie star. With only one independently made film to her credit, nineteen-year-old Calhoun obtained an introduction to Albert Smith in late 1919 and was hired on the spot. A year later, Calhoun was put under contract to star in minor features, but after her breakout role in *The Little Minister* she graduated to "Specials." Upon relocating to the Hollywood studio she started her own fan club, for which she published a bimonthly newsletter. Alice Calhoun was best described as "sometimes pretty," possessing a "rather slim" figure while "always aim[ing] to be natural" on screen. All of these qualities are on full display in surviving photographs from *Between Friends.*

Unlike Alice Joyce's model in *The Woman Between Friends*, Calhoun poses in the nude in Blackton's production. One production still shows Calhoun completely nude from the back; in another she is facing forward with an apple in hand, her slender figure draped in a transparent covering that fully reveals all of her natural charms. That Albert Smith would allow Blackton to film such a blatantly lascivious scene shows just how desperate Vitagraph's financial situation had become.

New York was one of six states in 1924 with its own movie censorship board. As with all of its productions, Vitagraph had to submit *Between Friends* to the State of New York Motion Picture Commission (SNYMPC) for approval before it could be exhibited. The SNYMPC ordered that the frontal shot of Calhoun be removed from the film but not the one showing her bare derrière. Additional edits required by the commission included "immoral suggestions" that the wife and friend have betrayed her husband; a title card quoting one of the characters saying "I don't believe in virgins spiritually or aesthetically"; the sculptor telling the model via intertitle "You don't have to believe in the annunciation to model the Virgin"; and two shots of the duplicitous friend putting a pistol to his head. Vitagraph complied with the order, and substituted a happy ending in which the sculptor stops his friend from killing himself at the last moment. *Between Friends* was resubmitted to the

SNYMPC and on April 23, 1924, received a license to be exhibited in New York. The company went through similar procedures with the other state censorship boards, but otherwise released the movie in its original form throughout the rest of the country.

VLSE booked *Between Friends* wherever and whenever it could. After its one-week premiere engagement at the Rivoli in Times Square the week of May 17, 1924, the film played mostly smaller neighborhood theaters scattered throughout the United States. Critical opinion was evenly divided, some considering *Between Friends* the best film Blackton ever made and others branding it "sordid."

On September 16, 1924, came word that the SNYMPC was revoking its license for *Between Friends* because of a complaint it received from associates of Cardinal Hayes, the Archbishop of New York. They objected to shots of partial nudity that the SNYMPC had previously approved, as well as to the suicide of the sculptor's wife, and to Calhoun being kissed and embraced by both the sculptor and his friend while posing for a statue of the Virgin Mary. The SNYMPC demanded *Between Friends* be withdrawn from exhibition, labeling it "immoral and indecent." Vitagraph's attorney responded that eleven prints of *Between Friends* were currently circulating in New York State, and that the SNYMPC had no legal authority to revoke any movie's license after one had already been granted. The company did, however, end up removing most of the inflammatory shots from all of the prints in circulation to placate the director of the National Catholic Welfare Council (NCWC), who had lodged a more measured complaint. For all its notoriety, *Between Friends* only netted a relatively modest $160,000 in exhibitor rentals.[32]

Johnnie Rock replaced John Quinn as Vitagraph sales manager after the latter suffered a fatal heart attack early in 1924. Rock lost much of the money he had inherited eight years earlier from his father's estate to bad business and real estate investments. Lately he had taken to financing individual Vitagraph productions in partnership with Albert Smith. With ten years at the helm of Vitagraph's Chicago office, Rock was well known and liked by exhibitors throughout the country. More importantly, Albert Smith trusted him. Having inherited his father's stock in the company, Rock was sufficiently motivated to sell Vitagraph product while keeping expenses down. Prodigal brother Victor Smith returned to assist Rock in his duties. At the time, Albert had his hands full overseeing production of the biggest film of his career.[33]

During his visit to London in late 1923, Albert Smith purchased the screen rights to Rafael Sabatini's best-selling novel *Captain Blood: His Odyssey* for a purported $30,000. Set during the Glorious Revolution of 1688, it is the story of an Irish surgeon sold into slavery on Barbados after providing medical assistance to rebel soldiers. He escapes, captures a Spanish ship, and becomes a pirate, preying on non-British naval vessels in the Caribbean. After thwarting an attack by a French warship on Jamaica, he is made governor of that British colony and marries the niece of his nemesis, the former governor.

Smith acquired *Captain Blood* following the success of Metro's adaptation of Sabatini's *Scaramouche*, directed by former Vitagraph player Rex Ingram (née Hitchcock) and released in the autumn of 1923. While *Scaramouche* was in production, First National purchased the motion picture rights to another Sabatini novel, *The Sea Hawk*.

Albert Smith commissioned three movie treatments of the book, choosing Jay Pilcher's for its "original touches" and his availability to work with Smith on the final shooting script. While it was still being written came the announcement that the actor to play Captain Blood would be chosen from a poll of "fans as well as . . . motion picture editors of all newspapers throughout the country." VLSE branch managers also solicited the opinions of the exhibitors they served. It was a gimmick inspired to generate nationwide interest in a movie not yet in production and was indicative of Albert Smith's caution in doing everything he could to insure box office success. The 2,876 fan votes mirrored the opinion of 387 newspaper critics. The top three choices were Rudolph Valentino, Douglas Fairbanks, and J. Warren Kerrigan. The majority of exhibitors preferred Kerrigan due to his starring role in *The Covered Wagon*, the highest-grossing movie of 1923. This presented a dilemma for Smith. Valentino was already tied up for the year under contracts to Famous Players and Ritz Productions, while Fairbanks only wrote and produced his own movies. That left Kerrigan, who Albert Smith thought "a little too effeminate" to convincingly portray Captain Blood; he preferred instead John Barrymore. In the end he deferred to the exhibitors' choice in the belief that they were better informed to predict the actor that would best fill their theaters.

The initial plan was to surround Kerrigan with an "important and expensive cast," but during the preproduction phase it became evident that *Captain Blood* was going to cost much more than originally anticipated. Consequently, Jean Paige came out of retirement to play Blood's love interest, and Vitagraph veterans James Morrison and Wilfrid North were cast as his loyal friend and nemesis, respectively.

Smith wanted *Captain Blood* to "travel with the speed of greased lightning and be full of punch, pep and thrills, with a scattering of pathos and heart interest." With his flair for handling fast-moving action, Dave Smith was the logical choice to direct. But days after production commenced in mid-May 1924, Dave alerted brother Albert that he was unsure whether his fragile health would hold up through the end of production. J. Stuart Blackton was in the midst of making his own film and, thus, was unable to lend a hand. Besides, *Captain Blood* was Albert Smith's personal super-production, his *The Battle Cry of Peace*, on which he staked Vitagraph's future survival. Albert dropped everything to step in as second unit director and take as much of the load off his brother as possible, with both companies shooting day and night. It was the first time the boss had actually directed anything since 1907.

Because Albert Smith wanted his movie to look as real as possible, it was necessary for Vitagraph to obtain seaworthy boats. Two three-masted schooners were purchased for $7,000 and a third two-masted ship was rented from producer-actor Charles Ray, built for *The Courtship of Miles Standish*. The ships were revamped to resemble seventeenth-century battleships, and Blood's boat, the *Arabella*, was outfitted with distinctive accoutrements. A fleet of miniature boats was constructed for shots requiring more ships, photographed in a specially built shallow tank. Each of the models rested in cradles that were attached to wheels fitted onto toy railroad tracks on the bottom of the tank. Electric motors controlled the movement of the miniatures through the water.

Steve Smith was in charge of principal photography and supervised a team of eleven additional cameramen. The most expensive and difficult shots in the film occur at the climax, during a duel to the death between the *Arabella* and a French warship. Captain Blood's crew pulls alongside and boards the enemy ship to engage in a spectacular sword fight, which Warner Bros. copied for their 1940 remake of *The Sea Hawk*. Blood's victory is signaled with a close-up of the lowering of the French flag and hoisting of the Union Jack in its place. The shot pays homage to Vitagraph's first great success, *Tearing Down the Spanish Flag* from 1898. Just before the *Arabella* departs, a long fuse is lit, which ignites a spectacular explosion that utterly destroys the French ship. No model or CGI effect has ever come close to the devastation wrought by the one hundred pounds of dynamite and fifty pounds of magnesium flash powder used to blow up the three-masted ship, which occurred off Catalina Island. The camera crews were pelted with wood, bits of iron, and other debris. This is followed by a separate shot of the *Arabella* slowly sinking into the sea after all aboard have safely abandoned ship. For the British release, the sinking of the *Arabella* is accompanied by a

Captain Blood. Albert E. Smith Papers (Collection 2004). Library Special Collections, Charles E. Young Research Library, UCLA.

shot of one of Captain Blood's men rescuing the Union Jack flag moments before the stern disappears under the sea.

A few days after production wrapped, Albert Smith brought the work print and negative to New York to supervise Bert Jordan's final edit, which brought the movie down to eleven reels. Jordan had been one of the editors on D. W. Griffith's *Intolerance*, and would go on to edit most of the Laurel and Hardy productions for Hal Roach. Throughout production and postproduction, Vitagraph inundated its branch offices in Chicago, London, and Paris with publicity stills and posters to forward to their exhibitors. Albert Smith explained that because *Captain Blood* was "the biggest and most expensive picture we have ever put on . . . the only way we will be able to get our money back is to let the exhibitor and the public know what we are doing." Victor Smith lined up approximately two hundred newspapers throughout the states to run an adaptation of the screenplay in serial form. Grosset and Dunlap simultaneously published a special edition of *Captain Blood* illustrated with stills from the movie.

Captain Blood had its world premiere on September 8, 1924, at the Astor Theatre in New York. Because the regular Broadway movie palaces were unavailable to him, Albert Smith had no alternative but to rent the Astor for $5,000 per week, in addition to paying for musicians, stagehands, and even the marquee lights. The president and his wife, the other stars, and the director of the movie attended the premiere, along with many former Vitagraphers. Blackton sent a congratulatory telegram from Los Angeles, charging it to the *Capt. Blood* account. Following its big city premieres, *Captain Blood* was cut down to eight reels for wide release.

Albert Smith and Jean Paige sailed for London at the end of October to attend the premiere of *Captain Blood* at the Palace Theatre in Leicester Square. Within a year, the London office booked *Captain Blood* into 1,239 theaters across the country, with net billings totaling £50,698. At the Paris office, Ronald Reader enjoyed just as much success booking the film throughout all of Western, Central, and Eastern Europe, the Scandinavian countries, and Egypt, Syria, and Palestine. The dividends from *Captain Blood* were used to pay off most of the remainder of the loan from Guaranty Trust and funds drawn from Albert Smith's personal savings that were used to meet payroll while *Captain Blood* was in production.

According to Albert Smith, on the night of *Captain Blood*'s premiere at the Astor Theatre, Adolph Zukor hosted a dinner party for New York's leading movie critics. Zukor presented each of the guests with expensive wristwatches and told them "his feelings wouldn't be hurt if [they] decided that *Captain Blood* was a lousy picture." This accounts for the unusual disparity in the reviews. On the one hand there were those echoing the sentiments of the *New York Bulletin*, which called *Captain Blood* "one of the greatest films since *The Birth of a Nation*," and others offering backhanded compliments like the *New York World*, which proclaimed, "This new Sabatini picture, which is neither so pictorially effective as *Scaramouche* nor so vitally alive as *The Sea Hawk*, is a good adaptation."

Comparisons with *The Sea Hawk* were inevitable since that film had just completed a fourteen-week run at the Astor Theatre when *Captain Blood* took over the house. When production wrapped, Smith enthused to brother George, "Praise the Lord . . . I can say without hesitation [*Captain Blood*] is the greatest [movie] ever produced." He repeatedly told his inner circle that he expected *Captain Blood* to do as well as *The Sea Hawk*, which took in two million dollars at the box office to become the highest-grossing film of 1924. *Captain Blood* earned $600,000 in exhibitor rentals in the United States, which translates into box office receipts of roughly $1.2 million.

Even though *Captain Blood* was far and away the highest-grossing film in Vitagraph's history, Albert Smith's plans for the company going forward were predicated on substantially higher earnings. He blamed Adolph Zukor for impeding the movie's box office potential, not without justification. Not only had Zukor exercised considerable influence regarding critical response, *Captain Blood* played in only two of the approximately 450 theaters in North America controlled by Paramount, for one week apiece. Zukor's policy of exclusion was akin to that of others of the era for whom imposing their prejudice was seemingly more important than their bottom line.[34]

Going into December, Albert Smith instructed brother Victor to discontinue all trade paper advertising until after the New Year in order to economize, well aware that doing so would negatively affect the company's likelihood of receiving positive publicity of any kind. Once again, most of the staff employed by the Hollywood studio was laid off from Christmas until well after New Year's. The company couldn't afford to pay them, finding itself $238,098 in the red after conscientiously paying off the majority of its bank loans.[35]

Entering 1925, Albert Smith couldn't help but reflect on the disappointments of the previous year. The truce with Paramount was a sham, a public relations ploy serving the interests of Adolph Zukor and MPPDA president Will Hays. Rather than deter Zukor from his quest to ruin Vitagraph, it provided him with a smokescreen from which to carry on his campaign. Even worse was Zukor's success in hindering the box office potential of *Captain Blood.* Albert Smith knew that his film was at least as good as if not better than *The Sea Hawk. Captain Blood* would have earned much more had Zukor allowed it to be booked into his theaters to replace underperforming Paramount releases. It was the kind of behavior that thirteen years earlier had resulted in a lot of bad press for the MPPC and incurred the wrath of the Justice Department; only now, no one seemed to care.

Smith and especially Blackton were no doubt also exasperated by the double standard that existed regarding Paramount's exclusionary tactics and salacious content in many of its movies. Although Vitagraph was forced to make several edits to *Between Friends,* Paramount releases of 1924 seemed to be protected from such attacks, including *Sinners in Heaven*, which featured "nude stuff . . . with Bebe Daniels . . . bathing in a tropical pool" in extended shots "so one can see considerable of Bebe"; *Lily of the Dust*, which concluded on a shot of Pola Negri "quite nude"; and *The Alaskan*, wherein "Estelle Taylor jumped from the steamer and started to swim, very apparently naked."[36]

The MPPDA ostensibly functioned as the industry's lobbyist, public relations arm, arbitrator, and self-censorship board. Albert Smith realized long before anyone else that the primary purpose of the MPPDA was to protect the interests of Zukor and other emergent industry leaders in the post–World War I era. Vitagraph attorney William Seabury, after making a careful study of the FTC's investigation into Famous Players, concurred, referring to them as "a bunch of crooks . . . from Zukor down," abetted by "the Hays organization . . . working with them."

Disgusted with Zukor's sanctioned chicanery and Hays's hypocrisy, Vitagraph resigned from the MPPDA in January 1925, explaining that it did so "because it does not believe that justice to the distributors and to the public and to those independent producers who are not theater-owning exhibitors can be obtained through the labors of the MPPDA." With a veiled knock against Paramount's strong-arm tactics and block booking, the statement concluded, "Vitagraph owns no theatres, therefore it can give the public what it wants without strings tied to it." Once again the other independent production companies were too cowed by Zukor to publicly support Vitagraph.

Sydney S. Cohen, the founder of Motion Picture Theatre Owners of America, was another target of Adolph Zukor, who ordered, "Cohen must be destroyed and his organization broken down." Cohen understood as well as anyone the plight of the independent producer and exhibitor: "Producer-owned theatres use no independent picture product save in rare emergencies. Through this sinister control and their ability to terrorize and coerce independent theatre owners, they force the latter to also refuse the product of independent producers, and thus through these unfair business methods force independent producers out of business."

An immediate benefit of the resignation was that Vitagraph would no longer be paying dues in support of an organization that was in fact working against it. For the moment Albert Smith could return his attention to making movies.[37]

Vitagraph produced seven features in 1925 and released at least eleven others made by independent filmmakers. The company's most significant production of the year was *Pampered Youth*, adapted from Booth Tarkington's Pulitzer Prize–winning novel *The Magnificent Ambersons*. Albert Smith acquired the motion picture rights to the book in 1921 but the project was shelved until the autumn of 1924, with Dave Smith directing Jay Pilcher's adaptation.

Alice Calhoun, the last player under contract to Vitagraph, was cast in the leading role of Isabel Amberson Minafer. Calhoun had never before played such a complex character, and over the course of the story progressed from her mid-teens to middle age. Allan Forrest played her longtime suitor Eugene Morgan and Cullen Landis was Isabel's adult son George. Fourteen-year-old Ben Alexander played George as a child and, according to at least one critic, walked away with the picture.

Jay Pilcher's screenplay changed the climax of Tarkington's story, introducing a massive tenement fire from which Morgan rescues Isabel. That act of heroism results in George repenting for repeatedly interfering with Eugene's romance with his mother. A four-story brick apartment building was constructed for the film. During the magnificent fire sequence the brick facade was designed to convincingly collapse in three stages. Although the movie was originally budgeted at $85,000, the spectacular sets and fire effects pushed the final cost up to $130,000. Production on *The Magnificent Ambersons* wrapped a few days before Christmas 1924, and a final cut was completed within days. By January 1, *The Magnificent Ambersons* was renamed *Pampered Youth.*

Moving Picture World lauded David Smith's direction, especially his fidelity to "bygone days" and the "finely handled fire sequence," which was deemed preferable to Tarkington's original ending. Most of the New York newspaper critics agreed. Today all that remains of the film is a half-hour condensation for the home movie market released in 1931 under the title *Two to One.* The production design is of a high order, as are Dave Smith's compositions and Steve Smith's gorgeous camera work and lighting. Tracking shots of a harness race are as fluid as those on the dance floor of the Amberson's enormous ballroom. The stunt work in the tenement fire, a horse and buggy spill, and George Minafer's car accident are equally impressive.

Pampered Youth grossed nearly $100,000 during its first five weeks in limited release. In several respects *Pampered Youth* approaches Orson Welles's *Magnificent Ambersons.* However, the performances in the latter film, especially Dolores Costello in her swan song as Isabel Amberson Minafer, are so accomplished as to render the Vitagraph players amateurish by comparison. It is ironic that both of the cinematic *Ambersons* exist today only in severely truncated form.[38]

While stepping up efforts to liquidate as much of Vitagraph's tangible assets as possible, Albert Smith instructed nephew Frank to take out a mortgage on the Hollywood property for $88,000 in order to finance Jim Blackton's latest production, $1,000 of which was paid at Blackton's insistence to two musicians providing mood music on the set for the actors—a first, and last, for Vitagraph.

While Blackton fiddled, Vitagraph burned. In late January, Albert Smith confided to Ronald Reader that it would take a financial miracle for the company to survive. Reader offered to help out by giving Smith 30,000 francs from his personal savings, the equivalent of a year's salary. Along with his selfless offer Ronald Reader expressed how grateful he was to his old friend for providing him with a career at Vitagraph. Smith was so deeply touched by Reader's kindness that later in the year he named his newborn son Ronald Albert Smith.

When George Smith in London got wind of Vitagraph's dire financial predicament he offered to mortgage all of his personal real estate and bonds in order to help pay off the company's outstanding loans, which as of February 14 totaled $415,989. Albert turned down brother George and friend Ronald's offers of assistance because exhibitor rentals in the United States for Vitagraph films in release during the month of February totaled $333,000, led by *Captain Blood*, *Pampered Youth*, and *The Beloved Brute*. George Smith contributed an additional $45,000 from earnings on his side of the pond.

At the beginning of April 1925, Vitagraph finally paid off the million-dollar loan from Guaranty Trust taken out in 1916 during the Benjamin Hampton debacle. Per the original agreement, stock in Vitagraph that had been held by Guaranty Trust during the term of the loan was reassigned to Albert Smith. Vitagraph still owed roughly $250,000 on other loans it had taken out to finance individual pictures. The company needed to step up its production of features in the hope of paying down the remaining debt and to enable it to compete with better-financed competitors.[39]

Publicly, Albert Smith announced in the trades that Vitagraph would be producing twenty features for the coming season. Privately, Vitagraph put the word out at the beginning of 1925 that it was interested in selling its studios. Offers poured in from a variety of interested parties including Sydney Cohen, former president of the MPTOA, who wanted to become an equal producing partner with Vitagraph. Johnnie Rock and Victor Smith urged Albert Smith to accept Cohen's offer after learning that MGM and First National had recently joined Famous Players' scheme to put Vitagraph out of business. Smith believed that a partnership involving Vitagraph, Cohen, and perhaps another producer like Warner Bros. could result in parity with the "Big Three," but Cohen was having difficulty securing an investment partner.

Another serious offer came from Herbert J. Yates, owner of Consolidated Film Industries and later founder of Republic Studios, who was willing to pay $250,000 cash for the processing laboratory at the Brooklyn studio. Vitagraph attorney A. I. Siegel advised Smith to reject the offer, instead advocating a proposal for a preferred stock issue from the Hamilton National Bank that could yield as much as one million dollars. The bank's representative was trying to rush the deal, which would involve a reorganization of the company that to Albert Smith must have seemed eerily familiar to the Hampton fiasco.

Sidney Cohen, the Hamilton National Bank, and Herbert J. Yates were each under the impression that they were on the verge of partnering with or purchasing a portion of Vitagraph. During the second week of April, Albert Smith prepared to make a deal, gaining the consent of Jim Blackton, who until then may not have been aware of the various proposals. Financial reports were prepared. For the week ended April 11, 1925, Vitagraph netted $47,765 in exhibitor rentals: $18,928 from domestic rentals, $15,483 from foreign rentals through the London office, and the remainder coming from the company's share of films made by six small independents that it distributed. That week Vitagraph only had $88,000 in the bank.[40]

A contract was prepared to bring Sidney Cohen into the fold, but Albert Smith stalled in executing it. He realized that partnering with Cohen would mean having to convince a significant number of independent exhibitors to align themselves with Vitagraph, which wasn't a sure thing. That wasn't nearly as daunting as the inevitable retribution it would bring from Adolph Zukor and the other monopolists. Smith was about to turn fifty years old and his doctor warned that he was driving himself to an early grave. He dreaded the workload and battles that lay ahead. On April 18 he received a telephone call from Harry Warner, president of Warner Bros. Warner wanted to know if Smith would be interested in selling him Vitagraph's distribution arm, formerly known as VLSE. Smith responded that in order to acquire Vitagraph's sales organization Warners would have to purchase the entire company "lock, stock and barrel." The next day while Harry Warner was getting approval from his brothers and their bank, Johnnie Rock and Jim Blackton gave Smith their approval to sell the company. Albert Smith and Harry Warner then spent the night hammering out the details of the sale in Smith's Manhattan hotel room.

On April 20, 1925, Warner Bros. purchased Vitagraph and all of its subsidiaries for $735,000, about $10,657,000 in 2020 dollars. The proceeds were split evenly among Albert Smith, Jim Blackton, and Johnnie Rock; however, Smith received an additional $25,000 from Warners for the common and preferred capital stock relinquished to him by Guaranty Trust less than three weeks earlier, and $40,880 on behalf of himself and Johnnie Rock as reimbursement for having personally financed two productions currently in release.

Warner Bros. also agreed to take over payments of outstanding bank loans used to finance Vitagraph features, along with mortgages on the Brooklyn and Los Angeles studios, and to honor oral and written commitments Vitagraph had with independent producers and stars. The Vitagraph partners received a down payment of $300,000 in cash, with the balance spread out in regular installments over the next few years.[41]

Virtually all of the newspapers and trades reporting on the sale noted that with the acquisition of Vitagraph's twenty-six exchange branches in the United States, four in Canada, ten in England, and ten in continental Europe, Warner Bros. was now one of the biggest producers and international distributors of motion pictures in the world. Within a week Vitagraph's advertising and publicity departments were moved from the Brooklyn studio to the Manhattan offices of Warner Bros. Warners also made the wise decision to retain Vitagraph's sales staff. In addition, Warners retained the Vitagraph trademark. Henceforth "Vitagraph" was used primarily as the name of Warner Bros.' distribution subsidiary.

Of the few Vitagraph productions released by Warner Bros. after the sale, the best was *Tides of Passion* directed by J. Stuart Blackton. *Tides of Passion* stars D. W. Griffith veteran Mae Marsh as the long-suffering wife of an errant sailor with a girl in every port. After her husband's death Marsh helps care for the baby born to one of his lovers, and saves the despondent mother from drowning herself in a raging sea. Blackton's half brother, William Stuart Adams, and Nick Musuraca photographed the climactic sequence amidst violent ocean waves and dangerous seaside rock formations. It is genuinely suspenseful because it was executed without special effects or stunt doubles.

Ten days after signing the contract with Warner Bros. and receiving a check for $100,000 as his share of the down payment, Jim Blackton borrowed $10,000 from Albert Smith. The Blacktons always lived beyond their considerable means. Paula Blackton was reportedly "still doing the social stuff from all accounts [and] doing her damndest to get in the [Los Angeles] smart set." Her husband signed a contract with Warner Bros. at the end of June to direct four feature films over the next twelve months budgeted at $75,000 apiece. He earned $500 per week for the first fifty-one weeks and $4,000 for the final week of his contract. Blackton was also guaranteed a minimum of $30,000 from the films' total gross, though Warners charged him a fee of $15,000 for studio and equipment rental on each production. Warners hired Marion Constance Blackton as scenario writer of her father's features, paying $1,500 per script. Blackton's casts included Dolores Costello, Julia Swayne Gordon, Florence Turner, and Wilfrid North.[42]

While Blackton was busy making his four movies at Warner Bros., Albert Smith kept tabs on Vitagraph productions still in circulation through colleagues who had been retained by Warners. During October and November 1925, Warners received 85,000 francs from Ronald Reader in Paris and $250,000 from London, mostly profits of *Captain Blood.* The London office continued to report on bookings and billings for *Captain Blood* and the other Vitagraph releases still in circulation, even after Warners terminated George Smith early in 1926. By 1927 *Captain Blood* had played in nearly two-thirds of England's movie theaters, far surpassing the bookings for *The Sea Hawk.*

Although he wasn't contractually obligated to do so, Albert Smith evenly divided the proceeds of the sale with Blackton and Johnnie Rock because it seemed the ethical thing to do. Motivated by the same sense of fairness, he prevailed on them to join him in paying George Smith and Ronald Reader for the small amount of stock they were forced to relinquish in the sale. By the end of the year Smith was comfortably dividing his time between his home in Hollywood and the cattle ranch, helping to raise the son and daughter he had with Hazel Neason and the two baby boys Lucille (aka Jean Paige) had given birth to.[43]

6

1926 and Beyond

Two months after purchasing Vitagraph, Warner Bros. acquired audio technology for synchronized sound in movies recently developed by Western Electric and Bell Laboratories. The familiar Vitagraph name was exploited in naming Warners' new talking picture production arm the "Vitaphone Corporation." The name change represented a fundamental shift in the emphasis of motion pictures over the next several years: no longer "life pictures" but now "living sounds."

The new owners converted one of Vitagraph's Brooklyn studios to a *soundstage*, but too much outside noise from automobile traffic and the elevated railroad leaked in, so new soundstages were built directly across the street from the Vitagraph property. Warner Bros. utilized the Vitagraph studio's processing lab, editing bays, and administrative offices until 1957. The Technicolor Corporation took over the property until 1964, when the facility was sold and converted into Yeshiva high schools for boys and girls. In 1982 it became a girls-only Orthodox Jewish school. The Vitagraph property was then sold in 2014 to a developer who demolished all of the buildings, most dating from 1907 to 1915. In its place a 302-unit apartment building, the "Vitagraph," was constructed. The only surviving structure from the original property is the brick smokestack with the inlaid lettering.

Vitagraph's Hollywood studio, renamed the Warner East Hollywood Studio Annex (WEHSA), was Warner's hub for motion picture production until 1929. Legend has it that Al Jolson's nightclub sequence for *The Jazz Singer* was photographed in WEHSA Stage Two. For most of its existence WEHSA served as a Warner Bros. back lot, its large tank utilized for Warners' remakes of *Captain Blood* and *The Sea Hawk*. In 1948 the fledgling ABC television network purchased the former Vitagraph studio for $350,000. Albert Smith and Antonio Moreno participated in ceremonies that renamed the facility ABC Television Center. For more than fifty years it was the home of the Los Angeles ABC-TV affiliate as well as of studios that broadcast such

The iconic smokestack, all that remains of the Brooklyn studio. Jeremy Hung, July 2016.

long-running network programs as *The Lawrence Welk Show*, *American Bandstand*, and *General Hospital*. The facility, currently known as The Prospect Studios, is still utilized for the production of television programs.

Warner Bros. retained "Vitagraph" as a trade name for the distribution of low-budget John Wayne Westerns in the early 1930s, some British imports, and Frank Capra's *Meet John Doe*, among others. Warners' last utilization of the Vitagraph name was in the on-screen closing credits for half of the Looney Tunes and Merry Melodies cartoons produced during the 1960s. It seems fitting that the longest-running series of animated motion pictures should conclude its final decade by displaying the name of the studio where the art form was invented.[1]

Not long after purchasing the rights to the technology that became Vitaphone, Harry Warner notified Blackton, Smith, and Rock that his company had to extend the length of the payment plan to them, which increased their premium by 6 percent. Commodore Blackton's directorial career ended in 1926 with the completion of the final film under his contract with Warners. The following year he began directing a wide-screen film produced by former Essanay chief George Spoor, but it was never completed, Spoor deeming it "an inferior picture." In 1928, several months before Warners had even completed their $300,000+ payments to Blackton, he was selling memberships in Chicago and Southern California Athletic Clubs, which quickly failed.

Vitagraph Hollywood studio front gate in 1924 and 2020. *Motion Picture Magazine*, July 1924; Kris and Celine Young, April 2020.

For his share of Vitagraph, the Commodore received the equivalent of $4,400,000 in 2020 dollars. According to his daughter, Blackton invested the money in a variety of risky business ventures, always first consulting his astrologer. By 1930 the Commodore was broke but kept it from wife Paula, who passed away that year from cancer. In order to pay the rent and put food on the table, Blackton began selling off the hundreds of silver trophies he had won as a yacht and motorboat racer. In 1931 when J. Stuart Blackton filed for bankruptcy he was unable to pay the filing fee.

Within a year Commodore Blackton was back in the movie game. Though living in poverty, he possessed a small collection of his old films, which served as the foundation for a documentary history of the movies. *The Film Parade* (aka *The March of the Movies*) was Blackton's "labor of love." Who better than someone that was there from the very beginning to tell its story? What movies he didn't have were recreated. Former director William P. S. Earle, Blackton's most loyal friend, lost all of his savings in the stock market crash and was reduced to selling vacuum cleaners door to door. But he still owned a movie camera, which he used to photograph the recreations. Blackton directed and appeared in the film as various fictional and historical characters, along with his now-adult children and their friends.

What survives of *The Film Parade* reveals Blackton's effort to inform and entertain. The recreations and some of the narration are played for laughs, executed in the same over-the-top manner as *And the Villain Still Pursued Her* and *Goodness Gracious.* The highlight of *The Film Parade* is Jim Blackton and A.E. Smith recreating the making of *The Battle of Manila Bay.* The old partners are obviously having the time of their lives. Blackton's daughter reported that Smith seldom saw her father after his "financial nosedive"; but that day seemed like old times, with plenty of reminiscing, laughter, and a few tears. According to Anthony Slide, *The Film Parade* played for only one day on the bottom of a double bill at Loew's Theatre in New York City, possibly its only theatrical screening. Blackton spent the rest of his life tinkering with the film and showing it to churches, fraternal orders, and women's clubs whenever he could hustle a booking.

Blackton was living with two of his children when youngest daughter Violet returned home following her brief marriage to pulp fiction writer extraordinaire Cornell Woolrich. In the mid-1930s Blackton wrote an autobiography, but his literary agent was unable to secure a publisher or even get it serialized in the *Saturday Evening Post.* The failure of *The Film Parade* and his autobiography seemed to indicate that no one was yet interested in looking back at the dawn of motion pictures. Undeterred, Blackton took a second stab at an autobiography, but that also failed to generate interest. Adding insult to injury, Blackton was photographed for a *March of Time* newsreel history of the movies but was left on the cutting room floor in favor of such "pioneers" as the Schenck brothers and Harry Warner.

The Commodore married twice after Paula's death. In the mid-1930s he talked his way into supervising a WPA project that enabled his large brood to move into a "charming rooming house," but the job lasted only eight months. For the rest of his life Blackton tried in vain to get a plethora of low-budget and oddball movie projects off the ground. Despite his dire poverty he remained cheerfully optimistic about making a comeback.

On a late afternoon while jaywalking across a busy Los Angeles boulevard, Blackton was struck by a car and died from his injuries four days later on August 17, 1941. Every obituary remembered him as one of the pioneers of the movies, who earned a million dollars from the sale of Vitagraph in 1925, declared bankruptcy in 1931, and went on relief in 1935. The editor of *Motion Picture Herald* recalled that Blackton's penchant for wearing lots of emerald jewelry during Vitagraph's salad days once caused General Film president Frank Dyer to arrive at a board meeting wearing sunglasses. Albert Smith eulogized his old friend as "an artist and a courageous experimenter.... What came from his hand had a gentle, subtle sweep."[2]

Ronald Reader, the man who had introduced Jim Blackton and Albert Smith, maintained friendships with both in the post-Vitagraph years, primarily via correspondence. Reader was Smith's closest friend, and many of their letters reflect their concern for Blackton's professional and financial well-being. Reader was also close with other members of the Smith family, including Albert's elderly father, to whom he mailed copies of the British humor magazine *Punch* every week; Dave Smith, who died in 1930 after years of suffering from tuberculosis of the kidneys; and "Uncle" George Smith, who distributed Cecil B. DeMille's independent films in England after getting the axe from Warner Bros. Reader was also a longtime friend of Georges Méliès, who endured financial hardship, much like Blackton, after making his last film in 1912. At the time of his second wedding in 1926, which Reader attended, Méliès was selling toys and candy from a stall at a Paris railway station. Albert Smith and Georges Méliès kept in touch with each other through Reader; it also appears that Reader was instrumental in spurring the French film industry to honor Méliès, which led to a major retrospective of his work at the Salle Pleyel in 1929.

Ronald Reader was the last of Vitagraph's old guard to be employed by Warner Bros., remaining in charge of the Paris office until December 1927. He and his wife retired to the Isle of Wight but wintered in warmer climates, including an extended visit to the Smiths in 1929. Reader wrote of that time "it will always be our best memory of America." Through the years,

Smith supplied "Dear Old Ron" with photos and updates of his namesake, whom the doting father called "the sweetest dispositioned" of all his children. The same could be said of his oldest friend.[3]

Albert Smith took a fatherly interest in Johnnie Rock long before Pop Rock's death in 1916. Like Ronald Reader, Rock was concerned about Jim Blackton, and maintained friendships with Dave, Vic, and George Smith. Rock and his wife spent their first post-Vitagraph winter living on a boat while deep-sea fishing off the Florida Keys. He eventually retired to the colder climes of upstate New York after failing to heed Albert Smith's advice and losing most of his Vitagraph payout to unscrupulous business partners.[4]

Unlike Jim Blackton and Johnnie Rock, Albert Smith fared better with his investments, though it didn't start out that way. Late in 1925 Smith finally found a buyer for his Oyster Bay, Long Island estate. He sold it at a loss, but at least he was paid cash. Smith then built a twenty-room home and added a hundred-acre orange grove and reservoir to the ranch in San Diego County. He acquired a forty-eight-unit Hollywood apartment building "and gave it new life with his artistic touches, turning a white elephant into a swank money-making operation." In 1931 Smith purchased a mostly vacant apartment building that had the misfortune of opening just months before the stock market crash of 1929. He purportedly paid $750,000 for the Chateau Marmont and turned it into a hotel, redecorating each room with valuable antique furniture he and wife Lucille purchased at estate sales in the midst of the Great Depression. From the moment Smith repurposed the Chateau Marmont, it became a destination for celebrities and bohemians, and has remained so ever since.

Although they continued to reside at their Hollywood home, after church on Sundays the Smith family would dine on lamb in Chateau Marmont's main floor drawing room overlooking the garden, the patriarch impeccably dressed "from starched collar to spats." When America entered World War II Smith's three sons enlisted, and the last of his daughters got married. At sixty-seven and suffering from high blood pressure, Smith sold the hotel and began spending most of his time at his home in Hollywood.

Albert occasionally regaled Lucille's women's clubs with stories of his adventures with the Rough Riders in the Spanish-American War and with Richard Harding Davis during the Boer War. In 1944 he began a friendship with Twentieth Century Fox cinematographer Charles G. Clarke. Clarke's hobby was early cinema and he preferred learning its history directly from the pioneers. Smith's letters to Clarke were more detailed and informative than the colorful yarns he spun at the women's clubs or in occasional newspaper interviews.

Charles Clarke was instrumental in Albert Smith, Col. Selig, Thomas Armat, and George K. Spoor receiving honorary Academy Awards for their pioneering contributions to the American motion picture industry. On March 20, 1948, from the stage of the Shrine Auditorium, Academy president Jean Hersholt choked back tears as he introduced his former employer Albert Smith to the audience. Smith told the audience about starting Vitagraph with Blackton on a shoestring and how two years later they made *The Battle of Santiago Bay.* He concluded his remarks by thanking "the Academy for remembering the forgotten man."

Shortly after receiving the award, Albert Smith sat for a series of oral history interviews conducted in his Hollywood home by Howard Walls, curator of the Academy of Motion Picture Arts and Sciences motion picture collection. Most of the interview, totaling nearly eight hours, consists of Walls reading titles from Thomas Edison rental catalogs from 1903 to 1904 and asking for Smith's recollections. In spite of that incongruity, Smith relates many personal experiences, and provides knowledge and insight regarding the development of motion pictures in general and Vitagraph in particular. This information isn't available anywhere else.

Coming on the heels of the honorary Oscar and Academy interviews, Doubleday asked Smith to write his autobiography. Smith was clearly more concerned with entertaining than he was in getting the facts straight. When *Two Reels and a Crank* was published in 1952, critics noted Smith's affability and decency in not maligning anyone. The *Los Angeles Times* called the book "the best ever to come from a pioneer." However, the review presumes to correct the book on several points. Unfortunately, these "corrections" are often inaccurate themselves. The *New York Times*'s movie critic wrote that *Two Reels* will "fascinate and delight anyone who has the slightest interest in screen history," but the greater part of the review is spent correcting errors while characterizing Smith and the other pioneers as "candid opportunists . . . not a great deal more respectable than train robbers." By comparison, the reviews for the biography that William Fox paid Upton Sinclair to write about him, and Adolph Zukor's autobiography that came out a year after *Two Reels* do not call attention to *any* of those books' copious self-serving prevarications, many of which express malevolence toward Vitagraph and many others.

Two Reels and a Crank inspired historians, former colleagues, and fans to reach out to Albert Smith, but he was often slow in responding. In 1954

Smith wrote *Shakespeare in Silent Film* author Robert H. Ball: "All the pep I used to have is now like the last rose of summer and I have been physically ailing for the last year." Albert Smith died at his Hollywood home on August 1, 1958, at the age of eighty-three, survived by wife Lucille. He was remembered as the "inventor of the early Vitagraph projector and one of the real motion picture pioneers."[5]

Between 1926 and 1956, Commodore Blackton and Albert Smith organized several reunions in Los Angeles for their Vitagraph colleagues. At the first gathering Blackton screened scenes featuring Florence Turner, Maurice Costello, James Morrison, Earle Williams, and Anita Stewart, all of whom were in attendance, as well as clips of "absent friends" John Bunny and Wallace Reid that "elicited much applause." It was a jolly affair with everyone laughing at the clothing and hairstyles they used to wear, as well as the corny intertitles of the films that Blackton confessed to have written. For some of the attendees, the April 1926 reunion and the one that followed in December were the highpoints of their year.

Florence Turner had become destitute following the collapse of her London-based production company in 1916. Marion Davies learned of Turner's plight in 1924 and came to her rescue, giving the former Vitagraph Girl a role in one of her films, and briefly engaging her as a scenario reader for her production company. Throughout the remainder of the silent era Florence Turner had small roles in a number of forgotten movies, an exception being her appearance as Buster Keaton's mother in *College.* Her sporadic work in talkies was confined to noncredited extra work until her health deteriorated and she became a ward of the Motion Picture Country Home, where she died in 1946.

Maurice Costello had also fallen on hard times prior to the 1926 reunion. His only motion picture employment in 1925 was a supporting role in an independent film in which Florence Turner also appeared. As was the case with the majority of silent movie stars who clung to the business, Costello worked mostly as an extra in talkies. He moved into the Motion Picture Country Home in 1946 and died four years later. Costello and Turner, the first international movie stars, were also the first casualties of a fickle public that discarded them for new favorites. As the *New York Times* noted, the former "idol of American girlhood . . . was romantic and dashing and he had his day in the sun."

Vitagraph's last great international star, Larry Semon, died in 1928. One year after leaving the company Semon realized his longtime ambition of directing, cowriting, coproducing, and starring (as the Scarecrow) in a feature-length slapstick version of *The Wizard of Oz.* It was a colossal failure that Semon never really recovered from, professionally or emotionally. Nearly $500,000 in debt, Semon suffered a nervous breakdown and died in a desert sanitarium at the age of thirty-nine.

In 1936 Commodore Blackton reunited his underemployed former colleagues with a more practical purpose in mind: to raise their visibility in the hope that it would lead to work in an industry that had forgotten them. Blackton called the endeavor the Associated Cinema Stars' Club. The initial gathering was held on May 27, 1936. A dinner dance took place at the end of August in the grand ballroom of the Biltmore Hotel. It was attended by "more than a hundred stars of yesterday," as well as D. W. Griffith and many current movie favorites. Among the attendees were Flora Finch and Florence Lawrence, both earning weekly salaries of $75 as extras at MGM.

After Vitagraph dismissed Flora Finch in 1916, she set up her own production company but that venture failed after one year. For the remainder of her career Finch freelanced as an uncredited extra or bit player, with a few exceptions, most notably as Laura LaPlante's Aunt Susan in the seminal haunted house comedy *The Cat and the Canary.* When Finch died in 1940 she was eulogized as "the cinema's first immensely popular comedienne."

After leaving IMP, Florence Lawrence starred in short films for Lubin and other companies. In 1915 she suffered severe burns and other injuries while filming a scene, which incapacitated her for several years. Upon regaining her health Lawrence discovered the movies had moved on without her. Three days after Christmas 1938 Florence Lawrence swallowed a fatal combination of ant paste and cough syrup. Her suicide note read, in part, "I am tired. Hope this works." She was five days shy of her fifty-third birthday.

On October 21, 1956, Albert and Lucille Smith organized an afternoon tea party in their Hollywood home to celebrate the sixtieth anniversary of the founding of Vitagraph. Over one hundred members of the Vitagraph family attended what turned out to be their final reunion. A veteran *Los Angeles Times* correspondent noted the "heart-warming intimacy" of the gathering, as friends and colleagues who hadn't seen each other in years pored over photo albums, recalling what had been for nearly all the best years of their professional lives. No longer the aloof studio executive, Albert Smith expressed gratitude for his Vitagraph family. "You only need to meet today the personnel we had in former years to realize what wonderful people they are." Among those in attendance were Paul Kelly, Paul Panzer, Clara Kimball Young, and Anita Stewart.

Two and a half weeks after the Vitagraph reunion Paul Kelly suffered a fatal heart attack at his Beverly Hills home. He had been one of the few child actors to make the successful transition to adult roles. However, in the late 1920s Kelly's career came to an abrupt halt when he served two years in prison for killing the husband of his lover during a drunken brawl. He survived the tragedy and scandal to resume his career as a character actor in such classic films as *The Roaring Twenties* and *The High and the Mighty.* Kelly also enjoyed a long and fruitful career on Broadway, culminating in the Tony Award for Best Actor in *Command Decision.*

Paul Panzer's first movie was shot at Vitagraph's rooftop studio on Nassau Street. He starred as Romeo opposite Florence Lawrence's Juliet, was the recipient of *The Thieving Hand,* and played the beleaguered smoker in *Princess Nicotine.* Panzer's most notable post-Vitagraph role was as the villain in the 1914 serial *The Perils of Pauline.* In 1934 Panzer became a salaried extra under contract to Warner Bros. He outlived Albert Smith by two weeks, passing away in August 1958.

A Vitagraph star that attended the 1920s reunions but was unable to make it to the 1956 gathering was Norma Talmadge, who by then was living in seclusion; she was confined to a wheelchair, suffering from acute arthritis. Talmadge was one of the few performers to enjoy even greater success after Vitagraph, thanks to the acumen of her producer-husband Joseph M. Schenck. Director Clarence Brown called Talmadge "a tragedy of talking pictures." Her Brooklyn accent is on full display in 1929's *New York Nights.* Her attempt to mask the accent the following year in *Du Barry, Woman of Passion* resulted in "a very affected imitation of stage speech . . . highly self conscious and artificial." It was Talmadge's last performance and may have served as an inspiration for the Lina Lamont character in *Singin' in the Rain.* Norma Talmadge died on Christmas Eve 1957.

After leaving Vitagraph, Clara Kimball Young was sued for divorce by husband James following the revelation of her affair with Lewis Selznick. She in turn sued Selznick for withholding profits from her movies. Her career was over by the early 1920s. After auctioning off her estate in 1932 Young returned in talkies doing extra work and occasional supporting roles, such as the 1938 exploitation film *The Wages of Sin,* playing bordello madam "Fat Pearl." Her most widely seen work is as the society matron in the 1936 Three Stooges short *Ants in the Pantry.* Clara Kimball Young died penniless in 1960 at the Motion Picture Country Home.

Anita Stewart was more fortunate than most of her colleagues. She continued to freelance through the end of the silent era and then retired from the screen, having married a wealthy banker following her divorce from Rudolph Cameron. Stewart died in 1961 in her Beverly Hills home.

James Morrison appeared in only seven films after *Captain Blood* before returning to the New York stage. He lived modestly in a Greenwich Village apartment and taught speech and drama for seventeen years at a private girls' school in Brooklyn. Morrison died on his eighty-sixth birthday at a New York nursing home.

Pretty Margaret Gibson served two stints with Vitagraph, from 1913 to 1915 and 1917 to 1918. In early 1917 while under contract to another company, Gibson, clad only in a brief kimono, was arrested in a raid on a "house of ill fame" that catered to Japanese clientele in downtown Los Angeles. During the investigation that followed she was linked to an opium dealer also apprehended at the house. Despite much damaging evidence, a jury found her not guilty of "lewd and immoral conduct." As Patricia Palmer she appeared in at least one film opposite Mary Miles Minter at Paramount in 1922. The following year Gibson was arrested for extortion after coercing a man to accompany her to Tijuana and then blackmailing him for violating the Mann Act. In court it was learned that she was part of a blackmail ring that included her mother, but less than a week into the proceedings the district attorney abruptly dropped the charges. In 1924 Gibson and the opium dealer were arrested for robbery following a gunfight with police. Ten years later the troubled woman fled the country for Singapore. She married an oil executive but returned to the States ahead of her husband, who died in a Japanese air attack in 1940. In 1964 Margaret Gibson suffered a fatal heart attack. In the throes of death she told a neighbor to call for a priest because she needed to confess to killing her former costar William Desmond Taylor. She died before the priest could hear her confession.

Within days of its purchase of Vitagraph, Warner Bros. signed the beautiful Costello sisters to contracts. Helen, who now went by Helene, had the distinction of starring in the last movie released as "A Vitagraph production," which commenced shooting shortly after the takeover. She also starred in *Lights of New York*, the first all-talking feature. As an adult, Helene's performances were wooden and self-conscious, and her career short-lived. She died at age fifty from alcohol and drug abuse with sister Dolores at her side. Dolores was one of Warner Bros.' biggest stars during the late silent era, during which time she was married to John Barrymore. Following in her

Margaret Gibson. *Who's Who in the Film World*, 1914.

grandmother's footsteps, Drew Barrymore was already acting at the age of four when Dolores died in 1979.

Though never placing among the top ten in popularity polls, Corinne Griffith was regarded as one of the biggest movie stars of the 1920s. Griffith's production company released through First National. She purportedly earned $10,000 per week in the post-Vitagraph years and invested wisely, eventually owning a "Los Angeles real estate firm and athletic club for men, as well as considerable property, including all four corners of the intersection of South Beverly Drive and Wilshire Blvd," which commanded some of the highest rental fees in America. An autobiography of her early years, *Papa's Delicate Condition*, was made into a motion picture starring Jackie Gleason in 1963.

Corinne Griffith was married four times, including a twenty-two-year union to George Preston Marshall, founder and owner of the Washington Redskins football team. In 1965 she married dancer-singer Danny Scholl. The groom was forty-four years old, the bride seventy-one. After five weeks of marriage they separated and Griffith filed for divorce. Scholl asked for alimony and Griffith countered, revealing that the marriage was never consummated. She testified in court as being "approximately 51" years old. She also claimed she was not Corinne Griffith at all but actually the actress's former stand-in who replaced the real Griffith after she died in Mexico in the 1930s. Griffith's old Vitagraph pal Betty Blythe was brought into the courtroom and testified that the woman was in fact Corinne Griffith. The judge brushed aside Griffith's prevarications to grant her a divorce and deny Scholl's claim for alimony. Her courtroom antics inspired Tom Tryon's novella *Fedora*, which served as the basis for Billy Wilder's penultimate film. Corinne Griffith died in 1979 at the age of eighty-four, alone in a Santa Monica hospital not far from where her movie career began at the original western Vitagraph studio. Her estate was valued at $150 million.[6]

When Larry Semon stopped making films, his loyal cinematographer Hans Koenekamp found a new career creating and photographing special effects at Warner Bros., beginning with Max Reinhardt's production of *A Midsummer Night's Dream*. Other credits include *The Sea Hawk*, *The Fountainhead*, *Strangers on a Train*, and the truly amazing *Beast with Five Fingers*, of which he was justifiably proud. For years Koenekamp was the last surviving link to Vitagraph until he passed away at the age of one hundred in 1992.

By the time Hans Koenekamp died, Vitagraph had long since disappeared from the public consciousness. If mentioned at all in histories of the cinema, Vitagraph is usually lumped together with other meaningless names, Selig and Lubin, as members of Edison's Trust, a cabal of bigoted ignoramuses whose involvement in the movies was so inconsequential it does not merit further investigation. "They had never been showmen; they had not understood the public because they were not in tune with the public; they had stood on the side-lines and watched the procession stream by, never suspecting the longings and aspirations hidden beneath the mob's mental laziness. They were scientists, businessmen, and lawyers; they had been stripped of their power by men of the people." The quote is from *A History of the Movies*, published in 1931. The preface to a 1969 reissue declares, "That it is the best history of the movie business to date there can be no doubt." *A History of the Movies* superseded two earlier tomes to become the primary text upon which later accounts of early American cinema are based, such as Bardèche and Brasillach's *Histoire du Cinéma*, originally published in 1935. The author of *A History of the Movies* was Benjamin Hampton.

Hampton's principal reasons for writing *A History of the Movies* were to generate income and create a false narrative that would mask both his failure to secure control of Vitagraph and his later washout as a filmmaker. Hampton was a promoter; *A History of the Movies* promotes Hampton. His version of the events involving his association with Vitagraph and the Mary Pickford affair are utterly at odds with the surviving correspondence, memoranda, and business records to which he was a party. *A History of the Movies* also fails to reveal Hampton's role as a covert informant in the FTC's case against Adolph Zukor. Paradoxically, Hampton's *History* attributes Adolph Zukor's dominance in the industry not to any illegalities but rather to his being "an incomparable showman with an amazing flair for sensing audience reactions long before the movie audiences themselves knew what they wanted. [Zukor] persistently outsmarted all other players of the game."

Hampton's lionization of Zukor and repudiation of Vitagraph and the other pioneers has been accepted as irrefutable because of his "status as an industry insider, his intimate knowledge of its business practices, and his clear, journalistic prose." It is indicative of a problem that has plagued film history scholarship from the very beginning: the tendency to accept the statements of the moguls and other professionals operating in the "studio era" as true, especially when their assertions support the dominant historical narrative, a narrative that they themselves created. Adolph Zukor mischaracterized Vitagraph as "producing rude pictures," and echoed Benjamin Hampton's mendacities by claiming, among other things: "What [the members of The Trust] were making belonged entirely to technicians. What I [made]—that was show business. That required actors, producers, a script—which of course was strange to these people. . . . With them the idea didn't develop from the showman angle."[7]

The truth is that Albert Smith and J. Stuart Blackton, along with fellow pioneer William Selig, are the only American producers to have hands-on experience with every facet of filmmaking, from building their own cameras and projectors, to writing, directing, photographing, editing, and acting in their own productions, to developing the negative and projecting the results to paying audiences. Adolph Zukor never engaged in *any* of these activities. He was a furrier who, like Pop Rock, got involved with the movies because it seemed like a good investment.

In the end Zukor didn't crush Vitagraph but his many ploys hastened its departure from the motion picture industry. Hampton's meddling was just as destructive to Vitagraph's financial health, though not fatal. Adolph Zukor and Benjamin Hampton did, however, set in motion nearly a century of erroneous film scholarship by disparaging Vitagraph and the other pioneer producers. Sharing in culpability are Zukor's contemporaries who claimed the achievements of the pioneers as their own, and their many biographers and historians who "print the legend" without bothering to check if it is true. Hampton, Zukor, et al. may not have destroyed Vitagraph and the others, but they did deny them their rightful place in the historical record.

Albert Smith and J. Stuart Blackton alone were responsible for Vitagraph's demise.

Long before embarking on his five-and-a-half-year hiatus from the company, Blackton abdicated his responsibility as co-owner by deferring to Smith in all business matters, even when he believed his partner was wrong. Greed compelled Smith to put his trust in outsiders who knew nothing about the motion picture industry. There were other missteps. Smith, Blackton, and Rock should never have kept all of Vitagraph's foreign profits for themselves. Had they taken less and dedicated a percentage to theater acquisition and higher salaries for key creative personnel, Zukor wouldn't have been able to touch them. Smith was also guilty of overreacting to the Hampton fiasco by putting his trust only in family and old friends. Early on, he and Blackton trained cameramen, projectionists, directors, and writers. However, neither man mentored anyone to succeed himself or even share the load.

Vitagraph reflected the attitudes and values of the generation that came of age in the early twentieth century more successfully than any other studio. But as the partners grew older, they and their movies grew more sentimental. After World War I Albert Smith produced fewer contemporary dramas in favor of more historical stories. For the first dozen years of cinema J. Stuart Blackton was the most brilliantly creative filmmaker in America. As he grew older and more prosperous, Blackton became less inventive and, instead, stodgier and more complacent. Audiences have always gravitated toward stories with characters that share their sensibilities. Unfortunately neither Smith nor Blackton understood or attempted to reach the Jazz Age generation. Thus it seems likely that Vitagraph would never have survived the advent of the talkies, with or without interference from Hampton or Zukor.

In 1927 the FTC found Paramount guilty of operating as a monopoly and, thus, in violation of the Clayton Antitrust Act. It ordered Adolph Zukor to divest himself of his theaters, but he ignored the edict and carried on as usual, knowing that the FTC had no legal authority to enforce its decision. It wasn't until 1948 that the Supreme Court finally declared that Paramount, MGM/Loews, Warner Bros., Twentieth Century Fox, and RKO constituted a monopoly. In what became known as the Paramount Decision, the Big Five consequently divested themselves of the exhibition component of their business, after which they more closely resembled the MPPC. Precious few have ever criticized or castigated any of the Big Five for monopolizing production, distribution, and exhibition. However, Vitagraph and the other reluctant members of the Patents Company have been subjected to unceasing criticism for far less. Faulty scholarship has resulted in one of the most egregious double standards tainting the canon of film history. There is no reason why it should be allowed to continue.[8]

For all of their shortcomings, J. Stuart Blackton, Albert Smith, and William T. Rock, like William Selig and Siegmund Lubin, were honorable men, and, with few exceptions, were well liked. Earle Williams remarked that Vitagraph wasn't "like the usual run of actors and actresses. . . . We are just like one huge family." James Morrison concurred. "It was a family. It really was. The people there were very fond of each other." Anita Stewart confessed, "Working for [Louis B.] Mayer was not like working at the Vitagraph. There we were like one big happy family. Here, it was all work and no play and I guess I was a little spoiled." Vitagraph's happy family was the product of Blackton, Smith, and Rock.[9]

Like every other production company, Vitagraph's most tangible legacy is the motion pictures it made. Early in its history the company maintained prints and negatives of its movies in two storerooms across the hall from its film rental offices in the Morton Building at 116 Nassau Street. On Saturday afternoon, July 2, 1910, nitrate films erupted in flames in one of the storerooms. The fire spread rapidly. Within an hour Vitagraph lost all of its pre-1910 movies, over one thousand reels in all. All the company had left were the movies that happened to be playing in theaters at the time of the fire and a handful of prints Blackton kept for home screenings.

The fire prompted Vitagraph to build fireproof storage vaults in Brooklyn and Hollywood. In 1925 Warner Bros. took possession of the surviving Vitagraph films. Until 1948 Albert Smith was unaware that Warners had cut down a dozen or so of the later Vitagraph features and sold 10-to-30-minute abridgments to the home market in the late 1920s and early 1930s. There is no record of Warner Bros. ever having informed Smith of an even more deplorable practice, its destruction of the Vitagraph film archive during the 1940s. In 1942 the original eleven-reel domestic negative of *Captain Blood* was deliberately incinerated; the following year a Warner bureaucrat ordered the liquidation of *The Saw Mill* and several other Larry Semon comedies, as well as *A Woman's Sacrifice* starring Corinne Griffith. Albert Smith must have had an inkling of what happened because he died believing there were no longer any prints of Vitagraph movies in existence.

As it turns out, 20 percent of the approximately thirty-five hundred productions made by Vitagraph are known to have survived into the present. This includes sixteen prints of *The Sawmill* scattered throughout archives in North America, Western Europe, Scandinavia, and South America; a new print struck from what may have been the 35-mm foreign release negative of *A Virgin's Sacrifice*; and a new 35-mm print of *Captain Blood* that was created in 2017 by combining surviving copies, though it is still nearly two and a half reels shy of its original running length.

The British Film Institute is the largest archive of Vitagraph films in the world, with over three hundred titles, a testament to the company's popularity in the United Kingdom. The Library of Congress archive contains nearly two hundred Vitagraph titles in addition to thirteen one-reel compilations of brief fragments from 398 films produced between 1905 and 1909 that were originally deposited on paper prints for copyright protection. In terms of length, the fragments average only about 5 percent of a given film.

In the mid-1980s the international film community learned that the Netherlands Filmmuseum (aka Eyefilm) possessed 120 Vitagraph titles in its archive, the third-largest collection in the world. Eighty of the prints originally belonged to Dutch film distributor and cinema owner Jean Desmet, many of which are beautifully preserved in their original color tints. The Desmet Collection helped spur a major retrospective, *Cinema Under the Vitagraph Flag*, the centerpiece of the 1987 "Days of Silent Film" (Giornate) Festival in Pordenone, Italy. Eyefilm has recently made the Desmet Collection available for viewing free of charge on the Internet. Many private collectors around the world have also posted their Vitagraph films. It is hoped that more will follow suit so that cinephiles can discover for themselves the joys and wonders of the company that more than any other defined American cinema.[10]

Conclusion

Vitagraph's success was rooted in the knowledge gained by J. Stuart Blackton and Albert E. Smith as vaudeville entertainers. Partnering different family-friendly performance skills made them more marketable. That same consideration guided the variety of films they made, which was fundamental in defining commercial cinema during its most prosperous era. That variety, stemming from their diversity of opinions, values, and talents, helped them reach a much larger audience than either man could have otherwise achieved alone.

Blackton was a humanist, raising daughter Marian to be "a nice little atheist." He once said of *The Battle Cry of Peace*: "The purpose of this picture is to make people think—to realize that preparedness cannot be half-hearted. . . . To prepare half-hearted is like saying, 'God Bless You,'" a meaningless salutation to Blackton's way of thinking.[1]

Smith, on the other hand, was a man of Christian faith, which guided much of his conduct and understanding. One time some friends rewarded an unsuspecting Smith with the proceeds of a bet they made on a boat race that he won. He promptly gave one-third of the winnings to his crew, one-third to the opposing crew, and one-third to the man that designed the boat. Smith explained, "My folks were very religious. To bet was a very wicked thing to do. To take money that you hadn't really earned was a terrible sin. . . . I'm a grown man now but I still feel that I couldn't take money that I didn't earn."[2]

The diversity of the partners resulted in a variety of subjects and sensibilities that in its totality represented far more of the moviegoing public than perhaps any other production company in history.

It took nearly twenty years to define and establish the American motion picture. Albert Smith was justified in believing that the generation of filmmakers that followed, "the so-called pioneers" of the history books, merely copied "everything we had done." Laemmle, Fox, Zukor, Mayer, and the

Warner Bros. succeeded *because* they copied and fine-tuned so much of what the actual pioneers had created.[3]

Maurice Costello best described what it was like to be a member of Vitagraph when the movies were new. "It was warm in those days, folksy and intimate. . . . It wasn't 'What have you done?' that counted, then, it was 'What can you do?' We weren't dealing in pasts, you see, but in futures."[4]

Unlike the Vitagraph pioneers, we now have 125 years of motion picture history to learn from. As attendance and interest in the movies continues to decline, it might well be worth considering a return to the strategies that were originally utilized by Vitagraph in order to recapture a larger audience that is inclusive of all.

Acknowledgments

In addition to his friendship and encouragement, Kevin Brownlow generously shared his print and photographic archives, and collection of 9.5 films, some of which were projected at London's amazing Cinema Museum. Thanks to Martin Humphries, Bob Goeghegan, Caroline Buck Brownlow, and everyone else who made those screenings such a memorable experience.

Thank you to the unsung heroes of the archives: Faye Thompson, Kristine Krueger, Jenny Romero, and all my friends at the Academy of Motion Picture Arts and Sciences Margaret Herrick Library; May Hong Haduong, AMPAS Film Archive; Michael Pogorzelski, AMPAS Pickford Center for Motion Picture Study; Jerry Hatfield, Josie Walters-Johnson, Rob Stone, Library of Congress; Kathleen Dickson, British Film Institute Reuben Library; Anne Simon, Lobster Films; Brett Service, Warner Bros. Archives at USC; Julianna Jenkins, James Fiala, Javier Garibay, Molly Haigh, Cesar Reyes, Charles E. Young Library, UCLA; Mark Quigley, UCLA Film & Television Archive; Carey Stumm, National Archives at New York City; Sophia Lorent, George Eastman Museum; Paul Israel, Thomas A. Edison Papers, Rutgers University; Ashley Swinnerton, Museum of Modern Art; Betty Uyeda, Beth Werling, John Cahoon, Natural History Museum of Los Angeles County Seaver Center; Marc Wanamaker, Bison Films; Edward R. Murrow High School; Christina Rice and Edward Acosta, Los Angeles Public Library.

This book couldn't have been written without the love and support of my family, beginning with my mother, Sandra, brothers Jay and Ricci, nephew Josh, Corey Floyd, Tony and Susan Frangello, Deni Garlitz, Desi Harris, and Terry Edlen, and Toni Romano, as well as friends William Ahearn, Mike Bencivenga, Randy Carter, Cornerstone Community Church of God, the Covells, Robert Crane, Mark Dickens, Joel Dinerstein, Tom Gammill, Frank Garrett, Mark Gleason, Jeremy Hung, Jim Kenah, Pancho Mansfield, Rich Nathanson, Henry Parke, Bruce Pross, Max Pross, Brenda Salmon, Nick Searcy, Ray Tennenbaum, Karl Tiedemann, Jerome Vered, Brandon Wade,

Neal Wilde, Kris and Celine Young, and absent friends Jim Eiseman, Lou Filosa, John Mandel, and Ken Skapik. God Bless you all!

Thanks also to Patrick McGilligan, Anne Dean Dotson, Stephen Bottomore, and everyone at the University Press of Kentucky, especially Ashley Runyon, Victoria Robinson, Sarah Olson, and Janet Yoe for making *Vitagraph: America's First Great Motion Picture Studio* a reality.

Notes

Introduction

1. For instance, see David A. Cook, *A History of Narrative Film*, 3rd ed. (New York: W. W. Norton, 1996), 32, 36, 47; Louis Giannetti and Scott Eyman, *Flashback: A Brief History of Film*, 5th ed. (Upper Saddle River, NJ: Prentice Hall, 2006), 22, 37; David Bordwell, Janet Staiger, and Kristin Thompson, *The Classical Hollywood Cinema: Film Style and Mode of Production to 1960* (New York: Columbia University Press, 1985), xv, 10, 136, 143; Douglas Gomery, *The Hollywood Studio System* (New York: St. Martin's, 1986), 2, 5, 193; Thomas Schatz, *The Genius of the System: Hollywood Filmmaking in the Studio Era* (New York: Pantheon, 1988), 4, 7–8, 15; and Neal Gabler, *An Empire of Their Own: How the Jews Invented Hollywood* (New York: Doubleday, 1989), 1–2, 5, 7, 24–26, 30–31, 40–44, 53, 59–61, 66–69. These texts rely on such foundational work as Benjamin B. Hampton, *A History of the American Film Industry* (New York: Covici-Friede, 1931), 31–33, 36, 56, 63, 67, 69, 73, 77, 79, 83, 85, 87, 90, 108, 119, 125, 137; Maurice Bardèche and Robert Brasillach, *The History of Motion Pictures*, ed. and trans. Iris Barry (New York: W. W. Norton and the Museum of Modern Art, 1938), 9–29, 32, 82; and Lewis Jacobs, *The Rise of the American Film* (New York: Harcourt, Brace, 1939), 8, 49–50, 84–86, 90–91, 93, 159, 204, 263.

1. 1875–1904

1. J. Stuart Blackton, "'Hollywood with Its Hair Down' or Hollywood Memories; Forty Years of the Movies," ms., unnumbered page, 1, J. Stuart Blackton papers, Special Collections, Margaret Herrick Library, Academy of Motion Picture Arts and Sciences; Donald Dewey, *Buccaneer, James Stuart Blackton and the Birth of the American Movies* (Lanham, MD: Rowman & Littlefield, 2016), 1, 4–5, 9–10, 12; Anthony Slide and Alan Gevinson, *The Big V: A History of the Vitagraph Company* (Metuchen, NJ: Scarecrow, 1987), 17; Albert Smith audio interview, tapes 1, 6, Albert E. Smith Papers (Collection 2004), Department of Special Collections, Charles E. Young Research Library, University of California, Los Angeles; "The Story of the Film, A Faversham Pioneer," *Faversham Worth East Kent News*, Mar. 8, 1924, Box 1, Albert E. Smith Papers (Collection 2004), Department of Special Collections, Charles E.

Young Research Library, University of California, Los Angeles; Albert E. Smith, *Two Reels and a Crank* (Garden City, NY: Doubleday, 1952), 26–27.

2. Joe Laurie, Jr., *Vaudeville, from the Honky-Tonks to the Palace* (New York: Henry Holt, 1953), 333–41.

3. Smith, *Two Reels and a Crank*, 26–27, 28; Smith tape 9; Letter Feb. 12, 1953, Smith to Al Munroe, Box 10, Albert E. Smith Papers (Collection 2004), Department of Special Collections, Charles E. Young Research Library, University of California, Los Angeles.

4. Dewey, *Buccaneer*, 14; William Basil Courtney, "History of Vitagraph," *Motion Picture News*, Feb. 7, 1925, 542; Letter Feb. 23, 1953, Smith to JL Moran, Box 10, Albert E. Smith Papers (Collection 2004), Department of Special Collections, Charles E. Young Research Library, University of California, Los Angeles; Smith, *Two Reels and a Crank*, 27, 28; Blackton, "Hollywood with Its Hair Down," unnumbered page.

5. Smith, *Two Reels and a Crank*, 13; Albert F. McLean, Jr., *American Vaudeville as Ritual* (Lexington: University Press of Kentucky, 1965), viii.

6. Smith, *Two Reels and a Crank*, 28–31; Smith tape 9.

7. Letter, Smith to Munroe; Letter Apr. 29, 1944, Smith to Clarke, Box 10, Albert E. Smith Papers (Collection 2004), Department of Special Collections, Charles E. Young Research Library, University of California, Los Angeles; Blackton, "Hollywood with Its Hair Down," 37, 46; "Saturday Church News," *Brooklyn Eagle*, Oct. 12, 1895, 4; "Boys' Brigade Entertainment," *Brooklyn Eagle*, Feb. 28, 1896, 7; "Benefit to Mr. Bedingfield," *Brooklyn Eagle*, Jul. 9, 1896, 4; Albert Smith testimony, United States of America vs. Motion Picture Patents Company et al., Nov. 18, 1913, 1740.

8. Shadow imagery is an essential component of Plato's "Allegory of the Cave" in Book 7 of *The Republic.* Richard Abel, ed., *Encyclopedia of Early Cinema* (London: Routledge, 2004), 565, 566; Charles Musser, "American Vitagraph 1897–1901," *Cinema Journal* 22, no. 3 (Spring 1983): 7.

9. Smith, *Two Reels and a Crank*, 33–34, 38; Letter, Smith to Clarke; Smith tape 1.

10. Gordon Hendricks, *The Edison Motion Picture Myth* (Berkeley, CA: University of California Press, 1961), 172.

11. Erik Barnouw, *The Magician and the Cinema* (New York: Oxford University Press, 1981), 41–43, 47, 58, 66; Abel, *Encyclopedia of Early Cinema*, 261; Smith, *Two Reels and a Crank*, 80.

12. Armond Fields, *Tony Pastor, Father of Vaudeville* (Jefferson, NC: McFarland, 2007), 159; "Koster and Bial's," *New York Dramatic Mirror*, Jan. 18, 1896, 19, Mar. 21, 1896, 19, May 2, 1896, 19; "Proctor Gets the Kintographe," *New York Dramatic Mirror*, Apr. 18, 1896, 19; "Edison's Vitascope," *New York Dramatic Mirror*, Apr. 25, 1896, 20; "Edison's Vitascope Cheered," *New York Times*, Apr. 24, 1896, 5; Epes Winthrop Sargent, "New York City Holds Record for Earliest Exhibiting," *Moving Picture World*, Jul. 15, 1916, 370; Deems Taylor, *A Pictorial History of the Movies* (New York: Simon and Schuster, 1943), 4.

13. Blackton, "Hollywood with Its Hair Down," 37, 40; Smith, *Two Reels and a Crank*, 38; Musser, "American Vitagraph 1897–1901," 6–7; Albert E. Smith, "Flatbush

and Vine," ms., Jan. 1951, 183, Charles G. Clarke Collection, Margaret Herrick Library, Academy of Motion Picture Arts and Sciences.

14. Musser, "American Vitagraph 1897–1901," 6–8; Denis Gifford, *The British Film Catalogue: Fiction Film, 1895–1994*, vol. 1 (Abingdon: Routledge, 2016), 00004–00005; *Phonoscope*, Nov. 15, 1896, 12, 13, 16; Smith, *Two Reels and a Crank*, 33–34; *New York Dramatic Mirror*, Jul. 18, 1896, 17, Aug. 1, 1896, 17, Sep. 19, 1896, 17, Oct. 17, 1896, 17, Nov. 7, 1896, 17, Dec. 5, 1896, 17.

15. Albert E. Smith Appointment Calendar 1896 [*sic*], Box 11, Albert E. Smith Papers (Collection 2004), Department of Special Collections, Charles E. Young Research Library, University of California, Los Angeles; Smith tape 1; Terry Ramsaye, "The Romantic History of the Motion Picture," *Photoplay*, Oct. 1922, 56–57, 89–92; Blackton, "Hollywood with Its Hair Down," 46–47; Smith, *Two Reels and a Crank*, 34, 39.

16. Smith Appointment Calendar 1896.

17. Smith, *Two Reels and a Crank*, 33–34, 38; Letter, Smith to Clarke; Smith tape 1; Albert Smith testimony, Greater New York Film Rental Company vs. Biograph Company and General Film Company, Aug. 6, 1913, 2705, Motion Picture Patents Company and General Film Company collection, Margaret Herrick Library, Academy of Motion Picture Arts and Sciences. Musser dates the partnership's founding to March 1897 and gives its original name as the Edison Vitagraph Company. This name doesn't appear to have ever been used in New York City, though it was briefly utilized to promote some shows outside of the city. Musser, "American Vitagraph 1897–1901," 9, 19.

18. Smith Appointment Calendar 1896; Marian Blackton Trimble, *J. Stuart Blackton: A Personal Biography by His Daughter* (Metuchen, NJ: Scarecrow, 1985), 9–10; "Smith-Arthur," *Brooklyn Eagle*, May 21, 1897, 7.

19. Smith Appointment Calendar 1896; *New York Dramatic Mirror*, Jun. 27, 1897, 16, Jul. 24, 1897, 16, Sep. 25, 1897, 18; *Moving Picture World*, Jul. 15, 1916, 370–71; Smith, *Two Reels and a Crank*, 42–43, 95.

20. Smith tapes 1, 3, 9; Smith, *Two Reels and a Crank*, 34–38, 40–41, 250; Letter, Smith to Clarke; Courtney, "History of Vitagraph," 542; Albert E. Smith deposition, Thomas A. Edison vs. J. Stuart Blackton and Albert E. Smith, April 9, 1900, Equity Nos. 6990, 6991, U. S. Circuit Court, Southern District of New York, National Archives at New York City; Albert Smith testimony, United States of America vs. Motion Picture Patents Company et al., Nov. 14, 1913, 1713, 1715–1717.

21. Film strips purporting to be two Vitagraph productions from 1897, *Boot Blacks* and *Street Scene in Brooklyn*, from the scrapbook of Eugene Lauste, are reprinted in Paul C. Spehr, "The Apparatus Unaltered to Date: Developing 35mm Film," *Moving Images: From Edison to the Webcam*, eds. John Fullerton and Astrid Söderbergh Widding (Bloomington: Indiana University Press, 2000), 21; "Where They Exhibited Last Month," *Phonoscope*, Feb. 1898, 10; *New York Dramatic Mirror*, Jan. 22, 1898, 18, Feb. 26, 1898, 16; Smith tape 5; Blackton, "Hollywood with Its Hair Down," 50.

22. Smith, *Two Reels and a Crank*, 137–39. It is not known if there was a paying audience for the rooftop exhibition in Harlem, nor was the program of movies

recorded for posterity. Courtney, "History of Vitagraph," 661; Musser, "American Vitagraph 1897–1901," 10–11; Terry Ramsaye, *A Million and One Nights, A History of the Motion Picture* (New York: Simon and Schuster, 1926), 378; "The Stage," *Munsey's*, Oct. 1897, 146.

23. Smith, *Two Reels and a Crank*, 54; J. Stuart Blackton, "The World in Motion," ms., 1932, 6–7, Box 1, Albert E. Smith Papers (Collection 2004), Department of Special Collections, Charles E. Young Research Library, University of California, Los Angeles; Blackton, "Hollywood with Its Hair Down," 52; *Phonoscope*, Apr. 1898, 17.

24. Blackton, "The World in Motion," 6–7; Musser, "American Vitagraph 1897–1901," 12; *New York Dramatic Mirror*, Apr. 30, 1898, 16, May 7, 1898, 18.

25. Blackton, "The World in Motion," 6–7; Blackton, "Hollywood with Its Hair Down," 53–56; Smith, *Two Reels and a Crank*, 11, 53–68; "Cuban War Pictures," *Phonoscope*, Apr. 1898, 7; *Phonoscope*, 17, May 1898, 6; "Bill Paley, the Kinetoscope Man," *Phonoscope*, Aug. 1898, 7; Kirk J. Kekatos, "Edward H. Amet and the Spanish-American War Film," *Film History* (2002): 405–17; Musser, "American Vitagraph 1897–1901," 12–16; Terry Ramsaye, "The Romantic History of the Motion Picture," *Photoplay*, Dec. 1922, 73; George Blaisdell, "Making Screen's Initial Feature—In Miniature," *Exhibitors Trade Review*, Dec. 15, 1923, 1–2; Stephen Bottomore, "Filming, Faking and Propaganda: The Origins of the War Film, 1897–1902" (PhD diss., Utrecht University, 2007), chap. 5, 8–29. According to Bottomore's meticulously researched dissertation, Biograph cameraman Arthur Marvin photographed Spanish–American war activities at Puerto Rico.

26. J. Stuart Blackton, "'Silence was Golden,' The Story of My Forty Movie Years," ms., 53, 56, 65, J. Stuart Blackton papers, Special Collections, Margaret Herrick Library, Academy of Motion Picture Arts and Sciences; Smith, *Two Reels and a Crank*, 56–68; Charles Musser, *The Emergence of Cinema: The American Screen to 1907* (New York: Charles Scribner's Sons, 1990), 260; Smith 1898 check ledger, Box 1, Albert E. Smith Papers (Collection 2004), Department of Special Collections, Charles E. Young Research Library, University of California, Los Angeles; Kekatos, "Edward H. Amet," 405–17.

27. Musser, "American Vitagraph 1897–1901," 12; *New York Dramatic Mirror*, Apr. 30, 1898, 12, 16; "Where They Were Exhibited Last Month," *Phonoscope*, Feb. 1898, 10, May 1898, 6, Oct. 1898, 16, *New York Clipper*, May 7, 1898, 160, 168, May 28, 1898, 221; Letter, Smith to JL Moran; Blackton, "Silence Was Golden," 56; "Brooklyn Was the Cradle of Film Industry," *Brooklyn Eagle*, Feb. 15, 1933; Courtney, "History of Vitagraph," 661–62; Smith tape 6.

28. Letter, George J. Mitchell, Jr., to Smith, Mar. 2, 1954, and response from Smith, Mar. 7, 1954, Box 10, Albert E. Smith Papers (Collection 2004), Department of Special Collections, Charles E. Young Research Library, University of California, Los Angeles; Smith 1898 check ledger; "Death of William T. Rock, Pioneer Picture Man," *Moving Picture World*, Aug. 12, 1916, 1078; *Moving Picture World*, Jul. 15, 1916, 368, 379; F. H. Richardson, "Projection," *Moving Picture World*, Aug. 13, 1921, 737–40; *Phonoscope*, Dec. 15, 1896, 8–9; *Moving Picture World*, Feb. 21, 1914, 936; Courtney, "History of Vitagraph," 542, 661–62; William T. Rock deposition, Thomas A. Edison vs. J. Stuart Blackton and Albert E. Smith, Apr. 9, 1900, Equity Nos. 6990,

6991, U. S. Circuit Court, Southern District of New York, National Archives at New York City; Richard Brown, "England Is Not Big Enough," *Film History* (1998): 22–24; Ramsaye, *A Million and One Nights*, 269; Andrew Kahrl, "The Making, Unmaking, and Memory of White and Black Beaches in New Orleans," *Louisiana Cultural Vistas* 23 (Spring 2012): 68–81.

29. *Moving Picture World*, Jul. 15, 1916, 379; Rock deposition, Apr. 9, 1900; Smith, *Two Reels and a Crank*, 69, 71, 92; Blackton, "Hollywood with Its Hair Down," 87, 89; Terry Ramsaye, "The Romantic History of the Motion Picture," *Photoplay*, Aug. 1922, 115.

30. Musser, "American Vitagraph 1897–1901," 18; Richard Abel, *The Red Rooster Scare: Making Cinema American, 1900–1910* (Berkeley, CA: University of California Press, 1999), 3.

31. Hendricks, *Edison Motion Picture Myth*, 176–88; Smith, *Two Reels and a Crank*, 75; Neil Baldwin, *Edison, Inventing the Century* (New York: Hyperion, 1995), 46, 61, 125–27, 272–73.

32. *New York Clipper*, May 28, 1898, 220, Jun. 4, 1898, 234; Smith deposition, Apr. 9, 1900; J. Stuart Blackton deposition, Thomas A. Edison vs. J. Stuart Blackton and Albert E. Smith, Apr. 9, 1900, Equity Nos. 6990, 6991, U. S. Circuit Court, Southern District of New York, National Archives at New York City; Affidavit of S. O. Edmonds, Apr. 18, 1900, Equity Nos. 6990, 6991, U. S. Circuit Court, Southern District of New York, National Archives at New York City; Eugene Elmore deposition, Thomas A. Edison vs. J. Stuart Blackton and Albert E. Smith, Jul. 15, 1898, Equity No. 6989, U. S. Circuit Court, Southern District of New York, National Archives at New York City; Legal Notices, *Phonoscope*, Aug. 1898, 13; Frank L. Dyer testimony, United States of America vs. Motion Picture Patents Company et al., Nov. 11, 1913, 1553.

33. Charles Musser, *Before the Nickelodeon: Edwin S. Porter and the Edison Manufacturing Company* (Berkeley, CA: University of California Press, 1991), 115–16; Tino Balio, "A Novelty Spawns Small Businesses: 1894–1908," *The American Film Industry*, ed. Tino Balio (Madison: University of Wisconsin Press, 1976), 7–8; Smith, *Two Reels and a Crank*, 11.

34. Rock deposition, Apr. 9, 1900; Smith, *Two Reels and a Crank*, 72, 92; Smith tape 9; Barnouw, *The Magician and the Cinema*, 75.

35. Smith, *Two Reels and a Crank*, 95; Musser, "American Vitagraph 1897–1901," 21; *Mahatma*, Feb. 1899, Smith Box 1, Albert E. Smith Papers (Collection 2004), Department of Special Collections, Charles E. Young Research Library, University of California, Los Angeles.

36. *Moving Picture World*, Jul. 15, 1916, 370–71; Smith tape 8; Letter Feb. 18, 1927, Ronald Reader to Smith, Box 9, Albert E. Smith Papers (Collection 2004), Department of Special Collections, Charles E. Young Research Library, University of California, Los Angeles; Barnouw, *The Magician and the Cinema*, 6–7.

37. Smith, *Two Reels and a Crank*, 44; Blackton, "Hollywood with Its Hair Down," 57–58; Smith tape 4; Musser, "American Vitagraph 1897–1901," 21–22; Ramsaye, *A Million and One Nights*, 331.

38. Smith, *Two Reels and a Crank*, 11–25, 250; Blackton, "Hollywood with Its Hair Down," 94–96; Blackton deposition, Apr. 9, 1900.

39. Kemp R. Niver, *Motion Pictures from the Library of Congress Paper Print Collection, 1894–1912* (Berkeley, CA: University of California Press, 1967), xiv, 258.

40. "A Visit to a Spiritualist," *Phonoscope*, Sep. 1899, 9; Blackton, "Hollywood with Its Hair Down," 67; Smith, *Two Reels and a Crank*, 51.

41. *Brooklyn Eagle*, Jul. 2, 1899, 21, Jul. 16, 1899, 20; Smith tape 8; Joseph P. Eckhardt, *The King of the Movies: Film Pioneer Siegmund Lubin* (Madison, NJ: Farleigh Dickinson University Press, 1997), 24, 70–71; Terry Ramsaye, "The Romantic History of the Motion Picture," *Photoplay*, Aug. 1922, 115; Blackton, "Silence Was Golden," 244.

42. Smith tape 7; *New York Clipper*, May 13, 1899, 217; Mae Noell, "Recollections of Medicine Show Life," *American Popular Entertainment*, ed. M. Matlaw (Westport, CT: Greenwood, 1979), 215–25; "The Kickapoo Indian Medicine Company of New Haven Entertains the Masses (But Doesn't Cure Them)," www.newenglandhistorical-society.com/the-kickapoo-indian-medicine-co (accessed June 24, 2017).

43. Gregory A. Waller, "Situating Motion Pictures in the Prenickelodeon Period: Lexington, Kentucky, 1897–1906," *Velvet Light Trap* (Spring 1990): 21–24.

44. *New York Clipper*, May 13, 1899, 217; Musser, "American Vitagraph 1897–1901," 28; *Brooklyn Eagle*, Feb. 19, 1899, 23, Oct. 9, 1900, 5, Jan. 31, 1899, 5, Nov. 26, 1900, 4.

45. Laurie, Jr., *Vaudeville, from the Honky-Tonks to the Palace*, 333–37; Fields, *Tony Pastor, Father of Vaudeville*, 159, 161, 169; *New York Dramatic Mirror*, Sep. 19, 1896, 17, Aug. 7, 1897, 16, Dec. 4, 1897, 18, Aug. 20, 1898, 16, Jun. 17, 1899, 18; Blackton, "Hollywood with Its Hair Down," 90; Blackton, "Silence Was Golden," 101; Smith, *Two Reels and a Crank*, 46; Courtney, "History of Vitagraph," 661.

46. Smith, *Two Reels and a Crank*, 165; Musser, *Before the Nickelodeon*, 155; Smith deposition, Apr. 9, 1900; Letter, Smith to Clarke; J. Stuart Blackton testimony, United States of America vs. Motion Picture Patents Company et al., Nov. 20, 1913, 1879.

47. An earlier Certificate of Incorporation may have been filed in October 1899. If so, it was nullified by the 1900 filing. See *Phonoscope*, Nov. 1899, 11; Smith, *Two Reels and a Crank*, 72, 250; Musser, *Before the Nickelodeon*, 143, 154–55; "Death of William T. Rock," 1078; James H. White deposition, Thomas A. Edison vs. J. Stuart Blackton and Albert E. Smith, Apr. 30, 1900, Equity No. 6991, U. S. Circuit Court, Southern District of New York, National Archives at New York City; Smith deposition, Apr. 9, 1900; Blackton deposition, Apr. 9, 1900; Rock deposition, Apr. 9, 1900; Smith 1898 check ledger, Box 1, Albert E. Smith Papers (Collection 2004), Department of Special Collections, Charles E. Young Research Library, University of California, Los Angeles; Musser, *Emergence of Cinema*, 283; Blackton testimony, Nov. 20, 1913, 1879, Dec. 1, 1913, 1984–1987 and 1994–1996.

48. Smith, *Two Reels and a Crank*, 51; Letter Nov. 27, 1956, Smith to George Pratt, Box 10, Albert E. Smith Papers (Collection 2004), Department of Special Collections, Charles E. Young Research Library, University of California, Los Angeles; Smith tape 5.

49. According to Albert Smith, the stop-action movement in *The Humpty Dumpty Circus* inspired James Blackton to conceive of *The Enchanted Drawing*. Smith tape 5.

50. Smith, *Two Reels and a Crank*, 126–28; Albert Smith Diary 1900, Box 11, Albert E. Smith Papers (Collection 2004), Department of Special Collections, Charles

E. Young Research Library, University of California, Los Angeles; Musser, "American Vitagraph 1897–1901," 38; Musser, *Emergence of Cinema*, 283; Blackton testimony, Dec. 1, 1913, 1987–1988.

51. Smith, *Two Reels and a Crank*, 97–125; *Brooklyn Eagle*, Jan. 28, 1900, 24, Jan. 29, 1900, 8, Jan. 30, 1900, 9; "Theatres and Music Halls," *New York Times*, Oct. 31, 1899, 5; Allston T. Brown, *A History of the New York Stage from the first performance in 1732 to 1901*, vol. 3 (New York: Dodd, Mead and Co., 1903), 575–77; *New York Dramatic Mirror*, May 5, 1900, 18; *Motion Picture News*, Mar. 7, 1925, 996; "List of New Films, American and Imported, Boer War, Comedy and Mysterious Subjects, American Vitagraph Company," Exhibit G, Equity No. 6991, Thomas A. Edison vs. J. Stuart Blackton and Albert E. Smith, U. S. Circuit Court, Southern District of New York, National Archives at New York City; John Barnes, *Filming the Boer War, The Beginnings of Cinema in England, 1894–1901*, vol. 4 (London: Bishopsgate Press Ltd., 1992), 159–79, 233–93; Stephen Bottomore, "Joseph Rosenthal: The Most Glorious Profession," *Sight and Sound* (Fall 1983): 260–65; Warwick Trading Company, Ltd., 1901 Catalogue, 52, Box 1, Albert E. Smith Papers (Collection 2004), Department of Special Collections, Charles E. Young Research Library, University of California, Los Angeles; Dewey, *Buccaneer*, 259–64; *Adventures and Letters of Richard Harding Davis*, ed. Charles Belmont Davis (New York: Charles Scribner's Sons, 1917), 261; Bottomore, "Filming, Faking and Propaganda," chap. 9.

52. Musser, "American Vitagraph 1897–1901," 36, 39; Eckhardt, *King of the Movies*, 39; Musser, *Before the Nickelodeon*, 177; Fields, *Tony Pastor, Father of Vaudeville*, 170; Smith, *Two Reels and a Crank*, 133–34; *Brooklyn Eagle*, Jan. 16, 1900, 6; Warwick Catalogue and Charles Urban 1904 Catalogue, Box 1, Albert E. Smith Papers (Collection 2004), Department of Special Collections, Charles E. Young Research Library, University of California, Los Angeles; Letter Jan. 31, 1908, Rock and Blackton to Smith, Box 2, Albert E. Smith Papers (Collection 2004), Department of Special Collections, Charles E. Young Research Library, University of California, Los Angeles; Charles Musser, "Vitagraph 1901–1905, The Lost Years," *Vitagraph Co. of America, Il Cinema prima di Hollywood*, ed. Paolo Cherchi Usai (Pordenone, Italy: Edizioni Studio Tesi, 1987), 89–90; Abel, *Red Rooster Scare*, 2, 3; Blackton testimony, Dec. 1, 1913, 1989–1991.

53. Hendricks, *Edison Motion Picture Myth*, 174–75; Musser, *Emergence of Cinema*, 305–6; Musser, *Before the Nickelodeon*, 196–97, 239; Eckhardt, *King of the Movies*, 44, 46; Letter Jun. 18, 1902, W. R. Baird to Dyer, Edmonds & Dyer, D0226; 187:842, Thomas A. Edison Papers, Rutgers University; Letter Jun. 20, 1902, S. O. Edmunds to W. R. Baird, D0226; 187:842, Thomas A. Edison Papers, Rutgers University; Letter May 6, 1902, Dyer, Edmonds and Dyer to William Gilmore, 187:833, Thomas A. Edison Papers, Rutgers University; Smith testimony, United States of America vs. Motion Picture Patents Company et al., Nov. 18, 1913, 1711; Blackton testimony, Nov. 20, 1913, 1879.

54. *New York Clipper*, Mar. 21, 1903, 108; *New Vitagraph Features*, PAM 1696, Margaret Herrick Library, Academy of Motion Picture Arts and Sciences; *Brooklyn Eagle*, Aug. 27, 1901, 5; "Gala Night of the Elks at the Orpheum Theater," *Brooklyn Eagle*, Jun. 13, 1901, 5; "Did You Bathe at Brighton?" *Brooklyn Eagle*, Sep. 1, 1901, 13.

55. "The Theatres Last Night: Kyrle Bellew Appears in 'A Gentleman of France,'" *New York Times*, Dec. 31, 1901, 5; "News of the Players," *New York Times*, Sep. 23, 1902, 9.

56. *New Vitagraph Features!*, 10; Smith tapes 3, 9; Musser, *Emergence of Cinema*, 335.

57. Musser, *Before the Nickelodeon*, 333; Eckhardt, *King of the Movies*, 48, 55.

58. Musser, *Emergence of Cinema*, 364; Musser, *Before the Nickelodeon*, 239, 241, 277; Letter, Rock and Blackton to Smith; Letter Nov. 10, 1904, Delos Holden to W. E. Gilmore, 189:367, Thomas A. Edison Papers, Rutgers University; McCoy Report on Pathé Cinematograph Company, Nov. 1, 1904, 189:368, Thomas A. Edison Papers, Rutgers University.

59. Morton Building Lease with American Vitagraph Company, Box 1, Albert E. Smith Papers (Collection 2004), Department of Special Collections, Charles E. Young Research Library, University of California, Los Angeles; Smith, *Two Reels and a Crank*, 251; Report by the Examinations Corporation, Mar. 31, 1917, 2–3, Box 10, Albert E. Smith Papers (Collection 2004), Department of Special Collections, Charles E. Young Research Library, University of California, Los Angeles; Supreme Court, County of New York, Guaranty Trust Company of New York vs. The Vitagraph Company of America, Box 7, Albert E. Smith Papers (Collection 2004), Department of Special Collections, Charles E. Young Research Library, University of California, Los Angeles.

2. 1905–1908

1. McCoy Report on Pathé Cinematograph Company, Nov. 1, 1904, 189:368, Thomas A. Edison Papers, Rutgers University; Richard Abel, *The Red Rooster Scare: Making Cinema American, 1900–1910* (Berkeley, CA: University of California Press, 1999), xi, xii, 25; Richard Abel, "'Pathé Goes to Town': French Films Create a Market for the Nickelodeon," *Cinema Journal* (Fall 1995): 12–13; Charles Musser, *Before the Nickelodeon: Edwin S. Porter and the Edison Manufacturing Company* (Berkeley, CA: University of California Press, 1991), 335.

2. Albert E. Smith, *Two Reels and a Crank* (Garden City, NY: Doubleday, 1952), 92–94, 170–71; Albert Smith Appointment Calendar 1902, Box 11, Albert E. Smith Papers (Collection 2004), Department of Special Collections, Charles E. Young Research Library, University of California, Los Angeles.

3. Smith, *Two Reels and a Crank*, 171–76; J. Stuart Blackton, "'Hollywood with Its Hair Down' or Hollywood Memories; Forty Years of the Movies," ms., 107, J. Stuart Blackton papers, Margaret Herrick Library, Academy of Motion Picture Arts and Sciences; Original Studio Hermance Parcel File #1, Box 16064B, Warner Bros. Archives at USC; *Views and Film Index*, Aug. 25, 1906, 6; Albert Smith audio interview, tape 7, Albert E. Smith Papers (Collection 2004), Department of Special Collections, Charles E. Young Research Library, University of California, Los Angeles; Charles Musser, *The Emergence of Cinema: The American Screen to 1907* (New York: Charles Scribner's Sons, 1990), 337, 470, 473; Barry Salt, "The Early Development of Film Form," *Film before Griffith*, ed. John L. Fell (Berkeley, CA: University of California Press, 1983),

286; Jon Gartenberg, "Vitagraph before Griffith: Forging Ahead in the Nickelodeon Era," *Studies in Visual Communication* 10, no. 4 (Fall 1984): 8.

4. Smith, *Two Reels and a Crank*, 165–71; Blackton, "Hollywood with Its Hair Down," 90; Smith tapes 7 and 9; Letter Mar. 19, 1906, William T. Rock to Selig Polyscope Co., Scrapbook #2, MS Collection #47, Charles G. Clarke Collection, Margaret Herrick Library, Academy of Motion Picture Arts and Sciences; Letters Mar. 7, 1908 and Mar. 27, 1908, Rock to Selig, Folder 460, William Selig Collection, Special Collections, Margaret Herrick Library, Academy of Motion Picture Arts and Sciences.

5. Robert C. Allen, "Motion Picture Exhibition in Manhattan, 1906–1912: Beyond the Nickelodeon," *Cinema Journal* (1979): 2; Musser, *Emergence of Cinema*, 428; Robert Grau, *The Theatre of Science* (New York: Broadway Publishing Co., 1914), 16, 27; Abel, *Red Rooster Scare*, 80–82.

6. Eileen Bowser, *The Transformation of Cinema, 1907–1915* (Berkeley, CA: University of California Press, 1990), 2; Musser, *Emergence of Cinema*, 412; Musser, *Before the Nickelodeon*, 327–28.

7. Andrew A. Erish, *Col. William N. Selig, the Man Who Invented Hollywood* (Austin, TX: University of Texas Press, 2012), 15–18, 35–39; Joseph P. Eckhardt, *The King of the Movies: Film Pioneer Siegmund Lubin* (Madison, NJ: Farleigh Dickinson University Press, 1997), 50–51; Musser, *Before the Nickelodeon*, 254–59; Barry Salt, "Film Form 1900–1906," *Early Cinema: Space, Frame, Narrative*, ed. Thomas Elsaesser (London: BFI, 1990), 32–44.

8. "Kyrle Bellew as Raffles," *New York Times*, Sep. 21, 1903, 7; Smith, *Two Reels and a Crank*, 159–60; Albert E. Smith, "Flatbush and Vine," ms., Jan. 1951, 149b, 176, 183, Charles G. Clarke Collection, Margaret Herrick Library, Academy of Motion Picture Arts and Sciences; Blackton, "Hollywood with Its Hair Down," 68–69; Smith tapes 3, 6; *Brooklyn Eagle*, Sep. 3, 1905, 8; Musser, *Emergence of Cinema*, 406, 410.

9. Blackton, "Hollywood with Its Hair Down," 69; Smith, *Two Reels and a Crank*, 160–61; Telegram Mar. 18, 1925, Smith to Barran Lewis, Box 9, Albert E. Smith Papers (Collection 2004), Department of Special Collections, Charles E. Young Research Library, University of California, Los Angeles; *New York Clipper*, Sep. 23, 1905, 795, Sep. 30, 1905, 39; Musser, *Emergence of Cinema*, 406; Smith tape 6. For more on exhibitor resistance to long films, see Erish, *Col. William N. Selig*, chap 8.

10. Smith tapes 4, 5; Musser, *Emergence of Cinema*, 406, 410; Smith, *Two Reels and a Crank*, 134; Theodore Waters, "Out With a Moving Picture Machine," introd. Richard Koszarski, *Film History* (2003): 396–99.

11. William Shea, "Twelve Years in One Studio—A Record," *Moving Picture World*, Mar. 10, 1917, 1507; "Veteran William Shea Is Dead," *Moving Picture World*, Nov. 23, 1918, 840; Smith, *Two Reels and a Crank*, 141; Donald Dewey, *Buccaneer, James Stuart Blackton and the Birth of the American Movies* (Lanham, MD: Rowman & Littlefield, 2016), 110; Smith tape 9.

12. Katherine Glover, "Moving Pictures Amuse and Instruct," *Brooklyn Eagle*, Sep. 9, 1906, 21; Blackton, "Hollywood with Its Hair Down," 100–101, 108, 111; Waters, "Out With a Moving Picture Machine," 396; Paul Panzer, "The Actor in the Early Days," *Moving Picture World*, Mar. 10, 1917, 1509; Smith, *Two Reels and a Crank*, 135, 141; Dewey, *Buccaneer*, 110.

13. Smith, *Two Reels and a Crank*, 136; Shea, "Twelve Years in One Studio," 1507.

14. Smith, *Two Reels and a Crank*, 189, 251; Musser, *Emergence of Cinema*, 410; Smith, "Flatbush and Vine," 173; Smith tape 7; Panzer, "The Actor in the Early Days," 1509; Shea, "Twelve Years in One Studio," 1507.

15. Smith tape 7; David Kiehn, *Broncho Billy and the Essanay Film Company* (Berkeley, CA: Farwell Books, 2003), 5; Smith, *Two Reels and a Crank*, 204.

16. *New York Clipper*, Apr. 7, 1906, 212.

17. Letter Nov. 27, 1956, Smith to George Pratt, Box 10, Albert E. Smith Papers (Collection 2004), Department of Special Collections, Charles E. Young Research Library, University of California, Los Angeles; *New York Clipper*, Apr. 7, 1906, 212. The foreign release version of *Humorous Phases of Funny Faces*, titled *Comedy Cartoons* in Charles Urban's catalog, is approximately thirty seconds longer and contains some additional shots that include a man's head that splits "from crown to chin" out of which "proceed champagne and liquor in bottles, cigars, cigarettes and glasses."

18. "W. V. Ranous Dead," *Moving Picture World*, Apr. 17, 1915, 366; Panzer, "The Actor in the Early Days," 1509; Robert Hamilton Ball, *Shakespeare on Silent Film* (London: Allen and Unwin, 1968), 40; Terry Ramsaye, *A Million and One Nights, A History of the Motion Picture* (New York: Simon and Schuster, 1926), 442; Smith tapes 7, 9; Musser, *Emergence of Cinema*, 410, 473; Smith, *Two Reels and a Crank*, 189; Abel, "Pathé Goes to Town," 12–13; Gartenberg, "Vitagraph before Griffith," 8.

19. Gartenberg, "Vitagraph before Griffith," 8, 10; Smith tape 6.

20. Gartenberg, "Vitagraph before Griffith," 8, 12–13; Salt, "Early Development of Film Form," 287; Robert Spadoni, "The Figure Seen from the Rear, Vitagraph, and the Development of Shot/Reverse Shot," *Film History* 11, no. 3 (1999): 321, 327; Blackton, "Hollywood with Its Hair Down," 112; Musser, *Emergence of Cinema*, 471.

21. Glover, "Moving Pictures Amuse," 21; Smith tape 3.

22. Musser, *Emergence of Cinema*, 424; Abel, "Pathé Goes to Town," 16; Abel, *Red Rooster Scare*, 82, 84; Bowser, *Transformation of Cinema*, 4.

23. *Billboard*, Feb. 17, 1906, back cover; *New York Clipper*, Feb. 3, 1906, 29; *Billboard*, Feb. 10, 1906, 31; Abel, *Red Rooster Scare*, 52; Smith, *Two Reels and a Crank*, 251.

24. Abel, *Red Rooster Scare*, xi–xii; J. Stuart Blackton testimony, United States of America vs. Motion Picture Patents Company et al., Dec. 1, 1913, 1991–1992.

25. *Billboard*, Dec. 5, 1905, 80; *Billboard*, Feb. 10, 1906, 31; Smith tape 7; Letter Oct. 16, 1906, John Hardin to Alexander T. Moore, D0624: 190:749, Thomas A. Edison Papers, Rutgers University; Smith, "Flatbush and Vine," 253; *New York Clipper*, Oct. 27, 1906, 972; Musser, *Before the Nickelodeon*, 328–29.

26. *New York Clipper*, May 5, 1906, 310, Aug. 11, 1906, 680; Smith tape 5; Musser, *Before the Nickelodeon*, 319; Letter Jan. 31, 1908, Rock and Blackton to Smith, Box 2, Albert E. Smith Papers (Collection 2004), Department of Special Collections, Charles E. Young Research Library, University of California, Los Angeles; Report by the Examinations Corporation, Mar. 31, 1917, 41, Box 10, Albert E. Smith Papers (Collection 2004), Department of Special Collections, Charles E. Young Research Library, University of California, Los Angeles.

27. Albert Smith Appointment Calendar 1906, Smith Pocket Diary and Date Book 1907, Box 11, Albert E. Smith Papers (Collection 2004), Department of Special Collections, Charles E. Young Research Library, University of California, Los Angeles; Smith, *Two Reels and a Crank*, 176, 184; "The Story of the Film, A Faversham Pioneer," *Faversham Worth East Kent News*, Mar. 8, 1924, Box 1, Albert E. Smith Papers (Collection 2004), Department of Special Collections, Charles E. Young Research Library, University of California, Los Angeles; Gartenberg, "Vitagraph before Griffith," 9; J. Frank Brockliss, "Early Motion Picture Days in London," *Moving Picture World*, Apr. 17, 1915, 379; Gordon Hendricks, *The Edison Motion Picture Myth* (Berkeley, CA: University of California Press, 1961), 157; Eckhardt, *King of the Movies*, 32; Musser, *Emergence of Cinema*, 473; Erish, *Col. William N. Selig*, 132–46.

28. Gartenberg, "Vitagraph before Griffith," 9, 12; Letter, Smith to Pratt; Erik Barnouw, *The Magician and the Cinema* (New York: Oxford University Press, 1981), 90; Donald Crafton, *Before Mickey: The Animated Film 1898-1928* (Chicago, IL: University of Chicago Press, 1993), 13–20; Frederick Talbot, *Moving Pictures: How They Are Made and Worked* (Philadelphia, PA: J. B. Lippincott, 1912), 242; Smith, *Two Reels and a Crank*, 183.

29. Smith Pocket Diary and Date Book 1907.

30. Eileen Bowser, "Toward Narrative, 1907: *The Mill Girl*," *Film before Griffith*, ed. John L. Fell (Berkeley, CA: University of California Press, 1983), 330–38; Gartenberg, "Vitagraph before Griffith," 13; Bowser, *Transformation of Cinema*, 60.

31. "Interviews with Manufacturers, No. 2—Vitagraph," *Moving Picture World*, Feb. 8, 1908, 95; "Francesca di Rimini," *Moving Picture World*, Feb. 8, 1908, 103; Musser, *Emergence of Cinema*, 472; William Uricchio and Roberta E. Pearson, "'Films of Quality,' 'High Art Films,' and 'Films De Luxe': Intertextuality and Reading Positions in the Vitagraph Films," *Journal of Film and Video* (Winter 1989): 18–29.

32. Smith tape 7; Smith, *Two Reels and a Crank*, 187, 209; Eugene Michael Vazzana, *Silent Film Necrology* (Jefferson, NC: McFarland, 2001), 530; Anthony Slide and Alan Gevinson, *The Big V: A History of the Vitagraph Company* (Metuchen, NJ: Scarecrow, 1987), 34; Grau, *Theatre of Science*, 209; Blackton, "Hollywood with Its Hair Down," 111–12; Terry Ramsaye, "The Romantic History of the Motion Picture," *Photoplay*, Aug. 1924, 65; "Picture Personalities, Miss Florence E. Turner: The Vitagraph Girl," *Moving Picture World*, Jul. 23, 1910, 187–88.

33. Kelly R. Brown, *Florence Lawrence, The Biograph Girl* (Jefferson, NC: McFarland, 1999), 2, 7–18, 25; Blackton, "Hollywood with Its Hair Down," 111; Smith tape 7; Musser, *Emergence of Cinema*, 473; Florence Lawrence and Monte M. Katterjohn, "Growing Up with the Movies," *Photoplay*, Nov. 1914, 28–29, 35–36, 40, Dec. 1914, 91–100, Jan. 1915, 99–100; Frank E. Woods, "Why Is a Star?" *Photoplay*, Oct. 1919, 71.

34. Smith 1908 Appointment Calendar, Box 11, Albert E. Smith Papers (Collection 2004), Department of Special Collections, Charles E. Young Research Library, University of California, Los Angeles; Letters Feb. 11, 14, and 21, 1908, Vic Smith to Albert Smith, Letter, Rock and Blackton to Smith, Letters Feb. 11, 21, and 25, 1908, Rock to Smith, Letter Feb. 15, 1908, Blackton to Smith, Box 1, Albert E. Smith Papers

(Collection 2004), Department of Special Collections, Charles E. Young Research Library, University of California, Los Angeles; Robert Jack Anderson, "The Motion Picture Patents Company" (PhD diss., University of Wisconsin-Madison, 1983), 80, 146; "Vitagraph Co. to Print in Paris," *Moving Picture World*, Mar. 7, 1908, 186–87.

35. Letter Feb. 27, 1908, George Smith to Albert Smith, Box 1, Albert E. Smith Papers (Collection 2004), Department of Special Collections, Charles E. Young Research Library, University of California, Los Angeles; Report by the Examinations Corporation, 17; Smith 1908 Appointment Calendar; Musser, *Emergence of Cinema*, 473; Smith, *Two Reels and a Crank*, 177, 251; Abel, *Red Rooster Scare*, xiii, 151; Letter Feb. 11, 1908, Vic Smith to Albert Smith, Letter Feb. 2, 1909, Reader to Smith, Box 2, Albert E. Smith Papers (Collection 2004), Department of Special Collections, Charles E. Young Research Library, University of California, Los Angeles.

36. Marian Blackton Trimble, *J. Stuart Blackton: A Personal Biography by His Daughter* (Metuchen, NJ: Scarecrow, 1985), 26; *Moving Picture World*, Oct. 24, 1908, 317; *Moving Picture World*, Dec. 5, 1908, 447; "An Interview with J. Stuart Blackton," *Moving Picture World*, Dec. 19, 1908, 497.

37. Letter Jun. 3, 1908, Reader to Smith, Box 1, Box 11, Albert E. Smith Papers (Collection 2004), Department of Special Collections, Charles E. Young Research Library, University of California, Los Angeles.

38. Panzer, "The Actor in the Early Days," 1509; Ball, *Shakespeare on Silent Film*, 39–60; W. Stephen Bush, "The Film of the Future," *Moving Picture World*, Sep. 5, 1908, 172; "Comments on Film Subjects," *Moving Picture World*, Oct. 3, 1908, 253, Nov. 14, 1908, 379–80; Musser, *Before the Nickelodeon*, 432; Bowser, *Transformation of Cinema*, 48; Ramsaye, *A Million and One Nights*, 484–85; W. Stephen Bush, "Shakespeare in Moving Pictures," *Moving Picture World*, Dec. 5, 1908, 446–48.

39. "The Female Politician," *Moving Picture World*, Jul. 25, 1908, 92; "An Auto Heroine," *Moving Picture World*, Oct. 17, 1908, 307–8.

40. Robert C. Toll, *On with the Show!: The First Century of Show Business in America* (New York: Oxford University Press, 1976), 231, 280, 302; "Salome; or, The Dance of the Seven Veils," *Moving Picture World*, Aug. 29, 1908, 163–64; "Romances of Old Studios," *Pictures and the Picturegoer*, Mar. 1924, 17; "A Child's Prayer," *Moving Picture World*, Mar. 14, 1908, 219.

41. "Levitsky's Insurance Policy; or, When Thief Meets Thief," *Moving Picture World*, Jul. 25, 1908, 71; "Leah the Forsaken," *Moving Picture World*, Oct. 10, 1908, 289.

42. "The Air-Ship, or, One Hundred Years Hence," *Moving Picture World*, Apr. 25, 1908, 377; "The Air-Ship, or, One Hundred Years Hence," Box 11, Albert E. Smith Papers (Collection 2004), Department of Special Collections, Charles E. Young Research Library, University of California, Los Angeles.

43. Gartenberg, "Vitagraph before Griffith," 8; *New York Dramatic Mirror*, Nov. 14, 1908, 10; David Bordwell, Janet Staiger, and Kristin Thompson, *The Classical Hollywood Cinema: Film Style and Mode of Production to 1960* (New York: Columbia University Press, 1985), 135–36; Smith tape 7.

44. Armond Fields, *Tony Pastor, Father of Vaudeville* (Jefferson, NC: McFarland, 2007), 191–92; "Trade Notes," *Moving Picture World*, Jun. 20, 1908, 527.

45. "Earmarks of Makers," *New York Dramatic Mirror*, Nov. 14, 1908, 10; Glover, "Moving Pictures Amuse," 21; Erish, *Col. William N. Selig*, 31–56; "S. Lubin A Pioneer," *New York Dramatic Mirror*, May 1, 1909, 37; Neil Baldwin, *Edison, Inventing the Century* (New York: Hyperion, 1995), 339; Gartenberg, "Vitagraph before Griffith," 8–9; Musser, *Before the Nickelodeon*, 310, 329, 466; Kevin Brownlow, *The Parade's Gone By* (New York: Alfred A. Knopf, 1968), 386, 388.

46. Musser, *Before the Nickelodeon*, 333; Letter Mar. 26, 1907, Gilmore to Edison, D0728; 191:583, Thomas A. Edison Papers, Rutgers University; Albert Smith testimony, Greater New York Film Rental Company vs. Biograph Company and General Film Company, Aug. 5, 1913, 2671, Motion Picture Patents Company and General Film Company collection, Margaret Herrick Library, Academy of Motion Picture Arts and Sciences; Blackton testimony, Dec. 1, 1913, 1993–1994.

47. "Film Firm Enjoined," *Moving Picture World*, Nov. 9, 1907, 580; Erish, *Col. William N. Selig*, 25–26; J. Stuart Blackton, "'Silence Was Golden,' The Story of My Forty Movie Years," ms., 159–61, J. Stuart Blackton papers, Special Collections, Margaret Herrick Library, Academy of Motion Picture Arts and Sciences; Frank L. Dyer testimony, United States of America vs. Motion Picture Patents Company et al., Nov. 11, 1913, 1558–1561.

48. Smith testimony, Greater New York Film Rental Company vs. Biograph Company and General Film Company, Aug. 5, 1913, 2671 and Aug. 6, 1913, 2759, Motion Picture Patents Company and General Film Company collection, Margaret Herrick Library, Academy of Motion Picture Arts and Sciences; Bowser, *Transformation of Cinema*, 22–23, 28; Letter, Rock and Blackton to Smith; Abel, *Red Rooster Scare*, 89–90; Letter Feb. 11, 1908, Rock to Smith, Box 1, Albert E. Smith Papers (Collection 2004), Department of Special Collections, Charles E. Young Research Library, University of California, Los Angeles; Frank L. Dyer testimony, Nov. 11, 1913, 1562–1563, 1569.

49. Ramsaye, *A Million and One Nights*, 468–69; Bowser, *Transformation of Cinema*, 24–26; Frank L. Dyer testimony, Nov. 11, 1913, 1561, 1569; Letter, Rock and Blackton to Smith; Letter Feb. 21, 1908, Rock to Smith, Box 1, Albert E. Smith Papers (Collection 2004), Department of Special Collections, Charles E. Young Research Library, University of California, Los Angeles; Anderson, "Motion Picture Patents Company," 8.

50. Smith testimony, Greater New York Film Rental Company vs. Biograph Company and General Film Company, Aug. 6, 1913, 2704; "Moving Pictures in Tight Trust," *Moving Picture World*, Feb. 15, 1908, 116; "Edison Company's Statement to Exhibitors of Moving Pictures in the United States," *Moving Picture World*, Feb. 29, 1908, 158–59; Smith, *Two Reels and a Crank*, 236; "USA vs. MPPC," *Film History*, Jan. 1, 1987, 196.

51. Bowser, *Transformation of Cinema*, 28; Smith testimony, Greater New York Film Rental Company vs. Biograph Company and General Film Company, Aug. 5, 1913, 2671–2672.

52. Blackton, "Silence Was Golden," 163; Bowser, *Transformation of Cinema*, 29; Patent drawings, Box 1, Albert E. Smith Papers (Collection 2004), Department of Special Collections, Charles E. Young Research Library, University of California, Los Angeles; Smith testimony, Greater New York Film Rental Company vs. Biograph Company and General Film Company, Aug. 5, 1913, 2668–2670; Smith, Two Reels

and a Crank, 237; "USA vs. MPPC," 202, 205, 268; Motion Picture Patents Company Balance Sheet, Profit and Loss Account and Report of Treasurer, Jul. 3, 1911, 214:622, Thomas Edison Papers.

53. Bowser, *Transformation of Cinema*, 23–24; Musser, *Before the Nickelodeon*, 445; Anderson, "Motion Picture Patents Company," xiii, 268.

3. 1909–1913

1. "An Interview with J. Stuart Blackton," *Moving Picture World*, Dec. 19, 1908, 497–98; Marian Blackton Trimble, *J. Stuart Blackton: A Personal Biography by His Daughter* (Metuchen, NJ: Scarecrow, 1985), 50; "Vitagraph High-Art Production," *Film Index*, Apr. 10, 1909, 14.

2. Blackton Trimble, *J. Stuart Blackton*, 50–52; Donald Dewey, *Buccaneer, James Stuart Blackton and the Birth of the American Movies* (Lanham, MD: Rowman & Littlefield, 2016), 111; "Vitagraph High-Art Production," 14; Albert Smith audio interview, tape 7, Albert E. Smith Papers (Collection 2004), Department of Special Collections, Charles E. Young Research Library, University of California, Los Angeles; Roberta E. Pearson and William Uricchio, "'How to Be a Stage Napoleon': Vitagraph's Vision of History," *Persistence of Vision* 9 (1991): 82–84.

3. "The Vitagraph Napoleon," *Moving Picture World*, Apr. 10, 1909, 439; "Comments on Film Subjects," *Moving Picture World*, Apr. 17, 1909, 477.

4. "Notes of the Trade," *Moving Picture World*, Aug. 28, 1909, 278; Letter Nov. 27, 1956, Smith to George Pratt, Box 10, Albert E. Smith Papers (Collection 2004), Department of Special Collections, Charles E. Young Research Library, University of California, Los Angeles; Anthony Slide and Alan Gevinson, *The Big V: A History of the Vitagraph Company* (Metuchen, NJ: Scarecrow, 1987), 144; "Mirror Interviews: Charles Kent," *New York Dramatic Mirror*, Jan. 1, 1898, 2; Robert Grau, *The Theatre of Science* (New York: Broadway Publishing Co., 1914), 120–21; Blackton Trimble, *J. Stuart Blackton*, 39–40; *Moving Picture World*, Nov. 6, 1909, 634.

5. *Moving Picture World*, Feb. 26, 1910, 304; "Special Lecture on The Life of Moses," *Moving Picture World*, Dec. 18, 1909, 878, 886; "Vitagraph Notes," *Moving Picture World*, Jan. 8, 1910, 18, Feb. 19, 1910, 260; Eileen Bowser, *The Transformation of Cinema, 1907–1915* (Berkeley, CA: University of California Press, 1990), 196. In 1911 *The Life of Moses* played to fifty thousand people over a two-week period at the Majestic Theatre in the Philippines. "From the Other Side of the World," *Moving Picture World*, Feb. 4, 1911, 236. For later rentals, see Letter Jul. 9, 1924, Siegel to Smith, Box 12660A, Warner Bros. Archives at USC.

6. "Fails to Hold the Interest of the Spectators," *Moving Picture World*, Apr. 3, 1909, 397; "Shakespeare on the Screen," *Moving Picture World*, Jan. 8, 1910, 10–11; Letter Feb. 12, 1954, Smith to Robert H. Ball, Box 10, Albert E. Smith Papers (Collection 2004), Department of Special Collections, Charles E. Young Research Library, University of California, Los Angeles; Albert E. Smith, *Two Reels and a Crank* (Garden City, NY: Doubleday, 1952), 263; Robert Hamilton Ball, *Shakespeare on Silent Film* (London: Allen and Unwin, 1968), 53–55.

7. Letter, Smith to George Pratt; L. Gardette, "Some Tricks of the Moving Picture Maker," *Nickelodeon*, Aug. 1909, 53–56; Erik Barnouw, *The Magician and the Cinema* (New York: Oxford University Press, 1981), 100; Frederick Talbot, *Moving Pictures: How They Are Made and Worked* (Philadelphia, PA: J. B. Lippincott, 1912), 242–53.

8. Thomas Bedding, "The Sentiment of the Picture," *Moving Picture World*, Nov. 12, 1910, 1100; Letter Dec. 8, 1909, Horace G. Plimpton to Frank L. Dwyer, quoting Carl Lewis Gregory and *The Bioscope*, D0934; 193:1087, Thomas A. Edison Papers, Rutgers University; Letter Nov. 23, 1910, Frank Dyer to Thomas Graf, D1045; 196:228, Thomas A. Edison Papers, Rutgers University; Bowser, *Transformation of Cinema*, 23; Albert Smith testimony, Greater New York Film Rental Company vs. Biograph Company and General Film Company, Aug. 7, 1913, 2802, Motion Picture Patents Company and General Film Company collection, Margaret Herrick Library, Academy of Motion Picture Arts and Sciences; *Moving Picture World*, Nov. 13, 1909, 675, Sep. 18, 1909, 374.

9. Max Alvarez, "The Origins of the Film Exchange," *Film History* 17 (2006): 438, 439; "USA vs. MPPC," *Film History* (Jan. 1, 1987): 268–69; Bowser, *Transformation of Cinema*, 4; Robert Jack Anderson, "The Motion Picture Patents Company" (PhD diss., University of Wisconsin-Madison, 1983), viii, ix, xv.

10. Letters Feb. 2, 1909 and Feb. 5, 1909, Ronald Reader to Smith, Box 2, Albert E. Smith Papers (Collection 2004), Department of Special Collections, Charles E. Young Research Library, University of California, Los Angeles.

11. Neal Gabler, *An Empire of Their Own: How the Jews Invented Hollywood* (New York: Doubleday, 1989), 50–54; Anderson, "Motion Picture Patents Company," 23; *Moving Picture World*, Apr. 17, 1909, 467, 472–73, 480–81, 494; "New Film Factories," *Moving Picture World*, Aug. 29, 1908, 155; *Moving Picture World*, May 8, 1909, 613; "Laemmle Becomes a Manufacturer," *Moving Picture World*, Jun. 5, 1909, 740, 750.

12. "The Combine and its Policy," *Moving Picture World*, Jan. 9, 1909, 29; "The New Order of Things," *Moving Picture World*, Jan. 30, 1909, 113; "The Independent Film Protective Association," *Moving Picture World*, Jan. 30, 1909, 116; Anderson, "Motion Picture Patents Company," v–vi, xv; Bowser, *Transformation of Cinema*, 76; *Moving Picture World*, Oct. 23, 1909, 594; Terry Ramsaye, *A Million and One Nights, A History of the Motion Picture* (New York: Simon and Schuster, 1926), 496; *Moving Picture World*, Oct. 30, 1909, 594; Gabler, *An Empire of Their Own*, 61; "Willat Will Make Pictures," *Moving Picture World*, Dec. 27, 1913, 1553; "Jules Stern, "Reminiscences of a Studio Manager," *Moving Picture World*, Jun. 5, 1915, 1592; "Tony G. Gaudio," *American Cinematographer*, Feb. 1, 1922, 45; Letter Mar. 3, 1910, Smith to Edison Mfg. Co., CK916B; 215:87, Thomas A. Edison Papers, Rutgers University; Kelly R. Brown, *Florence Lawrence, The Biograph Girl* (Jefferson, NC: McFarland, 1999), 41.

13. Smith, *Two Reels and a Crank*, 76; *Scientific American*, Sep. 1940, 145, Box 1, Albert E. Smith Papers (Collection 2004), Department of Special Collections, Charles E. Young Research Library, University of California, Los Angeles.

14. "Vitagraph Notes," *Moving Picture World*, Jan. 8, 1910, 18, Jan. 15, 1910, 59; Ramsaye, *A Million and One Nights*, 550; "Vitagraph Company of America Entertain Their Employees," *Moving Picture World*, Jan. 22, 1910, 86–88.

15. Terry Chester Schulman, *Film's First Family: The Untold Story of the Costellos* (Lexington: University Press of Kentucky, 2019), 7, 15, 26–28, 38–41; Gladys Hall, "Maurice Costello: What it Was to Be a Star in 1911," ms., 2, Gladys Hall Collection, Folder 118, Margaret Herrick Library, Academy of Motion Picture Arts and Sciences; John Montgomery, *Comedy Films 1894–1954* (London: George Allen & Unwin Ltd., rev. ed. 1968), 69–70.

16. Smith tape 7; Smith, *Two Reels and a Crank*, 175, 187; Ramsaye, *A Million and One Nights*, 443; J. Stuart Blackton, "'Hollywood with Its Hair Down' or Hollywood Memories; Forty Years of the Movies," ms., 112, J. Stuart Blackton papers, Special Collections, Margaret Herrick Library, Academy of Motion Picture Arts and Sciences; Vitagraph Bulletin, Aug. 1915, 42, Margaret Herrick Library, Academy of Motion Picture Arts and Sciences; "Chats with the Players: Maurice Costello," *Motion Picture Story Magazine*, Apr. 1912, 138.

17. Ball, *Shakespeare on Silent Film*, 56; Hall, "Maurice Costello," 4; Smith, *Two Reels and a Crank*, 175.

18. Price Waterhouse accounts report for five years to 1913, Box 2, Albert E. Smith Papers (Collection 2004), Department of Special Collections, Charles E. Young Research Library, University of California, Los Angeles; "Vitagraph Company Will Issue Three Reels," *Moving Picture World*, Jan. 29, 1910, 120; "Vitagraph Executive Offices Move to Factory," *Moving Picture World*, Aug. 27, 1910, 472; Bowser, *Transformation of Cinema*, 103; William H. Jackson, "A Casual Visit to the Vitagraph Plant," *Moving Picture World*, Sep. 17, 1910, 624.

19. *Moving Picture World*, Jul. 31, 1909, 150, 152, Nov. 6, 1909, 656; "Texas Now the Stamping Ground for Moving Picture Artists," *Moving Picture World*, Jan. 22, 1910, 93; "Méliès in California," *Moving Picture World*, May 13, 1911, 1070; Smith tape 8; Certificate No. 6 from Méliès Mfg. Co. for 34 shares purchased by Albert E. Smith Apr. 8, 1910, Box 2, Albert E. Smith Papers (Collection 2004), Department of Special Collections, Charles E. Young Research Library, University of California, Los Angeles; Paul Hammond, *Marvellous Méliès* (New York: St. Martin's, 1975), 74–76.

20. "F. S. A. Convention Notes," *Moving Picture World*, Feb. 12, 1910, 204, 211; F. H. Richardson, "The Home of Vitagraph," *Moving Picture World*, Jan. 24, 1914, 402–3; Blackton, "Hollywood with Its Hair Down," 89.

21. J. Stuart Blackton, "'Silence Was Golden,' The Story of My Forty Movie Years," ms., 164–66, J. Stuart Blackton papers, Special Collections, Margaret Herrick Library, Academy of Motion Picture Arts and Sciences; Anderson, "Motion Picture Patents Company," 196, 229; Bowser, *Transformation of Cinema*, 81; "USA vs. MPPC," 188–89, 244; "Observations by Our Man About Town," *Moving Picture World*, Aug. 27, 1910, 459–60; Smith tape 7; "Vitagraph Executive Offices Move to Factory," 472; Smith, *Two Reels and a Crank*, 238.

22. Brown, *Florence Lawrence, The Biograph Girl*, 41, 43–44, 47, 50–51; *Moving Picture World*, Feb. 19, 1910, 268, Mar. 12, 1910, 365; Andrew A. Erish, *Col. William N. Selig, the Man Who Invented Hollywood* (Austin, TX: University of Texas Press, 2012), 86–87; Bowser, *Transformation of Cinema*, 103, 106, 109, 112; Andrew Shail, "Max

Linder and the Emergence of Film Stardom," *Early Popular Visual Culture* 14, no. 1 (2016): 55–86.

23. Letter May 6, 1909, Blackton to Dyer, D0912; 193:426, Thomas A. Edison Papers, Rutgers University; Letter May 7, 1909, Dyer to Blackton, D0912; 193:428, Thomas A. Edison Papers, Rutgers University; Smith tape 8; Smith, *Two Reels and a Crank*, 210; Norman Zierold, *The Moguls* (New York: Coward-McCann, 1969), 83; Gabler, *An Empire of Their Own*, 48; Letter Dec. 15, 1908, Laemmle to Selig, Scrapbook #2, MS Collection #47, Charles G. Clarke Collection, Margaret Herrick Library, Academy of Motion Picture Arts and Sciences; Letter Feb. 5, 1909, Laemmle to Selig Polyscope Co., Letter Oct. 28, 1909, Laemmle to Selig, Folder 459, William Selig Collection, Special Collections, Margaret Herrick Library, Academy of Motion Picture Arts and Sciences; Anderson, "Motion Picture Patents Company," 185–88; Thomas Schatz, *The Genius of the System: Hollywood Filmmaking in the Studio Era* (New York: Pantheon, 1988), 18.

24. John Drinkwater, *The Life and Adventures of Carl Laemmle* (New York: G. P. Putnam's Sons, 1931), 110; Richard Dyer MacCann, *The First Tycoons* (Metuchen, NJ: Scarecrow, 1987), 32; Gabler, *An Empire of Their Own*, 59, 61; Anderson, "Motion Picture Patents Company," 135–36, 188–93, 250; Fred J. Balshofer and Arthur C. Miller, *One Reel a Week* (Berkeley, CA: University of California Press, 1967), 17, 21, 38–41, 59–60; Peter Bogdanovich, *Allan Dwan, the Last Pioneer* (New York: Praeger, 1971), 18–19; Kevin Brownlow, "An Introduction to Silent Film," *Journal of the Royal Society of Arts* (Mar. 1984): 264–65.

25. Anderson, "Motion Picture Patents Company," 188–90; McCoy Report on American Vitagraph, Nov. 7, 1904, 189:376, Thomas A. Edison Papers, Rutgers University; Blackton, "Silence Was Golden," 157–58; Gabler, *An Empire of Their Own*, 59; Douglas Gomery, *The Hollywood Studio System* (New York: St. Martin's, 1986), 3–4; "Doings in Los Angeles," *Moving Picture World*, Jul. 20, 1912, 235, Jul. 27, 1912, 335; "Bison Plant Attacked," *Moving Picture World*, Aug. 10, 1912, 533; Albert Smith testimony, United States of America vs. Motion Picture Patents Company et al., Nov. 14, 1913, 1713, Nov. 18, 1913, 1753–1754.

26. J. M. Bradlet, "A Reply to Some Enemies of the Motion Picture," *Moving Picture World*, Oct. 1, 1910, 744; J. Stuart Blackton, "Morality and Film Censorship," *New York Telegraph*, Mar. 20, 1910, D1046; 196:245, Thomas A. Edison Papers, Rutgers University; Gladys Hall, "Maurice Costello," 7–8.

27. Sam Spedon, "Ten Years of Film Publicity," *Moving Picture World*, Mar. 10, 1917, 1530.

28. "Moving Picture Gods and Goddesses," *Moving Picture World*, Mar. 26, 1910, 468; Richard Abel, *The Red Rooster Scare: Making Cinema American, 1900–1910* (Berkeley, CA: University of California Press, 1999), 148; Bowser, *Transformation of Cinema*, 112–14; "Vitagraph Notes," *Moving Picture World*, Apr. 2, 1910, 515; "Vitagraph Girl Feted," *Moving Picture World*, Apr. 23, 1910, 644; "On the Screen by Lux Graphicus," *Moving Picture World*, Oct. 8, 1910, 807; "Ten Years of Film Publicity," 1530; *Moving Picture World*, May 21, 1910, 825; "Vitagraph Notes," *Moving Picture World*, Aug. 13, 1910, 360; "Miss Florence E. Turner: The Vitagraph Girl," *Moving*

Picture World, Jul. 23, 1910, 187–88; F. H. Richardson, "A Vitagraph Girl Night," *Moving Picture World*, Dec. 31, 1910, 1521.

29. *Moving Picture World*, Jun. 4, 1910, 947; *Moving Picture World*, Jun. 11, 1910, 1024; "How Championships Are Won and Lost," *Moving Picture World*, Jun. 18, 1910, 1063; Vitagraph Life Portrayals Jun. 1 to Jun. 15, 1910, Box 3, Albert E. Smith Papers (Collection 2004), Department of Special Collections, Charles E. Young Research Library, University of California, Los Angeles; "Comments on the Films," *Moving Picture World*, Jul. 2, 1910, 24; Terry Ramsaye, "The Romantic History of the Motion Picture," *Photoplay*, Aug. 1924, 65. This was the debut film for Corbett's sparring partner Tom Kennedy, who in a career spanning fifty-five years provided comic support for the Marx Brothers, Laurel and Hardy, W. C. Fields, Bob Hope, the Three Stooges, and Abbott and Costello.

30. "Observations by Our Man About Town," *Moving Picture World*, Nov. 26, 1910, 1223; "Success of the Park Theater in Brooklyn," *Moving Picture World*, Mar. 4, 1911, 474; "Costello Theater," *Moving Picture World*, May 30, 1914, 1269; Gladys Hall, "Maurice Costello," 3–6; transcript of Dolores Costello interview by Sue McConachy and David Gill for *Hollywood* documentary, Kevin Brownlow to author.

31. Smith, *Two Reels and a Crank*, 175, 224; "Miss Florence E. Turner," 187–88; Ramsaye, *A Million and One Nights*, 545–46; Blackton Trimble, *J. Stuart Blackton*, 44, 46; Blackton, "Hollywood with Its Hair Down," 160–61; "Miss Hayes and Films," *New York Times*, Mar. 15, 1931, 116.

32. Letters Nov. 26, 1910, Blackton to Dyer, CK925; 215:398, Dec. 23, 1910, Dyer to Blackton, CK925; 215:400, Jan. 14, 1911, Blackton to Edison, E1163; 250:206, Thomas A. Edison Papers, Rutgers University; Blackton, "Hollywood with Its Hair Down," 332–33; *Motion Picture Story Magazine*, Jan. 1913, 121–23; Letter Aug. 24, 1911, Blackton to Dyer, CK925; 215:413, Thomas A. Edison Papers, Rutgers University; Gladys Hall, "Maurice Costello," 3; "Chats with the Players: Maurice Costello," 138; "Popular Player Contest," *Motion Picture Story Magazine*, Jun. 1912, 146; Andrew Shail, "The *Motion Picture Story Magazine* and the Origins of Popular British Film Culture," *Film History* 20, no. 2 (2008): 181–97; Grau, *Theatre of Science*, 255.

33. *Moving Picture World*, Jun. 10, 1911, 1304; "Four Vitagraph Reels," *Moving Picture World*, Jul. 1, 1911, 1506; "Another Three-Reel Vitagraph Life Portrayal Coming," *Moving Picture World*, Jun. 24, 1911, 1429; "Vitagraph Notes," *Moving Picture World*, Jul. 15, 1911, 49; "A Glimpse behind the Scenes," *Moving Picture World*, Aug. 12, 1911, 380.

34. "Jealousy," *Moving Picture World*, Sep. 23, 1911, 889; Louis Reeves Harrison, "Superior Plays," *Moving Picture World*, Aug. 12, 1911, 361; *Moving Picture World*, Sep. 9, 1911, 680; Vitagraph Life Portrayals, Aug. 27, 1911 to Sep. 14, 1911, Margaret Herrick Library, Academy of Motion Picture Arts and Sciences; Ramsaye, "The Romantic History of the Motion Picture," *Photoplay*, Aug. 1924, 65.

35. Gladys Hall, "Maurice Costello," 7; "Chats with the Players: Maurice Costello," 138; "Vitagraph Play," *Moving Picture World*, Feb. 25, 1911, 427; "Comments on the Films," *Moving Picture World*, Mar. 4, 1911, 483; "Comments on the Films," *Moving Picture World*, Mar. 11, 1911, 540; "Three Reel Subjects," *Film Index*, Feb. 25,

1911, 3, 7; "Three Reel Pictures a Success," *Moving Picture World*, Mar. 25, 1911, 640; "Film Criticism in the Lay Press," *Moving Picture World*, May 20, 1911, 1113; Letter Mar. 27, 1952, James Morrison to Smith, Box 1, Albert E. Smith Papers (Collection 2004), Department of Special Collections, Charles E. Young Research Library, University of California, Los Angeles; Kevin Brownlow, *The Parade's Gone By* (New York: Alfred A. Knopf, 1968), 16; Michael Eaton, "Notes on *A Tale of Two Cities*," Catalogue (Pordenone, Italy: Le Giornate Del Cinema Muto, Oct 6–13, 2012), 52–53, 55–57.

36. Norma Talmadge, "Close-Ups," *Saturday Evening Post*, Mar. 12, 1927, 6–7, 115–16, 121–22; Arthur Hornblow, Jr., "Norma Talmadge," *Photoplay*, Aug. 1915, 99–101; Elsie Vance, "Norma Talmadge—the Adorable," *Photoplay*, Feb. 1915, 68–70; Smith, *Two Reels and a Crank*, 190–92; Smith tapes 5, 8; Brownlow, *Parade's Gone By*, 145–46.

37. "Miss Turner Goes to California," *Moving Picture World*, Dec. 9, 1911, 811; Jerome D. Mitchell, "Miss Turner Gaining in Health," *Moving Picture World*, Mar. 2, 1912, 770; "Florence Turner Gets Ovation in Portland," *Moving Picture World*, Mar. 30, 1912, 1147; Transcript of Dec. 1964 audio interview between Kevin Brownlow and James Morrison, Kevin Brownlow to author.

38. "The Battle Hymn of the Republic," *Moving Picture World*, Jul. 1, 1911, 1497; Vachel Lindsay, *The Art of the Moving Picture* (New York: MacMillan Company, 1916), 58, 73–78, 187, 192; "The Battle Hymn of the Republic," *Motography*, Jul. 1911, 42; Blackton Trimble, *J. Stuart Blackton*, 48; J. Stuart Blackton, "Yesterdays of Vitagraph," *Photoplay*, Jul. 1919, 29; Grau, *Theatre of Science*, 91; "The Vitagraph Editress," *Moving Picture World*, Nov. 9, 1912, 550; Smith, *Two Reels and a Crank*, 204; Smith tape 7.

39. Vitagraph Bulletin Nov. 1-Nov. 15, 1909, Nov. 16–Dec. 1, 1911, Box 3, Albert E. Smith Papers (Collection 2004), Department of Special Collections, Charles E. Young Research Library, University of California, Los Angeles.

40. "Father and Son," *Moving Picture World*, Jan. 13, 1912, 142; "Comments on the Films," *Moving Picture World*, Nov. 8, 1913, 612; "Kenneth Casey Bound for Africa," *Moving Picture World*, Jul. 18, 1914, 447. Years later the former "Vitagraph Boy" composed the lyrics to "Sweet Georgia Brown."

41. Steve Massa, *Lame Brains & Lunatics: The Good, the Bad and the Forgotten of Silent Comedy* (Duncan, OK: Bear Manor Media, 2013), 93; "Jimmie's Job," *Moving Picture World*, Sep. 23, 1911, 891.

42. "John Bunny," *Screen Club Annual*, 1913, 14, Margaret Herrick Library, Academy of Motion Picture Arts and Sciences; "Mr. John Bunny," *Moving Picture World*, Oct. 14, 1911, 112; Slide and Gevinson, *The Big V*, 44–51; Smith tape 8; Smith, *Two Reels and a Crank*, 205–7; Grau, *Theatre of Science*, 118–19.

43. For instance, compare number of American production companies listed in "Daily Licensed Releases" and "Daily Independent Releases" in *Motography*, Dec. 1911, 295, 296; MPPC Balance Sheet, Profit and Loss Account and Report of Treasurer, Jul. 3, 1911, 214:622, Thomas A. Edison Papers, Rutgers University; Anderson, "Motion Picture Patents Company," xvi; Bowser, *Transformation of Cinema*, 217.

44. Anderson, "Motion Picture Patents Company," xvi, xvii, 38, 90–91, 229; Vanda Krefft, *The Man Who Made the Movies* (New York: HarperCollins, 2017), 36–44, 53, 92–97, 108; Smith, *Two Reels and a Crank*, 239–49; Smith testimony, United States of America vs. Motion Picture Patents Company et al., Nov. 14, 1913, 1697–1698; Smith testimony, Greater New York Film Rental Company vs. Biograph Company and General Film Company, Aug. 5, 1913, 2618, 2623, 2629; "No Injunction against Patents Co.," *Moving Picture World*, Feb. 10, 1912, 470; "Agitation and Alarm," *Moving Picture World*, Mar. 12, 1910, 370; "Alliance Executive Committee in Session, Projected Sales Company Seeks to Regulate the Business of the Independents," *Moving Picture World*, Apr. 9, 1910, 549; "More on the Open Market," *Moving Picture World*, Mar. 18, 1911, 586; Bowser, *Transformation of Cinema*, 217.

45. Report of Audit, Vitagraph Co. of America, Dec. 31, 1911, Box 2, Albert E. Smith Papers (Collection 2004), Department of Special Collections, Charles E. Young Research Library, University of California, Los Angeles.

46. "Comments on the Films," *Moving Picture World*, Sep. 28, 1912, 1277.

47. Dorothy Scott, "A Tip for Pershing," *Photoplay*, Jun. 1918, 39; Blackton, "Hollywood with Its Hair Down," 166–67; Smith, *Two Reels and a Crank*, 188–89; "Vitagraph Notes," *Moving Picture World*, Jun. 15, 1912, 1135; George Blaisdell, "Clara Kimball Young, Artist," *Moving Picture World*, Oct. 3, 1914, 41–42; "Jimmy Morrison, Versatile Vitagraph," *Moving Picture World*, May 6, 1916, 978; Brownlow, *Parade's Gone By*, 14; "Clara Kimball Young Wins Popularity Prize," *Moving Picture World*, Sep. 26, 1914, 1791.

48. Louis Reeves Harrison, "Studio Saunterings," *Moving Picture World*, Feb. 17, 1912, 557, Jun. 8, 1912, 906; Blackton Trimble, *J. Stuart Blackton*, 57–58, 61; "Observations by our Man About Town," *Moving Picture World*, Apr. 22, 1911, 879; "Commodore Blackton Sails South," *Moving Picture World*, Feb. 10, 1912, 493; "Vitagraph Studio Notes," *Moving Picture World*, Jul. 6, 1912, 28.

49. James S. McQuade, "Chicago Letter," *Moving Picture World*, Nov. 25, 1911, 630; Jul. 10, 1915, 218; "Mecca of the Motion Picture," *Moving Picture World*, Jul. 10, 1915, 218; Vitagraph Life Portrayals, Dec. 17, 1911–Jan. 1, 1912, Margaret Herrick Library, Academy of Motion Picture Arts and Sciences; Smith, *Two Reels and a Crank*, 229–30; Smith tape 7; Edwin LaRoche, "A New Profession for Women," *Motion Picture*, May 1914, 83–88; Blackton, "Hollywood with Its Hair Down," 134; Epes Winthrop Sargent, "The Literary Side of Pictures," *Moving Picture World*, Jul. 11, 1914, 200.

50. "How States Are Made," *Moving Picture World*, Feb. 17, 1912, 565.

51. *Moving Picture World*, Mar. 30, 1912, 1185, Aug. 10, 1912, 515; "Six Vitagraphs a Week," *Moving Picture World*, Aug. 10, 1912, 747; *Moving Picture World*, Sep. 7, 1912, 962.

52. Memo Sep. 25, 1912, Dyer to Edison, CK911; 214:990, Thomas A. Edison Papers, Rutgers University; Letter Jan. 23, 1912, Paul Cromelin to Dyer, CK918; 215:165, Thomas A. Edison Papers, Rutgers University; Memo Apr. 17, 1912, Dyer to Edison, CK911; 214:947, Thomas A. Edison Papers, Rutgers University; Anderson, "Motion Picture Patents Company," 285; Smith testimony, United States of America vs. Motion Picture Patents Company et al., Nov. 14, 1913, 1723–1724.

53. "Comments on the Films," *Moving Picture World*, Apr. 6, 1912, 40; "Lillian Walker," *Moving Picture World*, Aug. 15, 1914, 962; Moe Howard, *Moe Howard & the 3 Stooges* (Secaucus, NJ: Citadel, 1977), 19–21.

54. "John Bunny Sails for England," *Moving Picture World*, Jun. 8, 1912, 911; "Comments on the Films," *Moving Picture World*, Nov. 2, 1912, 450; Hugh Hoffman, "John Bunny Abroad," *Moving Picture World*, Sep. 21, 1912, 1157; "John Bunny in Merrie England," *Moving Picture World*, Jul. 20, 1912, 252; "A Vitagraph Screamer," *Cinema*, Jan. 15, 1913, 17–18; "Comments on the Films," *Moving Picture World*, Nov. 9, 1912, 553; Hugh Hoffman, "John Bunny as Pickwick," *Moving Picture World*, Feb. 15, 1913, 663; "On the Outside Looking In," *Motography*, Aug. 22, 1914, 265–66.

55. Robert L. Patten, "Introduction," *The Posthumous Papers of The Pickwick Club* (Harmondsworth, England: Penguin, 1972), 11–30; "John Bunny Abroad," 1157; Montgomery, *Comedy Films 1894–1954*, 32–40, 68; Cecil M. Hepworth, *Came the Dawn: Memories of a Film Pioneer* (London: Phoenix House Ltd., 1951), 111, 113; "John Bunny Returns from Europe," *Moving Picture World*, Sep. 14, 1912, 1083; Hoffman, "John Bunny as Pickwick," 663; "Comments on the Films," *Moving Picture World*, Sep. 20, 1913, 1283; Smith, *Two Reels and a Crank*, 208; Blackton, "Hollywood with Its Hair Down," 164; *Moving Picture World*, May 20, 1911, 1118; "Screen Club a Winner," *Moving Picture World*, Sep. 28, 1912, 1283.

56. "Industry's Chiefs Honor Brady," *Moving Picture World*, Mar. 15, 1919, 1451–1454; Dolores Costello interview, Brownlow to author; "Comments on the Films," *Moving Picture World*, Jun. 15, 1912, 102.

57. "Chats with the Players: Maurice Costello," 138; Vitagraph Life Portrayals, Jun. 1–Jun. 15, 1912, Margaret Herrick Library, Academy of Motion Picture Arts and Sciences; "Comments on the Films," *Moving Picture World*, Jun. 22, 1912, 1126, Nov. 8, 1913, 612; G. F. Blaisdell, "At the Sign of the Flaming Arcs," *Moving Picture World*, Aug. 10, 1912, 761; Smith, *Two Reels and a Crank*, 188.

58. "Chats with the Players: Hazel Neason," *Motion Picture Story Magazine*, Sep. 1912, 131–32; Dewey, *Buccaneer*, 143; Slide and Gevinson, *The Big V*, 34; *Motography*, Feb. 1, 1913, 102.

59. "Vitagraph Studio Notes," *Moving Picture World*, Jul. 6, 1912, 28; "Vitagraph's Christmas Stocking," *Moving Picture World*, Jan. 11, 1913, 143; Smith, *Two Reels and a Crank*, 252.

60. "The Vitagraph Globe Trotters," *Moving Picture World*, Jan. 4, 1913, 55; Peter Wade, "A Girdle of Film Round the World," *Motion Picture Story Magazine*, Aug. 1913, 101–6; Hugh Hoffman, "Picture Making in the Far East," *Moving Picture World*, Jun. 21, 1913, 1231; Smith, *Two Reels and a Crank*, 232–33; Bowser, *Transformation of Cinema*, 153–54; "The Joys of a Jealous Wife," *Moving Picture World*, Aug. 23, 1913, 843; Dolores Costello interview, Brownlow to author; Smith tape 8; "British Notes," *Moving Picture World*, May 31, 1913, 900; Dolores Costello, *How I Broke Into the Movies*, Hal. C. Herman, ed. (Hollywood, CA: Everett L. Sanders, 1930), 53.

61. "Observations by Our Man About Town," *Moving Picture World*, Apr. 5, 1913, 51; 10; Hugh Hoffman, "Florence Turner Going to England," *Moving Picture World*, Mar. 22, 1913, 1225.

62. Blackton, "Hollywood with Its Hair Down," 164–65; "Picture Face Gets $1,000," *Variety*, Jan. 10, 1913, 1; "John Bunny in Vaudeville," *Moving Picture World*, Feb. 1, 1913, 473; Grau, *Theatre of Science*, 119; Newspaper clipping: "Bunny's Smile a Winner at Keith's, Much Photographed Man Tells Experience in 'Movies,'" *Boston Journal*, Mar [9?], 1913, 0314, Thomas A. Edison Papers, Rutgers University.

63. "Sidney Drew," *Moving Picture World*, May 15, 1915, 1078; Slide and Gevinson, *The Big V*, 97–98; Ward Morehouse, *Matinee Tomorrow* (New York: Whittlesey House, 1949), 77; Joe Laurie, Jr., *Vaudeville, from the Honky-Tonks to the Palace* (New York: Henry Holt, 1953), 50, 51, 146; Smith, *Two Reels and a Crank*, 195–96; "Sidney Drew," *Moving Picture World*, May 15, 1915, 1078; Louis Reeves Harrison, "A Regiment of Two," *Moving Picture World*, May 24, 1913, 792, Jun 28, 1913, 1358.

64. Vitagraph Life Portrayals, Aug. 17–Sep. 1, 1912, Margaret Herrick Library, Academy of Motion Picture Arts and Sciences; "Doings at Los Angeles," *Moving Picture World*, Mar. 22, 1913, 1207; *Moving Picture World*, Apr. 5, 1913, 34; "From the Vitagraph Western Studio," *Moving Picture World*, Aug. 16, 1913, 722; Antonio Moreno vs. Vitagraph, deposition of William Steven Smith, May 23, Jun. 22, 1922, Box 7, Albert E. Smith Papers (Collection 2004), Department of Special Collections, Charles E. Young Research Library, University of California, Los Angeles.

65. "Comments on the Films," *Moving Picture World*, Aug. 16, 1913, 743; "Doings at Los Angeles," *Moving Picture World*, Oct. 5, 1912, 17; Slide and Gevinson, *The Big V*, 52; "Vitagraph Notes," *Moving Picture World*, Jul. 5, 1913, 52; Mabel Condon, "Sans Grease Paint and Wig," *Motography*, Aug. 13, 1914, 241–42.

66. Smith testimony, Greater New York Film Rental Company vs. Biograph Company and General Film Company, Aug. 6, 1913, 2746; "W. Steve Smith, Jr.," *American Cinematographer*, Feb. 1, 1922, 24; Dewey, *Buccaneer*, 10; Spedon, Sam, "Keeping in Personal Touch," *Moving Picture World*, Dec. 4, 1920, 582.

67. "Tony G. Gaudio," *American Cinematographer*, 45; Letter Mar. 3, 1910, Smith to Edison Mfg. Co, CK916B; 215:87, Thomas A. Edison Papers, Rutgers University; George Turner, "Cinemasters: Milton Krasner, ASC, *American Cinematographer*, Sep. 1986, 38; George Turner, "Out of the Past," *American Cinematographer*, Mar. 1984, 65:3, 32; John Bailey, "Nicholas Musuraca, Cat People and RKO Film Noir," *American Cinematographer*, Oct. 9, 2016.

68. For an astute analysis of film noir, see "The Death of Film Noir" at www.williamahearn.com.

69. *Film Index*, Aug. 25, 1906, 6; Barry Salt, "The Early Development of Film Form," *Film before Griffith*, ed. John L. Fell (Berkeley, CA: University of California Press, 1983), 286; Jon Gartenberg, "Vitagraph before Griffith: Forging Ahead in the Nickelodeon Era," *Studies in Visual Communication* 10, no. 4 (Fall 1984): 8; Barry Salt, *Film Style and Technology: History and Analysis* (London: Starword, 1992), 76–77.

70. "Learned Business from Bottom Up," *Moving Picture World*, Jul. 11, 1914, 285; "Ralph Ince Killed in Crash in London," *New York Times*, Apr. 12, 1937, 1; Julian Johnson, "Ince of the Atlantic," *Photoplay*, Aug. 1915, 103–7; Florence Lawrence and Monte M. Katterjohn, "Growing Up with the Movies," *Photoplay*, Dec. 1914, 98; "Two Vitagraph Headliners," *Moving Picture World*, Mar. 30, 1912, 1150.

71. Barry Salt, "The Unknown Ince," *Sight and Sound* 57, no. 4 (Fall 1988): 268–72; Robert Spadoni, "The Figure Seen from the Rear, Vitagraph, and the Development of Shot/Reverse Shot," *Film History* 11, no. 3 (1999): 11, 319–41; Ben Brewster, "Deep Staging in French Films, 1900–1914," *Early Cinema: Space—Frame—Narrative*, ed. Thomas Elsaesser (London: British Film Institute, 1990), 50; Noel Burch, *Life to Those Shadows*, ed. and trans. Ben Brewster (Berkeley, CA: University of California Press, 1990), 131; Salt, *Film Style and Technology*, 76–77, 93–95, 137, 238; Bowser, *Tranformation of Cinema*, 187, 262; Sam Spedon, "Keeping in Personal Touch, *Moving Picture World*, Dec. 4, 1920, 582.

72. Salt, "Unknown Ince," 268–70; "Vitagraph Notes," *Moving Picture World*, Jul. 5, 1913, 52.

73. "Chats with the Players: Anita Stuart, of the Vitagraph Company," *Motion Picture Story Magazine*, Dec. 1913, 109–10; *Moving Picture World*, Oct. 12, 1912, 143; Vitagraph Life Portrayals, Aug. 1915, 6, Margaret Herrick Library, Academy of Motion Picture Arts and Sciences; "The Wood Violet," *Moving Picture World*, Nov. 23, 1912, 808; Julian Johnson, "Anita Stewart a Star in Law," *Photoplay*, Apr. 1915, 50–55; "Learned Business from Bottom Up," 285; Smith tape 9; Blackton, "Yesterdays of Vitagraph," 29–30; Smith testimony, Greater New York Film Rental Company vs. Biograph Company and General Film Company, Aug. 7, 1913, 2798.

74. Smith tape 7; Smith, *Two Reels and a Crank*, 171; "Sordid Suit, Court Says," *New York Times*, Dec 3, 1913, 5.

75. George Blaisdell, "At the Sign of the Flaming Arcs," *Moving Picture World*, Apr. 12, 1913, 175; "Vitagraph Men Abroad," *Billboard*, May 3, 1913, 10; "Commodore Blackton Re-elected," *Moving Picture World*, Dec. 20, 1913, 1390; Blackton Trimble, *J. Stuart Blackton*, 61–63; Karl K. Kitchen, "Running the Art," *Photoplay*, Dec. 1915, 111–13.

76. Mrs. Beta Breuil, "The Reward for Reading," *Moving Picture World*, May 3, 1913, 482; "A New Profession for Women," 83–88; Smith testimony, Greater New York Film Rental Company vs. Biograph Company and General Film Company, Aug. 6, 1913, 2746; Report by the Examinations Corporation, Mar. 31, 1917, 18–19, Box 10, Albert E. Smith Papers (Collection 2004), Department of Special Collections, Charles E. Young Research Library, University of California, Los Angeles; Folder stamped 00088, Box 9, Albert E. Smith Papers (Collection 2004), Department of Special Collections, Charles E. Young Research Library, University of California, Los Angeles; David Bordwell, Janet Staiger and Kristin Thompson, *The Classical Hollywood Cinema: Film Style and Mode of Production to 1960* (New York: Columbia University Press, 1985), 135–36; Smith tape 7.

77. W. Stephen Bush, "Notes from Italy," *Moving Picture World*, Jun. 21, 1913, 1229; W. Stephen Bush, "The Film in France," *Moving Picture World*, Jul. 12, 1913, 179; "Vitagraph Notes," *Moving Picture World*, Aug. 23, 1913, 848; Report by the Examinations Corporation, 16–17, 42–43; "Ronald Reader Sails," *Moving Picture World*, Sep. 20, 1913, 1268; "Paris Letter," *Moving Picture World*, Oct. 25, 1913, 369; "Foreign Trade Notes," *Moving Picture World*, Jul. 5, 1913, 51; *Cinema*, Jan. 15, 1913, 52; "Vitagraph's New London Offices," *Moving Picture World*, Sep. 20, 1913, 1268; Smith testimony, United States of America vs. Motion Picture Patents Company et al., Nov. 14, 1913, 1724.

78. Smith testimony, Greater New York Film Rental Company vs. Biograph Company and General Film Company, Aug. 5, 1913, 2614, Aug. 6, 1913, 2747–2748; Anderson, "Motion Picture Patents Company," 284; "Interviews with F. S. A. Members and Others: Mr. William T. Rock, of the Vitagraph Company of America," *Moving Picture World*, Mar. 28, 1908, 260; Memo May 14, 1914, Carl Wilson to Edison, CK912; 214:1032, Thomas A. Edison Papers, Rutgers University; "Exposition Notes," *Moving Picture World*, Jun. 28, 1913, 33; Smith, *Two Reels and a Crank*, 252; Net Income Vitagraph Company, Box 1, Albert E. Smith Papers (Collection 2004), Department of Special Collections, Charles E. Young Research Library, University of California, Los Angeles; "A Hundred Thousand Miles of Film," *Motography*, May 16, 1914, 343–44; Accountant's report Dec. 31, 1913, Box 2, Albert E. Smith Papers (Collection 2004), Department of Special Collections, Charles E. Young Research Library, University of California, Los Angeles.

79. "Princely Christmas Gift for Picture Men," *Moving Picture World*, Jan. 3, 1914, 29; "'Pop' Rock is Sixty—Goes Like Forty," *Moving Picture World*, Jan. 10, 1914, 182; Krefft, *Man Who Made the Movies*, 111.

4. 1914–1918

1. *Moving Picture World*, Jan. 3, 1914, 15, 21; Robert Grau, *The Theatre of Science* (New York: Broadway Publishing Co., 1914), vi, 114, 271; "'Quo Vadis' at the Astor," *Moving Picture World*, May 3, 1913, 467; Robert E. Welsh, *A-B-C of Motion Pictures* (New York: Harper & Brothers, 1916), 10.

2. Louis Reeves Harrison, "The Christian," *Moving Picture World*, Mar. 28, 1914, 1656–1657; George Blaisdell, "At the Sign of the Flaming Arcs," *Moving Picture World*, Apr. 11, 1914, 219; Christian, Box 12700A, Warner Bros. Archives at USC.

3. "Vitagraph to Have Broadway Theater," *Moving Picture World*, Jan. 3, 1914, 60; Albert Smith audio interview, tape 9, Albert E. Smith Papers (Collection 2004), Department of Special Collections, Charles E. Young Research Library, University of California, Los Angeles; "Vitagraph Picture Theater," *Moving Picture World*, Feb. 14, 1914, 786; "Great Reels at New Vitagraph Says Alan Dale," *New York American*, Feb. 8, 1914, Box 2, Albert E. Smith Papers (Collection 2004), Department of Special Collections, Charles E. Young Research Library, University of California, Los Angeles; "Vitagraph to Abandon Theater," *Moving Picture World*, Jan. 1, 1916, 87.

4. Louis Reeves Harrison, "A Million Bid," *Moving Picture World*, Feb. 7, 1914, 658; "Opened with Éclat," *Moving Picture World*, Feb. 21, 1914, 931; "Vitagraph Theater Opens," *Motography*, Feb. 21, 1914, 142.

5. "Vitagraph New York Theater," *Billboard*, May 2, 1914, 52; Report by the Examinations Corporation, Mar. 31, 1917, 36–37, Box 10, Albert E. Smith Papers (Collection 2004), Department of Special Collections, Charles E. Young Research Library, University of California, Los Angeles. There was an unaffiliated Vitagraph Theater in Chicago owned by exhibitors Lubliner & Trinz. *Moving Picture World*, Oct. 3, 1914, 74; Albert E. Smith, *Two Reels and a Crank* (Garden City, NY: Doubleday, 1952), 253–54, 258.

6. Eileen Bowser, *The Transformation of Cinema, 1907–1915* (Berkeley, CA: University of California Press, 1990), 131, 134; J. Stuart Blackton testimony, United States of America vs. Motion Picture Patents Company et al., Nov. 20, 1913, 1886, 1887; "Vitagraph's New Bill," *Billboard*, Apr. 25, 1914, 53; George Blaisdell, "Mr. Barnes of New York," *Moving Picture World*, May 2, 1914, 651; Letter Dec. 14, 1914, Brown and Dion to Percival Waters, CK912; 214:1037, Thomas A. Edison Papers, Rutgers University.

7. W. Stephen Bush, "The Screen Children's Gallery," *Moving Picture World*, Mar. 14, 1914, 1371; *Moving Picture World*, Sep. 4, 1915, 1659; Leah Weinberg, Film Notes, An Easter "Lily" (1914), www.filmpreservation.org/preserved-films/screening-room /an-easter-lily-1914.

8. "Brevities of the Business," *Motography*, May 16, 1914, 356; Blackton testimony, Nov. 20, 1913, 1886–1887; A Florida Enchantment, Box 12701B, Warner Bros. Archives at USC; "Sidney Drew's Vitagraph Co. Flies North," *Moving Picture World*, Jun. 13, 1914, 1521; R. Bruce Brasell, "A Seed for Change: The Engenderment of 'A Florida Enchantment,'" *Cinema Journal* 36, no. 4 (Summer 1997): 3–21; Constance Severance, "Alone with a Mirror," *Photoplay*, May 1916, 84–85; Smith tape 8; The Professional Scapegoat, Box 12697A, Warner Bros. Archives at USC; Louis Reeves Harrison, "Vitagraph Theatre Program Changes," *Moving Picture World*, Nov. 14, 1914, 908; "Novelty at Vitagraph Theater," *Motography*, Dec. 19, 1914, 838.

9. Bowser, *Transformation of Cinema*, 232–33; Charles Barr, "Before Blackmail: Silent British Cinema," *The British Cinema Book*, ed. Robert Murphy (London: BFI, 1997), 9; "Paris Letter," *Moving Picture World*, Mar. 28, 1914, 1664; "British Notes," *Moving Picture World*, Jul. 11, 1914, 245; Smith, *Two Reels and a Crank*, 259; "The War and the Pictures," *Moving Picture World*, Aug. 15, 1914, 963; Report by the Examinations Corporation, 17; "Vitagraph's History Is History of World's Greatest Industry," *Exhibitor's Herald*, Dec. 29, 1923, 147; "Motion Picture Trade Abroad," *Moving Picture World*, Oct. 3, 1914, 79; "A. J. D. Wallace, Chilean Exhibitor," *Moving Picture World*, Oct. 17, 1914, 312; "Philippine Film Man Here," *Moving Picture World*, Oct. 24, 1914, 468.

10. "Clara Young Entertains Vitagraphers," *Motography*, Mar. 21, 1914, 188; Louis Reeves Harrison, "My Official Wife," *Moving Picture World*, Jun. 6, 1914, 1390; "Clara Kimball Young Wins Popularity Prize," *Moving Picture World*, Sep. 26, 1914, 1791.

11. J. Stuart Blackton, "'Hollywood with Its Hair Down' or Hollywood Memories; Forty Years of the Movies," ms., 167–68, J. Stuart Blackton papers, Special Collections, Margaret Herrick Library, Academy of Motion Picture Arts and Sciences; Smith, *Two Reels and a Crank*, 189–90; "Peerless Feature Company," *Moving Picture World*, Sep. 19, 1914, 1652.

12. "Christmas of the Vitagraphers," *Moving Picture World*, Jan. 16, 1915, 344; *Motion Picture News*, Dec. 19, 1914, 18.

13. Vitagraph Life Portrayals, Jun. 1–Jun. 30, 1914, Margaret Herrick Library, Academy of Motion Picture Arts and Sciences; Louis Reeves Harrison, "Captain Alvarez," *Moving Picture World*, May 9, 1914, 799; "Vitagraph Theater Changes Bill," *Moving Picture World*, May 30, 1914, 1239; "Doings at Los Angeles," *Moving Picture World*, Apr. 18, 1914, 348; "William D. Taylor," *Moving Picture World*, Oct. 3, 1914, 44; "Myrtle Gonzalez, of the Vitagraph Company," *Motion Picture Story*, Mar. 1914, 105.

14. "Vitagraph Western Players," *Moving Picture World*, Jul. 10, 1915, 247; "Doings at Los Angeles," *Moving Picture World*, Jul. 31, 1915, 981; Smith, *Two Reels and a Crank*, 231; *Motography*, Sep. 18, 1915, 586; Vitagraph Life Portrayals, Oct. 1915, Margaret Herrick Library, Academy of Motion Picture Arts and Sciences; "Vitagraph Company Has Now Moved to Hollywood," *Moving Picture World*, Dec. 11, 1915, 1995; "Stretch of 11 Acres for Vitagraph in Hollywood," *Motion Picture News*, Sep. 11, 1915, 39.

15. Letter Jan. 16, 1915, Carl Wilson to Chas. Edison, CK912; 214:1049, Thomas A. Edison Papers, Rutgers University; Smith tape 9; Smith, *Two Reels and a Crank*, 259–60; "Big Feature Exchange Launched," *Moving Picture World*, Apr. 17, 1915, 366; Articles of Agreement Apr. 8, 1915 for V-L-S-E, Box 12647B, Warner Bros. Archives at USC; "Scope of the 'V-L-S-E,'" *Moving Picture World*, May 1, 1915, 703; "President Smith Discusses New Policies," *Motography*, May 1, 1915, 695–96; "V-L-S-E Cuts Fat Melon," *Moving Picture World*, Nov. 6, 1915, 1152.

16. "Vitagraph's The Juggernaut," *Motography*, Apr. 17, 1915, 611; Barry Salt, "The Unknown Ince," *Sight and Sound* 57, no. 4 (Fall 1988): 270; Barry Salt, "The Early Development of Film Form," *Film before Griffith*, ed. John L. Fell (Berkeley, CA: University of California Press, 1983), 295.

17. Earle Williams, "Good Friends, Good Wages, Good Fun, Good Work!" *Pictures and the Picturegoer*, Oct. 30, 1915, 90; The Tattler, "A Day with Earle Williams," *Motion Picture*, May 1914, 105–8; Earle Williams, "Sweethearts," *Photoplay*, May 1915, 44–47; Smith, *Two Reels and a Crank*, 213.

18. "Ince Takes Company To Georgia," *Moving Picture World*, Mar. 27, 1915, 1937; "Paul Scardon," *Photoplay*, Sep. 1915, 22; Vitagraph Life Portrayals, Apr. 1–Apr. 30, 1915, Margaret Herrick Library, Academy of Motion Picture Arts and Sciences.

19. Julian Johnson, "Ince of the Atlantic," *Photoplay*, Aug. 1915, 103–7; "1,000 Actors Appear in Vitagraph Fire Scene," *Motion Picture News*, Jun. 19, 1915, 60; King Vidor, *A Tree is a Tree* (New York: Harcourt, Brace, 1953), 41–42.

20. Letter Nov. 16, 1915, Leonard McChesney to Thomas and Charles Edison, E1558; 263; 280, Thomas A. Edison Papers, Rutgers University; Max Alvarez, "The Origins of the Film Exchange," *Film History* 17 (2006): 458–59; "'Goddess' Popularity Shown in 1,000 Prints," *Motion Picture News*, Jun. 12, 1915, 61; Report by the Examinations Corporation, Memorandum #4; Vitagraph Company of America, Plaintiff, against Anita Stewart and Louis B. Mayer, Defendants, 1917, 52, 111, New York Supreme Court, Appellate Division—First Dept., Papers on Appeal from Order, 1917; Bowser, *Transformation of Cinema*, 209; Letter Mar. 3, 1916, Benjamin Hampton to Smith, Box 4, Albert E. Smith Papers (Collection 2004), Department of Special Collections, Charles E. Young Research Library, University of California, Los Angeles.

21. Blackton, "Hollywood with Its Hair Down," 212–29, 333; Marian Blackton Trimble, *J. Stuart Blackton: A Personal Biography by His Daughter* (Metuchen, NJ: Scarecrow, 1985), 75–77, 81; The Battle Cry of Peace, Box 12698B, Warner Bros. Archives at USC; Lynde Denig, "The Battle Cry of Peace," *Moving Picture World*, Aug. 21, 1915, 1291; "Vitagraph's Patriotic Picture," *Moving Picture World*, Jul. 31, 1915,

795; "Prepare against Invasion, Is Vitagraph Film Lesson," *Motion Picture News*, Jul. 31, 1915, 49; "Vitagraph Has Eight-Reel on Invasion of America," *Motography*, Jul. 31, 1915, 216; Anthony Slide and Alan Gevinson, *The Big V: A History of the Vitagraph Company* (Metuchen, NJ: Scarecrow, 1987), 72–81; "Lecture by Commodore J. Stuart Blackton at USC, Feb. 20, 1929," *Introduction to the Photoplay*, ed. John C. Tibbetts (Shawnee Mission, KS: National Film Society, 1977), 36; Smith, *Two Reels and a Crank*, 191, Smith tape 8; "'The Battle Cry of Peace' and other Releases of the Week Reviewed," *Motography*, Aug. 21, 1915, 361; "Big Opening for Vitagraph Feature," *Moving Picture World*, Sep. 25, 1915, 2158; "Vitagraph Produces Remarkable Film," *Billboard*, Aug. 14, 1915, 54; "'The Battle Cry of Peace'—a Super-Film," *Motography*, Nov. 6, 1915, 967; "Stirring Photo Drama of War," *Evening Sun*, Sep. 10, 1915, Box 2, Albert E. Smith Papers (Collection 2004), Department of Special Collections, Charles E. Young Research Library, University of California, Los Angeles; "New York Shelled on 'Movie' Screen," *New York Times*, Aug. 7, 1915, 8; Hugo Münsterberg, *The Film, A Psychological Study* (New York: Dover, 1970), viii, 81; Nov. 6, 1970 letter from Wm. P. S. Earle to Mr. Peters, photocopy from Kevin Brownlow to author; "A Country-Wide Propaganda," *Motography*, Nov. 27, 1915, 1109; Contracts for The Battle Cry of Peace, Box 12647B, Warner Bros. Archives at USC; Melvyn Stokes, *D. W. Griffith's Birth of a Nation* (New York: Oxford University Press, 2007), 118, 138–44, 287; Joel W. Finler, *The Hollywood Story* (London: Wallflower, 2003), 356; "Actors Play Cut-Out," *Motography*, Mar. 11, 1916, 564; Scott Eyman, *Lion of Hollywood: the Life and Legend of Louis B. Mayer* (New York: Simon & Schuster, 2005), 41–42; Blackton, "Hollywood with Its Hair Down," 225; Report by the Examinations Corporation, Exhibit E.

22. Smith, *Two Reels and a Crank*, 191; "National Engages Norma Talmadge," *Moving Picture World*, Jul. 10, 1915, 312; *Photoplay*, Dec. 1915, 160; Richard Koszarski, *Hollywood on the Hudson* (Piscataway, NJ: Rutgers University Press, 2008), 63, 72; Adela Rogers St. John, "Matrimony and Meringue," *Photoplay*, Jul. 1919, 82; Kevin Brownlow, *The Parade's Gone By* (New York: Alfred A. Knopf, 1968), 430; "Norma Talmadge, Selznick Star," *Moving Picture World*, Oct. 21, 1916, 410.

23. Slide and Gevinson, *The Big V*, 49; Mabel Condon, "Sans Grease Paint and Wig," *Motography*, Jul. 4, 1914, 23–24; Blackton, "Hollywood with Its Hair Down," 118; "Bunny Show Well Made," *Variety*, Sep. 11, 1915, 10; *Variety*, Oct. 24, 1914, 35; "John Bunny Show," *Variety*, Mar. 19, 1915, 16; "Bunny a Favorite in St. Louis," *Moving Picture World*, Apr. 3, 1915, 53; "Observations by Our Man About Town," *Moving Picture World*, May 15, 1915, 1062; "British Notes," *Moving Picture World*, Apr. 17, 1915, 383; Smith, *Two Reels and a Crank*, 207–9; Smith tape 8; "Death of John Bunny," *Moving Picture World*, May 8, 1915, 876; "John Bunny Dies at the Age of Fifty-two," *Motion Picture News*, May 8, 1915, 40; "Throng at Bunny's Funeral," *Moving Picture World*, May 15, 1915, 1048; "Last Tribute to Bunny," *Motography*, May 15, 1915, 771; "The Pictures Lose a Famous Droll," *Kinematograph and Lantern Weekly*, May 16, 1915, Box 13, Albert E. Smith Papers (Collection 2004), Department of Special Collections, Charles E. Young Research Library, University of California, Los Angeles; "On and Off the Screen," *Pictures and the Picturegoer*, May 15, 1915, 111; "South African Letter," *Moving Picture World*, Aug. 14, 1915, 1173; "John Bunny

Dead. Rise to Fame of the World's Funniest Fat Man," *Star*, 28 H. 1915, Box 13, Albert E. Smith Papers (Collection 2004), Department of Special Collections, Charles E. Young Research Library, University of California, Los Angeles; "The Art of John Bunny," *Bioscope*, May 6, 1915, Smith Box 13, Albert E. Smith Papers (Collection 2004), Department of Special Collections, Charles E. Young Research Library, University of California, Los Angeles; "The World's Loss," *Punch*, May 12, 1915, Box 13, Albert E. Smith Papers (Collection 2004), Department of Special Collections, Charles E. Young Research Library, University of California, Los Angeles.

24. Robert Jack Anderson, "The Motion Picture Patents Company" (PhD diss., University of Wisconsin–Madison, 1983), ix–x, xiii, 196, 271–72; Charles Musser, *Before the Nickelodeon: Edwin S. Porter and the Edison Manufacturing Company* (Berkeley, CA: University of California Press, 1991), 471; Vanda Krefft, *The Man Who Made the Movies* (New York: HarperCollins, 2017), 114–15.

25. Letter Mar. 3, 1916, Hampton to Smith; Report by the Examinations Corporation, 7; "Vitagraph's New Release Schedule," *Moving Picture World*, Dec. 18, 1915, 2189; Albert E. Smith, "The Survival of the Fittest," Vitagraph Life Portrayals, Jan. 1916, Margaret Herrick Library, Academy of Motion Picture Arts and Sciences.

26. *Brooklyn Eagle*, Dec. 21, 1915, 24, Jun. 29, 1916, 18; Smith tape 7; Smith, *Two Reels and a Crank*, 187–88; "Movies Actor Buys Farm," *Brooklyn Eagle*, Jul. 9, 1915, 6; "Notes on the New York Ball," *Motography*, Nov. 23, 1912, 392; "World's Greatest Film Artistes Contest (exclusive of British-born players)," *Pictures and the Picturegoer*, Nov. 6, 1915, 112; *Photoplay*, Mar. 1916, 122.

27. Report by the Examinations Corporation, 3; Letter Mar. 6, 1916, Smith to Hampton, Box 4, Albert E. Smith Papers (Collection 2004), Department of Special Collections, Charles E. Young Research Library, University of California, Los Angeles.

28. Letter Mar. 3, 1916, Hampton to Smith; "Ralph Ince to Remain with Vitagraph," *Moving Picture World*, Jan. 23, 1915, 492; Johnson, "Ince of the Atlantic," 103–8; "Ince Has Housewarming," *Motography*, Jan. 1, 1916, 29; "Lucille Lee Stewart," *Moving Picture World*, Mar. 18, 1916, 1811.

29. "Beta Breuil with Mirror," *Moving Picture World*, Jan. 15, 1916, 431; "Vitagraph Employs Woman Director," *Moving Picture World*, Aug. 5, 1916, 935; "The Devil's Prize," *Motography*, Nov. 11, 1916, 1096; Vitagraph Company of America, Plaintiff, against Anita Stewart and Louis B. Mayer, Defendants, 72, 111; *Moving Picture World*, Feb. 19, 1916, 1115.

30. "Hearst with Vitagraph," *Moving Picture World*, Dec. 4, 1915, 1802; Andrew A. Erish, *Col. William N. Selig, the Man Who Invented Hollywood* (Austin, TX: University of Texas Press, 2012), 153–56; Letter Mar. 3, 1916, Hampton to Smith; "Tom Powers, Cartoonist," *Moving Picture World*, Jan. 8, 1916, 251; Koszarski, *Hollywood on the Hudson*, 312–13; "International Takes Over V-L-S-E Business," *Moving Picture World*, Jun. 24, 1916, 2269, 2271; Report by the Examinations Corporation, Exhibit E.

31. Blackton, "Hollywood with Its Hair Down," 233, 236–39; *Moving Picture World*, Feb. 26, 1916, 1275; "Decision in Vitagraph-Metro Case," *Moving Picture World*, Mar. 25, 1916, 2015; W. Stephen Bush, "Film Hosts in Battle Array," *Moving*

Picture World, Jan. 22, 1916, 566–69; W. Stephen Bush, "Motion Picture Men Greet President," *Moving Picture World*, Feb. 12, 1916, 923–30.

32. "Blackton Denies Rumors," *Moving Picture World*, Jan. 15, 1916, 388; Smith Memo, Box 4, folder 3, Albert E. Smith Papers (Collection 2004), Department of Special Collections, Charles E. Young Research Library, University of California, Los Angeles; "Hampton Explains," *Moving Picture World*, Apr. 15, 1916, 411; Blackton, "Hollywood with Its Hair Down," 257–58; Bound Agreements, Smith Box 2, Folder 6, Albert E. Smith Papers (Collection 2004), Department of Special Collections, Charles E. Young Research Library, University of California, Los Angeles; "Millions for Vitagraph," *Moving Picture World*, May 20, 1916, 1305–1306; "Tobacco Men Are Important Factors in the New Vitagraph," *Billboard*, May 27, 1916, 3, 70; Adolph Zukor with Dale Kramer, *The Public Is Never Wrong* (New York: G. P. Putnam's Sons, 1953), 4, 54, 61–62, 66, 97–98, 170–71, 176; "Rock, Smith and Blackton Were Pioneer Exhibitors," *Moving Picture World*, Jul. 15, 1916, 379; "'Pop' Rock Convalescing," *Moving Picture World*, Jun. 17, 1916, 2049; "Death of William T. Rock, Pioneer Picture Man," *Moving Picture World*, Aug. 12, 1916, 1078; "The Death of a Pioneer," *Moving Picture World*, Aug. 19, 1916, 1220; "Vitagraph Founder Dead," *Motography*, Aug. 5, 1916, 356; Smith, *Two Reels and a Crank*, 261; "Old Vitagraph Office to Close," *Moving Picture World*, Aug. 19, 1916, 1222; Letter Aug. 2, 1916, Hampton to Smith, Box 4, Albert E. Smith Papers (Collection 2004), Department of Special Collections, Charles E. Young Research Library, University of California, Los Angeles; Mary Pickford, *Sunshine and Shadow* (New York: Doubleday & Co., 1955), 103–4; Letters Jul. 27, 1916, Hampton to Nicholas G. Roosevelt, Jul. 27, 1916, Hampton to Smith, Jul. 21, 1916, George K. Spoor to Smith, Jul. 20, 1916, Hampton to Smith; Jul. 15, 1916, Hampton to Smith, Mar. 27, 1916, Hampton to Smith, Mar. 3, 1916, Hampton to Smith, Letter Mar. 19, 1916, Hampton to Mary Pickford, Memo prepared by Hampton, Apr. 20, 1916, Box 4, Albert E. Smith Papers (Collection 2004), Department of Special Collections, Charles E. Young Research Library, University of California, Los Angeles.

33. The Vitagraph Family, Jul. 28, 1917, 36, Box 6, Albert E. Smith Papers (Collection 2004), Department of Special Collections, Charles E. Young Research Library, University of California, Los Angeles; Report by the Examinations Corporation, 42–43; "British Notes," *Moving Picture World*, Jan. 8, 1916, 237, Feb. 12, 1916, 969, Feb. 26, 1916, 1291.

34. *Cine Mundial*, Jan. 1916, cover; Doval Albino, "La 'Vitagraph,'" *Cine Mundial*, Apr. 1916, 148; F. G. Ortega, "Los de la Risa," *Cine Mundial*, Apr. 1916, 142; Gil Pérez, "Gidugas de la Nueva Escena," *Cine Mundial*, Aug. 1916, 332. Virtually every issue of *Cine Mundial* from 1916 through 1925 contains articles pertaining to Vitagraph in various countries of Latin America.

35. "New Vitagraph Outdoor Studio," *Moving Picture World*, Jan. 1, 1916, 57; "Vitagraphers Snowbound," *Moving Picture World*, Jan. 22, 1916, 578–79; "William Duncan," *Motography*, Jul. 24, 1915, 151; Thomas C. Kennedy, "God's Country and the Woman," *Motography*, May 6, 1916, 1051; Lynde Denig, "God's Country and the Woman," *Moving Picture World*, May 6, 1916, 983.

36. *Motography*, Mar. 18, 1916, 657, Apr. 1, 1916, 774, Apr. 29, 1916, 1005; *Motion Picture News*, Nov. 20, 1915, 75; "Comments on the Films," *Moving Picture World*, Sep. 9, 1916, 1688; Mosgrove Colwell, "Something New in Pictures," *Motion Picture*, Sep. 1916, 53–59; John P. Welle, "Film on Paper: Early Italian Cinema Literature, 1907–1920," *Film History* 12, no. 3 (2000): 295–96; "The Yellow Girl," *Moving Picture World*, Sep. 2, 1916, 1590; Smith, *Two Reels and a Crank*, 213; Corinne Griffith, *How I Broke into the Movies*, ed. Hal C. Herman (Hollywood, CA: Everett L. Sanders, 1930), 97; "Popular Picture Personalities," *Moving Picture World*, Dec. 29, 1917, 1933; Vidor, *A Tree is a Tree*, 64–66.

37. Report by the Examinations Corporation, 16; "Vitagraph Lessens Production," *Moving Picture World*, Aug. 19, 1916, 1231; Letter Sep. 29, 1916, Rollin S. Sturgeon to Col. W. N. Selig, Charles G. Clarke Collection, Margaret Herrick Library, Academy of Motion Picture Arts and Sciences; "News from Santa Barbara," *Moving Picture World*, Feb. 10, 1917, 853; Doris Schroeder would go on to write many of the Hopalong Cassidy films of the 1930s and 1940s.

38. "Sam Spedon Leaves Vitagraph," *Motography*, Aug. 19, 1916, 412; *Moving Picture World*, Jan. 6, 1917, 51; "Flora Finch Has Own Company," *Moving Picture World*, Dec. 23, 1916, 1793; "Kate Price Now a Vim Star," *Moving Picture World*, Oct. 14, 1916, 245; Transcript of Dec. 1964 audio interview between Kevin Brownlow and James Morrison, Kevin Brownlow to author; "Ralph Ince Leaves Vitagraph," *Moving Picture World*, Nov. 11, 1916, 876; Salt, "Unknown Ince," 272.

39. Smith, *Two Reels and a Crank*, 210; Report by the Examinations Corporation, Memorandum #4; Letter Mar. 3, 1916, Hampton to Smith; "Antonio Moreno," *Photoplay*, Dec. 1915, 21.

40. "Vitagraph Beefsteak," *Moving Picture World*, Apr. 8, 1916, 264; *Motography*, Jan. 6, 1917, 31.

41. "Vitagraph Announces Six Week Schedule," *Motography*, Jan. 6, 1917, 15–16; Report by the Examinations Corporation, 21–22; "Vitagraph De Luxe Re-issues," *Motography*, Apr. 7, 1917, 721; "Vitagraph Issues 'A Million Bid,'" *Motography*, Feb. 17, 1917, 358; "New Vitagraph Brand," *Motography*, Jun. 2, 1917, 1168; "To Reissue Bunny Pictures," *Moving Picture World*, Jun. 23, 1917, 1941; "Greater Vitagraph Plans," *Motography*, Mar. 10, 1917, 518; "Vitagraph Promotions," *Motography*, Mar. 24, 1917, 625.

42. Report by the Examinations Corporation, 4, 6–11, 14, 16–22, 26, 30–31, 34, 42; Smith memo, Box 4, Albert E. Smith Papers (Collection 2004), Department of Special Collections, Charles E. Young Research Library, University of California, Los Angeles; May 17, 1917 Smith memo, Box 5, Albert E. Smith Papers (Collection 2004), Department of Special Collections, Charles E. Young Research Library, University of California, Los Angeles; Telegrams Apr. 20, 1917 Harold Boetler to Smith, Apr. 25, 1917 Blackton to Smith, Box 5, Albert E. Smith Papers (Collection 2004), Department of Special Collections, Charles E. Young Research Library, University of California, Los Angeles; "President Smith Recovering," *Motography*, Apr. 14, 1917, 764; "Edith Storey Goes to Metro," *Moving Picture World*, Jul. 7, 1917, 63; "Lillian Walker Has Not Renewed Vitagraph Contract," *Moving Picture World*, Feb.

17, 1917, 1018; "Ex-Postmaster General Joins Vitagraph," *Moving Picture World*, May 19, 1917, 1099; Special Interest—R. C. Sr., Memo from the President, Box 6, Albert E. Smith Papers (Collection 2004), Department of Special Collections, Charles E. Young Research Library, University of California, Los Angeles; *New York Dramatic Mirror*, Jun. 23, 1917, 20; Letter Jul. 11, 1917, Smith to Prentiss, Box 5, Albert E. Smith Papers (Collection 2004), Department of Special Collections, Charles E. Young Research Library, University of California, Los Angeles.

43. Letter Jul. 11, 1917, Smith to Hampton, Box 5, Albert E. Smith Papers (Collection 2004), Department of Special Collections, Charles E. Young Research Library, University of California, Los Angeles; "Ben B. Hampton Heads General Film Company," *Moving Picture World*, Dec. 2, 1916, 1303; Letter Nov. 14, 1916, Carl Wilson to Edison, CK913; 214:1091, Letter May 10, 1917, George Kleine to Wilson, CK920; 215:207, Thomas A. Edison Papers, Rutgers University; Report by the Examinations Corporation, 9, 26; Vitagraph Reports and Accounts Mar. 31, 1919 by Price, Waterhouse & Co., Box 6, Albert E. Smith Papers (Collection 2004), Department of Special Collections, Charles E. Young Research Library, University of California, Los Angeles; "Hampton Resigns G. F. Presidency," *Moving Picture World*, Apr. 28, 1917, 601.

44. "Alice Joyce Joins Vitagraph," *Moving Picture World*, Jun. 3, 1916, 1670; "Popular Picture Personalities," *Moving Picture World*, Mar. 3, 1917, 1355; Report by the Examinations Corporation, Memorandum #4; "Womanhood," *Motography*, Apr. 7, 1917, 731; "Extra Prints Necessary to Fill Demand for 'Womanhood,'" *Motion Picture News*, Jun. 9, 1917, 3597.

45. "Blackton Quits Vitagraph to Produce Films for Paramount," *Billboard*, Jul. 21, 1917, 3, 79; Blackton Trimble, *J. Stuart Blackton*, 86–88, 94; Barnard F. Dick, *Engulfed: The Death of Paramount Pictures and the Birth of Corporate Hollywood* (Lexington: University Press of Kentucky, 2001), 9–12; Contract Jul. 5, 1917 between J. Stuart Blackton and Paramount Pictures Corporation, J. Stuart Blackton Papers, Special Collections, Margaret Herrick Library, Academy of Motion Picture Arts and Sciences; Grebben Bakker, "The Decline and Fall of the European Film Industry: Sunk Costs, Market Size and Market Structure, 1890–1927," Working Paper No. 70/03, London School of Economics, Feb. 2003, 25, http://eprints.lse.ac.uk/22366/1/wp70; Smith tape 9; J. Stuart Blackton, "A Glimpse into the Past," *Moving Picture World*, Mar. 10, 1917, 1527–1528; Koszarski, *Hollywood on the Hudson*, 108; "Blackton to Produce For Paramount," *Moving Picture World*, Jul. 28, 1917, 630.

46. "Blackton Quits Vitagraph," 3, 79; Letter Apr. 29, 1944, Smith to [Chas. B.] Clarke, Box 10, Albert E. Smith Papers (Collection 2004), Department of Special Collections, Charles E. Young Research Library, University of California, Los Angeles; Smith, *Two Reels and a Crank*, 260, 262; "To Picture Romance of the War," *Motography*, Sep. 1, 1917, 448; "Vitagraph Speeding Up," *Billboard*, Jun. 2, 1917, 58; "Special Interest—R. C. Sr."; From the Manger to the Cross, Box 12647B, Warner Bros. Archives at USC; Itemized Statement of Net Billings Per Subject week ended Nov. 6, 1920, Box 5, Albert E. Smith Papers (Collection 2004), Department of Special Collections,

Charles E. Young Research Library, University of California, Los Angeles; *Moving Picture World*, Mar. 3, 1923, 66, Mar. 10, 1923, 140, 145, Apr. 7, 1923, 65, May 2, 1925, 76; "Kalem Studio Properties Absorbed by Vitagraph," *Moving Picture World*, Feb. 22, 1919, 1048.

47. "British Notes," *Moving Picture World*, Feb. 24, 1917, 1202; Report by the Examinations Corporation, 42; "War and Exports," *Moving Picture World*, Sep. 29, 1917, 1988; *Moving Picture World*, Aug. 25, 1917, 1352; "Another Smith in Service," *Moving Picture World*, Oct. 5, 1918, 68.

48. "Anita Stewart Starts Work with S. Rankin Drew," *Moving Picture World*, Feb. 26, 1916, 1288; Vitagraph Company of America, Plaintiff, against Anita Stewart and Louis B. Mayer, Defendants, 22, 72, 77–78, 83, 91, 112–14, 132, 170, 182–85, 188; "S. Rankin Drew of Vitagraph," *Motography*, Dec. 25, 1915, 1324; "Anita Stewart Convalescent," *Moving Picture World*, Sep. 23, 1916, 1952; Fred Schaefer, "S. Rankin of the Clan Drew," *Photoplay*, Apr. 1917, 115–18; *Motion Picture News*, Dec. 23, 1916, 3905; "At the Leading Picture Theaters," *Moving Picture World*, Jan. 13, 1917, 211; Edward Weitzel, "The Girl Philippa," *Moving Picture World*, Jan. 20, 1917, 356; "Anita Stewart in New One," *Motography*, Jan. 6, 1917, 16; "Anita Stewart Play," *Motography*, Feb. 10, 1917, 307; Smith, *Two Reels and a Crank*, 196; "Director Drew Joins Metro Forces," *Motography*, Oct. 21, 1916, 944; "Cameron Opposite Anita Stewart," *Motography*, Feb. 3, 1917, 245; "Sidney Drew Now Counted as Dead," *Moving Picture World*, Jun. 29, 1918, 1854; *Life and Letters of Sidney Rankin Drew*, ed. Mrs. Sidney Drew (New York: Cheltenham, 1921), 5, 6, 11–12, 13, 14, 33, 36, 47, 66; S. Rankin Drew Marker, www.nycgovparks.org/ parks/central-park/monuments/406; "Sidney Drew Dies," *Motion Picture News*, Apr. 19, 1919, 2445.

49. "Improvements at Vitagraph Western Studio," *Moving Picture World*, Jul. 20, 1918, 387; Koszarski, *Hollywood on the Hudson*, 108; "Earle Williams Party Reach Coast," *Motography*, Jan. 12, 1918, 71; "Vitagraph to Send More Companies West," *Moving Picture World*, Aug. 24, 1918, 1100; "Vitagraph to Do Four Serials a Year," *Motography*, Jul. 6, 1918, 19; "William Duncan Vitagraph' s Popular Serial Director," *Moving Picture World*, Nov. 16, 1918, 725.

50. List of O. Henry Stories, Box 12696A, Warner Bros. Archives at USC; "O. Henry's Stories in Pictures," *Moving Picture World*, Feb. 24, 1917, 1196; *Moving Picture World*, Apr. 7, 1917, 61; "'Wolfville Tales' Filmed," *Motography*, Oct. 6, 1917, 723.

51. "David Smith to Direct 'Baree, Son of Kazan,'" *Motography*, Apr. 20, 1918, 747; "Nell Shipman Leaves Vitagraph," *Moving Picture World*, Nov. 9, 1918, 669, 678.

52. Norman Zierold, *The Moguls* (New York: Coward-McCann, 1969), 275–77; Henry, "The New England Invasion," *Moving Picture World*, Dec. 2, 1911, 718; Eyman, *Lion of Hollywood*, 22–28, 29, 30–31, 41–42, 50–53; Richard Schickel, *D. W. Griffith: An American Life* (New York: Simon & Schuster, 1984), 273–74; Bosley Crowther, *Hollywood Rajah* (New York: Holt, Rinehart and Winston, 1960), 48–50, 55–56, 58, 62–64; "Anita Stewart in New Company," *Moving Picture World*, Sep. 15, 1917, 1668; "Vitagraph Seeks Injunction," *Moving Picture World*, Sep. 22, 1917, 1835; Smith tape 9; Smith, *Two Reels and a Crank*, 211; "Vitagraph Wins Anita Stewart

Suit," *Motography*, Apr. 13, 1918, 695; "Vitagraph Goes After Louis B. Mayer," *Motography*, May 4, 1918, 843; "Anita Stewart Completes Picture," *Moving Picture World*, Jul. 20, 1918, 405; "Vitagraph Settles Anita Stewart Case," *Moving Picture World*, Aug. 3, 1918, 667; "Anita Stewart Starts," *Wid's Daily*, Aug. 27, 1918, 1.

53. Condon, "Sans Grease Paint and Wig," *Motography*, Jul. 4, 1914, 23–24; "Hughie Mack," *Moving Picture World*, Oct. 17, 1914, 343; Vitagraph Life Portrayals, Jul. 1–31, 1915, Margaret Herrick Library, Academy of Motion Picture Arts and Sciences; "Trailers," *Moving Picture World*, Jan. 27, 1917, 539.

54. Claudia Sassen, *Larry Semon, Daredevil Comedian of the Silent Screen* (Jefferson, NC: McFarland & Company, 2015), 10, 15,18, 20, 21, 25, 28, 35, 37, 41, 44–45, 54, 56, 59, 63–65; Blackton, "Hollywood with Its Hair Down," 152–54; Smith, *Two Reels and a Crank*, 194–95; Steve Massa, *Lame Brains & Lunatics: The Good, the Bad and the Forgotten of Silent Comedy* (Duncan, OK: Bear Manor Media, 2013), 94, 276; Buster Keaton, *My Wonderful World of Slapstick* (New York: Doubleday, 1960), 176; "Graham Baker Many Sided," *Moving Picture World*, Sep. 15, 1917, 1672; Report by the Examinations Corporation, Memorandum #4; Rob Stone, *Laurel or Hardy: The Solo Films of Stan Laurel and Oliver "Babe" Hardy* (Manchester, NH: Split Reel Books, 1996), 413–18.

55. "Figures Show Drop in Film Exports," *Moving Picture World*, Jan. 4, 1919, 54; *Moving Picture World*, Oct. 19, 1918, 441; Musser, *Before the Nickelodeon*, 465, 472; Erish, *Col. William N. Selig*, 209; William Franklyn Grisham, "Modes, Movies, and Magnates: Early Filmmaking in Chicago" (PhD diss., Northwestern University, 1982), 261–62; Bakker, "The Decline and Fall of the European Film Industry," 42–43; André Rossel-Kirschen, "Charles Pathé and His Scapegoat: Bernard Natan," 1895, 55/2008, accessed Nov. 2019, http://journals.openedition.org/1895/ 4109; DOI:10.4000/1895.4109.

56. "Mary Maurice, Screen Mother, Dies," *Moving Picture World*, May 18, 1918, 986; "Veteran William Shea Is Dead," *Moving Picture World*, Nov. 23, 1918, 840; "Bobby Connelly Dead," *New York Times*, Jul. 7, 1922, 13.

57. "Walter Irwin Resigns from Vitagraph Company," *Moving Picture World*, Dec. 21, 1918, 1322; Vitagraph Company of America, Plaintiff, against Anita Stewart and Louis B. Mayer, Defendants, 89, 134; Memo by Albert Smith on The Homestead, Hot Springs stationery, Box 6, Albert E. Smith Papers (Collection 2004), Department of Special Collections, Charles E. Young Research Library, University of California, Los Angeles; Slide and Gevinson, *The Big V*, 70.

58. "A New Era in Vitagraph Blue Ribbon Features and Service, Season of 1918–1919" Box 6, Albert E. Smith Papers (Collection 2004), Department of Special Collections, Charles E. Young Research Library, University of California, Los Angeles; "Producers Decide to Close Shop," *Moving Picture World*, Oct. 26, 1918, 491; "Influenza Epidemic Working West," *Moving Picture World*, Nov. 2, 1918, 571, 573, 574; "Influenza Hits Vitagraph Forces," *Moving Picture World*, Nov. 16, 1918, 723; "Death of Myrtle Gonzales" [*sic*], *Moving Picture World*, Nov. 16, 1918, 727.

59. "Vitagraph Busy," *Moving Picture World*, Dec. 7, 1918, 1061; "Special Interest—R. C. Sr."

5. 1919–1925

Note: Unless otherwise noted, data regarding gross and profit for post-1920 Vitagraph productions are taken from Itemized Statement of Net Billings per Subject for week ended Apr. 11, 1925, Box 12726A, Warner Bros. Archives at USC.

1. "Vitagraph Chiefs Hold Convention," *Moving Picture World*, Jan. 18, 1919, 333; "Vitagraph's Eastern and Western Plants Are Very Active—Will Make One Super-film a Month," *Moving Picture World*, Sep. 20, 1919, 1812; Letter, Mar. 15, 1919, Smith to Board of Directors, Box 6, Albert E. Smith Papers (Collection 2004), Department of Special Collections, Charles E. Young Research Library, University of California, Los Angeles; Archives at USC; "George Randolph Chester Is Vitagraph Script Chief," *Moving Picture World*, Feb. 8, 1919, 757; "Albert E. Smith Goes West to Attend Family Reunion," *Moving Picture World*, Mar. 22, 1919, 1624; "Vitagraph Increases Size of Studios on West Coast," *Moving Picture World*, Jul. 26, 1919, 533; "Vitagraph Buys More Land," *Moving Picture World*, Nov. 22, 1919, 422; Giebler, "Rubbernecking in Filmland," *Moving Picture World*, Aug. 23, 1919, 1117–18; "Vitagraphers in Four Different Places," *Moving Picture World*, Aug. 16, 1919; Vitagraph Itemized Statement of Net Billings per Subject week ended Nov. 6, 1920, Box 5, Albert E. Smith Papers (Collection 2004), Department of Special Collections, Charles E. Young Research Library, University of California, Los Angeles; "Vitagraph Wants Theatre," *Moving Picture World*, May 31, 1919, 1334; "Bunny Theatre Bills Vitagraph," *Moving Picture World*, Jun. 28, 1919, 1998; "Los Angeles Theatre Books Vitagraph," *Moving Picture World*, Jul. 19, 1919, 423.

2. 1919 Albert E. Smith affidavit, Letters Aug. 19, 1919 and Sep. 29, 1919, Lawrence Langner to Seabury, Massey & Lowe, Memorandum Aug. 25, 1919, Box 12970B, Warner Bros. Archives at USC; Denis Gifford, *The British Film Catalogue: Non-Fiction Film, 1888–1994*, vol. 2 (Abingdon: Routledge, 2016), 170, 220–22, 226–28, 345–47, 349; John Barnes, *The Rise of the Cinema in England, 1894–1901:* vol. 2, *1897* (London: Bishopsgate Press, Ltd., 1983), 41; John Barnes, *The Rise of the Cinema in England, 1894–1901:* vol. 3, *1898* (London: Bishopsgate Press, Ltd., 1983), 63; Richard Abel, ed., *Encyclopedia of Early Cinema* (London: Routledge, 2004), 538.

3. "George Smith Sailing for London," *Moving Picture World*, May 3, 1919, 642; "Vitagraph Buys British Exchange," *Moving Picture World*, Aug. 16, 1919, 975; *Moving Picture World*, Jun. 21, 1919, 1767; "Ronald A. Reader Back from Europe," *Moving Picture World*, Sep. 27, 1919, 1984; "To Show Vitagraphs South of Line," *Moving Picture World*, May 31, 1919, 1336; Australasian Films, Ltd., *Moving Picture World*, Jul. 5, 1919, 32–33; "American Movies in Japan," *Photoplay*, May 1919, 68, 109; Thomas S. Imrie, "Sends Representative to Far East," *Moving Picture World*, Sep. 20, 1919, 1792; Dorothy Kingdon van Raven, "Made-In-India Film Sells for Big Price Despite Great Production Difficulties," *Moving Picture World*, Jul. 10, 1920, 185.

4. Itemized Statement of Net Billings per Subject week ended Nov. 6, 1920; Memo from President, Box 5, Albert E. Smith Papers (Collection 2004), Department of Special Collections, Charles E. Young Research Library, University of California, Los

Angeles; "Vitagraph Starts Posting 24-Sheet Stands Widely Advertising its Six Feature Players," *Moving Picture World*, Jul. 12, 1919, 191; Vitagraph Inc.—Story or Play Contracts, Box 12647B, Warner Bros. Archives at USC; "Rialto Books Vitagraph Feature," *Moving Picture World*, Feb. 22, 1919, 1056.

5. William J. Reilly, "The Cambric Mask," *Moving Picture World*, Apr. 5, 1919, 126; "The Cambric Mask," *Photoplay*, Jul. 1919, 102; Tom Rice, *White Robes, Silver Screens: Movies and the Making of the Ku Klux Klan* (Bloomington: Indiana University Press, 2015), 171, 178–79.

6. Itemized Statement of Net Billings per Subject ended Nov. 6, 1920; Vitagraph and VLSE invoices for the Palace Theatre, Antigo, Wisconsin, accessed from eBay Dec. 4, 2019, https://www.ebay.com/itm/Movie-Billhead-Vitagraph-1919-The-Lion-and-the-Mouse-Alice-Joyce-Conrad-Nagel/163103971412?hash=item25f9c11854:g:U6MAAOSwGNxbHI6t; https://www.ebay.com/itm/Movie-Letterhead-Vitagraph-1919-Smashing-Barriers-Serial-William-Duncan-Johnson/153364680231?hash=item23b53f4e27:g:v0EAAOSwyPFcRiKU; "Books All Vitagraph's Serials," *Moving Picture World*, Mar. 1, 1919, 1188; The Counter Jumper, Box 12700B, Warner Bros. Archives at USC; "Vitagraph's Serial Pictures Gaining in Popularity," *Moving Picture World*, Nov. 9, 1918, 681; Letter Sep. 23, 1919, WS Smith to A. Smith, Box 7, Albert E. Smith Papers (Collection 2004), Department of Special Collections, Charles E. Young Research Library, University of California, Los Angeles; William Duncan, "The Business of Making Thrills," *Photoplay*, Feb. 1922, 109; "Jack Pierce Sustains Burns," *Moving Picture World*, Jul. 5, 1919, 58; "Vitagraph Serial Soon Available as Feature," *Moving Picture World*, Jun. 16, 1923, 595; Daily Report Sheet Aug. 25, 1919, Box 8, Albert E. Smith Papers (Collection 2004), Department of Special Collections, Charles E. Young Research Library, University of California, Los Angeles; "His Own Boss on the Lot," *Photoplay*, Nov. 1919, 86–87.

7. Marian Blackton Trimble, *J. Stuart Blackton: A Personal Biography by His Daughter* (Metuchen, NJ: Scarecrow, 1985), 94; Contract Jun. 26, 1919 between Blackton and Sanford Samuel, J. Stuart Blackton papers, Special Collections, Margaret Herrick Library, Academy of Motion Picture Arts and Sciences; J. Stuart Blackton, "Yesterdays of Vitagraph," *Photoplay*, Jul. 1919, 28–33; Letters Dec. 30, 1919 and n.d. marked "Absolutely Personal and Private," Cyrus Townsend Brady to Smith, Box 6, Albert E. Smith Papers (Collection 2004), Department of Special Collections, Charles E. Young Research Library, University of California, Los Angeles; "Dr. Cyrus Townsend Brady, Vitagraph Scenarist, Dies Victim of Pneumonia," *Moving Picture World*, Feb. 7, 1920, 862.

8. All Branches week ended Apr. 2, 1920, Feature Star Contracts and Total Value per Subject, Average net billings for 26 weeks ending Mar. 27, 1920, Weekly Statement of Cash Receipts and Disbursements week ended Mar. 26, 1920, Box 6, Albert E. Smith Papers (Collection 2004), Department of Special Collections, Charles E. Young Research Library, University of California, Los Angeles; Itemized Statement of Net Billings per Subject week ended Nov. 6, 1920.

9. Number of Contracts and Total Value of Subjects, week ended Apr. 2, 1920, Box 5, Albert E. Smith Papers (Collection 2004), Department of Special Collections,

Charles E. Young Research Library, University of California, Los Angeles; Daily Shipping Report week ended Apr. 24, 1920, Box 5, Albert E. Smith Papers (Collection 2004), Department of Special Collections, Charles E. Young Research Library, University of California, Los Angeles; "Coast Brevities," *Wid's Daily*, Dec. 22, 1919, 2; Claudia Sassen, *Larry Semon, Daredevil Comedian of the Silent Screen* (Jefferson, NC: McFarland & Company, 2015), 59–60, 63, 75–76, 82, 84, 91–93 117; Steve Massa, *Lame Brains & Lunatics; the Good, the Bad and the Forgotten of Silent Comedy* (Duncan, OK: Bear Manor Media, 2013), 20, 38, 276–79; "The Expressions of Larry Semon," *Picture Show*, May 8, 1920, 7; Horace Gladstone, "Charlie Chaplin's Rival," *Cinema Chat*, 40, Feb. 23, 1920, 3–6; "Larry Semon Renews His Contract with Vitagraph," *Moving Picture World*, Dec. 6, 1919, 655; *Kinematograph Weekly*, Jan. 6, 1921, qtd. in John Montgomery, *Comedy Films 1894–1954* (London: George Allen & Unwin Ltd., rev. ed. 1968), 125; "The Expressions of Jimmy Aubrey," *Picture Show*, Sep. 18, 1920, 19; "Jimmy Aubrey Begins on New Comedy Series for Vitagraph," *Moving Picture World*, Jul. 24, 1920, 494; Rob Stone, *Laurel or Hardy: The Solo Films of Stan Laurel and Oliver "Babe" Hardy* (Manchester, NH: Split Reel Books, 1996), 225–30, 237, 258, 271; Report by the Examinations Corporation, Mar. 31, 1917, Memorandum #4, Box 10, Albert E. Smith Papers (Collection 2004), Department of Special Collections, Charles E. Young Research Library, University of California, Los Angeles; Vitagraph and VLSE invoices for the Palace Theatre, Antigo, Wisconsin, eBay, accessed Dec. 4, 2019, https://www.ebay.com/itm/Movie-Billhead-Vitagraph-9-18-1919-Spooks-Spasms-Earl-Montgomery-Larry-Semon/153349620665?hash=item23b45983b9:g:xDgAAOSws05cR8Jk, https://www.ebay.com/itm/Movie-Billhead-Vitagraph-8-18-1919-Stowaways-Strategy-Earl-Montgomery/163460898098?hash=item260f075d32:g:vT0AAOSwybtcHFI0; Letters Sep. 3, 1919 and Sep. 23, 1919, WS Smith to AE Smith, Box 7, Albert E. Smith Papers (Collection 2004), Department of Special Collections, Charles E. Young Research Library, University of California, Los Angeles; "Vitagraph to Star Separately Earl Montgomery and Joe Rock," *Moving Picture World*, Mar. 20, 1920, 1992; A. H. Giebler, "Joe Rock Forms Producing Company," *Moving Picture World*, Jul. 3, 1920, 93.

10. New York City exhibitor reports for Sep. 1920 conducted by F. W. Smith, Box 11, Albert E. Smith Papers (Collection 2004), Department of Special Collections, Charles E. Young Research Library, University of California, Los Angeles.

11. Daily Shipping Report week ended Apr. 24, 1920; Letters Feb. 5, 1920, Sep. 3, 1919, Jun. 22, 1920, WS Smith to AE Smith, Box 7, Albert E. Smith Papers (Collection 2004), Department of Special Collections, Charles E. Young Research Library, University of California, Los Angeles; Letter Aug. 19, 1919, WS Smith to AE Smith, Box 5, Albert E. Smith Papers (Collection 2004), Department of Special Collections, Charles E. Young Research Library, University of California, Los Angeles; Note re: Moreno-Bowman unit ca. Jul. 1920, Box 6, Albert E. Smith Papers (Collection 2004), Department of Special Collections, Charles E. Young Research Library, University of California, Los Angeles; *Photoplay*, Feb. 1921, 77; *Photoplay*, Sep. 1920, 94; "Jesse Lasky Appoints Walter Wanger to Position of F.P.-L. Production Head," *Moving Picture World*, Jun. 12, 1920, 1448; Telegram May 2, 1920, Victor Smith to A. Smith,

Box 6, Albert E. Smith Papers (Collection 2004), Department of Special Collections, Charles E. Young Research Library, University of California, Los Angeles.

12. "Mrs. Albert Smith Dies," *Moving Picture World*, Feb. 7, 1920, 914; "Vitagraph Head Weds Film Star," *Los Angeles Times*, Dec. 13, 1920, II4; "Jean Paige Signs Vitagraph Contract," *Moving Picture World*, Jul. 13, 1918, 216; Grace Kingsley, "Flashes: Albert Smith Visits," *Los Angeles Times*, Sep. 8, 1920, III4; Edwin Schallert, "Radios: Vitagraph Head Here," *Los Angeles Times*, Nov. 4, 1920, III4.

13. "1920 Proves Vitagraph's Biggest Year with 32 Percent Business Increase," *Moving Picture World*, Jan. 8, 1921, 163; Total net billings for 1920, Box 5, Albert E. Smith Papers (Collection 2004), Department of Special Collections, Charles E. Young Research Library, University of California, Los Angeles; Net Income for 1920, Box 1, Albert E. Smith Papers (Collection 2004), Department of Special Collections, Charles E. Young Research Library, University of California, Los Angeles.

14. "President Smith, of Vitagraph, Back from Coast with Negative of Black Beauty," *Moving Picture World*, Dec. 18, 1920, 896; Memo, Dec. 2, 1920, Black Beauty, Box 12698B, Warner Bros. Archives at USC; Vitagraph Story Contracts, Box 12647B, Warner Bros. Archives at USC; Black Beauty script, Box 2410B, Warner Bros. Archives at USC; "Vitagraph to Film 'Black Beauty' Famous Horse Story, as a Special," *Moving Picture World*, Aug. 21, 1920, 1055; Transcript of Dec. 1964 audio interview between Kevin Brownlow and James Morrison, Kevin Brownlow to author; Anthony Slide and Alan Gevinson, *The Big V: A History of the Vitagraph Company* (Metuchen, NJ: Scarecrow, 1987), 96, 114; "Flashback to Yesteryear," *American Cinematographer*, Oct. 1963, 608; "Cuts and Flashes," *Wid's Daily*, Aug. 9, 1918, 2; "Reginald E. Lyons," *American Cinematographer*, Feb. 3, 1922, 44; "Reggie Lyons, A.S.C., Re-joins J. Stuart Blackton," *American Cinematographer*, Mar. 1924, 18; *Motion Picture News*, Mar. 10, 1917, 1538; Earl Theisen, "The Photographer in the World War," *International Photographer*, Nov. 1933, 4, 6; "Studio Shots," *Moving Picture World*, May 17, 1919, 1027; Harry Burns, "Chit, Chat and Chatter," *Camera!*, Jun. 8, 1919, 7; "Pickups By the Staff," *Camera!*, Mar. 5, 1921, 7; Ingmar Bergman with Stig Bjorkman, Torsten Manns, Jonas Sima, *Bergman on Bergman* (New York: Simon and Schuster, 1973), qtd. in Slide and Gevinson, *The Big V*, 105; Ingmar Bergman interview on *The Dick Cavett Show*, originally broadcast Aug. 2, 1971; Jessie Robb, "Vitagraph's 'Black Beauty' a Winner; Renowned Story is Finely Filmed," *Moving Picture World*, Jan. 29, 1921, 555; "What the New York Newspaper Critics Said about 'Black Beauty' Now Playing at the Strand Theatre," *Moving Picture World*, Mar. 5, 1921, 41; Jan. 31, 1921 letter from manager Poli's Capitol Theatre, *Moving Picture World*, Feb. 12, 1921, 799; "'Black Beauty,' Autobiography of a Horse, Being Produced By Vitagraph," *Exhibitors Herald*, Aug. 28, 1920, 69; *Motion Picture News*, Oct. 6, 1917, 2263; *Film Year Book 1922–23* (New York: Wid's Films and Film Folks, Inc., 1922), 329, 372; "Federal Decision Too Late for Value," *Variety*, Nov. 3, 1922, 46.

15. Edwin Schallert, "Radios: Smith Here to Stay," *Los Angeles Times*, Mar. 16, 1921, III4; A. H. Giebler, "Smith Buys Cattle Ranch," *Moving Picture World*, Apr. 2, 1921, 477; Letter Feb. 18, 1927, Ronald Reader to Smith, Box 9, Albert E. Smith Papers (Collection 2004), Department of Special Collections, Charles E. Young Research

Library, University of California, Los Angeles; Grace Kingsley, "Vitagraph to Resume Here," *Los Angeles Times*, Apr. 5, 1923, II6.

16. "Big Demand for Pictures Keeps Studios Humming with Activity," *Moving Picture World*, Apr. 23, 1921, 872; Adele Whitely Fletcher, "Across the Silversheet: What's Your Reputation Worth?" *Motion Picture Magazine*, Jul. 1921, 102; Herbert Howe, "Whose Beauty Reigns upon the Screen?" *Photoplay*, Jul. 1921, 33–34; Three of the other seven most beautiful actresses were former Vitagraph players: Anita Stewart, Betty Blythe, and Florence Vidor; "The Broadway Bubble," *Photoplay*, Dec. 1920, 123; "The Broadway Bubble," *Wid's Daily*, Nov. 21, 1920, 13–14; Pearl Gaddis, "The Broadway Bubble," *Motion Picture News*, Nov. 27, 1920, 4163; *Exhibitors Herald*, Oct. 23, 1920, 52, 90; Ethel Sands, "A Girl's Adventures in Movieland," *Picture-Play Magazine*, Mar. 1921, 46–48; Margaret Reid, "Corinne as She Is," *Picture-Play Magazine*, May 1928, 74, 107; Delight Evans, "The Girl on the Cover," *Photoplay*, Jan. 1922, 38–39, 105.

17. "Charles Graham Baker Succeeds Chester as Vitagraph's Chief Scenario Editor," *Moving Picture World*, Dec. 3, 1921, 557; "Cousin Kate—Vitagraph," *Photoplay*, Mar. 1921, 62.

18. Letter Jun. 22, 1920, WS Smith to A. Smith, Box 7, Albert E. Smith Papers (Collection 2004), Department of Special Collections, Charles E. Young Research Library, University of California, Los Angeles; "Larry Semon Finishes Comedy and with New Leading Woman Starts New One, All within Thirty-Six Hours," *Moving Picture World*, Dec. 25, 1920, 1060; Sassen, *Larry Semon*, 72, 78, 84; Massa, *Lame Brains and Lunatics*, 277–79; Stone, *Laurel or Hardy*, 270–79; "Hans F. Koenekamp," *American Cinematographer*, Feb. 1, 1922, 51; "In Memoriam," *American Cinematographer*, Nov. 1992, 106; Kevin Brownlow, *The Parade's Gone By* (New York: Alfred A. Knopf, 1968), 216; Larry Semon, "It's No Laughing Matter," *Photoplay*, May 1922, 24; Buster Keaton, *My Wonderful World of Slapstick* (New York: Doubleday, 1960), 176.

19. Stock agreements Dec. 19, 1921 and Jun. 8, 1922, Box 7, Albert E. Smith Papers (Collection 2004), Department of Special Collections, Charles E. Young Research Library, University of California, Los Angeles; "Financial Statements Issued during 1922, Famous Players-Lasky Corporation," *Film Year Book 1922–23* (New York: Wid's Films and Film Folks, Inc., 1922), 335–36.

20. "A. E. Smith Back," *Moving Picture World*, Aug. 12, 1922, 494.

21. J. Stuart Blackton, "'Silence Was Golden,' The Story of My Forty Movie Years," ms., 370, 375, 380, 387, J. Stuart Blackton papers, Special Collections, Margaret Herrick Library, Academy of Motion Picture Arts and Sciences; J. Stuart Blackton, "'Hollywood with Its Hair Down' or Hollywood Memories; Forty Years of the Movies," ms., 242, 291–307, J. Stuart Blackton papers, Special Collections, Margaret Herrick Library, Academy of Motion Picture Arts and Sciences; Marian Blackton Trimble, *J. Stuart Blackton*, 102–5, 108; Diana Cooper, *Rainbow Comes and Goes* (Boston, MA: Houghton Mifflin, 1958), 236–37; *The Duff Cooper Diaries: 1915–1951*, ed. John Julius Norwich (London: Weidenfeld & Nicolson, 2005), 131, 143, 170; Russell Mallinson, "Filming Lady Di," *Pictures and the Picturegoer*, Jul. 1921, 10–11; The Glorious

Adventure—Legal 1921–1922, Memorandum of Agreement Jul. 10, 1922, Margaret Herrick Library, Academy of Motion Picture Arts and Sciences.

22. "Greatest Production Activity in Its History Under under Way by Vitagraph," *Exhibitors Herald*, Mar. 11, 1922, 65; "The Chicken Parade," *Exhibitors Herald*, Jan. 5, 1924, 76; "Too Much Business," *Photoplay*, Jun. 1922, 58.

23. Semon, "It's No Laughing Matter," 24; Sassen, *Larry Semon*, 85, 87, 114–16, 121, 123–25; "The Sawmill," *Moving Picture World*, Mar. 18, 1922, 297; Letter Oct. 26, 1921, A. Smith to WS Smith, Box 7, Albert E. Smith Papers (Collection 2004), Department of Special Collections, Charles E. Young Research Library, University of California, Los Angeles; "Coast Picture News," *Variety*, Jul. 14, 1922, 41; "Plays and Players," *Photoplay*, Apr 1922, 94; Contract May 12, 1922, Larry Semon and Vitagraph, Box 12702A, Warner Bros. Archives at USC; Letter May 12, 1922, Smith to Semon, Box 7, Albert E. Smith Papers (Collection 2004), Department of Special Collections, Charles E. Young Research Library, University of California, Los Angeles.

24. Albert E. Smith, *Two Reels and a Crank* (Garden City, NY: Doubleday, 1952), 213–16; Richard Koszarski, *Hollywood on the Hudson* (Piscataway, NJ: Rutgers University Press, 2008), 109; Reid, "Corinne as She Is," 74, 107; Arabella Boone, "Why Bob Your Hair?" *Photoplay*, Jul. 1920, 67–68; "A Virgin's Sacrifice," *Exhibitors Herald*, Nov. 4, 1922, 79; "A Woman's Sacrifice," *Exhibitors Herald*, Oct. 21, 1922, 86; A Virgin's Sacrifice, Box 2442B, Warner Bros. Archives at USC; "Corinne Griffith Quits Vitagraph Organization," *Exhibitors Herald*, Dec. 2, 1922, 31; *Pictures and the Picturegoer*, Jun. 1923, 54.

25. Telegram Jan. 20, 1922, A. Smith to WS Smith, Letter Dec. 26, 1922, Smith to William M. Seabury, Telegram Jan. 24, 1922, Bradley J. Smollen to Smith, undated memo by David Smith, Letter Feb. 8, 1922, WS Smith to A. Smith, Telegram Mar. 15, 1922, Smith to Frank Voller, Letter Oct. 22, 1921, Bradley J. Smollen to WS Smith, Letter Oct. 26, 1921, A. Smith to WS Smith, Box 7, Albert E. Smith Papers (Collection 2004), Department of Special Collections, Charles E. Young Research Library, University of California, Los Angeles; May 23 and Jun. 22, 1922 depositions of WS Smith, Box 7, Albert E. Smith Papers (Collection 2004), Department of Special Collections, Charles E. Young Research Library, University of California, Los Angeles; "Questions and Answers," *Photoplay*, Jun. 1922, 84; "In the Courts," *Film Daily*, Aug. 19, 1923, 4; Letter Mar. 12, 1923, A. Smith to WS Smith, Box 8, Albert E. Smith Papers (Collection 2004), Department of Special Collections, Charles E. Young Research Library, University of California, Los Angeles.

26. "Vitagraph Plans Big Production Based on New Wallingford Tale," *Exhibitors Herald*, Feb. 14, 1920, 52; "Albert E. Smith and George Randolph Chester Go to Coast to Make 'The Son of Wallingford,'" *Moving Picture World*, Feb. 19, 1921, 917; "Judge Won't Enjoin Famous Players From Issuing 'Get Rich Quick Wallingford,'" *Moving Picture World*, Apr. 23, 1921, 819; "Film Magnates Fete Champions of Sunday Shows," *Evening World*, Jun. 19, 1919, retrieved Jan 9, 2020, from sydneyscohen.wordpress.com; Supreme Court, New York County, Star Company vs. Vitagraph and Pathé Freres, Box 6, Albert E. Smith Papers (Collection 2004), Department of Special Collections, Charles E. Young Research Library, University of California, Los Angeles;

JRM, "'The Son of Wallingford' a Winner," *Exhibitors Herald*, Oct. 8, 1921, 45; "Vitagraph's 'Son of Wallingford' Booked by Many Leading Theatres," *Moving Picture World*, Oct. 29, 1921; Letter Oct. 26, 1921, A. Smith to WS Smith, Box 7, Albert E. Smith Papers (Collection 2004), Department of Special Collections, Charles E. Young Research Library, University of California, Los Angeles; *Moving Picture World*, Dec. 21, 1921, 636; "The Little Minister," *Photoplay*, Mar. 1922, 60; MMF, "The Little Minister," *Visual Education*, Apr. 1922, 221–22; "Across the Silversheet," *Motion Picture Magazine*, Mar. 1922, 117; "As to The Little Minister," *Boston Evening Transcript*, Jan. 21, 1922; Bill of Complaint Nov. 28, 1922, United States District Court, SDNY, Vitagraph Company of America, plaintiff, Against Famous Players-Lasky Corporation, Adolph Zukor, et al., Box 7, Albert E. Smith Papers (Collection 2004), Department of Special Collections, Charles E. Young Research Library, University of California, Los Angeles; "Allege Monopoly," *Film Daily*, Nov. 29, 1922, 1, 3; "Vitagraph Suit for Millions on Grounds of Monopoly Awakens Unusual Interest," *Film Daily*, Dec. 1, 1922, 1, 8; "Denies Charges," *Film Daily*, Mar. 5, 1923, 1–2; "Vitagraph Sues Paramount, Seeks $6,000,000 Damages," *Exhibitors Herald*, Dec. 16, 1922, 31–32, 44; Letter Jan. 31, 1922, SR Kent to MS Wilson, Letter Feb. 6, 1922, MS Wilson [to salesmen], Letter Apr. 10, 1922, William Marston Seabury to John E. Quinn, Letters Nov. 21, 1922, William Marston Seabury to Smith, Aug. 18, 1922, Smith to F. H. Sisson, Sep. 14, 1922, Blackton to Smith, Box 7, Albert E. Smith Papers (Collection 2004), Department of Special Collections, Charles E. Young Research Library, University of California, Los Angeles; Thomas Schatz, *The Genius of the System: Hollywood Filmmaking in the Studio Era* (New York: Pantheon, 1988), 72; "Zukor and Kent in Tomorrow," *Film Daily*, Apr. 12, 1923, 1; Smith, *Two Reels and a Crank*, 259; Mae D. Heuttig, "The Battle for Theaters," *The First Tycoons*, ed. Richard Dyer MacCann (Metuchen, NJ: Scarecrow, 1987), 168–71; Michael Conant, "Antitrust in the Motion Picture Industry," *The First Tycoons*, 179–80; Smith memo ca. September 1922, Box 4, Albert E. Smith Papers (Collection 2004), Department of Special Collections, Charles E. Young Research Library, University of California, Los Angeles; "The Important Twelve," *Film Year Book 1922–1923*, 267; Blackton, "Silence Was Golden," 255–57; "Independents Sue Lasky," *Scenario Bulletin-Digest*, Jan. 1923, 21; "Bayshore Vitagraph Studio Destroyed," *Film Daily*, Dec. 5, 1922, 1; "Film Inquiry Continues," *New York Times*, Jun. 19, 1923, 24; "Denies Charges," *Film Daily*, Mar. 5, 1923, 1–2; Letters Apr. 15, 1924, Smith to Rock, Jun. 13, 1923, A. Smith to Frank L. Smith, Box 8, Albert E. Smith Papers (Collection 2004), Department of Special Collections, Charles E. Young Research Library, University of California, Los Angeles; MPPDA Committee on Public Relations, 01–0193–01–0194, MPPDA Digital Archive, https://mppda.flinders.edu.au/records/85; "Suit Dropped," *Film Daily*, Jun. 13, 1923, 1.

27. Mark Lynn Anderson, "The Historian Is Paramount," *Film History* 26, no. 2 (2014): 9–10, quoting confidential complaint to the FTC from Famous Players Lasky attorney Paul Cravath, Nov. 15, 1922, FTC, Auxiliary Case Files, National Archives; Negative Costs, Billings and Booking to Mar. 7, 1925, Box 12726A, Warner Bros. Archives at USC; "J. Stuart Blackton Returns to Vitagraph as Vice-President," *Moving Picture World*, Apr. 7, 1923, 614; *The Duff Cooper Diaries: 1915–1951*, 170; "Albert E.

Smith on Coast to Supervise Vitagraph Production," *Exhibitors Trade Review*, Feb. 17, 1923, 610; On the Banks of the Wabash, Box 12696A, Warner Bros. Archives at USC; "Blackton Penciling Own Production," *Moving Picture World*, Sep. 15, 1923, 272; "On the Banks of the Wabash," *Photoplay*, Jan. 1924, 101; Blackton Trimble, *J. Stuart Blackton*, 148–49.

28. "Vitagraph to Resume Here," II6; Letter Nov. 17, 1923, Frank L. Smith to Alice Calhoun, Box 8, Albert E. Smith Papers (Collection 2004), Department of Special Collections, Charles E. Young Research Library, University of California, Los Angeles.

29. Letters Mar. 12, 1923, AE Smith to WS Smith, Jan. 24, 1924, Smith to AI Siegel, Telegram Mar. 16, 1923, AE Smith to WS Smith, Box 8, Albert E. Smith Papers (Collection 2004), Department of Special Collections, Charles E. Young Research Library, University of California, Los Angeles; "What the Picture Did for Me, Verdicts on Films in Language of Exhibitor," *Moving Picture World*, Feb. 3, 1923, 417; *Cine Mundial*, Dec. 1923, 721; Sassen, *Larry Semon*, 125–26, 128, 130–32.

30. "Albert E. Smith Goes to Look Over Conditions in Europe," *Moving Picture World*, Oct. 27, 1923, 725; Letters Nov. 20, 1923, Frank Vollor to Frank Smith, Nov. 28, 1923, AE Smith to Frank Smith, Jun. 13, 1923, AE Smith to Frank L. Smith, Box 8, Albert E. Smith Papers (Collection 2004), Department of Special Collections, Charles E. Young Research Library, University of California, Los Angeles; Letter Dec. 27, 1923, JS Blackton to Frank Smith, Box 7, Albert E. Smith Papers (Collection 2004), Department of Special Collections, Charles E. Young Research Library, University of California, Los Angeles; "Vitagraph Celebrates This Month," *Los Angeles Times*, Mar. 12, 1924, A9; Epes Winthrop Sargent, "Sigmund Lubin," *Moving Picture World*, Sep. 22, 1923, 326; "Fund for Lubin," *Variety*, Aug. 2, 1923, 18.

31. Letter Mar. 31, 1924, AE Smith to Rock and Vic Smith, Box 8, Albert E. Smith Papers (Collection 2004), Department of Special Collections, Charles E. Young Research Library, University of California, Los Angeles; Billings and Bookings to Mar. 7, 1925, Box 12726A, Warner Bros. Archives at USC; Koszarski, *Hollywood on the Hudson*, 108; Letters Feb. 8, 1924, Reader to Smith, Mar. 13, 1924, Smith to Reader, Jan. 24, 1924, Smith to John M. Quinn, Jan. 30, 1924, Smith to Willis C. Bright, Telegram Jun. 14, 1924, Blackton to George H. Smith, Box 8, Albert E. Smith Papers (Collection 2004), Department of Special Collections, Charles E. Young Research Library, University of California, Los Angeles; Letter Dec. 27, 1923, Blackton to Frank Smith, undated telegram, George Smith to Blackton, Box 7, Albert E. Smith Papers (Collection 2004), Department of Special Collections, Charles E. Young Research Library, University of California, Los Angeles; The Beloved Brute, Box 12726A, Warner Bros. Archives at USC.

32. "Vitagraph Engages Alice Calhoun," *Moving Picture World*, Jan. 3, 1920, 74; Edward Weitzel, "Alice Calhoun, of Vitagraph, Tells How to Become a Screen Star at Seventeen," *Moving Picture World*, Feb. 12, 1921, 801; OMS, "All about Alice," *Pictures and the Picturegoer*, Sep. 1923, 46; "Concerning Alice Calhoun," *Pictures and the Picturegoer*, Jul. 1924, 38–39; "Between Friends," *Film Daily*, Apr. 20, 1924, 13; MPPDA Digital Archive, Between Friends file, 01–1675, Letter Apr. 17, 1924, EMH of SNYMPC to Vitagraph, 01–1676–1677, Letter Sep. 16, 1924, George H. Cobb, NYS

Mot Pict Commission to R. Horsley, 01–1670, Synopsis Sep. 18, 1924, by FL Herron, 01–1669, Memorandum Sep. 18, 1924, Courtland Smith MPPDA to WHH, 01–1665–1667, Letter Sep. 19, 1924, AI Siegel to George H. Cobb, 01–1661–01662, Letter Sep. 24, 1924, Charles A. McMahon to Smith, 01–1660, Letter Sep. 25, 1924, Smith to McMahon, 01–1643, Letter Oct. 19, 1924, AI Siegel to Courtland Smith, https://mppda.flinders.edu.au/records/170; "Vitagraph Studio in Full Swing," *Los Angeles Times*, Mar. 2, 1924, B14; *Film Year Book 1925* (New York: Film Daily, 1925), 15, 27, 267, 269; *Exhibitors Herald*, Jun. 28, 1924, 66; *Moving Picture World*, Jun. 28, 1924, 806; *Film Daily*, Jul. 17, 1924, 4; *Exhibitors Herald*, Aug. 9, 1924, 78; "Effective Reverse on Vitagraph Play," *Moving Picture World*, Aug. 16, 1924, 537; J. M. Wright, "The Film Mart," *Exhibitors Herald*, Sep. 13, 1924, 54; "Newspaper Opinions," *Film Daily*, May 14, 1924, 6; "Between Friends," *Photoplay*, Aug. 1924, 88; Billings and Bookings to Mar 7, 1925, Box 12726A, Warner Bros. Archives at USC.

33. Letters, Apr. 26, 1924, AE Smith to Victor Smith, Jan. 23, 1924, Smith to Graham Baker, Telegram Jun. 18, 1924, Smith to Frank Voller, Telegram Feb. 5, 1924, AE Smith to Frank Voller, Letters Mar. 5, 1924, Smith to William Wright, Dec. 11, 1924, Smith to Victor Smith, Jun. 20, 1924, Smith to Clinton T. Miller, Box 8, Albert E. Smith Papers (Collection 2004), Department of Special Collections, Charles E. Young Research Library, University of California, Los Angeles; "J. B. Rock to Manage Vitagraph," *Los Angeles Times*, Feb. 19, 1924, A10; "Rock New General Manager of Vitagraph," *Exhibitors Herald*, Mar. 1, 1924, 28.

34. "Vitagraph Chief Back from English Trip," *Exhibitors Trade Review*, Dec. 15, 1923, 12; "Three 'Scaramouche' Premieres," *Film Daily*, Sep. 26, 1923, 1; "Newspaper Opinions," *Film Daily*, Oct. 3, 1923, 2; *Exhibitors Trade Review*, Jan. 26, 1924, 17; Letters Feb. 28, 1924, unknown sender to Smith, Apr. 22, 1924, AE Smith to Victor Smith, Mar. 19, 1924, Smith to Rock, Apr. 11, 1914, Smith to Rock, May 28, 1924, AE Smith to George Smith, Jun. 12, 1924, Smith to Rock, Jun. 19, 1924, ELS to Victor Smith, Telegrams Jun. 17, 1924, Smith to Rock, Jul. 25, 1924, Frank Vollor to Smith, Aug. 2, 1924, Smith to Rock, Letters May 28, 1924, Smith to Francis H. Sisson, Jun. 8, 1924, Smith to DJ McDonald, Sep. 30, 1924, Frank L. Smith to Victor Smith, Jun. 18, 1924, AE Smith to Victor Smith, Aug. 7, 1924, AE Smith to George Smith, Jul. 1, 1924, AE Smith to George Smith and Reader, Aug. 6, 1924, Smith to Rock, Aug. 12, 1924, Victor Smith to Frank Smith, Sep. 13, 1924, Vic Smith to Frank Smith, Feb. 17, 1925, Reader to Smith, Telegram Sep. 8, 1924, Blackton to Smith, Box 8, Albert E. Smith Papers (Collection 2004), Department of Special Collections, Charles E. Young Research Library, University of California, Los Angeles; "Fans Will Choose Actor," *Exhibitors Trade Review*, Dec. 15, 1923, 33; "Vitagraph," *Exhibitors Herald*, Feb. 2, 1924, 63; Plans for 1925–1926 season, Box 9, Albert E. Smith Papers (Collection 2004), Department of Special Collections, Charles E. Young Research Library, University of California, Los Angeles; "Kerrigan in Tale by Sabatini," *Los Angeles Times*, Jun. 3, 1924, A11; "Vitagraph to Resume Here," II6; Letter Jun. 19, 1924, Smith to Reader, Box 8, Albert E. Smith Papers (Collection 2004), Department of Special Collections, Charles E. Young Research Library, University of California, Los Angeles; Steve Smith, Jr., "Pictorial Side of 'Captain Blood,'" *American Cinematographer*, Sep. 1924, 5–7, 20;

Albert E. Smith, "Flatbush and Vine," ms., Jan. 1951, 183, 256, Charles G. Clarke Collection, Margaret Herrick Library, Academy of Motion Picture Arts and Sciences; "Vitagraph Head Personally Editing 'Captain Blood,'" *Moving Picture World*, Aug. 30, 1924, 725; "Remarkable Exploitation Is Aiding 'Captain Blood,'" *Moving Picture World*, Sep. 6, 1924, 22; "Big Releases and Future Plans Are Announced by Vitagraph," *Moving Picture World*, Sep. 13, 1924, 147; "$5,000 Weekly for Bare Walls Shubert Wants Pay for Extra Shows," *Variety*, Oct. 1, 1924, 21; "Many Stars Attend Rialto Performance," *Los Angeles Times*, Sep. 25, 1924, A9; *Film Year Book 1925*, 7, 15, 267; *Moving Picture World*, Nov. 1, 1924, 26; Josie P. Lederer, "He, She, and It," *Pictures and the Picturegoer*, Dec. 1924, 64; *Moving Picture World*, Nov. 1, 1924, 26; "'Capt. Blood' Grips England; Book, Music, Magazine Tie-ups," *Moving Picture World*, May 2, 1925, 70; Letters Nov. 9, 1925, John Pearson to Smith, Apr. 14, 1925, Reader to Smith, Dec. 20, 1924, Al Siegel to Vitagraph France, Feb. 12, 1925, Rock to Smith, Feb. 18, 1925, Rock to Smith, Box 9, Albert E. Smith Papers (Collection 2004), Department of Special Collections, Charles E. Young Research Library, University of California, Los Angeles; Smith, *Two Reels and a Crank*, 270; "Newspaper Opinions," *Film Daily*, Sep. 11, 1924, 7; C. S. Sewell, "Captain Blood," *Moving Picture World*, Sep. 20, 1924, 244; "National Board of Review Praises Vitagraph Pictures," *Moving Picture World*, Jan. 17, 1925, 272; Joel W. Finler, *The Hollywood Story* (London: Wallflower, 2003), 356.

35. Letters Mar. 13, 1924, Smith to G. Miller, Feb. 17, 1924, Reader to Smith, Jun. 20, 1924, Smith to Clinton T. Miller, Dec. 11, 1924, Smith to Rock, Dec. 22, 1924, AE Smith to Victor Smith, Telegrams Jun. 16 and 17, 1924, Frank L. Smith, Dec. 10, 1924, AE Smith to Victor Smith, Dec. 27, 1924, Smith to Rock, Box 8, Albert E. Smith Papers (Collection 2004), Department of Special Collections, Charles E. Young Research Library, University of California, Los Angeles; New Income Vitagraph Company for year ending 1924, Box 1, Albert E. Smith Papers (Collection 2004), Department of Special Collections, Charles E. Young Research Library, University of California, Los Angeles.

36. "Oddities on B'way This Week," *Variety*, Sep. 10, 1924, 21; "The Movies and the Public," *Educational Screen*, Oct. 1924, 329; "The Alaskan," *Wid's Daily*, Dec. 25, 1924, 18.

37. Letter Feb. 8, 1924, to Smith, Box 8, Albert E. Smith Papers (Collection 2004), Department of Special Collections, Charles E. Young Research Library, University of California, Los Angeles; MPPDA Digital Archive, 02–0887, Jan. 28, 1925 memo by Will Hays, https://mppda.flinders.edu.au/records/1345; "Vitagraph Quits Hays Organization, Quoting 'Live and Let Live' Belief," *Moving Picture World*, Feb. 7, 1925, 547; "Disagreeing with Policies, Vitagraph Quits Hays Group," *Billboard*, Feb. 7, 1925, 6; "Will Hays the Target," *Kansas City Times*, Feb. 9, 1925, 5, Box 1, Albert E. Smith Papers (Collection 2004), Department of Special Collections, Charles E. Young Research Library, University of California, Los Angeles; "M. P. T. O. A. Congratulates Albert Smith and Vitagraph," *Moving Picture World*, Feb. 14, 1925, 654; Resolution Feb. 11, 1925, Motion Picture Theatre Owners of Canada, Box 10, Albert E. Smith Papers (Collection 2004), Department of Special Collections, Charles E. Young Research Library, University of California, Los Angeles.

38. Telegram Dec. 15, 1921, Smith to Frank Voller, Box 7, Albert E. Smith Papers (Collection 2004), Department of Special Collections, Charles E. Young Research Library, University of California, Los Angeles; "Greatest Production Activity in its History under way by Vitagraph," 65; Telegram Oct. 14, 1924, Frank L. Smith to AE Smith, Box 8, Albert E. Smith Papers (Collection 2004), Department of Special Collections, Charles E. Young Research Library, University of California, Los Angeles; Epes W. Sargent, "Pampered Youth," *Moving Picture World*, Feb. 21, 1925, 785; Letters Oct. 24, 1924, Frank L. Smith to Rock, Dec. 22, 1924, AE Smith to Victor Smith, Box 8, Albert E. Smith Papers (Collection 2004), Department of Special Collections, Charles E. Young Research Library, University of California, Los Angeles; "Alice Calhoun's Role," *Moving Picture World*, Jan. 3, 1925, 73; Telegram Jan. 3, 1925, Dave Smith to Rock, Box 9, Albert E. Smith Papers (Collection 2004), Department of Special Collections, Charles E. Young Research Library, University of California, Los Angeles; "New York City Reviewers Praise 'Pampered Youth,'" *Moving Picture World*, Feb. 28, 1925, 928; Pampered Youth Negative Cost Exclusive of Office Overhead and Billings to Mar. 7, 1925, Box 12726A, Warner Bros. Archives at USC.

39. Valuation of Vitagraph Company of America ca. 1925, Telegrams Jan. 27, 1925, Frank L. Smith to AE Smith, Feb. 25, 1925, Frank Vollor to Smith, Letters Jan. 29, 1925, Reader to Smith, Oct. 1, 1925, Rock to Smith, Feb. 12, 1925, Rock to Smith, Feb. 18, 1925, Rock and Vic Smith to AE Smith, Feb. 27, 1925, Rock to Smith, Mar. 3, 1925, George Smith to AE Smith, Feb. 21, 1925, Vic Smith to AE Smith, Apr. 9, 1925, DJ McDonald to AE Smith, Cablegram Apr. 27, 1925, Price Waterhouse, Paris, to Vitagraph, NY, Box 9, Albert E. Smith Papers (Collection 2004), Department of Special Collections, Charles E. Young Research Library, University of California, Los Angeles; "Control of Vitagraph Returns to Founders," *Billboard*, Apr. 4, 1925, 8; Letters Mar. 1925, from representatives of Guaranty Trust Co. resigning as officers/directors of Vitagraph, Document Apr. 13, 1925, Guaranty Trust acknowledging receipt of full payment by Vitagraph abolishing all indebtedness to the bank based on the original indenture dated May 24, 1916, Document Apr. 13, 1925, Guaranty Trust relinquishing its stock in Vitagraph to Smith, Box 16084A, Warner Bros. Archives at USC; Blackton, "Silence Was Golden," 260; "Vitagraph to Release 30 Productions, President Albert E. Smith Announces," *Moving Picture World*, Apr. 11, 1925, 587.

40. Letters Jan. 7, 1925, Blackton to Smith, Feb. 20, 1925, Rock to Smith, Feb. 27, 1925, Rock and Vic Smith to AE Smith, Feb. 11, 1925, Rock and Victor Smith to AE Smith, Feb. 14, 1925, AI Siegel to Smith, Feb. 16, 1925, AI Siegel to Smith, Mar. 13, 1925, Rock to Smith, Telegrams Feb. 11, 1925, Rock to Smith, Mar. 14, 1925, Smith to Rock, Apr. 10, 1925, Blackton to Smith, Apr. 11, 1925, Blackton to Smith, Statement Feb. 13, 1925, by Smith, Approximate cash on hand on Apr. 18, 1925, Box 9, Albert E. Smith Papers (Collection 2004), Department of Special Collections, Charles E. Young Research Library, University of California, Los Angeles.

41. Smith, *Two Reels and a Crank*, 272–73; Albert Smith audio interview, tape 9, Albert E. Smith Papers (Collection 2004), Department of Special Collections, Charles E. Young Research Library, University of California, Los Angeles; Unsigned contract

Vitagraph and Sydney Cohen, Telegrams Apr. 19, 1925, Blackton to Smith, Apr. 22, 1925, AE Smith and Rock to Blackton, David Smith and Frank Smith, Contracts Apr. 20, 1925, signed by Harry Warner and Albert Smith, Letter Apr. 20, 1925, H Warner to Smith, Agreement Warner Bros. Pictures, Inc. and Smith, Rock and Blackton made Apr. 20, 1925, to acquire stock and assets of Vitagraph, see especially Schedules A, E, G, H, X, receipts Apr. 22, 1925, for checks and promissory notes signed by Smith, Agreement Apr. 20, 1925, between Smith and WB purchasing negatives of *The Man from Brodney's* and *Behold This Woman*, Letter May 7, 1925, George Smith to AE Smith, Box 9, Albert E. Smith Papers (Collection 2004), Department of Special Collections, Charles E. Young Research Library, University of California, Los Angeles; Slide and Gevinson, *The Big V*, 122.

42. "Pioneer Vitagraph Sold to Warners," *New York Times*, Apr. 23, 1925, 24; "Warner Bros. Buy Vitagraph; Acquire 50 Branches throughout the World," *Moving Picture World*, May 2, 1925, 25; "Warner Bros. Will Retain Vitagraph Co. Trade Mark," *Moving Picture World*, May 9, 1925, 138; "Warners Will Not Disturb Vitagraph Exchange Staffs," *Billboard*, May 9, 1925, 52; Telegram Apr. 29, 1925, Rock to Smith, IOU Apr. 30, 1925, Blackton to Smith, Box 9, Albert E. Smith Papers (Collection 2004), Department of Special Collections, Charles E. Young Research Library, University of California, Los Angeles; Letter Jul. 20–21, 1924, Mae to Maurice Costello, Maurice Costello papers, Margaret Herrick Library, Academy of Motion Picture Arts and Sciences; Lin Bonner, "Screen 'Founder' Seeks Quiet Life," *Evening Herald*, Apr. 25, 1925, II13, Box 1, Albert E. Smith Papers (Collection 2004), Department of Special Collections, Charles E. Young Research Library, University of California, Los Angeles; Agreement Jun. 30, 1925, Warner Bros. Pictures, Inc and J. Stuart Blackton, Letter Agreement Aug. 6, 1925, JL Warner and J. Stuart Blackton, J. Stuart Blackton papers, Special Collections, Margaret Herrick Library, Academy of Motion Picture Arts and Sciences; Agreement Jul. 1, 1925, Warner Bros. and Marian Constance Blackton, Box 2729B, Warner Bros. Archives at USC.

43. Letters Nov. 9, 1925, John Pearson to Smith, Feb. 15, 1926, Dec. 15, 1926, Jul. 18, 1927, Oct. 4, 1925, Smith to Rock, Dec. 3, 1925, Dec. 3, 1925, Reader to Smith, Dec. 29, 1925, Oct. 1, 1925, Rock to Smith, Box 9, Albert E. Smith Papers (Collection 2004), Department of Special Collections, Charles E. Young Research Library, University of California, Los Angeles; *Pictures and the Picturegoer*, May 1925, 20.

6. 1926 and Beyond

1. Richard Koszarski, *Hollywood on the Hudson* (Piscataway, NJ: Rutgers University Press, 2008), 148–51, 153–54, 156, 401–6; Kevin Brownlow, *The Parade's Gone By* (New York: Alfred A. Knopf, 1968), 569; Sales contract Oct. 3, 1951 Vitagraph Corporation (aka Chestnut Studio Corporation) and NBC, Box 16064B, Warner Bros. Archives at USC; Gerd Wilcke, "Vitagraph Studio in Flatbush, A Cradle of Movies, Is Closing," *New York Times*, Aug. 31, 1957, 17; "Yeshiva Acquires Old Film Studios," *New York Times*, Jun. 3, 1964, 45; Matthew Taub, "Residents Fear for Vitagraph Smokestack, Last Remnant of Silent Film Studio," *Brooklyn Eagle*, Oct.

6, 2014; www.thevitagraphbk.com; Ron Hutchinson, "The Jazz Singer," http://www.loc.gov/ static/programs/national-film-preservation-board/documents/jazz_singer; "Telefile: Los Angeles' Seventh Outlet, KECA-TV Gets Off to Fast Start in the TV Race," *Broadcasting*, Nov. 28, 1949, 32; Marc Wanamaker, *Hollywood 1940–2008* (Charleston, SC: Arcadia, 2009), 108; Philip K. Scheuer, "ATCH," *Los Angeles Times*, Oct. 23, 1932, B13.

2. Letter Jul. 28, 1927, Warner to Blackton, Letter Aug. 3, 1928, Smith to Ruby Miller, Charles G. Clarke Collection, Margaret Herrick Library, Academy of Motion Picture Arts and Sciences; Letter Dec. 15, 1927, Warner to Smith, Box 9, Albert E. Smith Papers (Collection 2004), Department of Special Collections, Charles E. Young Research Library, University of California, Los Angeles; "The Changes with Years," *Variety*, Feb. 15, 1928, 12; "Spoor Takes $150,000 Loss When He Discards Third Dimension Picture," *Exhibitors Herald*, Oct. 1, 1927, 20; J. Stuart Blackton 1924 astrological forecast, Letters Nov. 3, 1936, Nov. 9, 1936, Henriette Herz to Lulu C. Russell, J. Stuart Blackton papers, Special Collections, Margaret Herrick Library, Academy of Motion Picture Arts and Sciences; Philip K. Scheuer, "ATCH," *Los Angeles Times*, Jul. 26, 1931, B13; J. Stuart Blackton, "'Silence Was Golden,' The Story of My Forty Movie Years," ms., 406, J. Stuart Blackton papers, Special Collections, Margaret Herrick Library, Academy of Motion Picture Arts and Sciences; Anthony Slide and Alan Gevinson, *The Big V: A History of the Vitagraph Company* (Metuchen, NJ: Scarecrow, 1987), 28–30; Marian Blackton Trimble, *J. Stuart Blackton: A Personal Biography by His Daughter* (Metuchen, NJ: Scarecrow, 1985), 168–75, 178, 184–90, 192–205; Letter Jun. 22, 1939, Blackton to Earl Theisen, GC 1091, Seaver Center for Western History Research, Natural History Museum of Los Angeles County; J. Stuart Blackton, "'Hollywood with Its Hair Down' or Hollywood Memories; Forty Years of the Movies," ms., cover note, J. Stuart Blackton papers, Special Collections, Margaret Herrick Library, Academy of Motion Picture Arts and Sciences; "J. Stuart Blackton," *Motion Picture Herald*, Aug. 23, 1941, 1; Albert E. Smith, *Two Reels and a Crank* (Garden City, NY: Doubleday, 1952), 262.

3. Letters Smith and Reader, Sep. 6, 1926, May 15, 1925, Dec. 3, 1925, Dec. 6, 1925, Dec. 29, 1925, Mar. 15, 1926, Feb. 18, 1927, May 10, 1927, Dec. 4, 1927, Aug. 1, 1925, May 3, 1929, Box 9, Albert E. Smith Papers (Collection 2004), Department of Special Collections, Charles E. Young Research Library, University of California, Los Angeles; Miriam Rosen, "Méliès, Georges," *World Film Directors*, vol. 1, *1890–1945*, ed. John Wakeman (New York: H. W. Wilson Company, 1987), 747–65; Erik Barnouw, *The Magician and the Cinema* (New York: Oxford University Press, 1981), 103.

4. Letters Smith and Rock, Sep. 25, 1926, Jan. 30, 1926, Letter May 10, 1927, Reader to Smith, Box 9, Albert E. Smith Papers (Collection 2004), Department of Special Collections, Charles E. Young Research Library, University of California, Los Angeles; "John B. Rock," *New York Times*, Nov. 25, 1948, 31.

5. Letter Dec. 29, 1925, Reader to Smith, Box 9, Albert E. Smith Papers (Collection 2004), Department of Special Collections, Charles E. Young Research Library, University of California, Los Angeles; "Site Near Lake Hodges Chosen for Residence," *Los Angeles Times*, Apr. 10, 1927, E4; Raymond Sarlot and Fred E. Basten, *Life at the*

Marmont (New York: Penguin, 2013), 5, 7–14, 82; "Apartments Justify Faith," *Los Angeles Times*, May 1, 1932, D2; Bess Wilson, "Glendale Clubwomen Learn Film History," *Los Angeles Times*, Mar. 2, 1939, A7; Letters Smith and Clarke, Apr. 29, 1944, Feb. 2, 1944, Box 10, Albert E. Smith Papers (Collection 2004), Department of Special Collections, Charles E. Young Research Library, University of California, Los Angeles; Smith, *Two Reels and a Crank*, 283–85; Ezra Goodman, "Record on Records," *New York Times*, Feb. 20, 1949, X4; H. D. Moria, "Vitagraph's Ex-Chief Cites Film Power Fight," *Los Angeles Times*, Dec. 7, 1952, D8; Bosley Crowther, "The Flickers and Mr. Smith," *New York Times*, Nov. 23, 1952, BR4; "When Hollywood Came to Wall Street," *New York Times*, May 14, 1933, BR4; Bosley Crowther, "Some of Those Days Were Colossal," *New York Times*, Oct. 18, 1953, BR7; Alan Thrasher, "Public Never Wrong, Film Pioneer's Motto," *Los Angeles Times*, Oct. 25, 1953, D6; Letter Feb. 12, 1954, Smith to Ball, Box 10, Albert E. Smith Papers (Collection 2004), Department of Special Collections, Charles E. Young Research Library, University of California, Los Angeles; "Pioneer Filmmaker Albert E. Smith Dies," *Los Angeles Times*, Aug. 3, 1958, 35; "Albert Smith, Inventor of Vitagraph, Is Dead," *Motion Picture Daily*, Aug. 5, 1958, 3.

6. Rosalind Shaffer, "Stars Laugh over Old Time Movies," *Chicago Tribune*, Jan. 31, 1926, H5; clipping, *Saturday Evening Post*, Apr. 9, 1927, Brownlow to author; "Screen Stars of Another Day Honored: Breakfast Club Fetes Group of Silent Film Celebrities," *Los Angeles Times*, Oct. 12, 1933, A16; "Sentimental Directors Go for Old-Time Favorites," *Los Angeles Times*, Mar. 26, 1939, C4; Frederick James Smith, "Unwept, Unhonored and Unfilmed," *Photoplay*, Jul. 1924, 64–67, 101–5; "Florence Turner, Top Film Star in '15," *New York Times*, Aug. 30, 1946, 15; "Costello Girls with Warner," *Moving Picture World*, May 9, 1925, 228; Terry Chester Schulman, *Film's First Family: The Untold Story of the Costellos* (Lexington: University Press of Kentucky, 2019), 74–76, 104–6, 129, 188, 208–10, 216–18; "Maurice Costello Dies in Hollywood," *New York Times*, Oct. 30, 1950, 27; "An Idol Not Forgotten," *New York Times*, Oct. 31, 1950, 26; Claudia Sassen, *Larry Semon, Daredevil Comedian of the Silent Screen* (Jefferson, NC: McFarland & Company, 2015), 142–43, 152, 172, 177, 179–81; Blackton, "Hollywood with Its Hair Down," cover note; "Memorial for Silents by Film Vets," *Variety*, Jun. 3, 1936, 3; "Blackton Founds Organization of Screen Pioneers," *Motion Picture Herald*, Sep. 5, 1936, 36; Steve Massa, *Lame Brains & Lunatics: The Good, the Bad and the Forgotten of Silent Comedy* (Duncan, OK: Bear Manor Media, 2013), 14; "Flora Finch, Star of Film Comedies," *New York Times*, Jan. 5, 1940, 23; "Florence Lawrence a Suicide on Coast," *New York Times*, Dec. 29, 1938, 15; Kelly R. Brown, *Florence Lawrence, The Biograph Girl* (Jefferson, NC: McFarland, 1999), 142, 146; Edwin Schallert, "Vitagraph Stars Turn Back Clock at Reunion," *Los Angeles Times*, Oct. 22, 1956, 2; "Paul Kelly, Actor on Stage, Screen," *New York Times*, Nov. 7, 1956, 31; Philip K. Scheuer, "Earliest of Screen Villains Looks Back Over Career of 40 Years," *Los Angeles Times*, Jun. 18, 1944, C1; "Paul Panzer, Silent Screen Actor, Dies," *Los Angeles Times*, Aug. 17, 1958, 28; Ezra Goodman, "Stars of Yesteryear," *New York Times*, Apr. 25, 1943, X5; Anthony Slide, *Hollywood Unknowns* (Jackson: University Press of Mississippi, 2012), 167, 176; Brownlow, *Parade's Gone By*, 14, 146; "Norma Talmadge, Film Star, Dead," *New York Times*, Dec. 25, 1957, 31; Greta de Groat,

"DuBarry, Woman of Passion," the Norma Talmadge website, https://web.stanford.edu/~gdegroat/NT/home.htm; "Clara Kimball Young," *Variety*, Oct. 19, 1960, 63; Karen Ward Mahar, "Clara Kimball Young," Women Film Pioneers Project, doi.org/10.7916/d8-1tst-hf20; "Anita Stewart, Silent-Film Star," *New York Times*, May 5, 1961, 29; "James W. Morrison," *New York Times*, Nov. 22, 1974, 42; *Moving Picture World*, Aug. 1, 1914, 694; "Miss Margaret Gibson," *Moving Picture World*, Oct. 3, 1914, 42; "Star Comedienne Caught in a Raid," *Los Angeles Times*, Aug. 26, 1917, I10; "Former Film Star Will Be Tried as a Vagrant," *Los Angeles Times*, Aug. 28, 1917, II3; "Pair Held for Taking Property," *Los Angeles Times*, Mar. 1, 1924, 1; "Screen Star Faces Judge," *Los Angeles Times*, Nov. 3, 1923, II1; "Local Fugitive On Trial," *Los Angeles Times*, Nov. 23, 1923, II1; Bruce Long, "Margaret Gibson's Deathbed Confession: I Killed William Desmond Taylor," and Raphael F. Long, "What Did I Know and When Did I Know It," *Taylorology*, Dec. 1999, silentera.com/taylorology; Maureen Joyce, "Corinne Griffith, Film Star, Redskins Adviser, Dies," *Washington Post*, Jul. 15, 1979, B7; "Divorce Puzzler: Will Real Corinne Griffith Stand Up?" *Tampa Tribune*, May 6, 1966, 9; "Hubby Loses Alimony Plea, Actress Wins Her Divorce," *Tampa Tribune*, May 15, 1966, 10A; Anthony Slide, "Corinne Griffith," *Silent Players* (Lexington: University Press of Kentucky, 2002), 169; *American Cinematographer*, Nov. 1992, 108.

7. "B. B. Hampton, Promoter, Died in N. Y. Hospital," *Variety*, Feb. 2, 1932, 55; Benjamin B. Hampton, *A History of the American Film Industry* (New York: Covici-Friede, 1931), ix, 125, 150–65, 185. The autobiographies of Mary Pickford, Adolph Zukor, and Albert Smith are also at variance with the facts regarding Pickford's contract renewal with Zukor. Mary Pickford, *Sunshine and Shadow* (New York: Doubleday & Co., 1955), 102–4; Adolph Zukor with Dale Kramer, *The Public Is Never Wrong* (New York: G. P. Putnam's Sons, 1953), 21, 176; Smith, *Two Reels and a Crank*, 97–201; Reminiscences of Adolph Zukor: 1958, 4075134, 14/2146, Columbia Center for Oral History, Popular Arts Project, Columbia University; Mark Lynn Anderson, "The Historian Is Paramount," *Film History* 26, no. 2 (2014): 4, 7–13, 16–21. Mark Lynn Anderson points out that film historian Douglas Gomery, in "What Was Adolph Zukor Doing in 1927?" *Film History* 17, no. 2–3 (2005): 205, "portrays Zukor as a reliable source . . . since he 'established the first principles of the studio system.' We might term this version of the myth 'In the Beginning There Was Zukor.'" Gomery is not alone in propagating Zukor's statements as fact: e.g., Neal Gabler, *An Empire of Their Own: How the Jews Invented Hollywood* (New York: Doubleday, 1989), 12, 24–26, 30 and Richard Dyer MacCann, *The First Tycoons* (Metuchen, NJ: Scarecrow, 1987), 2–3, 32, 82–83.

8. Mark Lynn Anderson, "Historian Is Paramount," 3; Douglas Gomery, *The Hollywood Studio System* (New York: St. Martin's, 1986), 22.

9. Earle Williams, "Good Friends, Good Wages, Good Fun, Good Work!," *Pictures and the Picturegoer*, Oct. 30, 1915, 90; Dorothy Scott, "A Tip for Pershing," *Photoplay*, Jun. 1918, 39; Slide, *Silent Players*, "James Morrison," 251–54; Crowther, *Hollywood Rajah* (New York: Holt, Rinehart and Winston, 1960), 78; Scott Eyman, *Lion of Hollywood: the Life and Legend of Louis B. Mayer* (New York: Simon & Schuster, 2005), 10, 84.

10. "Vitagraph Company Lose All Their Old Reels," *Moving Picture World*, Jul. 16, 1910, 149; "Observations by Our Man About Town," *Moving Picture World*, Jul. 16, 1910, 139; Albert Smith audio interview, tapes 5, 9, Albert E. Smith Papers (Collection 2004), Department of Special Collections, Charles E. Young Research Library, University of California, Los Angeles; Inter-office memos Nov. 6, 1942, W. G. Wallace to J. H. Spray, Feb. 17, 1943, Wallace to S. Schneider, Box 12700B, Warner Bros. Archives at USC; Ivo Blom, "The Impact of the Desmet Collection: Pordenone and Beyond," *Journal of Film Preservation* 87 (October 2012): 34–50: Ben Brewster, "The Vitagraph fragments in the Library of Congress paper prints collection," *Screen Culture: History and Textuality* (London: John Libbey, 2004), 73–98.

Conclusion

1. James S. McQuade, "'The Battle Cry of Peace' Comes to Chicago," *Moving Picture World*, Oct. 30, 1915, 773; Marian Blackton Trimble, "The Man and the Movies," ms., 51, J. Stuart Blackton papers, Special Collections, Margaret Herrick Library, Academy of Motion Picture Arts and Sciences.

2. Albert Smith audio interview, tape 6, Albert E. Smith Papers (Collection 2004), Department of Special Collections, Charles E. Young Research Library, University of California, Los Angeles.

3. Letter Mar. 7, 1954, Smith to George J. Mitchell, Jr., Box 10, Albert E. Smith Papers (Collection 2004), Department of Special Collections, Charles E. Young Research Library, University of California, Los Angeles.

4. Gladys Hall, "Maurice Costello: What it Was to Be a Star in 1911," ms., 8, Gladys Hall Collection, Folder 118, Margaret Herrick Library, Academy of Motion Picture Arts and Sciences.

Selected Bibliography

Due to space limitations, the reader is directed to the endnotes for a complete listing of sources consulted. The following works have been particularly helpful in the preparation of this work.

Books, Manuscripts, and Dissertations

Anderson, Robert Jack. "The Motion Picture Patents Company." PhD diss., University of Wisconsin–Madison, 1983.

Blackton, J. Stuart. "'Silence Was Golden,' The Story of My Forty Movie Years," ms., J. Stuart Blackton papers, Special Collections, Margaret Herrick Library, Academy of Motion Picture Arts and Sciences.

Blackton, J. Stuart. "'Hollywood with Its Hair Down' or Hollywood Memories; Forty Years of the Movies," ms., J. Stuart Blackton papers, Special Collections, Margaret Herrick Library, Academy of Motion Pictures Arts and Sciences.

Blackton Trimble, Marian. *J. Stuart Blackton: A Personal Biography by His Daughter.* Metuchen, NJ: Scarecrow, 1985.

Bowser, Eileen. *The Transformation of Cinema, 1907–1915.* Berkeley, CA: University of California Press, 1990.

Brownlow, Kevin. *The Parade's Gone By.* New York: Alfred A. Knopf, 1968.

Cherchi Usai, Paolo, ed. *Vitagraph Co. of America, Il cinema prima di Hollywood.* Pordenone, Italy: Edizioni Studio Tesi, 1987.

Dewey, Donald. *Buccaneer, James Stuart Blackton and the Birth of the American Movies.* Lanham, MD: Rowman & Littlefield, 2016.

Erish, Andrew A. *Col. William N. Selig, the Man Who Invented Hollywood.* Austin, TX: University of Texas Press, 2012.

Koszarski, Richard. *Hollywood on the Hudson.* Piscataway, NJ: Rutgers University Press, 2008.

Massa, Steve. *Lame Brains & Lunatics: The Good, the Bad, and the Forgotten of Silent Comedy.* Duncan, OK: Bear Manor Media, 2013.

Musser, Charles. *The Emergence of Cinema: The American Screen to 1907.* New York: Charles Scribner's Sons, 1990.

Sassen, Claudia. *Larry Semon, Daredevil Comedian of the Silent Screen.* Jefferson, NC: McFarland, 2015.

Schulman, Terry Chester. *Film's First Family: The Untold Story of the Costellos.* Lexington: University Press of Kentucky, 2019.

Slide, Anthony, and Alan Gevinson. *The Big V: A History of the Vitagraph Company.* Metuchen, NJ: Scarecrow, 1987.

Smith, Albert E. *Two Reels and a Crank.* Garden City, NY: Doubleday, 1952.

Articles and Chapters in Books and Periodicals

Blackton, J. Stuart. "Yesterdays of Vitagraph." *Photoplay*, July 1919.

Gartenberg, Jon. "Vitagraph before Griffith: Forging ahead in the Nickelodeon Era." *Studies in Visual Communication* 10, no. 4 (Fall 1984).

Musser, Charles. "American Vitagraph 1897–1901." *Cinema Journal* 22, no. 3 (Spring 1983).

Salt, Barry. "The Unknown Ince." *Sight and Sound* (Fall 1988).

Salt, Barry. "Film Form 1900–1906," in *Early Cinema: Space, Frame, Narrative*, ed. Thomas Elsaesser. London: BFI, 1990.

Shail, Andrew. "The Motion Picture Story Magazine and the Origins of Popular British Film Culture." *Film History* 20, no. 2 (2008).

Spadoni, Robert. "The Figure Seen from the Rear, Vitagraph, and the Development of Shot/Reverse Shot." *Film History* 11, no. 3 (1999).

Collections

Albert E. Smith Papers (Collection 2004), Department of Special Collections, Charles E. Young Research Library, University of California, Los Angeles

J. Stuart Blackton papers, Special Collections, Margaret Herrick Library, Academy of Motion Picture Arts and Sciences, Beverly Hills, CA

J. Stuart Blackton collection, Natural History Museum of Los Angeles County, Seaver Center for Western History Research, and Material Culture, Los Angeles, CA

Charles G. Clarke collection, Margaret Herrick Library, Academy of Motion Picture Arts and Sciences, Beverly Hills, CA

Motion Picture Patents Company and General Film Company collection, Margaret Herrick Library, Academy of Motion Picture Arts and Sciences, Beverly Hills, CA

Warner Bros. Archives at University of Southern California, Los Angeles

Thomas A. Edison Papers, Rutgers University, Piscataway, NJ

Film Archives

British Film Institute, London, UK

Library of Congress, Washington, DC

Eye Filmmuseum, Amsterdam, the Netherlands

UCLA Film & Television Archive, Los Angeles, CA

Academy of Motion Picture Arts and Sciences, Los Angeles, CA

George Eastman House, Rochester, NY
Lobster Films, Paris, France

From 1897–1925 Vitagraph produced approximately 3,500 movies, about 20 percent of which are known to survive in public and private archives. A growing number of prints are also accessible on the Internet. Of the surviving films, 310 have been screened for this project, as well as the fragments of 398 productions made between 1905 and 1909 that constitute the paper prints Vitagraph submitted to the Library of Congress for copyright protection. For the most complete and accurate list of Vitagraph titles, the reader is directed to the filmography compiled by Anthony Slide in *The Big V.*

Index

Screen Classics

Screen Classics is a series of critical biographies, film histories, and analytical studies focusing on neglected filmmakers and important screen artists and subjects, from the era of silent cinema through the golden age of Hollywood to the international generation of today. Books in the Screen Classics series are intended for scholars and general readers alike. The contributing authors are established figures in their respective fields. This series also serves the purpose of advancing scholarship on film personalities and themes with ties to Kentucky.

Series Editor

Patrick McGilligan

Books in the Series

Olivia de Havilland: Lady Triumphant
Victoria Amador

Mae Murray: The Girl with the Bee-Stung Lips
Michael G. Ankerich

Harry Dean Stanton: Hollywood's Zen Rebel
Joseph B. Atkins

Hedy Lamarr: The Most Beautiful Woman in Film
Ruth Barton

Rex Ingram: Visionary Director of the Silent Screen
Ruth Barton

Conversations with Classic Film Stars: Interviews from Hollywood's Golden Era
James Bawden and Ron Miller

Conversations with Legendary Television Stars: Interviews from the First Fifty Years
James Bawden and Ron Miller

You Ain't Heard Nothin' Yet: Interviews with Stars from Hollywood's Golden Era
James Bawden and Ron Miller

Von Sternberg
John Baxter

Hitchcock's Partner in Suspense: The Life of Screenwriter Charles Bennett
Charles Bennett, edited by John Charles Bennett

Hitchcock and the Censors
John Billheimer

A Uniquely American Epic: Intimacy and Action, Tenderness and Violence in Sam Peckinpah's The Wild Bunch
Edited by Michael Bliss

My Life in Focus: A Photographer's Journey with Elizabeth Taylor and the Hollywood Jet Set
Gianni Bozzacchi with Joey Tayler

Hollywood Divided: The 1950 Screen Directors Guild Meeting and the Impact of the Blacklist
Kevin Brianton

He's Got Rhythm: The Life and Career of Gene Kelly
Cynthia Brideson and Sara Brideson

Ziegfeld and His Follies: A Biography of Broadway's Greatest Producer
Cynthia Brideson and Sara Brideson

The Marxist and the Movies: A Biography of Paul Jarrico
Larry Ceplair

Dalton Trumbo: Blacklisted Hollywood Radical
Larry Ceplair and Christopher Trumbo

Warren Oates: A Wild Life
Susan Compo

Improvising Out Loud: My Life Teaching Hollywood How to Act
Jeff Corey with Emily Corey

Crane: Sex, Celebrity, and My Father's Unsolved Murder
Robert Crane and Christopher Fryer

Jack Nicholson: The Early Years
Robert Crane and Christopher Fryer

Anne Bancroft: A Life
Douglass K. Daniel

Being Hal Ashby: Life of a Hollywood Rebel
Nick Dawson

Bruce Dern: A Memoir
Bruce Dern with Christopher Fryer and Robert Crane

Intrepid Laughter: Preston Sturges and the Movies
Andrew Dickos

Miriam Hopkins: Life and Films of a Hollywood Rebel
Allan R. Ellenberger

Vitagraph: America's First Great Motion Picture Studio
Andrew A. Erish

Jayne Mansfield: The Girl Couldn't Help It
Eve Golden

John Gilbert: The Last of the Silent Film Stars
Eve Golden

Stuntwomen: The Untold Hollywood Story
Mollie Gregory

Saul Bass: Anatomy of Film Design
Jan-Christopher Horak

Hitchcock Lost and Found: The Forgotten Films
Alain Kerzoncuf and Charles Barr

Pola Negri: Hollywood's First Femme Fatale
Mariusz Kotowski

Sidney J. Furie: Life and Films
Daniel Kremer

Albert Capellani: Pioneer of the Silent Screen
Christine Leteux

Ridley Scott: A Biography
Vincent LoBrutto

Mamoulian: Life on Stage and Screen
David Luhrssen

Maureen O'Hara: The Biography
Aubrey Malone

My Life as a Mankiewicz: An Insider's Journey through Hollywood
Tom Mankiewicz and Robert Crane

Hawks on Hawks
Joseph McBride

Showman of the Screen: Joseph E. Levine and His Revolutions in Film Promotion
A. T. McKenna

William Wyler: The Life and Films of Hollywood's Most Celebrated Director
Gabriel Miller

Raoul Walsh: The True Adventures of Hollywood's Legendary Director
Marilyn Ann Moss

Veit Harlan: The Life and Work of a Nazi Filmmaker
Frank Noack

Harry Langdon: King of Silent Comedy
Gabriella Oldham and Mabel Langdon

Charles Walters: The Director Who Made Hollywood Dance
Brent Phillips

Some Like It Wilder: The Life and Controversial Films of Billy Wilder
Gene D. Phillips

Ann Dvorak: Hollywood's Forgotten Rebel
Christina Rice

Mean. . .Moody. . .Magnificent!: Jane Russell and the Marketing of a Hollywood Legend
Christina Rice

Fay Wray and Robert Riskin: A Hollywood Memoir
Victoria Riskin

Lewis Milestone: Life and Films
Harlow Robinson

Michael Curtiz: A Life in Film
Alan K. Rode

Arthur Penn: American Director
Nat Segaloff

Film's First Family: The Untold Story of the Costellos
Terry Chester Shulman

Claude Rains: An Actor's Voice
David J. Skal with Jessica Rains

Barbara La Marr: The Girl Who Was Too Beautiful for Hollywood
Sherri Snyder

Buzz: The Life and Art of Busby Berkeley
Jeffrey Spivak

Victor Fleming: An American Movie Master
Michael Sragow

Hollywood Presents Jules Verne: The Father of Science Fiction on Screen
Brian Taves

Thomas Ince: Hollywood's Independent Pioneer
Brian Taves

Picturing Peter Bogdanovich: My Conversations with the New Hollywood Director
Peter Tonguette

Carl Theodor Dreyer and Ordet: *My Summer with the Danish Filmmaker*
Jan Wahl

Wild Bill Wellman: Hollywood Rebel
William Wellman Jr.

Clarence Brown: Hollywood's Forgotten Master
Gwenda Young